Henry George Keene

History of India from the Earliest Times to the Present Day

Vol. I

Henry George Keene

History of India from the Earliest Times to the Present Day
Vol. I

ISBN/EAN: 9783337060480

Printed in Europe, USA, Canada, Australia, Japan

Cover: Foto ©ninafisch / pixelio.de

More available books at **www.hansebooks.com**

HISTORY OF INDIA

FROM THE EARLIEST TIMES TO THE PRESENT DAY

FOR THE USE OF STUDENTS AND COLLEGES

BY

H G KEENE CIE

HON MA OXON

Author of " The Fall of the Mughal Empire" " The Turks in India" &c

Vol I

LONDON
W H ALLEN & CO LIMITED
Publishers to the India Office
13 WATERLOO PLACE SW
1893

PREFACE.

It is in no spirit of disparagement towards the works of predecessors that the following pages are offered to the reader. Many of those works are, in their several ways, of much value. Nevertheless, all are open to some objection: are too bulky; have grown obsolete owing to the discovery of new matter; or are insufficient for the purposes of the student. It is with a full sense of the difficulties of their task that the present work has been undertaken. The writer has endeavoured to give, without prolixity, a statement of the relevant facts at present available, both in regard to the origin of the more important Indian races, and in regard to their progress before they came under the unifying processes of modern administration: and the tracing of that evolution forms the subject of the first chapters. In the residue will be found the brief relation of that unprecedented series of events under which a remote commercial people have begun to weld those races into a single nationality.

The obstacles to success in both of these respects were perceived by Mr. Elphinstone, whose own labours have done so much for students of the subject. So far back as 1833, apparently contemplating a complete treatment of both the periods of Indian history, he wrote to Erskine, the translator of Babar's memoirs, endeavouring to convince him. that a history of the Mughal Empire would necessarily involve "a complete history of India," extending at least as far down as Warren Hastings, the inadequacy of whose record by James Mill he was the first to point out. Some years afterwards Elphinstone took in hand a portion of the task, and recorded in his diary the noble conception that sound knowledge and opinions ought to be diffused through India, till the people were capable of producing indigenous statesmanship for the government of themselves. "Should such a period arrive, the most interesting subject to the Indians—as they will then be—and to all the world, to which they will then become interesting, will be the progress of improvement and of liberal ideas among them. *A history, of little other merit, which shall preserve the otherwise perishable record of that progress, will be read with the deepest interest in India and with attention elsewhere.*"

Such was Elphinstone's ideal; not destined to be fully realised by him: and where so competent a man failed others may well feel anxious. The present writer, however, has found in his experience as an examiner that the ideal is still unattained; and he may add that he knows his own feeling to be widely shared by examiners and teachers, alike in India and in England. There is no work which relates the whole growth of India, from Chaos to Cosmos, in a consecutive order, so as to give students in both countries a rational view of the matter, mentioning really operative facts, yet not dwelling too minutely on the details of battles, sieges, or the intrigues and crimes of high-placed individuals.

Within the last few years, too, materials have accumulated to an extent which gives a further excuse for a new work. For the early periods we have the researches of Kaegi, Zimmer, and other German scholars, together with the Reports of the Archæological Survey of India. Ed. Thomas's works on Coins, and the writings of Messrs. Fleet, Sewell, and Burnell, have given solid results on mediæval chronology, while the late Professor Dowson's edition of Sir H. M. Elliot's "Muhamadan Historians" and Beale's "Oriental Biographical Dictionary" have supplied facts about the various Muslim dynasties to which Mr. Elphinstone had not the opportunity to refer. The edition of the first volume of the "Ain Akbari," by Prof. Blochmann, and the biography of the Emperor Akbar, by Count v. Noer, are exact and exhaustive, so far as they go. The rise of British power has been illustrated with much research by the posthumous papers of Elphinstone, edited by Sir E. Colebrooke; and the work of Sir James F. Stephen and of Sir J. Strachey has co-operated with Prof. Forrest's selections from Government records to throw much new light upon the career and conduct of the misunderstood and ungratefully treated Warren Hastings. The Wellesley and Wellington *Selections* of Mr. Sidney Owen are also valuable. Above almost all new matter should be mentioned the two great works of Sir W. Hunter, K.C.S.I.: namely, "The Indian Empire" (3rd Edition, 1893); and—still more—the "Imperial Gazetteer of India," a work which, by its completeness and accuracy, has filled a great vacuum, and is indeed essential to a due knowledge of Indian history.

In respect of the vexed question of spelling oriental words, the author can only trust to the indulgence of those who know the difficulties. There are Indian words which have taken their place in British history, consecrated by the glory of great deeds or by the pathos of great suffering. To write Bharatpúr, Kalighátá, Kánhpúr, Kodangalúr, or Shrirangapatanam, would be to offer readers a mystification which would be more likely to disgust than to edify. It is better to accept frankly the perversions which ignorance and a bad ear established in the last century, and to write "Calcutta," "Cawnpore," "Cranganore," and "Seringapatam." In other cases—proper names for example—it has appeared best to use a phonetic practice which might help in denoting the general sound without pedantic accuracy. The vowels—as in the Jones system, partially adopted by the Indian Government—have the Italian value rather than that usual in English: of which, however, instances occur in such English words as "rum*i*nant" and "*o*b*e*y." Where it seemed absolutely necessary to contrast one syllable with another, especially where an *(a)* was used, an acute accent appears over the long syllable, but the multiplication of accents has been avoided.* Where strange consonants are involved no attempt has been made to imitate the sound. What can be more unsightly in an English book than Qandahár? The rules followed, therefore, are three:—

1. Well-known words are represented by their conventional spelling, which, though sometimes absurd, is not always worse than the proposed substitutes (*e.g.*, "Masulipatam" sometimes rendered Machlipatanam).

2. Other words are given a kind of phonetic form, based upon the Italian use of vowels.

3. Consonants are expressed by their nearest English equivalents.

To those who are inclined to find fault with the small scale which has been applied to a vast matter it may be observed that, in our crowded time, a big book is more than ever in danger of being a big nuisance. The author

---

* The abuse of the accent is becoming almost as misleading a practice with Anglo-Indians as that of the aspirated consonant once was. Although we do not so often meet with the Baiza " Bhai," or the Dehra " Dhun" as we did formerly, there still occur such solecisms as Háfiz " Ráhmat " and Táj " Mahál."

would only hope that there will be readers who will welcome a miniature when they might look upon a wide canvas as occupying more space than they could spare. And especially he must plead that his book is declared upon the title-page to be, primarily at least, intended for the use of "students"; a class on whose attention too many claims are made to allow of undue importunity from one.

Finally, the author of this work has to acknowledge the courteous help of the India Office—alike in the use of books and of documents—and, more especially, the permission of the Secretaries of State for Foreign Affairs and for India, to refer to papers on the subject of the first Afghán war which had not before been accessible to the public, and which throw new light upon that unfortunate transaction.

CONTENTS OF VOL. I.

CHAPTER I.—INTRODUCTORY 1-24
    Description of country—Early inhabitants—Aryan settlement.

CHAPTER II.—PRÆ-MUSLIM TIMES.............. 25-50
    Rise of Buddhism—India as known to the Greeks—The Eve of the Conquest.

CHAPTER III.—THE MUSLIM CONQUEST 50-79
    Houses of Ghazni and Gur—Slave Dynasty—Aggressions in the Deccan.

CHAPTER IV.—END OF THE "PATHANS" 80-119
    House of Tughlak and Invasion of Tamerlane—Line of Lodi, and New Mughals—Adventures of Babar, etc.

CHAPTER V.—THE MUGHAL EMPIRE, I. 120-160
    Rise of Empire—Equilibrium—Early Europeans.

CHAPTER VI.—DECLINE OF MUGHAL EMPIRE 161-201
    Decline—Mahratta Confederacy—English Company.

CHAPTER VII.—HINDU REVIVAL AND RISE OF BRITISH 202-247
    English in Bengal—Restoration of Empire—First Ministry of Sindia.

CHAPTER VIII.—FINAL OVERTHROW OF FRENCH.. 248-282
    Haidar Ali—Second Mysore War; destruction of French power—Sindia.

CHAPTER IX.—THE END OF ANARCHY 283-321
    Cornwallis as a Reformer—Sindia's second Administration—Wars in Deccan and destruction of Tipu.

CHAPTER X.—THE WARS OF WELLESLEY 322-379
    India in 1799-1802—Mahratta Empire—Wellesley's conquests.

CHAPTER XI.—THE EVE OF EMPIRE 380-419
    Non-intervention—Minto's administration—Revenue, Justice, Public debt.

CHAPTER XII.—REVIEW OF FOREGOING.......... 420-450
    First Muslim period (1193-1398), Mughal Empire (1586-1748)—End of præ-British period.

LIST OF MAPS—VOL. I.

Sketch Map, to show places in Hindustan at the time of the first Muslim Invasion 57

State of Deccan, 12th Century .. 73

Hindustan and the Deccan, 1524-1526 .. 97

State of Deccan, 15th and 16th Centuries .. 108

Sketch Map, to shew Main Division of India, 1748-1803 189

Battle Fields of the Carnatic 205

Sketch of the Siege of Seringpatam 319

Sketch of the Seat of the War from 1803-1806 360

Map of Hindustan (with the Deccan) 428

HISTORY OF INDIA

CHAPTER I.

INTRODUCTORY.

Section 1: Description of the country.—Section 2: The early inhabitants and their descendants.—Section 3: The Aryan settlement.

SECTION 1.—India is the vast and varied Italy of Asia: a great promontory, imperfectly fenced on the north by a snowy highland, jutting southward into the ocean, with a detached island at its foot. Across the northern barrier invading hordes have poured in all ages, sometimes bringing rapine, sometimes conquest of a more or less beneficial kind. On the side of the sea the movement has been that of departure and emigration, traces of which are found not only in the adjacent island of Ceylon, but farther off, in Burma, Siam, and Cambodia, and in the islands of the Equatorial belt.

Of these movements, however, we possess but an indirect record. The early inhabitants were too rude and savage; the early conquerors took to other paths of learning, but had no taste for history. It is thus that we are driven to the study of the map when we would learn anything of the remote past; and to found our historical edifice on the shifting basis of conjecture.

The India, or "Hindustan," of geographers then is a vast triangular peninsula, lying between the 68th and 96th meridians of east longitude, and extended from the 36th parallel of north latitude to a point within 8° of the Equator. In respect of area and of population the country is about equal to all Europe west of the river Vistula; and its Alpine barrier is nearly twice as high as that of Italy, while its rivers are generally, whether for length or for area of drainage, among the greatest in the world. The base of the triangle is the above-mentioned Alpine barrier—a double range of enormous mountains, between whose almost parallel walls rise two rapid streams, running east and west until they break into the plains through which, on either side, they pursue their slackened but majestic course into the Bay of Bengal on the one hand, the Arabian Sea on the other. Of the detritus that these rivers bring down have been formed vast alluvial tracts as wide as an European kingdom. The mighty hills which are their cradle are known as Himála—or, popularly, Himalaya—the name being, perhaps, akin to the Greek "Haemus," and signifying "a land of snow," or of perpetual winter.* The width of this range is estimated at two hundred miles, and its extreme length at fifteen hundred; and it has been stated that if all the mountains of Switzerland could be thrown down there in one place the group would be hardly noticed at a short distance. To the north-east of the Himála are treeless plateaux tributary to the Emperor of China; on the western side are the countries subject to the Czar of Muscovy, and the hilly provinces under the direct administration of the Amir of Kábul. The higher crests are covered by glaciers and eternal snow, which terminate at a line higher on the Indian side than that which they attain to the northward, looking down on the plateau of Thibet or the valleys of the Oxus and the Zarafshán. Above the southern snow line are no fixed abodes

---

* The author once experienced a snow-storm on the 24th May at the source of the Jumna, on the south side of the range.

of man, barring a few holy places maintained as an attraction to pilgrims from India.

Through the gorges of this range the tribes of the north have often issued to ravage or take possession of the fertile lands below. Some of these invaders—and the most savage and destructive among them—were of Turanian blood, coming from Mongolia and the Siberian steppes. Others were of Aryan race, the overflow of the Medes and Persians. The one party has left fragments in the valleys between Kábul and Cashmere; the other is represented by the hill folk of Nipál and Bhután. Midway are mountain clans of more recent Hindu origin, and the fair-complexioned Brahmans and Rajputs of Kashmir, Kulu, and Kángra. The climate of these elevated regions is mild and temperate, except on the extreme heights, where the cold forbids human habitation, and in some of the valleys, which are close and malarious. But the important element, for India, of the Himalayan climate is the effect produced on the seasons by the condensing influence of the vast and eternal ice-fields and snow-beds upon the vapours arising out of the Indian Ocean. Towards the end of winter this appears to create a region of low pressure, lowest towards the east (where the greatest mass of snow is situated), and thus forming a slope down which the vapour-laden air flows from the north of the Equator. This current is the "south-west monsoon," which travels up until it meets the line of cold at an average height of 20,000 feet above sea level, where the vapours are turned back, condensed, to fall in the form of cloud and rain upon the thirsty plains below. Most rain ordinarily falls where the bulk of the current infringes on the greatest mass of snow and glacier, so that the cooling process is most rapidly effected: thus, in the hills bordering Bengal, and the area subtended by the great peaks and ranges, the rainfall is sometimes as much as 500 inches in the year—twenty or thirty times as much as falls at the other extremity. At the end of the rainy season the pressure on the mountains rises, and an anti-monsoon is generated, travelling from the north-east; and it is when this period, with the subsequent equilibrium, is unduly prolonged that those great droughts occur which have caused the terrible famines from which India has, from time to time, so severely suffered. Thus, the Himála range has had an influence upon the fortunes of the Indian races far beyond any action that it may have exercised in the way of protecting them against invasion. For, in the first place, it has rendered them dependent on a periodical supply of rain, which sometimes falls short or altogether fails; and secondly, the snows, dissolving under the sunshine of the hot season, fall down the southern slopes in great streams of water which—while they tear the upper hills and hinder vegetation in the steeper parts—produce an abundant supply lower down. Wherever a strong and wise government exists this supply can be directed and utilised, so that artificial irrigation can be positively depended on to supply (so far as it can extend) the occasional defect of nature. And this at the precise period when such a supply is most required.

Thus much as to the Himála region; the rest of the country may be most properly considered from the native point of view; that is to say, as divided into the alluvial tract and the southern peninsula, or "Hindustan and Deccan." The former comprises all those broad lands through which, after leaving their native mountains, the rivers flow, east and west, to the sea. Reference to a map will show that there is a watershed a few miles to the west of the river Jumna, in the region of Sirhind: the actual spot is in the State of Sirmur, a plateau about one thousand five hundred feet above sea-level in east longitude, 77·5 to 77·50. From this neighbourhood the rivers of the Punjab run to the west and join the Indus. Then comes a vast expanse of waterless desert, known as "Thur," to the south of which flow other rivers, the Luni, the

INTRODUCTORY. 5

Sabarmati, and the Mahi, all flowing into the "Runn" of Cutch or the Gulf of Canbay. On the other side of the Sirmur watershed run the rivers of Hindustan proper; the Jumna and Ganges —which, after forming a riverine tract known as the Duáb (= Mesopotamia, land between two rivers), unite at Allahabad; and all the minor drainage-lines which finally fall into the Bay of Bengal, in the channel of the Hughli, or Lower Ganges. Still farther east the rivers Sanpu and Dihong unite and cleave the hills at Dibrugarh, whence they descend into the mighty stream of the Barhamputar, take up the Meghna on the east and sink into the Gangetic Delta.

Finally, the south, or *Dakhan* ("Deccan" of English historians) is a wholly separate land, parted from the northern region by the Narbada river (west) and the Máhánadi (east) and having a river system entirely its own.

Of the northern region, with which the work before us will be principally concerned, it need only be added here that it consists of three great primary divisions: namely, the Punjab, or land of the "five-waters," between the Indus and the Jumna; the provinces of Hindustan proper, from Delhi to Benares; and those of Bihár, Bengal, and Orissa, making together what the native historians have called "The Eastern Subah." Many of the rivers of this wide expanse are navigable, especially the Indus on the westward and the Ganges to the east; and the fact—already mentioned—of their being fed by the melting of the mountain snows in summer causes them to be particularly useful for the purposes of agricultural irrigation. This is rendered almost necessary by two causes; the inequality of the level (amounting to one thousand five hundred feet) and the uncertainty of the rainfall. From the circumstance of the snow melting most when the heat is greatest it happens that the supply of water is greatest in the time of greatest need. So far all is well; but the rivers in descending from so great a height have scooped out their beds, so that they flow at levels constantly lower and lower than the level of the land. Hence it becomes important that their water-supply should be tapped at their highest points after leaving the hills; so that it may be delivered in the plains at appropriate spots by means of artificial channels. The earliest known attempts of this sort were made by some of the Muslim rulers; but the works of those days have been enormously developed and extended by the British in modern times. Thus, for example, the west Jumna Canal was opened about A.D. 1350 by Firoz Shah Tughlak, but had only a feeble irrigation: falling into neglect and decay after the irruption of Taimur, it was subsequently repaired in the reign of Akbar about the year 1558 A.D. And, finally—much improved and extended by order of the Emperor Shah Jahan some sixty years later—it delivered water into the palaces and streets of Delhi. Having quite ceased to flow in the great anarchy of the 18th century it was taken in hand by the British, under Lord Hastings, and now measures four hundred and thirty-three miles with two hundred and fifty-nine miles of distributing channels, irrigating nearly four hundred thousand acres of land and returning to the State an annual profit of over 10 per cent. The great Gangetic system—entirely new—can supply water to close upon one-and-a-half million acres: the cost has exceeded five millions of Rs.x.* But the interest returned is over 6 per cent. per annum, besides the action of the outlay as a famine insurance for so wide a tract of country. The Ganges Canals are navigable for at least eight hundred miles and afford a useful alternative to the railway, for the transport of heavy goods. The climate, however, of the country under notice is still dependent on the natural water supply; and the character

---

* That is the integer of Anglo-Indian finance; once (but not now) equivalent to £1. sterling.

INTRODUCTORY.

of the inhabitants has varied accordingly. Thus, in the Punjab and in the Indus desert, where the earth has only yielded her increase to strenuous labour, the peasantry are strong and warlike; in the eastern provinces, where the water supply is abundant, the inhabitants are densely packed but physically weak; in the central parts the conditions are of an intermediate character; a fertility somewhat less than in Bengal and with less certainty of rainfall, produces races which, from Audh to the Narbada, have always been robust and laborious, almost—but not quite—as much so as in the drier regions of the far west. In all the three regions the agricultural system is somewhat uniform: there is the autumn harvest, sown in the beginning of the spring and consisting of semi-tropical crops, such as cotton, sugar, millet, and rice; then the land has rest during the great dryness of the hot season; the crops are reaped at the end of the rainy season; and in the beginning of winter the fields reserved for the spring harvest are got ready for the cereals and other products of the temperate zone. Wheat, the chief spring crop of Upper India, is produced for the markets rather than for the consumption of the rural communities, who mostly share with their cattle the less valuable products: the wheat goes in large quantities to Bombay, and the exportation is becoming more and more important, alike to India which benefits by its sale and to Britain which is largely dependent on its purchase.* This region also produces several kinds of fruit-trees and of timber; and groves are usually to be met with near the villages and beside the wells and roads. To the S.W. of the Ganges the country is somewhat hilly, and the people—though belonging mostly to the races of Hindustan—are in a more backward condition and considerably less numerous by the square mile.

---

* During the past ten years the quantity of Indian wheat exported—chiefly to England—has averaged near twenty million cwt. per annum,

On the west of the Jumna are found the ancient principalities of the Rajputs, typical Hindus of the purest blood and most unquestioned orthodoxy: and still farther to south and west are the Mahratta States of Gujarat and Málwa, the valley of the Indus and the primitive principalities of the peninsular Kathiawár.

The South, or Deccan, is a triangular and sloping table, rising to considerable altitude on the west, so that all its more important rivers flow eastward into the Bay of Bengal. On that side also are mountains, though not continuous, and the eastern and western ranges meet in the peak of Dodabetta, 8,760 feet above sea-level, with the Nilghiri highlands to the east and the Arabian sea bathing the Malabar coast a few miles from its western foot. This country is of great area, stretching from the Tropic of Cancer to within eight degrees north of the Equator, and more than eight hundred miles across in its greatest breadth. It is inhabited by about one hundred millions of human beings, some of whom are Muslims by race, and some descended from northern Hindus; but the greater number are of races more resembling the Talaings of Burma, or the Malays of the Tropic islands, and the people of Ceylon. The rivers and mountains that separate the Deccan from the northern regions may have impeded immigration though they did not wholly prevent it; and the southern races have preserved much peculiarity of race and language, though they have adopted Hindu influence in matters of religious belief. Parallel to the Vindhya hills, though at some distance to the south of their course, flows the Narbada river, from its source in the Maikal range (about 82 degrees east longitude) traversing a breadth of nearly eight hundred miles, but rocky and rapid to an extent that makes it of little use to man, whether for agriculture or for irrigation. South of the Narbada runs another parallel river—the Tapti—and south of that another chain of hills of moderate elevation, called Sátpura;

the Maikals are held to be the easternmost link of this chain; and the two rivers here spoken of as running parallel to it are the only considerable streams of the south which do not flow into the Bay of Bengal. On the left, or southern, bank of the Tapti commence the western ghâts, and they run down the western coast in an unbroken line of some seven hundred miles. The chief points or peaks of this range are crowned by the almost inaccessible fastnesses from which in the days of their vigour the Mahratta hosts used to pour down on the plains, to levy blackmail or to defy the cumbrous armies of the Great Moghul. Those plains, watered by mighty rivers, were the seats of ancient Hindu kingdoms succeeded, in more recent times, by four or five Turkish States. The most northerly of those rivers is the Máhánadi, rising on the easterly slope of the same range which forms the cradle—on the other slope—in which the infant Narbada reposes: the course of the Máhánadi is almost due east for a distance of five hundred and twenty miles; and though rocks impede the navigation, boats and rafts use its waters in all but the very driest season of the year. The river is subject to occasional high floods; and the lower water has been diverted by weirs into four different canals, calculated, when complete, to irrigate a total of one million six hundred acres. South of this the next large river is the Godávari, the pass by which it cleaves the eastern ghâts being twenty miles in length. This river is nowhere used for navigation of any importance; but like the Máhánadi it has a vast delta which has long been filled with irrigation works that water half-a-million of acres, besides returning a handsome dividend to the state. The Krishna crosses the Deccan for a distance of eight hundred miles, and is formed out of two tributaries, the Bhima and the Tunga-Bhadra, which rise in the eastern ghâts: it flows into the Bay of Bengal, near Masulipatam, and, like the other rivers, has a delta full of canals. Farther south are the two Panárs, and the Kávari, four hundred and seventy-five miles in length, which passes through Mysore and the famous town known in military history as Seringapatam. Its lower waters divide, and the northern channel falls into the Bay near Tanjore, under the name of the Coleroon*; in this portion of its course it has been utilised to irrigate over eight hundred thousand acres of land. Like Hindustan, the Deccan is largely occupied by agriculturists; but it also produces gold, diamonds, iron, and coal; and it is thought that this mineral wealth is still capable of farther development. The interior hills and forests can hardly be said to have been hitherto fully explored or developed; but they are known to be inhabited by tribes of the aborigines who have never yet been completely assimilated to the manners and customs of the Hindus. The more civilised inhabitants are, for the most part, members of one or other of four great races, who are also, perhaps, indigenous; though they have been supposed to be descended from the ancient Medes, and to be of kin to the present inhabitants of the Indus Valley. The languages used by these races have received from European science the technical title of "Dravidian," and their occurrence may be traced in geographical succession; the Támil, which is regarded as the representative of cultivated Dravidian, is chiefly used in the south, from Tinevelli to Nellore; the Telugu, which from its sweet and musical sounds has been compared to the language of Tuscany, is found over the north from Nellore to the banks of the Máhánadi; the Kanarese and Malayálim are spoken from the head of the Malabar coast down to Travancore. The Dravidian races, if not aboriginal, probably entered the Deccan many centuries before the Aryan settlement of Hindustan to be hereafter described; and it is thought that they possessed

---

* In these Deccan names the conventional spelling has been retained, as the words are for the most part known in English literature.

rudiments of civilisation—and even of literature—so long ago as the tenth century before the Christian era. Of this there is no certainty, but some of their states, or kingdoms, were known to Ptolemy, the Greek geographer, who wrote in the second century after Christ, and who derived his information from earlier writers.*

It has appeared needful to give this slight description of the scene on which were acted the events which will be found briefly narrated in the following pages; and from what has been said it will be perceived that the land now known as "India" is by no means homogeneous in any respect. It is not positively known to have been ever united under one empire, or to have otherwise formed, in any period, the home of a combined nationality; but such words as "Bhartkhand" or "Jambudwipa" are found in old writings, and may, perhaps, be taken as indications of a sense that the peninsula *ought* to be united: and the later Hindu books (*Puránas*, hereafter described)† contain perhaps a similar ideal in the vain ascription to mythical rulers of the feat of bringing all the country "under one umbrella," the realisation of which was reserved for a race of remote foreigners in the distant future. It will be sufficient here to resume the main facts of the past. The Himalayan range is the wall which has maintained the specific existence of the Indian populations, while its gaps have admitted the occasional inroads of bold and hardy immigrants. These, following the courses of the rivers, have effected settlements upon the plains, as will presently appear. The central belt forms the arena on which these immigrants have lived and fought, and laid the foundations of their power. The southern triangle has also received colonists, and has formed a hunting-ground for adventurous foreigners for more than two hundred centuries.

* These were the States of Pandiya, Chera, and Chola (v. ch. II.)
† v. ch. II.

Having thus briefly sketched the landscape, let us now proceed to inquire what manner of people may have lived within its limits from the earliest times and prepared, by their thoughts and actions, the events and characters of later times.

SECTION 2. Peninsular India, or the Deccan and Vindhya region, is an old Palæozoic formation; and in such a situation aboriginal man may well have appeared in Miocene times and carried on his obscure and barren existence for ages, in the state in which the people of the Andaman islands were still living in the middle of the nineteenth century. Similar human beings spread northward in Asia and Europe after the retreat of the glaciers had begun in those regions; and they have left their traces in caves and stone weapons, and perhaps in the persons of the Finns and Basques and the less-favoured branches of European society. The characteristics of such races are short stature, straight black hair, dark eyes and skin. Flint implements, cup-marked stones, and such-like remains of man's ruder development, have been found in the Deccan and as far as the north scarp of the Narbada valley. After this "neolithic" period came one of iron-workers, who raised stone circles, and who buried their dead under earthen mounds and under slabs of rock; at some far-distant, though unfixable, epoch they had already learned the art of making round pots of hard, thin earthenware; and they knew how to provide themselves with rude ornaments and jewelry of gold and copper. These iron-workers appear to have protracted their form of existence down to the times of the Roman Emperors whose coins have been found in the cemeteries ascribed to them; unless, indeed, as we know to have occurred elsewhere, these cemeteries may have been used by others who succeeded them in the more accessible parts of India. Certain it is that of both these races, the neolithic and the early iron-workers, descendants are still found in the forest-clad mountains of central and southern India; and the bulk of the Hindu populations, with the exception of the Brahmans, is more or less supplied with their blood.

For, like most other nations of whose origin we have any adequate knowledge, the Hindus are easily seen to be of mixed descent. In India, as in Greece, Italy, and many other countries, the rude primæval occupants of fertile regions have been disturbed by visits from stronger races of men who killed or drove away their fighting men, married their women, and made slaves of their children. In this way was established a servile stratum of society held down by a higher one, which, like the Eupatrids and the Populus of European nations, originated a religious and civil aristocracy. Putting aside obscure and unimportant movements of Mongolians from the north-east, the Dravidian tribes may have entered India from the north in prehistoric times, although now only met with in the Deccan. But by far the most lasting and important conquests were those of the Aryan races who, coming through the Hindukush passes, brought their physical and mental superiority to bear in an irresistible and generally beneficial manner on the Punjab and Hindustan in succession; ultimately introducing their civilisation into the southernmost limits of the whole country. In the most ancient sacred songs of this people they are found calling themselves "Arya;" and the fact that a province of Persia was formerly known as as "Ariana," while the whole country is still denominated in the local language "Irán," serves to strengthen the inference that this was the old home of the conquerors of India. This conclusion is further affirmed by the evidence of language. The race was originally of agricultural habits; and its warlike energies were stimulated by the everlasting struggle with the pastoral nomads who, under the generic name of "Turán," figure as the perpetual enemies of the race.* The Aryans of

---

* The names of Irán and Turán will be found reproduced in comparatively recent Indian history to denote the chronic opposition between the Persian and Turkmán parties in the Moghul Empire.

Persia were a religious people; and their southward migration may have been due to one or both of these causes; dissidence of creed, and strife between the agricultural and the pastoral communities. The subject of the invasion of India by what may be conveniently styled the "Vedic Aryans" is dealt with more fully hereafter; we need only notice here that they were a mild and well-favoured race, whose relative advantages are still, to some extent at least, maintained by the Brahmans in India, who have ever since preserved a certain superiority over the other inhabitants of the country by means of the laws of caste. Other and later immigrations are thought to be traceable, which have left effects less evident, perhaps, but scarcely less important than those attributable to the Vedic Aryans. Such were those of the tribes known as Kagar, Takshak, Ját, etc., all described as "Scythians," although the word cannot be taken to have any precise scientific import. Assuming, however, that the Scythians were another branch of the Aryan race, the apparent identity of such names as "Oxydracae" and "Getae" has been taken as establishing their parentage of the Kshatryas and Játs, or Jats; in that case the Scythians have wandered over a great part of India, and have founded kingdoms everywhere, from the shores of the Arabian Sea to the banks of the Ganges. Reserving some further details of these successive invasions, we must for the present take notice of some of the more prominent of the non-Aryan tribes whom they disturbed and suppressed.

Beginning in the north we find tribes of non-Aryan blood in the Gakkars, Gonds, Bhars, Bundelas, Santals; while the once intractable Bhils are now almost completely reclaimed in the Narbada valley. Indeed, most of the tribes here named have embraced Hinduism, or, in rarer cases, the creed of Islam; the former being that with which they have been in most close and constant contact. Their total number has been estimated at over twenty millions, while their blood is mingled with that of perhaps one hundred and twenty more of the general population. Only about fifteen millions among the Hindus appear to be of pure Aryan descent.

Some of the non-Aryans rank, as we have already observed, with the dwarfish folk of the islands. These, so lately as 1855, were in a state of primal savagery; entirely unclothed, suspected of cannibalism, and prepared to repel the visits of strangers with poisoned arrows. This is what is known as the "Negrito" family; they have no sense of religion, except of a mysterious and malevolent power which delights to afflict mankind. That state of existence is still represented on the continent by a few scattered tribes of shy savages in the hilly forests of East and Central India. The rest of the non-Aryans are believed to be descended from invaders from the east and northeast; with the important exception of the Dravidians, already mentioned in connection with the Deccan as having been, perhaps, a north-western people. These are remarkable for having maintained a number of highly-developed non-Aryan languages, and for being of peaceful, docile, and intelligent character. The word "Drávida" in Sanskrit literature applies to populations not regarded as hostile, like the indigenous enemies encountered in other parts; and it has been thought that the mythic history of the hero, Ráma, as set forth in the epic poem to be hereafter noted, relates to a peaceful visit of the Aryans introductive of agriculture and other civilising arts. The Dravidian people seem to have welcomed such visits; and the memory of one at least of the Aryan missionaries is preserved near "Ráma's Bridge," at the extreme south, where the peak of Agastya towers over Cape Comorin. The date of the missionary whose name this mountain bears varies from the sixth century before Christ to the seventh century after that era: so hard is the task of introducing accuracy into these subjects. But it is to be noted that while the earliest scriptures of the Deccan are in Sanskrit, the people learned to use their own vernacular, and that this movement has been ascribed to the struggle of Buddhism, somewhat earlier than the later of the conjectured dates.

If at that time Buddhism was the popular creed its defenders would naturally adopt the popular language; and the Tamil was certainly employed in anti-Brahman writings at a later date, for the books are still forthcoming. The Dravidians--estimated at twenty million—are now Hindus, though not of the most orthodox type; they preserve the old mildness of their manners, though their lower lower castes have always produced good soldiers; and, with an admixture of northern blood, they have given rise to the enterprising Mahrattas of whom we hear so much in Indian history.

SECTION 3.—It is impossible to describe the conquest of Upper India by the Vedic Aryans in the same purely historical manner as that which is applied to the Hebrews in Palestine or the Normans in England. All that can be done, in the absence of actual contemporaneous records and dates, is to make use of such evidence as we have, and to complete our picture from conjecture and from the unanimous conclusions of the best modern authorities. Using such methods we find the proofs of Aryan colonisation, not only in the languages of Upper India but also in laws, customs, and religious beliefs. There was, probably, a time when the Aryan races—though now widely scattered over all the world—once had a common origin and a common home; and the fact that most words used in family life, and in peaceful occupations, are identical or closely similar in many of their most widely-separated tongues may be taken as a strong confirmation of this belief. Where the same name is used for the same idea by remote races, it can hardly be doubted that the subject was familiar to their forefathers before they were separated and dispersed. So also there are laws and customs amongst equally scattered nations which could hardly have arisen but from a similar state of things. And

INTRODUCTORY. 17

so again of some of the fundamental religious conceptions. "Diespitar" in the name of the Heavenly Father alike among the Romans and the Vedic Aryans; and the *patria potestas* of the former not only existed amongst the latter, but might have been described by almost the same name. Cattle, horse, water, the "daughter" who milked the cow, the king and his royal power, are all common objects described by cognate words alike in Greek and German, in Ancient Irish and in Archaic Indian. The very word "Aryan" is thought to come from a root which, in many Indo-Germanic languages, denotes the "earing" of "arable" land (earth), and points to the agricultural habits of the race. It is not possible to decide at what time the departure occurred among the Asiatic section of this race, whereby the Aryan empire was established in the Punjab and Hindustan. Early Anglo-Indian scholars, adopting the estimates of their Brahman guides, assigned a very ancient date to the first invasion; though we know hardly anything to warrant very positive conclusions. All that can be with any confidence asserted is that, under pressure of some disturbance in Balkh and Khorasán, whether social, political, or religious, some tribes or families of tall stature and comparatively fair complexion, speaking a language akin to the Zend, or ancient Persic, crossed the Hindukush passes, bringing with them some rude sacrificial hymns, and a simple faith in the sacredness of fire, and the value of propitiating certain elemental deities. But their social ideas held germs of useful development; the integer of society—as in the related societies of Germany, Greece, and Rome—was the corporate family whose head (the father) was also priest, and the mother an active and respected partner. These families were loosely tied together in the various tribes or clans who maintained the tradition of a common ancestry. Moreover, each clan was ruled by a chief, the head, perhaps, of what was believed to be the founding family; which chief had a sort of Bardic college as his assessors. Thus much has been gathered from

c

the Vedic hymns, which internal evidence shows to be of the highest antiquity. Most of the hymns, we are told, are in a language so rugged as to prove that they were written before the formation of classical Sanskrit, the later poems being in a style more conformed to classic usage, though still preserving an archaic form. No materials have been as yet discovered from which to form any approximate date, either for the earlier hymns or for the formation of the existing canon by virtue of which they have been incorporated with later texts to form the Vedic Scripture. The Hindu chronologers boldly claim for these books an origin in the 31st century before Christ; while modern European scholars place them at dates varying between the 14th and the 11th. All therefore that remains is, assuming that these hymns reveal the condition of the invaders a little before and a little after their migration, to extract from them some information as to the laws and manners of the founders of the Indian polity.

Now, in the first place, let it be borne in mind that the two elements already noted as existing in the Hindu scriptures call for caution on the part of those who would seek to learn from them the facts of ancient life. There may—for all we know—be as long a period between the old Vedic hymns and the later Brahman rubrics as there is between the oldest traditions of the Hebrew wanderings in the wilderness and the story of Ezra and his reforms. Thoughts and words, the structure of the language and the framework of society, all must vary in the course of centuries: and the condition of a Hindu kingdom in Bihár could not be reasonably expected to resemble that of a nomad tribe in the passes of the Hindukush. To take one simple illustration, the early hymns suggest fire-worship and the use of Bacchic rites in which fermented liquor played a part: there is neither priestly caste nor consecrated animal. Later accretions, made when the people had begun to settle in valleys and plains under a burning sun and subject to occasional drought, show the Godhead passing from the Spirit of the Fire to the Lord of Tempests, and provide ritual and calendar for the propitiation of the Rain-god and the worship of the rivers. Accumulated ceremonies will be found to have led to the existence of a special class of hereditary ministers, and the indispensable ox to have become a national totem, almost an Incarnation like Apis. But these changes were slow.

In those writings which linguistic and other evidence show to be oldest, a simple society is revealed, not unlike that attributed to ancient Germany. Each householder is the leader of his family's devotions, each family shares a common dwelling: a number of such dwellings forms the tribal town, enclosed by a palisade as a protection against the wandering of the herds and the depredations of the aborigines. The sexes are equal, and the women free, always under the control of the paterfamilias; widow-burning is unknown.

The Aryans are traceable as they slowly spread east and south from the Punjab towards the Ganges, exterminating those of the inhabitants who resist them, but accepting those who submit, as serfs and clients, and thus anticipating the policy of their kinsfolk the Romans, as laid down by Virgil. Their onward progress from the cold mountains to the sunny plains leads them to modify their worship of the sun and the Fire-God; they find that warmth may be taken for granted, while their welfare as husbandmen is become dependent upon clouds and rain. The brimming rivers where they bathe and water their cattle are named with gratitude and devotion; in the order of their march; in short, it was no longer needful, or even always agreeable, to pray for heat; but prayers for water would appear more and more appropriate, and, thus, the Rain-God, and the fertilising streams absorb their worship. Going still farther eastward their foremost tribes were pressed on to regions where a constant supply of water was yielded by the two monsoons, and by the great increase of the volume of drainage. The cloud-compelling Indra then, in his turn, retires, to make way for a triad of almost metaphysical powers, more suited to a community at last settled, amid the prodigal gifts of Nature, in the Gangetic valley; and, thus, the quasi-abstract conception of a triune Godhead, Creator, Destroyer, Preserver, took a place in popular estimation, and prepared a pantheon for the boundless mythology of the modern Hindus.*

Accordingly, we find the later portions of the sacred writings indicating, by a complication of ritual and of sacrificial observances the change that was coming over the once simple life of the conquerors; the language becomes more artificial, and a specialised class is evolved to commit the rites and rules to memory and carry them into practice. By degrees the tribes, multiplying and abandoning their wandering habits, grew into a nation; then the confederation of those tribes broke up, and separate states began to be created. Kings and hereditary families of chiefs were needed to judge the people and lead them in war; and a second class arose in addition to that of the sacrificers. The members of the general community were now regarded as confined to the care of herds and tillage; and the system of caste originated. The Brahmans, Kshatryas, and Vaisyas were the hereditary castes or classes of the "Twice born"; the subjugated clients, or Sudras, were "once-born," and were prohibited the use of the scriptures. We are reminded of the early society of Rome, and the distinction between Plebs and Populus.

The next literary monument of social progress is to be found in the political and legal writings of a considerably later period. It used to be thought that the *Dharm-shástar*, or "Code of Manu," afforded a complete picture of the state of Indian society in ancient times. But the opinion now usually sup-

* See next chapter.

ported by scholars is that this work is a compilation not much earlier than the Christian era. It is nevertheless of some value, as it is held to have been in great measure composed from older documents, and to represent the spirit and character of some part of the Hindu world after the caste system had been firmly and thoroughly organised. As a "code of laws" the work is of no great authority, being no more than the latest embodiment of the views of a school of commentators called Mánavas, from whom it takes its title. As a political treatise, however, it is believed to be a description, for the information of a southern chief, of society such as it existed, or ought to exist, in a Brahmanic ideal. It does this by marking off the employment of the castes in subordination to the Brahmans, and laying down regulations in the manner of an *Atlantis* or *Utopia*, for eating, marriage, social intercourse, education, government; in a word, for life and for death. Although such a work must have had great influence in fixing the habits and institutions of the Hindus, yet it must be taken rather as showing what was desired at the time of publication than what was always done. We may safely assume that the picture was one of an ideal which, though conceived by a man of genius as arising out of the needs of his society, was one for whose immediate fulfilment actual facts were still wanting, if not positively unfit. The author would not have assigned, for example, so much authority to the higher orders, so much docility to the lower, had those relations been already in full and unquestioned operation. What he could do was to draw an attractive picture, not at variance with the traditions of the past and capable of affording a pattern for the future.

From other sources it may be inferred that the Brahmans did not obtain their supremacy without considerable opposition, and that the caste system, in marriage especially, was not at first rigid. It is not improbable that by their almost exclusive possession of records and traditions the priestly class succeeded in making these subservient to their social and political ambitions. Nevertheless, the vigilance of modern criticism has detected in the old literature indications of a struggle between the two higher classes for the rights of sacrifice, and the general leadership of the simple but superstitious people. It is even thought that the Kshatrya, or military aristocracy, was so much worsted in these contentions as to be either destroyed or expelled from Hindustan; though it appears more likely that a large number of them settled in Máhárashtrá, Gujarát, and Central India, where they founded the famous Rájput dynasties of those regions, and by intermarriage with the earlier inhabitants gave birth to warlike races of mixed blood. The Brahmans alone of all the Aryan tribes have any claim to have preserved their purity of descent, having been enabled to keep themselves separate by the twofold superiority of religious and social privilege. On the whole, therefore, it may be concluded that the actual conditions of the four-fold division of the Aryans as described in "Manu" was originally rather ideal than actual.

Whatever may have been the frame of their early society, the Aryans soon became too numerous for the limits of the Punjab. Westward the Indus and the mountains held them in, combined with some dread of the populations of those quarters, who appear in the Vedic record as impure Aryans, contact with whom was a pollution. To the South, again, the way was blocked by various obstacles, of which the most formidable would be that great expanse of arid and uninviting sand, which extends from about the 30th parallel of latitude in a southerly direction for nearly four hundred miles to the Runn of Catch. Thus compressed, the migration would naturally take the line of least resistance, namely, the outlet afforded by the rivers trending towards the East. After crossing the Saraswati—which after a short attempt to seek the Indus is now lost in the sand—they would come to the

Jumna and the fertile plains between that river and the Upper Ganges. Here, between the Sutlej and the Ganges, they founded the famous cities of Indrápat and Hastinapur. And here are to be found the legendary scenes of the great epic of the Mahabhárat, and also the fields of real historic battles. After settlement of unknown duration in the *Madhya-Des*, or "Midland," the Aryans pushed forth fresh branches into Bihár, where Buddhism originated, and whence set forth the expedition to the Deccan already mentioned as forming the subject of the second great epic, the *Ramáyana*. The exact era of these movements is concealed by the mists which hang over all Hindu chronology, save at those rare points where India comes in contact with the history of other countries. We cannot even say whether the migration had any connection with the rise of Buddhism or not. All that can be certainly said is that there was a reformation of religion in Bihár, and that there was a migration from Bihár into the Deccan, but we cannot be sure which took place before the other. There is indeed a presumption that the migration preceded the reform; but it is not a very strong presumption; it rests upon the fact that Sanskrit was originally the language of science and religion among the Dravidians, who did not use the Tamil for those purposes until much later. Hence it may be plausibly argued that they used the language of their instructors as long as the authority of the latter was undisputed, and only fell back on the vernacular when driven to seek popular favour by the rise of controversy. Coming to the time of the Buddhist reform and to the almost immediately succeeding notices of Greek intercourse with India we meet with evidence that demands a somewhat more careful examination.

[Among authorities to be consulted on the subjects dealt with in this chapter are:—"The Imperial Gazetteer of India," 14 vols, Trübner and Co., 1887; "History of India," by M. Elphinstone (Cowell's Notes); the Maps contained in the

"Progress Statement" for 1882-3; Part. II. Hansard, 1885; Muir's "Sanskrit Texts," 3 vols.; "The Laws of Manu," Bühler ("Sacred Books of the East"), 1888; Max Müller's "Essays," *passim*; Weber's "Indian Literature" (Trübner's "Oriental Series"), 1878; "Altindisches Leben," H. Zimmer, Berlin, 1879; "Der Rigveda, die älteste Literatur des Inder," Leipzic, 1881; "Indo-Aryans," by Rajendradala Mitra, C.I.E, 2 vols, London, 1881. There are two editions of Dr. Muir's book, the latest published 1868-73.]

CHAPTER II.

PRÆ-MUSLIM TIMES.

Section 1: Rise of Buddhism.—Section 2: India as known to the Greeks.—Section 3: India on the eve of the Muslim conquest.

SECTION 1.—Up to the great religious schism we have—as has been already stated—no historical record in regard to the people in any part of India. The national mind, if such an expression may be permitted, has never shown any aptitude for that branch of letters. Reference has been already made to the ancient scriptural hymns, and to the scarcely less sacred commentaries of sages; and two great epic poems have been mentioned in which real events may be supposed to have afforded a groundwork for imaginative and mythologic embroidery. Of speculation there was no lack; and it can scarcely be doubted that there was a tendency towards many branches of science. But for concrete facts, the dates of events and their successive evolution, the Hindus have never shown the slightest taste or curiosity. Some admixture of possible biography in their poems, and one set of provincial annals,[*] are all that they have done in that kind during a period of, say, twenty centuries. This peculiarity may have been the result of the very love of speculative philosophy, the taste for abstract reasoning which bred a conviction of the unreality of matter and its appearances. Something, also, may be due to a turn for the marvellous acquired by the conquerors from the ruder

[*] The "Rájataranganí."

aborigines amongst whom their lives were led, and to the natural desire to give their own conditions a heroic scale of proportion. However caused, the scorn of facts and figures is undeniable; and it is likely to keep posterity from all detailed knowledge of the history of the Vedic Aryans. Our information shows them to us as a pastoral people, who also practised agriculture and made war on the aborigines and among themselves. Gradually settling in villages and towns, they built up a kind of cellular social tissue based on the family as a rudimental organ. The family: which with them meant a permanent incorporation whose managing partner was the father, while the mother was free, but kept to her particular sphere of labour. The sons also worked for the common good, with some voice in council, some latent claim to separate their respective shares of the joint estate; but ordinarily that estate was probably undivided at first, and the private property of the sons was confined to everything that they might earn without using family capital. The daughters, like their mother, had their prescribed occupation—the name is connected with the milking of cattle*—and were allowed some freedom in the choice of husbands. Monogamy was the rule; and when, in certain cases, a second wife could be taken, the original consort remained in the position of "Housewife." When the father became decrepit the eldest son took his place in the management; and when the father died the women came entirely under charge of him who kept the homestead, ordinarily the eldest son. The *manes* of fathers continued a hypothetic presence, but were not deified; and the performance of certain rites for their spiritual welfare was a necessary part and condition of the administration of the estate. The Deity was regarded as an immanent Power latent in Nature, but capable of representation by one force or

---

* Cf. "Dug," and "Dairy." The Aryan languages have the same word for daughter from East to West—Sanskrit, Persian, German, Greek, &c.

another, which became the object of what Professor F. M. Müller has called "henotheistic" worship. The typical manifestations of that power in the phenomenal universe were, as we have seen, chosen according to the varying pressure of environments; first ADITI, SAVITRI, or by whatever name the Sun might be indicated, and AGNI, or Fire, the Sun's agent on earth: then came INDRA, VAHU, the wind. And this early Trinity was the object of veneration and propitiation before the growth of a cumbrous ritual, and a specialised priesthood had begun to act and react upon each other, and to create the system of Vedantic Brahmanism contemplated in the "code of Manu," developing by degrees into an oppressive clericalism.

The exact period of the first reaction against this system is subject to much of the uncertainty that pertains to all Hindu chronology. According to the ordinary view, the Buddha was a Prince of Bihár, who died B.C. 543. The latest European estimates bring this date to B.C. 477. Some of these critics question if he ever existed at all; and the earliest date that can be actually determined is, perhaps, that of a great council convened at Patna B.C. 244, from which the establishment of Buddhism as a religion unquestionably dates. But this brings us to a date later than that of the Macedonian intercourse with Upper India, at which time the reformation had already begun. We shall, therefore, do well to examine its nature and probable origin before dealing with Hindustan as known to the Greeks.

Not only has the personal existence of the Reformer been doubted, but some scholars have gone so far as to question the existence of Buddhism itself, as a distinct Indian heresy, or counterblast to Brahmanism. It is urged by them that Buddhism is merely the name for a development of the "Sánkhya" philosophy, as taught by a sage named Kápila; a system too abstract for the apprehension of the masses unless it could be rendered concrete by being gathered round the person of some human being, however idealised. It is hopeless to seek for the era of Kápila, but there seems reason to believe that he lived at Hardwár—where the Ganges breaks out through the sub-Himalayan hills--which was a place of sanctity before any of the existing forms of religion had taken birth in India. Such sages and such heresies have never been unknown in the country: the Brahmo Somáj is an instance in our own times as the foundation of Jainism was in the days with which we are now dealing. The Jains—who still exist in India—assert that their reform is older than that of the Buddha; like him they reject the fetters of caste, and preach social and spiritual emancipation. It is to be noted that the earliest legends of the reformer represent him as the son of the King of Kápilávastu, which seems to favour the theory mentioned above.

Subject to such cautions as this, the accepted view of the matter may be abstracted as follows. The Reformer dying, about the time of the birth of Socrates, his disciples attempted to systematise his teaching in what is known as the First General Council. About a century later a second council is reported, at which certain controversies were brought forward, and an attempt was made for their reconciliation; but the proceedings only led to further dissidence. It was after this that the form known as "Northern Buddhism" arose; and, ere long the incursion of Alexander the Great began to throw Upper India open to foreign influence, while the Buddhist missionaries became enabled to penetrate into Central Asia, where the system still subsists, in a form considerably differing from southern and eastern developments. Judging from existing records we are enabled to form a plausible idea of what the nature of the original movement may have been. It sprang out of Brahmanism much as Christianity sprang out of Judaism, substituting a religion of emotion and sympathy for one of ceremonial and dogma. It promulgated the admission of universal sorrow and suffering, and the belief in transmigration as a punishment for the sins of the soul: two doctrines, however, that had long been taught by the Brahmans. But the system rejected the whole Hindu pantheon; and what was offered to mankind as an asylum in its place, was a prospect of ultimate extinction as a reward, to be earned by the accumulation of a capital of good works. There was no place in such a system either for a crowd of monstrous divinities, or for one supreme God in human form. Meanwhile ignorance, pain, and other aspects of evil were to be steadily encountered; and a general charity towards all sentient beings—animals as well as men—became a prominent feature. Such appears, in a few words, to have been the nucleus of ancient Buddhism; an attempt which succeeded, to a far greater extent than might have been expected, in the strange task of founding a system of holy living upon a basis of agnostic doctrine.

We are not to suppose the spread of Buddhism to have taken place suddenly, or even to have ever established a popular creed. Side by side with the orthodox hierarchy, which was its natural foe, was no doubt a mass of polytheistic—or, rather, polydæmonic—superstition, having its roots in the fear and fanaticism of myriads of abject savages, cowering in wild mountain-tracts, and seeking in stones and trees some object of propitiation. Such people would be indifferent to reform, and neither anxious for social progress nor conscious of moral evil; to them the philosophy of the Buddhist would appeal as vainly as would the theosophy of the Brahmans. All that the reformers could do, without a system of universal instruction, would be to kindle a lamp in the darkness, and wait for calls for aid.

SECTION 2. The people being such as they were—the majority gentle and laborious, though engrossed in abject superstition, the minority, a graded society of self-satisfied Pharisees—the refined and altruistic tenets of the reformers were necessarily confined to the schools and convents of Magadha, or slowly propagated amongst a few congenial souls. About the end of the 4th century, B.C., a new light came upon the dark Indian world, not from the East, but from the West. Alexander the Great, having conquered Persia, and marched through Khorasán and Kábul, crossed the Indus at Attok early in the year 327 B.C. He found the Punjab divided into a number of Hindu states, jealous of each other to a degree which kept them from uniting to oppose his progress. On the banks of the Jehlam, however, he was encountered by a considerable native army under a local Raja, whom the Greeks knew by the name of "Porus." But the tactics of the Macedonian were too much for the multitudinous array of the unpractised Asiatics. Leaving his camp in its original position, Alexander moved a strong division, unperceived, a few miles up the river to a ford. Here he crossed early in the morning, and fell upon the Indian host while they were engaged in opposing the portion of the Macedonian force that had been left in their front. Porus was entirely overthrown, near the scene of the modern battle of Chilianwala, half way between the bank of the Indus and the city of Lahore. The whole of Upper India seemed to lie open to the victors, and all Indian history might have been altered. But there were opposing forces far more powerful than the unskilled army of Porus. After another battle and a few onward marches, Alexander found himself on the banks of the Sutlej, with a diminished host, and under the fierce sun and fiery winds of the hot season. Rumours reached him that the King of Magadha was marching against him at the head of a mighty assemblage of six hundred thousand infantry, with a proportionate contingent of elephants and horse. To his military ambition and conscious skill, such news might be a fresh encouragement; but his men were unwilling. To the trials of heat were now added the depressing influences of the monsoon. "We have done enough," they said; "take us no farther from our homes; ask of us no further sacrifices to barren glory." Alexander was unable to restore the courage of the men, or to break their resolution. Much against his wishes he had to retrace his steps to the Indus, down which he marched with a great flotilla of rafts and boats, and left India for ever, having learned all that was possible, in so short a visit, from friendly natives of that vast, mysterious land.

Among the Indians who had visited the camp of the invaders was an adventurer, destined to exert a powerful influence upon the fortunes of his countrymen. This was Chandra Gupta, an exiled subject of the King of Magadha, and believed to have been an illegitimate scion of one of the Scythian races, whose "totem" was the serpent. The details of this man's proceedings are wanting; he appears to have had friends at the Court of Palibothra, or Pataliputra, near the site of the modern Patna, and to have succeeded by their help in obtaining the throne of Magadha soon after the departure of the Macedonians. Before the end of the century he had extended his power to the Punjab, where he found his possessions bounded by the Indus, on whose opposite bank was the south-eastern extreme of the Kingdom of Babylonia, ruled by Seleukos, the successor of Alexander. A collision ensued, evidently advantageous to the Indian leader, who made a treaty with the Greek, by virtue of which his power was recognised up to the Indus, and the daughter of Seleukos became his wife. A Macedonian envoy was deputed to reside at Palibothra.

The name of this envoy was Megasthenes, and he wrote an account, entitled, "*Indiké*," of the court and kingdom of Chandra, which is only known to us from fragments, and the use made of it by Arrian, the friend of Epictetus, four centuries later. He speaks of the city as twenty-four miles in circuit, surrounded by a deep moat, the walls having 570 towers and sixty-four gates. Buddhism must have been in an infant condition, as the only allusion Megasthenes seems to have made to it is in his enumeration of the various orders of sophists, amongst whom the "Srámans" of that system, perhaps, appear. Had the subject been sufficiently prominent to attract his attention, the portions of his work in which it would have been described, are thought to be among the fragments that are still forthcoming. The inference is strong that the Buddhist schism had not then assumed any very great prominence or any position of active hostility towards the Brahman orthodoxy of the period. Nor does any crying necessity for reform appear to have then existed, for Megasthenes found Magadha society in a very creditable condition. The envoy reports that the people were brave, honest, and truthful, while slavery was unknown among them. But it was evidently at the same time a society that was too complicated, strange, and extensive to be completely understood or correctly described by an outside observer, however intelligent, and however desirous of giving a faithful report. That Megasthenes intended to be accurate is evident from the one instance of his statement of the distance of Palibothra from the Indus, which is correct within a few miles; but he could not possibly understand all the peculiarities of a state of life so unlike anything previously known to himself. Reading his report through the medium of our present more exact knowledge we are enabled to form some estimate of what the facts may have been. We may conjecture, for example, that the four castes, or classes, of the Mánava code formed the basis of the social hierarchy, though to Megasthenes it seemed as if the people were divided into seven; the higher and lower classes alike beginning to recognise the need for a division of labour. Thus, there were philosophers who were not statesmen, and statesmen who were not philosophers, a distinction by no means confined to ancient India. There were one hundred and eighteen kingdoms; that of Chandra was called the empire of "the Prasii," and claimed a kind of federal superiority, but each township reminded the Greek of the little republics of his own land. The later conditions of political literature were hardly anticipated, for "the philosopher who is found mistaken in his predictions has to observe silence for the remainder of his life."

For purposes of war considerable forces were always in a state of mobilisation, inclusive of an establishment of ordnance, which consisted of war-chariots and fighting elephants: but it was characteristic of the mild and humane habits of the people that the husbandman was not to be disturbed in his operations by any military doings; and, as in the English Wars of the Roses, the pursuits of agriculture were allowed to continue amid the marchings and engagements of contending armies. The soldiers were of good courage and discipline; and such was the efficiency of the police, or the virtue of the population, that in a camp of 400,000 persons which followed the progress of the emperor like a moving city, the value of stolen property only averaged something like £3 daily. In matters of justice the ruler sate with a sort of jury, but none of our Greek authorities seem to have known of any written code of law. The revenue was derived from the rent of land rather than from taxation; and the expression of Strabo—"the whole land is royal"—must be taken as implying that the whole surplus produce was to be used for the common benefit. There was no private ownership; but after the necessities of the husbandman had been provided for, the net balance went to meet the wants of the public service. It seems that this balance was assumed to equal a fourth of the total yield, the remaining three-quarters being left for the subsistence of the cultivator, and for the replacement of stock, etc. In towns the artisans were expected to contribute to the public service by way of labour estimated sometimes at one day in every month: every unit, in town or country, was administered by the chief revenue officer. The use of brick and stone in building is not mentioned; and from this and other considerations it is believed that the efforts of architecture were confined to structures of timber, which was then, probably, very abundant. The fortifications of walled towns were made of earth. In most other respects the manners and customs of the people were those of the modern Hindu; their habit of cooking and eating, each caste apart from all others, is particularly noticed. They used but little fermented liquor, and were temperate and patient, ready for just warfare, but all lovers of peace.

Such is the golden age of Hinduism as seen by outsiders. The Emperor Chandra is said to have abdicated and gone to the Deccan, where he ended his days as a hermit. Of his son and successor, it is only known that his name was Mitra Gupta,* and that he renewed the alliance with his European kinsfolk. The Empire continued to expand; it embraced what have been called "the three *Kulingas*," or coasts; that is—(1st) the northern portion of what is now known as the Coromandel coast; (2nd) the sea-board of Bengal with its "Hinterland"; and (3rd) the Burmese coast from Chittagong to Arakan. This is accordingly taken as the era when Brahmanism first spread to the Straits, where an ancient form of that system is still existing, especially in the island of Bali, off the coast of Java. Of this, indeed, tradition is our only evidence; perhaps the real emigration was later, but it is in the time of Asoka, the son of Mitra, that the Empire received its chief aggrandisement: and the era of this monarch—B.C. 264-223—is the first firm ground in Indian history.

Of the period of Asoka's reign there can be no manner of

---

* But he is also named by some writers "Vindusára," which was perhaps a title.

doubt, any more than of the extent of his power. The subjoined summary of events in his career has been collected, chiefly from the authority of contemporaneous inscriptions. About 263 B.C. he was Viceroy for his father, in Málwa, having his seat of government at the famous old city of Ujjain. Soon after he was engaged in a struggle for the succession, by reason of his father's death; and he did not finally obtain the throne until 260, after a series of successful wars against his competing brothers. In 257 he publicly embraced the faith of the Buddhists; and in the following year pursued the policy of his family by concluding a treaty with his cousin Antiochus II., grandson of Seleukos Nikator. This Prince soon afterwards lost the kingdoms of Parthia and Bactria, which were never reunited to the Macedonian possessions. Asoka, convert and mighty Emperor, trusted to moral suasion for the spread of his new creed. Tradition asserts that he erected no less than eighty-four thousand doctrinal monuments; but the actual inscriptions hitherto discovered amount to no more than forty-two. Nevertheless, being in various characters and dialects, and in places far distant from each other, they afford considerable evidence of a widely-extended influence, and render it more than probable that there was, at that period, an Empire of India north of the Narbada and the Máhánadi at least; for these proclamations are found cut on rocks and stones, or inscribed on pillars erected for their reception, to the north of Pesháwar, and in Ganjam, in the hills of Dehra Dun, on the shores of Kathiawar, and in the forests south of Nágpur. Their contents are as honourable to the Imperial preacher as they are demonstrative of his power and influence; and they serve to show that Asoka—or Priyádási as he calls himself—(probably a religious title) cared for all the various classes of his people. He provided for the instruction of the aborigines and foreign neighbours, while continuing ever mindful of the more material interests of all the inhabitants of the country. Thus, the inscriptions set forth that the Emperor sent missionaries to "the utmost limits of barbarian lands to associate with all unbelievers for the spread of the faith." At the same time roads were made in India, and medical attendance provided for the sick, while care was taken to maintain the purity of belief and practice among the faithful. The doctrine was fixed, and a standard of orthodoxy formed at a council held in 244 B.C. The Canon of Buddhist Scripture was settled; and the Magadhi dialect, called Páli, became the language of tradition and worship in many distant lands—Ceylon, Burma, Siam. The slaughter of animals—whether for human food or sacrifice to the gods—was prohibited, though not apparently made penal; the edicts notice also the establishment of a kind of censorship of morals; they proclaim equality of rank among all believers; they earnestly invite to the practice of benevolence and virtue.

Many autocrats have traced their own moral portraits, some intending to do so, others not. We know, from similar memorials left in Persia and Assyria, what was the notion of themselves affected by despots in those countries; conquest, slaughter, captivity, and persecution continue down to recent times the pride and the delight of despots. But Asoka is the only oriental monarch who has sought to extend an empire of suasion, and to subdue men's minds to useful and holy life. In so doing, this mighty, if simple-hearted, emperor has shown his own nature, and the ideal of his age; nor can it be denied that the result is as pleasing as unexpected. So long as the system and influence of Asoka lasted there was peace, there was some degree of happiness for a large portion of the human race.

SECTION 3.—What was the exact political character of Asoka's power we cannot learn; possibly, in so wide a region, the various states and tribes continued to exercise a good deal of autonomy. About 225 B.C. the good Emperor retired from the world; but his house continued supreme, in Magadha at least, for seven generations. About the end of that time, or say, a little before the Christian era, Magadha fell into the hands of a dynasty known as "Andhras," who are mentioned by Pliny, but appear to have retired south, and to have ruled at Orangal, in Telingána, about the time of the preparation of the Roman itinerary known by the name of Peutinger. Meanwhile, the northern part of the Empire— Hindustan and the Punjab—became subject to incursions from the North. It has been already noticed that the Greek Provinces of Central Asia broke away from the Empire of Antiochus before the end of Asoka's reign. Great disturbances ensued, and "Scythian" tribes were precipitated upon Upper India who used, to some extent at least, the Greek character, insomuch that their coins —with such inscriptions—have been found as far east as Mathura (Muttra), on the Jumna. A so-called "Scythian" king, named Kanishka, who was a Buddhist, established that form of religion in this part of India, and held a general council there about 40 A.D. Kashmir is believed to have been the centre of this northern Empire, which extended as far north as Yarkand, and as far south as Sindh. The council assembled in Kashmir, and was attended by two of the members of the great college of Jetávana in what is now the Gonda District of Audh.*

Dim memories remain of a conflict between this dynasty and the people of Central India. The Arthur of Ujjain was Vikram Aditya, whose era still forms a date and base of calculation in Hindustan. But this era (*Sambat* 1. B.C. 57) is a little too early for the supposed victory over the

---

* This was near the famous city of Srávasti, the capital of the "northern Kosala," where the Buddha is said to have taught and where the founder of Jainism certainly had a school.

"Scythians," which seems more likely to have occurred at what is called the *Saka* (*q·d.* Scythian) era of A.D. 78. General Cunningham inclines to the opinion that the victor drove the Scythians back upon the northern hills, and established a Hindu, Anti-Buddhistic, Empire from Málwa to Pesháwar, and eastward to Bengal. We have, perhaps, here a trace of some fierce religious struggle which led to the emigration of some of the worsted leaders : at all events this is the era assigned by Javanese tradition to the introduction of Indian creeds into their island, from whence they were propagated into Bali. Here, as already noted, ancient traces of Buddhism and of Brahmanism are alike found, as they also are in Sumatra. The alphabet of Java—though it has lost most signs of Indian forms—has preserved the curious signs for the nasal and final aspirate, and retains the classification of letters peculiar to the *Devanágari* alphabet. The sacred language of Bali—also used to some extent in Java and Sumatra--is called *Kawi* (*q·d.* "Bardic"), and still contains 40 per cent. of Sanskrit words.

Hence it may be concluded that, whether founded by Asoka or propagated at the so-called era of Vikram Aditya, both Brahman and Buddhist settlements were made in the equatorial islands, and that they have left remains and impressions of the ancient thoughts and ways of the people of India before the birth of modern Hinduism. Especially to be noted is the curious fact that while Muslim conquest has eradicated Hinduism from Sumatra and Java, it continues to exist in the neighbouring island of Bali, where society is still divided into four classes known by the same names that are applied to them in the *Mánava* "Code." The three higher classes have kept a mark of their former connections by occasional intermarriage : the Brahmans do not practise widow-burning any more than they did in India, but among the rest the terrible rite is usual. In Java the Muslims warred against the Hindus—of both persuasions—with great and growing success until 1478 .A.D., when they completely and finally prevailed. It is possible that the Hindus were then expelled, or allowed to escape, into Bali ; but the system as it exists there, even if only propagated indirectly and in comparatively recent times, must be taken to express the ancient beliefs and practices as the mammoth in Siberia represents the palæozoic fauna of the world.

According to an Audh legend the empire of Vikram lasted eighty years and was then overthrown by a fanatic named Samudra Gupta who removed the seat of Government to Kanauj on the Jumna and founded a dynasty which is held by those who follow local tradition to have ruled for three or four hundred years. In the seventh century of the Christian era Kanauj was still the seat of a great monarchy as will be more particularly shown presently ; and during the interval between Samudra and this later period occurred the final propagation of Hinduism into Bengal, where all Brahmans to this day trace their descent to one or other of the five apostles who visited them from Kanauj. The age of the Gupta Kings—who are said to have been of the Vaisya, or third class of Hindus— has received some illustrations from their coins, and their true era seems to have been from about 120 to 320 A.D., when they were overthrown and succeeded by the Vallabhi dynasty. But it has been doubted whether this latter dynasty had any general power until more than a century and a half later ; the *seventh* ruler being the first of any importance. The Vallabhi era is therefore usually taken as commencing about 480 A.D. They were Buddhist in faith, and soon retired to the west of India where they were ultimately overthrown by the Arab invaders of Sindh.*

---

* It must be noted that the exact date and duration of these dynasties are most uncertain. " Mr. E. Thomas and General Cunningham are at issue

Meanwhile, the States of the Deccan were divided among Dravidian and Hindu potentates. The three old Dravidian powers have been called Pandiya, Chola, and Chera, or Kerala, while wild aborigines wandered over waste areas in the centre. The three coasts of the Bay of Bengal—Arakan, Bengal, and what is now Northern Madras—have been already spoken of as the Kulingas; the name became afterwards specialised; and "the Kingdom of Kulinga" figures in Buddhist legends as applied to the last alone. By degrees the Hindus began to encroach more and more. The Andhras established themselves in Orissa: the Chalukyas had their capital at Kalyán, near the site of the modern Bombay.

The original Dravida country was that where the Tamil language still prevails: the southern capital was Madura, and the kingdom of Pandiya—whose centre this formed—was known to the Greeks by the name of Pandion.* It occupied the south-eastern extremity of the peninsula.

The Karnáta, or Canarese country, was the seat of the Chera Kings—whose dynasty was also called Kerala, their capital being spoken of as Keralaputra in the edicts of Asoka. Of the third great southern division, the Chola kingdom, the capital was mostly at, or near, Tanjore in later days, having formerly been at Trichinopoli. This state was also mentioned by Asoka; and all three were known to Ptolemy. The sovereigns of Kulinga, called Gangas, are mentioned by the oldest chroniclers, Hindu and Buddhist, and also by the Greeks: hardy and adventurous, they traded by sea with distant lands, and ruled at home over a civilised country.

Of the life of the people of Hindustan during the period

as to the commencement of the Gupta era . . . . . the several dates assigned to Toramána (the last important monarch of the series) vary from 89 B.C. to the 7th century A.D." So says Bábu Rájendra Lála.

* This may be regarded as the "Bretagne Bretonnante" of India, where the conquered race made a stand with its back to the sea.

just before, and a few hundred years after, the Christian era, we have some evidence in the Hindu dramas—for though the dates of these are also uncertain, we know in a general way when and in what order they were composed. Of the same period we have likewise a glimpse in the meagre notice of India preserved in the narrative of Fa Hian, a Buddhist traveller who visited the cradle of his faith from China in the beginning of the 5th century A.D. Of the Chinese pilgrim, and of his follower of two centuries later, it has been said by a great scholar that they form "almost our only stepping-stones through a thousand years of fable."* The account of our earlier pilgrim, indeed, is only useful in a minor and relative degree. It does not much help us to answer the most interesting of all questions of the period—What was the normal relation of Buddhism to the older creed? But it helps us to see the beginnings of the decay of the Reformation, and to obtain some notion of the way in which the Brahmans recovered their lost ascendency. Fa Hian travelled from North to South, following the course of the Ganges to the sea, and spent fourteen years in India, from A.D. 399. At that time Buddhism was still very prevalent; but, true to its humane principles, it did not persecute; and the temples and colleges of the Brahmans existed side by side with the conventual establishments of the Reformers. Signs of decline were visible; at Srávasti, already mentioned as the great seat of Buddhist learning, Fa Hian found the college buildings in decay, and the town deserted by all but two hundred poor families. In the dramatic literature of the period we hear of no religious quarrels; but we find a romantic treatment of mythologic themes, and a domestic picture of a noble and humane social system.

We may pass rapidly over the next two hundred years; of

* Professor Cowell.

the events of which indeed but little is yet known, and that little vague and doubtful. Hindustan has no annals for that period; may we hope that the people were not unhappy! Literature, at least, was prosperous. Kálidása produced some exquisite poetical dramas, one of which—"*Sakuntala*, or the Lost Ring"—even in a most imperfect version, obtained the admiration of no less a judge than Goethe. Among the domestic plays "The Toy-Cart" is distinguished for its graceful delineation of gay and gentle manners. "The Cloud Messenger" and the *Gita Govinda* are fascinating idyls, full of warm sentiment, and idealised pictures of nature, such as we should seek in vain from modern Hindus. Grammars, lexicons, works on the abstract sciences, on music, medicine, and surgery, bear testimony to a time of taste and leisure. The so-called "Code of Manu" is believed to have taken its present form about A.D. 500. The great kingdom of Kanauj, where the Aditya dynasty ruled, was apparently the centre of this intellectual movement; but it is by no means clear how far its power and influence extended. Delhi—then called Indraprastha—was the seat of a Rajput monarchy, of which there were others in Ajmere and Gujarát. The Chálukya dynasty ruled in Maháráshtra, where they introduced a beautiful school of architecture, an art in which they had already been anticipated by the Buddhists. Chálukya architecture was perhaps a development from the Buddhist rock-cut temples of that part, but its later products are found north of the Narbada also. To the eastward there were other powerful states; the Kingdom of Orissa was invaded by a tribe of foreigners from the north, who were finally expelled by the Kesari family, A.D. 473. Farther south, Telingána became an independent kingdom under the Andhras, of whom something has been already said; here too the northern foreigners called "Yávana," effected a successful incursion, after their expulsion from Orissa. In the west was the Rajput (Jádu) State of Deogiri, whose rock-cut temples indicate a long and peaceful rule. Another Rajput kingdom in the Deccan is supposed to have had its capital at Paithan on the Upper Godávari, formerly the seat of the power which founded the "Saka" era (A.D. 77) still current in southern India.

When Hiwen Tsiang, the second of our Buddhist pilgrims, visited India (A.D. 629-645), there were no less than seventy of these kingdoms, or states; but, so far at least as Upper India was concerned, there was some sort of loose federation under the Empire of Kanauj, still held by a Prince of the old dynasty, whose name was Siláditya, and whom the pilgrim visited. Málwa was a seat of learned men, but there, as generally throughout India, the Buddhist establishments were becoming fewer than of old, and not only were the colleges and temples of Brahmanism increasing in number, but sects of fanatics were making their appearance—always a sign of religious fermentation. In Kápilavastha, the above-mentioned cradle of the Buddhist creed, the royal city was in ruins, and so were the convents. Near Benares there were numerous heretical votaries of Siva, mostly going about naked, or only covered with a paste made of the ashes of burnt cow-dung; in the city of Benares itself the worship of the same deity was established, the pilgrim saw a brazen statue of Siva nearly 100 feet in height. The monarch of Kanauj, though he professed to be a Buddhist, continued the tolerant practice of his predecessors; and the pilgrim was present when myriads of people were entertained by Siláditya without distinction of creed. The great Buddhist college of Sarnáth was still standing near Benares, but it was burnt not very long after the departure of the Chinese pilgrim.

Apart from such indications of violence, it would seem that Buddhism expired by slow degrees between the 8th and 9th centuries of our era. It was, doubtless, by the aid of combination with indigenous superstitions that Brahminism was enabled to supplant it in popular acceptation, though it is evident that Buddhism was not entirely extinguished. Its practice may have been too purely philosophical for the common people; but its principles had won too much favour to be destroyed; and a great deal of Buddhism was accordingly preserved, in the reorganised Hinduism which arose upon the ground so long occupied by the controversies of the rival faiths.

In spite of all recorded prohibitions against intermarriage, it is probable that, at an early period of the conquest, the Vaisyas had taken wives from among the Sudra women; the analogy of other conquests is too strong to admit of much doubt upon the matter. Marriage with Canaanitish women was practised by the followers of Moses and Joshua; the "Rape of the Sabines" is a familiar instance in Roman history; the Norman conquerors of England took English wives, as is shown in the story of Morville. And it cannot be supposed that the Vedic Aryans brought across the bleak and difficult passes of the Hindu Kush a large train of women and children—especially if driven away from their older seats by war. Their ancient marriage codes, after their arrival in Upper India, took cognisance of the offspring of unequal alliances; one ancient commentator on the Veda enumerates 159 castes, mostly distinguished by the relations between the families of their parents.

Out of the amalgamation thus begun, a solidarity must have arisen between the invaders and the friendly portions of the conquered populations; and it was for the spiritual government of this mixed multitude and of their chiefs that the sages of Buddhism competed with the priests of the *Vedánta* and the *Tantra*. And there is a considerable literature to our hands in which we can watch the controversy and gauge the renascence of Brahmanism, which became ultimately successful in the form of modern Hinduism. Of the religious books of the

Buddhists, nothing need here be said; whether in the canons of Thibet and Nipal, or in those of Ceylon, which teach a somewhat varying system, there is nothing that is now scriptural in India. The sacred literature of the modern Hindus is of comparatively modern date. Whatever respect be paid to the vague and venerable memory of the *Veda*, great as is the popular feeling for the tale of Ráma, it is to the *Puránas* that the ultimate appeal lies in matters of faith and in matters of practice. Symptoms of eclecticism had been already noticed in the seventh century A.D., when Siláditya, Emperor of Kanauj, held his great council—circ. 634 A.D.—at which Hiwen Tsiang was present; and the system went on for at least three centuries.

It may further the understanding of a rather dark matter if we agree to look upon the higher form of Hinduism as a synthesis of two views of the universe which have always presented themselves to reflective minds. Stated in terms of modern science, Brahmanism had been based upon the conception of nature as emanating from the compound action of a dual force; while Buddhism proceeded upon the relativity of human knowledge, teaching the "Sankhya" doctrine of evolution and the dependence of the phenomenal universe on the illusions of perception. The union of these two schemes is one great characteristic of Hindu philosophy. But something more was needed to popularise the system, and this was found in a compromise with the demon-worship of the conquered populations. The two-fold task was begun by Kumarila, a teacher who arose in Bihár—the very birth-place of Buddhism—about a century after the time of Hiwen Tsiang. He earnestly proclaimed the necessity of a personal deity; and—partly, at least, by force—extirpated the agnostic creed in his own part of the country. His doctrines were taken up by his disciple, Shankar Achárya, a native of Assam, or—according to some authorities—of the Deccan, who lived for some time at Benares; and who, after founding the Smarta school in the Deccan, is related to have proceeded on pilgrimage to Kidarnáth on the Himalaya, where he died, towards the end of the eighth century A.D. The Smarta Brahmans are worshippers of Siva, and whatever the esoteric teaching of their founder may have been, there is little doubt but that Kumarila conciliated the popular craving for concrete religion by adopting that worship.

This object of idolatry appears to have originated in a combination of the storm-god of the Vedic Aryans with some local demon: with his consort he forms the incarnation of the two "forces" above mentioned, and the phallic symbol of generation is consecrated to Siva, as are also the emblems of death. In him have full play those wilder elements usually hidden under the self-controlled surface of the Hindu character: he is shown, in painting and in sculpture, with an aspect of the sort most terrible to simple minds; and some of his votaries indulge in grotesque and disgusting practices. One of the gospels of this faith inculcates human sacrifice with detailed rites of the most unambiguous character. Some two hundred years after the period of Shankar, a more humane worship was set up—that of Vishnu, also founded on an Aryan conception originally representing the sun, and afterwards applied to a series of human and other incarnations, all of a beneficent character. The notion of a supreme creator being added, the theory of a new Trinity became substituted for the old Brahmanical theology; this is the famous triune Godhead of the Hindus, BRAHMA, the Creator; SIVA, the Destroyer; VISHNU, the Preserver. But the first of these impersonations never took the public imagination; and, in practice, the devotion of the Hindus is divided between Siva and Vishnu, the worship of the former being general in the south, the service of the latter more followed in the north of India:

Brahma seems to be too abstract a deity, and the only temple to his honour in all India is said to be that of Pohkar in Ajmere, by the side of a lake of great sanctity.

By thus adroitly adopting the superstitions of the multitude, the Brahmans wove the web of Hinduism on a familiar ground-work; and thus the mass of the people might think themselves advanced, both socially and spiritually, by professing an enlightened creed; while yet able to preserve the compassion of kindly village fairies who had been dear to their fathers, and to avert the wrath of malevolent demons that their mothers had taught them to fear and to propitiate.

At the same time not only some of the metaphysics of Buddhism, but its general spirit and, indeed, some of its practical principles also, were adopted in the new religious system. Among the results of the former was the doctrine of transmigration, which plays a large part in the belief of high and low among the modern Hindus; a survival of the latter is seen in an extreme scrupulosity about some forms of life, and a widespread objection to animal food. The followers of Vishnu—whose special gospel, the *Vishnu Purana*, has been provisionally dated about 1045 A.D.—at first denounced the Buddha as a teacher of atheism; but they afterwards found it advisable to adopt him as one of the incarnations of their favourite deity; and it has been asserted that their rules of religious life are little more than fragments of Buddhist precept, enforced by Brahmanic sanctions and arguments. The rival sect of Siva has borrowed elements from the hopes and fears of the lower classes, largely tinctured—as above said—with local superstition; and in such a compromise they too were following a path originally indicated by the Buddhists. Portions even of the archaic worship of trees and of serpents were adopted by the Buddhists: at the present day they are tolerated, if not taught, in Hinduism as now practised; while the sects of Vishnu use forms of fetish almost certainly traceable to a very old form of nature-worship. Besides all these concessions and compromises, Hinduism has always shown a prudent consideration for the reforming sects which have arisen out of its own body. Many of these have struck hard at the system of caste, and at polytheistic idol-worship, attempting to combine the omnipotence of the Supreme Being with the absolute equality of men. The heresy of Kabir, in the fourteenth century A.D., even showed a leaning towards the new and hostile creed of Islam; and it was imitated—if not developed—by the system of the Sikhs, which is professed by a hardy population even at the present day. Yet these heresies show themselves ready to submit when Hinduism takes their doctrines to itself, and adopts their prophets as apostles or even incarnations of its own deities. As a return for that hospitality many disciples of the reformers have shown readiness for reconciliation. The Sikhs, indeed, long held out, refusing all compromise. But history will show how much the Sikh movement was actuated by political motives. Now that the Sikhs have become foremost in accepting the government of the British, and have lost the fiery stimulus of persecution, their religious creed is also losing its aggressive character. It is probable that Sikhism will slowly, but surely, merge into a form of Hinduism; as has been the case with the creed of the Kabir Punthis, of the Satnámis, and of many other sects.

One denomination, indeed, there was which, to this day, neither yields nor disappears. The Jain or Sarawak denomination—a sect whose foundation is believed to be of an earlier date than Buddhism—has survived its more ambitious sister, and still numbers a petty, but not diminishing, fraction of the Indian people. The Jains are like the English Quakers, a small but prosperous community, of pure and simple tenets, tolerant, but tenacious.

Such as is the condition of Hinduism after centuries of Muslim persecution, it has yet to show its power of resisting the more subtle influences of modern science. For the present we have only to remark that the laws, literature, and religious practices, which are still prevalent in Hindustan, arose in the period between the decline of Buddhism and the introduction of Islam.

For the part of northern India, east of Benares—what is now known as "The Lower Provinces,"—a few more details have been provisionally determined, and Buddhism seems to have held out longer there than elsewhere. By careful collation of his own discoveries with those of the earlier epigraphists, Babu Rajendralal Mitra has arrived at the conclusion that there was a Buddhist dynasty, styled the House of Pála, whose capital was at Mangeer (Monghyr), about the middle of the ninth century A.D.; while a Brahmanic line bore rule in Bengal proper, having its capital at Bikrampur, near Dháka (Dacca).

Their surname was Sena, or Sen; and the ruins of their fortified palace are still shown with traces of a surrounding city. These latter kings were probably Kshatriyas of the lunar race, brave and intelligent men. They gradually supplanted the Buddhist line, and made their capital at Gaur, or Lakhnauti, until conquered in their turn by the advancing Muslims. The founder of the power of the Senas over Bengal and eastern Bihár, was Bállala, about 1000 A.D.; and it is believed to have been in his time that the five Brahmans came as missionaries from Kanauj, as above-mentioned.

[The books mentioned at the end of last chapter may be consulted for this. Also "The Dynasty of the Guptas," by E. Thomas, London, 1876 : "Sketch of the Dynasties of Southern India," by Robert Sewell, Madras, 1883; and the "Ancient Geography" and Archæological Reports of General Cunningham. For the islands of the Equator, see Crawford's "Dictionary of the Indian Islands," London, 1856; also Colonel H. Yule's "Sketch of Java," Calcutta, 1862.]

CHAPTER III.

THE MUSLIM CONQUEST.

Section 1: The houses of Ghaniz and of Gur.—Section 2: The Slave Dynasty.—Section 3: First Muslim aggressions in the Deccan.

SECTION I.—The domestic drama of the Hindus affords a picture of the life of the people during the centuries immediately preceding the invasion of the Muhamadans. The tenets of the Buddhists had produced a standard of character and conduct something similar to what is now existing in Burma and Siam, and, in many ways, very different from what is observable in modern India after ages of foreign domination. Brahmans were ceasing to be a sacerdotal class; although their religious ascendency was reviving with the birth of the new Hinduism, they were chiefly respected as an aristocracy of pure and ancient descent. Secular life was gay and luxurious; the world of sense, however denounced by sages, attracted the bulk of Indian mankind. But if the Hindus had not mastered the difficult lesson how to submit the cravings of the body to the aspirations of the soul, their sensuousness was not without the charm proceeding from refinement. Like their Greek contemporaries, they united the life of the family with the existence of female companions who were free but not degraded. Genial and gentle of mood, both sexes were generous and without fear. The fusion of races—always under the restrictions of the caste system—had been almost, if not quite, completed. It was thought by Megasthenes that slavery was unknown among them; in any case the servants were faithful and of independent bearing. The married ladies went abroad unveiled, like those of Theocritus; they received visitors, mixed in general society, but had to suffer serious competition from other women with whom their husbands associated without loss of reputation. In the grove of Káma—the Indian Eros—the respectable citizen met his equally respectable "professional beauty," who even became the friend of his wife. We are shown, in short, a world sufficiently advanced in civilisation to be amiably voluptuous, yet far from general corruption. Parasites and buffoons were tolerated; and the heroine of unlawful love, for all her equivocal position, was yet sweet and womanly, redeemed by affection, and glorified by devotion and fidelity.

How long such an Arcadian scheme of manners may have endured we cannot positively say. Under a sky bright without cloud during the long summer days, gorgeous in atmospheric pomps during the green luxuriance of the monsoon, breathing fresh and balmy airs upon the blossoming flower-trees of the cooler season—when the Bauhinia trails its purple glories over the flaming branches of the Butea, and the antelope browses under the scented shade of the Mango—the Hindus led their easy lives, relaxing slowly under the increasing influences of luxury and peace. In their mud-walled cities, the palaces of their chiefs and the temples of their gods bristled with multitudinous pinnacles and statues and carved turrets; and the processions of Royal marriages glittered in the crowded bazaars.

But a terrible time of change was being prepared. Far off, beyond the glaciers of the Himalaya, the home of the negligent gods, was a swarm of hardy, hungry nomads, constantly engaged in tribal conflicts for their wild pastures, or slowly gathering for defence in crowded towns. Devastation and invasion kept the north and north-western lands in constant ferment. Twenty years after the era of the Prophet's flight the

Persian State had been overthrown by his warlike lieutenants, and a Muslim Empire was established under the Khalif of Baghdad. The last vestige of this once mighty power disappeared before Tartar incursions; and the Seljuk conquest pushed out the old Muslims towards the east and south-east. The last of the Hindu dramas, written perhaps in the latter part of the 10th century, A.D., plainly indicates the effect of these movements on India. The old gay freedom was scared away, perhaps never to return. The Grove of Love became a wilderness, and the Hindu lady had to seclude herself from the pursuit of the invading foreigner. There is no female character visible throughout this play, the principal persons are politicians of a depraved school. Fraud and assassination are the crude expedients for liquidating inconvenient obligations. There is no mention, as in earlier works, of law or courts of justice. Chiefs and mercenary soldiers of foreign origin are mentioned, social and political anarchy are evidently at hand.

Such was the state of the country when first exposed to the influence of the new power that had been established on the north-western border. But the valiant Rajputs did not yield without a protracted struggle. The lands between the Oxus river and the Sulaiman mountains became subject to a Turkmán* dynasty, called Samanides, after the founder, *circ.* 860 A.D. The fifth chief of this house entrusted the government of the Helmand Valley to a favourite mameluke named Alptigin, who made himself independent, and who was succeeded by his own slave in 976. The name of this man was Nasir-ud-din Sabaktigin; and the centre of his sway was at Ghazni, between Kandahár and Kábul, reaching from the confines of the left bank of the Oxus to the foot of the Sulaiman range. On the other side of these mountains was the territory

---

* This word (= "Turk-like") is here used to denote the mixed race negendered by the fusion of the local races (called Tájik) with their Tartar conquerors.

of a Rajput chief, named Jai Pál, whose capital was at Lahore, but who had some ill-defined claims to sovereignty over the vast extent of country from Delhi to the Hindu Caucasus. Endeavouring to vindicate his northern frontier, Jai Pál marched an army up the celebrated defile of the Khaibar Pass; but he found the army of Sabaktigin ready to close with him near Kábul. The season was cold and stormy. Jai Pál's heart failed him; a negotiation was opened, the result of which was that he was allowed to depart in peace on paying a heavy ransom. A Muslim envoy was appointed to accompany the returning host of the Hindus; but on its arrival at Lahore the Rája, recovering his courage, threw the envoy into prison, and refused to pay the stipulated ransom. This act of perfidy naturally brought down the Muslim chief, who collected his followers and marched towards Peshawar. The Rája, on his side, appealed to the patriotism and feudatory obedience of the chiefs of Delhi, Ajmere, and Kanauj; and a gallant host once more crossed the Indus, hoping by a forward movement to repel the threatened danger. The action ended in the defeat of the Hindus; the Rája fled to Lahore, and committed suicide by cremation, like a second Sardanapalus. The conquerors returned, after plundering the Punjab, and leaving a garrison in in Peshawar; and some of the mountain tribes were converted to Islam. These events occurred in the very end of the 10th century A.D.

The son and successor of Sabaktigin was the famous Saltan Mahmud, known in eastern history as *Bhut Shikan*, or "The Iconoclast." He found the Hindus, under their new Rája, Anang Pál, resolved to dispute the possession of the Peshawar Valley. But he completed its conquest, and advanced his boundaries to the right bank of the Indus. On the other side Anang Pál, at the head of a strong Rajput confederacy, held his own during his lifetime, and on his death was succeeded by another Jai Pál. In the outset of this reign, however, Mahmud marched suddenly down from the mountains north of Lahore, and occupied the capital; on which the Rája fled from the Punjab, and took refuge at Ajmere after sustaining a severe defeat on the field of Chach, near Ráwal-Pindi. This was in 1008, and the victory laid the whole of Upper India open to the invaders. It was in such a state of affairs that the last Hindu dramatist said of his country that

> "This nurse of elemental life,
> Now harassed by barbarians, shall resort
> For safety to the bosom of her kings,
> And so escape a new annihilation."

But the aspiration was vain. Indian annals for the next century were to be written in blood. During a reign of thirty years Mahmud the Iconoclast invaded India no less than twelve times, causing carnage wherever he was resisted, desecrating the Hindu temples and destroying their idols. Mathura, in the centre; Kanauj, in the east; Somnáth, the gloomy shrine of Siva, on the coast of Kathiawar; in such distant and divergent spots he smote the Rajput; Mathura, or "Muttra," was sacked in 1017, Kanauj in the following year. Somnáth, which was under the sovereignty of the Chálukya House of Kalián, was captured after an assault of three days' duration. This was in 1025, when the great statue of Mahádeo is said to have been destroyed, and the doors of his temple carried away to fill the gateway where the conqueror was to be entombed. In 1030 A.D. that conqueror died, and the monument is still to be seen at Ghazni, whence Lord Ellenborough caused the doors to be removed in 1841* and brought to India.

Mahmud of Ghazni left a famous name. Full two centuries after his demise the celebrated Shaikh Saádi of Shiráz related

---

* This affair was the occasion of Macaulay's famous speech in Parliament on March 9, 1843. It has been since shown that the doors in question could not have been those of the Somnáth temple. They are now at Agra.

THE MUSLIM CONQUEST.   55

that the dead warrior had appeared to him in a vision, the eyes staring :—

"And still he gazes round,
Because his realm to other lords is bound."

But the manner of his house's fall was of the most customary kind. Great conquerors cannot always establish their dynasty; great leaders are apt to be succeeded by inadequate sons. Mahmud was no exception to such rules, though a favourable specimen of the successful soldier-king, an eastern Oliver or Napoleon. The offspring of a Tartar father by a Tajik mother, he combined the refined taste of the one race with the aggressive and predatory instincts of the other. Hence he was able to make extensive conquests and to rule them well and wisely. He also knew how to avoid the temptation of extending his conquests permanently beyond his means of administering them. Therefore, in India, he contented himself with the possessions of his father; and while amassing wealth by the plunder of the rest of the country, made no attempt to retain possession of the government. He is said to have accumulated more treasure than any of his predecessors.

But his treasury, his magnificent palace, his mosque of marble, were all inherited by unworthy heirs. His sons quarrelled with one another. Their armies failed to oppose the Seljuk advance; the Hindus profited by the confusion to resume their independence, and ventured even to lay siege to Lahore, the Muslim capital, although here they were foiled. Northward the Seljuk war went on with varying results, until, in 1118—little more than three-fourths of a century from Mahmud's decease—a descendant of better quality became the ruler of Ghazni under the title Sultan Bairám. He ruled ably for many years, and gave his daughter in marriage to the Satrap of Gur (the "Ghore" of English historians.)* This chief, who

* Gur is the country of the modern Hazáras, between Kandahar and Herat.

was called Kutb-ud-din, was of the famous Sur clan; one of three ambitious brothers. He ultimately quarrelled with his royal father-in-law, and the Sultan tarnished the splendour of his reign by the treacherous murder of the Satrap. On this he was attacked by the brother of that chief, and driven out of Ghazni. A war ensued, which ended by Ghazni being captured and recaptured till it was finally sacked in 1152. All the city was given up to arson, and the tomb of Mahmud is said to have been almost the only building of importance to escape the flames. The dynasty of Sabaktigin lingered a few years longer at Lahore, and the Hindus enjoyed some respite from rapine and persecution until 1186. Meanwhile, Alá-ud-din took possession of the empire, and made his capital at Firoz Koh in the hills of Gur.

At the time when the Ghazni dynasty took refuge in the Punjab their immediate neighbour was a Rajput, of the Chauhán tribe, named Rai Pithaura. He was descended, by the mother's side, from that Anang Pál whose spirited resistance to Muslim encroachment has been lately noticed. To the eastward were the federations of Kanauj and Bengal, under other Rajput chiefs; to the west the chief Rajput power was Gujarát, in alliance with Kanauj, but Rai Pithaura, who had originally been chief of Ajmere only, had dispossessed the Kanauj Rája of the Delhi territory, and claimed the title of *Pirthi Rája*, or Sovereign. He extended the fortifications of old Delhi, where his fortress is still to be seen, a circuit of 4½ miles surrounding the old fort, which stands on higher ground and forms an inner citadel. It also included 27 Hindu and Buddhist places of worship, hundreds of whose pillars still remain, converted into supports and ornaments of a mosque erected by the conquerors. The pedigree and power of Rai Pithaura were sung wherever men repeated the poems of his minstrel, Chand Bardai.

On the other side of the Punjab a Muslim kingdom had

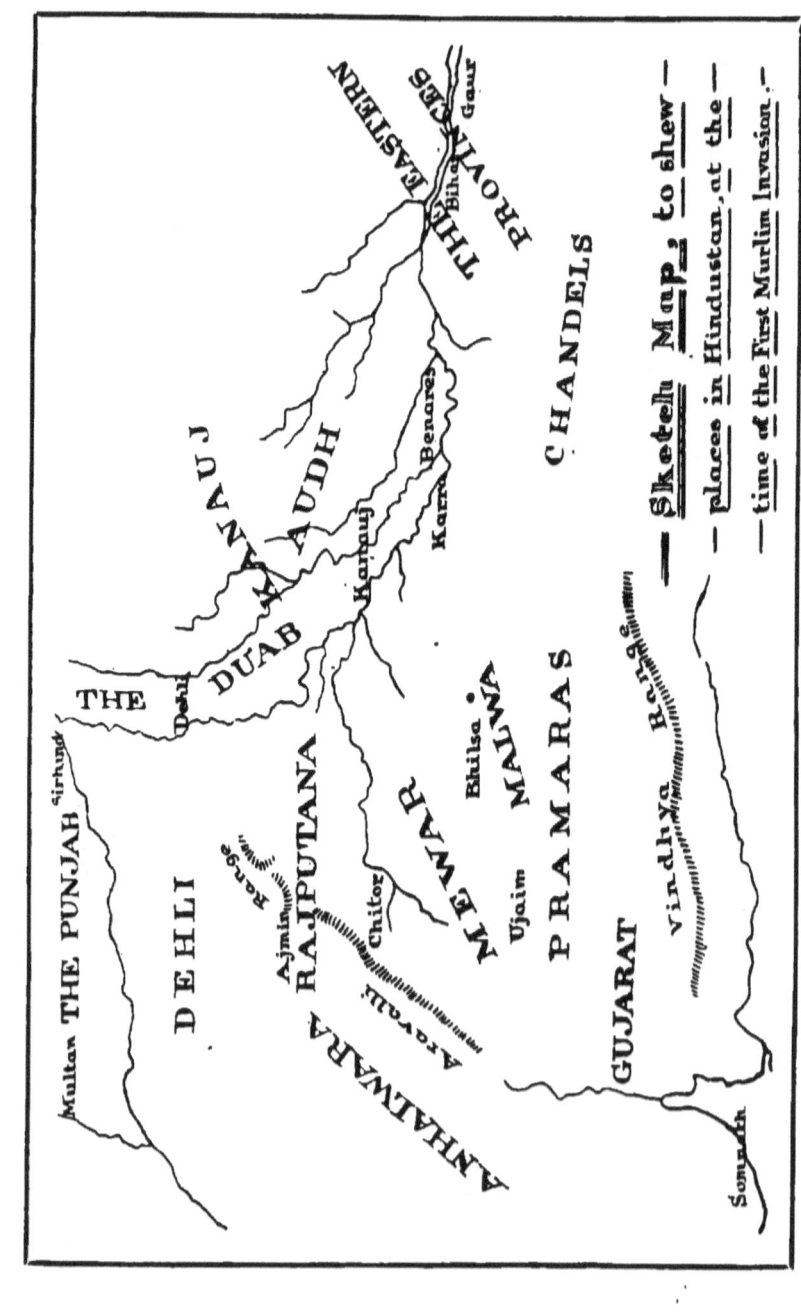

been set up in the hills of Gur, which extended over what is now the Amirate of Afghanistan. This state had been established by Alá-ud-din Jahánsoz, the "burner of the world" (*q.d.* burner of Ghazni). He died in 1156, being succeeded by his two nephews. These chiefs presented the rare spectacle among oriental rulers of brethren living together in unity; but their joint reign of thirty years was constantly disturbed by war, at first with the Seljuks, and—when these were finally repulsed—with the exiled Ghaznevides in the Punjab, assisted by the wild and warlike Ghakkars of those parts. At length, in 1186, the Ghaznevides were quite overcome; Lahore was occupied by the younger of the two brothers, Muhamad-bin-Sám, and all obstacles to the invasion of Hindustan were removed.

Shaháb-ud-din and *Muiz-ud-din* were titles of the first Muslim conqueror of Hindustan, an able warrior, whose name was Muhamad-bin-Sám. During the life of his brother, Ghyás-ud-din, he acted as Viceroy of the eastern part of the empire of Gur, having his capital at Ghazni. After the fall of the Muslim power in the Punjab he extended his sway to that country, and began to prepare for further conquest. But the strength of the Rajputs, though divided by the jealousies between their various states, indicated the need of careful marshalling of the Muslim forces; and it was not until 1190 that Shaháb-ud-din felt strong enough to cross the Sutlej. At this time the enmity between the Chauhán Rája and his unfriendly neighbour, the Rathor ruler of Kanauj, by name Jai Chandra, had broken out into a serious quarrel, the news of which may have emboldened the invader. Unsupported as he was, Rai Pithaura advanced to oppose the progress of the invader, and completely defeated him in a great battle south of the Sutlej, the famous scene of so many battles of Indian history. Shaháb-ud-din, wounded in the action, escaped with difficulty, and fell back on his capital of Ghazni, leaving the Punjab, as it would seem, to be occupied by the Hindus.

The defender of Hindustan had prevailed, but his success was of short duration. The next year (1192) Shaháb-ud-din passed at Ghazni, recruiting his forces, and proclaiming a holy war in the hills and dales around him. In 1191 he once more entered the Punjab at the head of a power which, however diverse in political obedience, was held together by the fanaticism of a common creed. According to the testimony of an eye-witness, the mounted men-at-arms alone numbered 120,000, clad in chain mail and riding good Turkmán horses; of light horse there were full forty thousand. Moreover, the Muslims had learned a lesson from their former defeat, and were prepared to meet the simple tactics of the enemy, which consisted in opening their line before a charge, while the flanks of the advancing host were enveloped on either side by the wheeling round of the ranks.

The armies met on the Sirhind plain, Rai Pithaura having allied and feudatory chiefs for support, but none from the eastward. He tried once more his famous flank-movement, but it availed him little. The Muslims affected to retreat before they had been enclosed; the Hindus breaking their order rushed on to pursue; but Muhamad had his cavalry in hand, and charged at their head under cover of a cloud of arrows. The Rajput host was broken; Pithaura, alighting from his elephant, sought to escape on horseback, but was overtaken and made prisoner. He was despatched to attend the conqueror's triumphal entry into Ghazni, but died on the way, perhaps by his own hand. His exploits and misfortunes were sung by Chand, his favourite minstrel, who long survived him.

The city of Delhi fell at once.* A year later the Rájas of Kanauj and Benares paid the penalty of their folly in holding back from the defence of their common country. The attention of Shaháb-ud-din was, however, distracted by the politics of

* For the date (A.H. 587) v. Thomas, "Pathan Kings," p 22-3.

his own land, and the turbulence of the Punjab where the Ghakkars continued to revolt and plunder. The gradual settlement of Hindustan was left to a lieutenant of named Aibak,* a Turkman slave, aided in the eastern districts by a Khilji officer named Bakhtyár. The nominal head of the empire died, and Muhamad-bin-Sám went to Gur leaving Ghazni in charge of another Mameluke named Yalduz (*mod. Turk.* Yildiz, "a star") while he engaged in wars, sometimes in Central Asia, sometimes in the valley of the Indus. In 1206 A.D. he was murdered in his tent by a band of Ghakkars, and Aibak assumed the dignity of Sultan at Delhi under the title of Kutb-ud-din. At the time of the accession of this fortunate adventurer a complete Muslim sovereignty only existed in the city and immediate neighbourhood of Delhi. At Ajmere a tributary Rája was maintained for a time, after which the Muslims attempted to substitute a garrison and governor of their own, who were, however, cut to pieces by the Rajputs in the fourth year of the reign. The grandson of Jai Chandra, the Rathor of Kanauj, refused submission, and emigrated, with the bulk of his people, to Márwar, where they founded the State of Jodhpur, which still subsists. In the eastern districts, where the Sena dynasty had become supreme from Benares to the sea, the Khilji general, Bakhtyár, drove the Raja from Lakhnauti —or Gaur, as it was called later—and forced him back on Bikrampur, where Billála Sena had his capital before the conquest of the Pála dynasty. The name of this unfortunate descendant is believed to have been Asoka, but the glorious patronymic did little for him. For a short time he clung to the fortified palace of his ancestors; then the Muslims made a further advance. Alarmed and helpless, the Rajput threw himself upon a burning pyre, with his family, and all perished in the flames. The successful adventurer established himself as an independent ruler at Sonárgaon, not far from the modern Dacca; but

* *Ai* = "*Moon*," and *Bak, Bek*, or *Beg* = "Lord."

being the Sultan's son-in-law, he probably, for the time, appeared in the light of a Satrap to the Court of Delhi.

Kutb-ud-din Aibak established that Court in the fortified palace of Rai Pithaura; but he overthrew the Hindu temples there, and built with the materials the great mosque of Kutb-ul Islám, which is still to be seen there, and still bears witness to the grand designs of the Muslim ruler, as much as to the skill of the Hindu artificers whose work he adopted.* The style of the columns is what is technically known as "Jain," but the arrangement is purely that of a Muslim cloister. In front of the chancel was an arcade, of whose arches only three are now standing. These, however, are not truly arched, but produced by brackets of spandril form jutting out from the pillars of the abutments, and meeting in the centre without key-stones. This peculiarity shows the employment of Hindu workmen, who had to comply with the desire of their employers for the form of the arch, yet did not know the principle of its construction. Within the arcade is a hall of 133 feet in length, covered by a roof supported by rows of pillars. The carvings are rich and sharp after the havoc of seven hundred years. Outside the south-east angle of the main building, like the campanile of an Italian church, stands the great minaret 258 feet high, sloping from the foot, where the diameter is 47·3 feet across, to a thickness of barely 9 feet at the summit. It is now in five storeys, the two lower divided from the rest by balconies, supported on rich pendentives going all round the circumference of the tower. Mosque and minar alike bear great arabesque inscriptions in honour of Muhamad-bin-Sám. The original tower was of two storeys only.

SECTION 2.—The year of Aibak's accession marks the era of a new dynasty. While he was conquering Bengal and beautifying the capital he was only a military Viceroy. But in

---

* Qutb (pop. Kutb) means "Pole Star." The mosque is also called *Quvvat-ul: Islám*

1206 his master died, and he received from headquarters the insignia of an independent Sultan. The dynasty of Mamelukes thus established receives in history the name of "Slave-Kings." (See opening paragraph of CHAPTER IV.)

During the rest of his short career Aibak showed himself as valiant and able a king as he had been a good and faithful servant. He engaged in war with Yalduz, in which neither side obtained any permanent advantage; and he died by an accident at the game now called "Polo," at Lahore, 1210 A.D. In his time the Muslim power was confirmed, at the expense, of course, of the Hindus. "The realm," says a chronicler, "was filled with friends and cleared of foes; his bounty was continuous, and so was his slaughter."

A striking instance of the contrast between the manners of the Hindus, and those of their northern conquerors, is afforded by the account given in this Muhamadan chronicle * of the taking of Bihár by Bakhtyár Khilji. A number of Hindu books were found, we are told; but it was impossible to get them examined because "all the men had been killed." Such a massacre indicates resistance, no doubt; indeed, we know that the people of the eastern provinces were not wholly subdued for more than two generations.

At the death of Kutb-ud-din Aibak, the Empire was divided into four loosely connected parts. The Khiljis held for Islám in such parts of the eastern provinces as they had been able to subjugate. They were a Turkmán clan, of some distinction, who had come down from the Trans-Oxus towards the end of the 10th century, A.D. and settled in the eastern part of Afghanistan, where they became the progenitors of the modern Ghilzi, or (popularly) Gilzai, tribe. At the period under notice, they still used the Turkish tongue, but were

---

* The *Tabakat-i-Nasiri*, composed by Minháj-i-Suráj in the last years of Nasir's reign; during which he was Chief Kazi of the empire.

somewhat ahead of their neighbours in civilisation. Their leader bore, as we have seen, the Persian name of Bakhtyár. The northern provinces were under the Mameluke Yalduz. The valley of the Indus was held by another of Muhamad-bin-Sám's promoted slaves, named Kabácha. An attempt was made in Hindustan to set up an incompetent son of the late Sultan Aibak; but a third Mameluke, called Shams-ud-din Iltimsh,* who had married one of the late Sultan's daughters, was invited to contest the succession. Having been sold by his brothers while yet young, he had passed through the hands of the Bokhára slave-dealers into the possession of Aibak; his qualities enabling him to attain early distinction, he was raised to the command of the body-guard; and, before the Sultan's decease, became his son-in-law and master-of-the-horse. Being in the prime of life, and supported by a party of influence, Iltimsh soon put down the movement in favour of his youthful brother-in-law, and assumed the Sultanate after a brief contest, in 1211. His first trouble was with Yalduz, who was defeated and made prisoner in 1215. Two years later Kabácha came up from Sindh, having enlisted some of the heathen Mughals in his army: those formidable barbarians being at that time in general movement under their famous leader Changez Khán, or Timujin. They had already occupied Khorásan, and were pouring into the Helmand valley when Iltimsh ruled in Hindustan. At first Kabácha seemed willing to make common cause with his brother Mameluke; and their joint forces opposed the fugitive King of Bokhara who, under Mughal pressure, was endeavouring to effect a settlement in the Punjab. In 1225, Sultan Iltimsh undertook an expedition to the eastward, where the Khiljis were attempting to set up an in-

* Thomas has some speculations on the meaning of this name (p. 213-14.) but comes to no conclusion. Elphinstone spells it Altamsh; in inscriptions it is found as given in the text; the Hindi die-sinkers got it on their coins as "Lititminsh"; neither meaning nor true sound is known.

dependent state in Bihár. The Sultan occupied Gaur, the chief city, and reduced the Khiljis to a temporary obedience. Proceeding from that centre he made further conquests over the Hindus, both north and south. The Khiljis of Bengal took the opportunity of his absence to raise another revolt; but they were put down by the Sultan's son, on which occasion Bakhtyár, the Khilji leader, was killed in battle. For the next three years the Sultan was constantly engaged. He took from the Rajputs the strong fort of Ranthambor, the key of the Málwa, and reduced that rich province, where he demolished the great Hindu temples of Bhilsa and Ujain. Gwalior was besieged and captured in the year 1232. All Hindustan, roughly speaking, was now reduced to the Muslim obedience; though isolated states were still left in the enjoyment of autonomy—which indeed has been maintained in several cases to this day. And even in those regions which lost their native chiefs, the Hindus maintained their own peculiar religions and legal systems; indeed, Professor H. H. Wilson believes that the evidence of coins goes to show that the spread of Islám was slow and gradual: partly supported in that opinion by the high numismatic authority of the late Edward Thomas.*

The early Turkmáns, though they showed no mercy to the actively hostile, were conciliatory towards the princes and peoples who did not attempt or show opposition; as may be inferred from the maintenance of Hindu symbols upon the public moneys. It is to the early part of this period that the final codification of Hindu law has been plausibly ascribed.†

---

* May this not, however, admit of the simple explanation of which the sham arches of the Kutb Mosque are suggestive? Namely, that the rude Muslim conquerors had to entrust their art work to Hindus.

† *Mitakshara:* circ. 1076 A.D. Jimata Váhana's commentary, ending in the *Dhayabhaga* schism, circ. 1325, *v. inf.*

It is at least remarkable that law-reform should have been found possible in such times.

With all his military occupations, the Sultan found time for the works of peace. He made his capital where his predecessor did, in the walled city of Rai Pithaura, and close by the great mosque are a college and mausoleum, destined to preserve the founder's name. He also made vast additions to the enclosing cloisters, which were made to take in the Kutb Minar; and that column likewise received an addition in height. Little, indeed, seems to have been wanting to the glory of Iltimsh. Always victorious in war, he reduced the whole of Hindustan, from the Himálaya to the Vindhya, and from the Indus to the Brahmaputra. But his position was not based on conquest alone, for it received the highest sanction and legitimacy by means of a patent of investiture from the Khálif of Bághdád, fallen in power, but still the acknowledged High Pontiff of Islám, and source of all true authority and honour through all the Eastern world. A wise minister from the Khálif's court resided at Delhi, and was heard with respect and reverence: men of letters were not absent.

All this prosperity laboured under the peculiar transience of the East. The mighty Sultan passed away in 1236; his eldest son, the victor of the Bengal campaigns, was already dead, a younger son, Rukn-ud-din, succeeded without a contest. He proved unequal to his high fortunes, and gave himself into the hands of his mother, a Turkmán lady of strong prejudices but narrow intellect. A palace revolution ensued; the Sultan and his mother were imprisoned; and the State came under the government of the Sultan's sister, Musamat Raziya. This princess, who is observable as the first and last female ruler who ever bore sway in the Muslim empire of Hindustan, was of quick intelligence and true courage; and maintained herself for some little time in the trying position to which she had attained. But the times were too stormy for a woman, or for any man but a very strong one. Assuming male attire, "Sultan" Raziya went abroad unveiled, and discharged the duties of a sovereign; seated on the judgment seat in durbar, and mounted on an elephant in battle.* Being overthrown by a successful rebellion, she was deposed and imprisoned, after a reign of three years; but she captivated the captor, who soon made her his wife. Meanwhile her younger brother, Bahrám, had assumed the Sultanate at Delhi, and Raziya marching against him was defeated and put to flight along with her husband; they were caught in the act of escaping and murdered by some villagers, near Kaithal, in the month of October, 1240.† Next year Lahore was taken by the heathen Mughals, with terrible slaughter. A series of trouble ensued; Bahrám, the new Sultan, soon learned of what cares he had relieved his ill-starred sister; the army which he raised for service against the Mughals besieged him in his palace. In May, 1242, the palace was stormed, and Bahrám was slain.

His successor was Alá-ud-din, son of Sultan Rukn-ud-din, the son of Iltimsh; incompetent and apathetic as is but too common with princes born in the purple. The land was once more partitioned by Muslim satraps, and wasted by heathen incursions; these overran the Punjab under Mangu Khán, grandson of the mighty marauder Changhez, and father to the famous Khublai Khán, the conqueror of China. The Sultan marched against them and achieved a partial triumph; but this success, turning into evil courses the little intellect he had, led to the formation of a plot which ended in his destruction. Alá-ud-din was killed, in June, 1246, and the Sultanate devolved on Násir-ud-din, another grandson of Iltimsh, his father having been the prince who subdued the Khiljis in Bengal dur-

---

* It is believed that it was with reference to these masculine habits that she is spoken of as "Sultan" and "Padshah," like a male sovereign.

† Her body was interred on the bank of the Jumna a league north of Delhi, and became a place of pilgrimage.

ing the reign of that Sultan. The new sovereign was a man of peaceful character and frugal habits, who would have probably failed to meet the difficulties of his position had he been left to his own resources. The Hindus were disaffected and rebellious; and the Mughals, who had by this time become possessed of Ghazni, kept the north-western parts of the empire in perpetual turmoil. But these perils were abated by the ability and energy of a great public servant who was rapidly rising into distinction, and for whom a still more glorious career was in the future. This was Ulagh Khán, of the ancient stock of the Turkish Khákáns of Albari, who had been sold by slave-dealers, with a number of other young Turkmáns, to Sultan Iltimsh who was, it will be remembered, their countryman, and prepared to give them employment and favour. This was in 1232, since when the Mamelukes had formed themselves into an association called "Shamsis," from the title of their royal master, Shams-ud-din. Under Sultana Raziya, Ulagh had risen to be grand huntsman, and retained the post during the subsequent troubles. Obtaining the fiefs of Riwári and Hánsi, he was made chamberlain by Alá-ud-din, and the elevation of that futile Sultan must have been partly due to his intervention. He conducted a campaign against the Hindus, in the Duáb, or Gangetic plain, east of the capital, at the outset of the reign, where, according to the chronicle, he "fought much against the infidels," that is to say the people of the country. In 1245 he led the Sultan's army against the Mughals in the Punjab; and on his return took an open and conspicuous part in the revolution which placed Nasir-ud-din upon the *Masnad* of Delhi.

The rest of the Sultan's history is nothing more than the record of the minister's exploits; but it is to his credit that he was content with a subordinate situation, and preserved constant fidelity to his harmless sovereign. Whether it be called duty or prudence this course was one of almost unbroken prosperity. Necessarily, the minister made enemies; and once at least his star appeared to wane. In the year 1252 he fell into disgrace; but after a struggle he prevailed and was restored to power; and it is noted by a contemporaneous writer that a drought of some duration ceasing on Ulagh Beg's return to Delhi, "it was no wonder that the citizens looked upon his return as a happy omen, and all were thankful to the Almighty."*

The next attempt of the minister's opponents was masked by a fresh rising of the Hindus, which they instigated in the Duáb; this was suppressed in 1255, and a similar attempt, having its base at Mount Abu in Rajputána, met with a like fortune in 1257. In the same year a dangerous conspiracy was discovered and frustrated in the metropolis itself. In 1259 a fresh incursion of the Mughals took place, by the route of Multan—which seems to have been one commonly adopted by them—and so formidable did it seem, that poets were commissioned to produce patriotic songs " in order to stir up the feelings of the Muslims." Having once more expelled the northern foe, the minister was again called upon to meet a fresh combination between his Turkmán rivals and the Hindus of the Duáb. The former were conciliated and invited to Court; and then the hand of the minister fell heavily upon the recalcitrant natives, whom the members of the opposition had made their instrument.

While these things were doing in Hindustan, Central Asia had been the scene of a new revolution. Huláku Khán, the chief of the Mughals of Transoxiana, and a grandson of the mighty Changhez Khán, took Baghdad in 1258, and put to death the last of the Abasside Khalifs. About this time the

* On a tower at Aligarh there used to be an inscription in which the Sultan recited the glories of his minister, dated in 1255. This interesting monument was unhappily destroyed in 1861 after standing six hundred years.

death of his brother Mangu, so long the leader of the southern horde, and perhaps some sense of the military superiority of the Indian minister, induced Huláku to think of withdrawing the Mughals from India and concentrating his power in Central Asia. Accordingly, not long after the last defeat of his deceased brother in the Punjab, he resolved to send a peaceful mission to the court of Delhi; and the minister there prepared to receive the Mughal envoys with all possible pomp and circumstance. By this time the residence of the Sultan had been removed from old Delhi to the suburb of Kilokhari, on the bank of the river Jumna; and it was there that the reception took place. Twenty lines of armed soldiers, horse and foot, guarded the approach to the palace, supported by ranks of caparisoned elephants; and it is characteristic of the stern policy of the minister that he caused the envoys to find the gate, which they reached through this warlike pageantry, decorated with the embalmed bodies of Hindu captives—slaughtered, perhaps, for the grim and ghastly purpose. They were conducted to the durbar-room, where they found the simple old sovereign splendidly attended; and having delivered their message, they were solemnly conducted to their lodgings. On their departure the ruthless minister led a fresh expedition against the Hindus, whom he drove into the mountains, after killing twelve thousand of them—men, women, and children.

In all this policy the minister made use of the Sultan's name, making him and his sons "a show," as was said of him by a later historian. The explanation of his conduct is to be found in the incessant competition of the Shamsis—"The Forty," as they were called. As these, however, became less formidable, from increasing years and repeated failure, the great services and abilities of the minister grew more and more conspicious, until the quiet old Nasir-ud-din passed away, and Ulagh became Sultan, in 1266, just forty-four years after he had entered Delhi as a slave.

His early career deserves notice, both as showing the gradual alienation of the Hindus, and as throwing light upon the curious state of society, in which it was possible to keep up a certain degree of efficiency in the Muslim State. From Sabaktigin downwards the slave markets of Central Asia had continued to produce men of remarkable energy for the conquest of the rich lands of India. These, without actually becoming an organised corps of Janisaries, for which their numbers were insufficient, formed a reserve of soldiers and statesmen, strong enough to lead the armies of the state and furnish a sort of administration. It cannot be believed that the people, even when abstaining from rebellion, were in a state of happiness or wealth; but there must have been a certain amount of agriculture and finance to render possible the court-pageants, the public works, and the pay of the troops. And the system by which the more eminent of the Mameluke officers were enabled to become ministers and sultans favoured a survival of the fittest, by which the momentum of the foreign empire was maintained. Nasir-ud-din is the only instance of a hereditary Sultan who had a long reign; but under the rule of the Mamelukes, Hindustan was a powerful state for a century and a quarter.

Ulagh Beg —or Khán—was about sixty years old when he became Sultan, under the title of Ghayás-ud-din Balban, by which he his best known in history. He had still many years of active life before him; and his reign as Sultan was marked by the same characteristics as his ministerial career, accompanied with the additional splendour becoming to his new situation. Zia-ud-din Barni, who wrote nearly a hundred years later, is the chief authority for Balban's reign; and the fact of his not being quite contemporaneous frees him from the suspicion of flattery. His record was a labour of love, designed, avowedly, as a continuation of the *Tabákát*, to which, hitherto, we have been mainly indebted. Barni asserts that he wrote the account of Balban's reign from information delivered to him by his own grandfather and others who had held high offices of state during the period.

No sooner had the sometime minister obtained plenary powers, than insubordination at once disappeared. The army was remodelled, commands being reserved for the ablest of the officers. Rigorous justice was enforced, from whose effects the offences of the Sultan's former comrades were not exempted. Spies were employed, by whose means the Sultan was to receive universal knowledge of all that went on. The Sultan allowed no light talk in his presence; he gave up wine to which he had been addicted, and was never seen to laugh. He desisted from aggressive warfare, husbanding all his resources for the defence of his territory against foreign foes, and combating all persuasions to the contrary from advisers, who urged that such an attitude was derogatory to the dignity of a great empire. It is probable that the Hindus were gainers by this new policy. "I have to prepare," said the Sultan, "to receive the Mughals: were that anxiety removed, I would soon reduce the *Rais* and the *Ranas*." Yet the troops were not kept idle. The quondam grand huntsman went into sport with his habitual solemnity. For forty miles round Delhi the country was kept as a strict preserve of game for the Sultan; and during the cold season he would beat it all day, accompanied by thousands of his soldiers. The Mughals heard of these hunts. "Balban is an old campaigner," cried their leader, "there is more in his hunting than a mere pastime of peace." Indeed, more serious hunting was soon to come, though the Mughals were not, at first, its objects. The Mewátis on one hand, to the south-west of the capital, and later the dakaits (gang robbers) of Patiáli, to the north-east, were the earliest human game of the Sultan: both were, not undeservedly, visited with chastisement. The Mughals were watched by the Sultan's eldest son, his headquarters being at Multan.

The name of this prince was Muhamad, a brave soldier like his father, and a man of decorous life, and a patron of arts and letters. The poet Amir Khusru (known in Indian literature as "Tota") was his favourite companion; and he is remarkable for encouraging conviviality at his Court without permitting excess. He governed the Punjab wisely and well, duly submitting to his father, at Delhi, his yearly reports and tribute. Second only, in point of danger, were the eastern provinces of Bihár and Bengal, always ripe for rebellion by reason of their distance from the central power. These were ruled by another son, named Mahmud, or Baghra Khán; and it was here that the first serious trouble arose. Unwarned by the Sultan's past severities, a general named Taghril Beg, after gaining a temporary success against some rebels, began to defy the authority of Baghra, and held quasi sovereign state at Sonárgaon. The old Sultan, after his son had failed, went to Gaur and made a campaign in person. The rebel chief was pursued into Tippera and killed, fighting or fleeing, in 1279. It is said that the Sultan intended to make his triumphal entry into Delhi through an avenue of impaled prisoners, but was persuaded to abandon the purpose by the prayers of the heads of Islám.

But disaster was at hand. Some five years later the Mughals entered the Punjab in great force; and, though they are said to have been repulsed, it is not the less certain that the blameless Prince Muhamad was killed and his companion the poet Khusru made prisoner; to which latter circumstance is due a curious description of the manners of the barbarians, of which something will be found on a later page. The misfortune was too much for the worn strength of the aged Sultan, which rapidly declined, he being nearly, or quite, 80 years of age. Calling a last council round his bedside he directed that the son of the late prince should be made his heir, to the exclusion of Baghra, the Viceroy of the East, in whom events had led him to expect weakness. The nobles promised compliance; but no sooner was the old man gone than they cancelled his orders, sent the prince to his father's post at Multan, and awarded the Sultanate to Baghra's son. The young man's accession took place early in 1287; and he bore the ancient Persian title of Kai Kubád; but he was destined to give another proof of the weakness of the hereditary principle, even when education has not been neglected. Trained by his stern and solemn grandfather, the young prince had never kissed girl or goblet, as we are told by Barni; but the sudden emancipation was too much for his acquired virtue. Abandoning himself to the most reckless indulgence, warring against his father, and causing the death of his cousin at Multan, he lost the confidence of those who had served his house so long. The Khiljis, though put down in Bengal, were still powerful at court: a revolution occurred, of which the details are not recorded: the wretched young Sultan sank into a premature decrepitude, brought on by his vices, and was slaughtered in bed at Kilokhari about three years after his accession. The leader of the Khiljis—Jalál-ud-din—found himself opposed by the head of the Mughal mercenaries, who wished to put forward a son of the deceased Kubád to carry on the line of Balban: but the opposition was unsuccessful, and the general, who was an old and seasoned warrior, became Sultan, and the founder of a new dynasty.

This closed the line of the Mamelukes, during which the Hindus had been, indeed, ill-treated; but their ill-treatment was less the result of religious persecution than of stern political repression. Chafing under the yoke of foreign conquest, they persisted in rebellion; and the Mamelukes put them down in the manner then universally adopted. With the accession of the Khiljis a new system began, which destroyed the country and slowly sapped the Muslim power.

SECTION 3.—It is to be regretted that we have so little

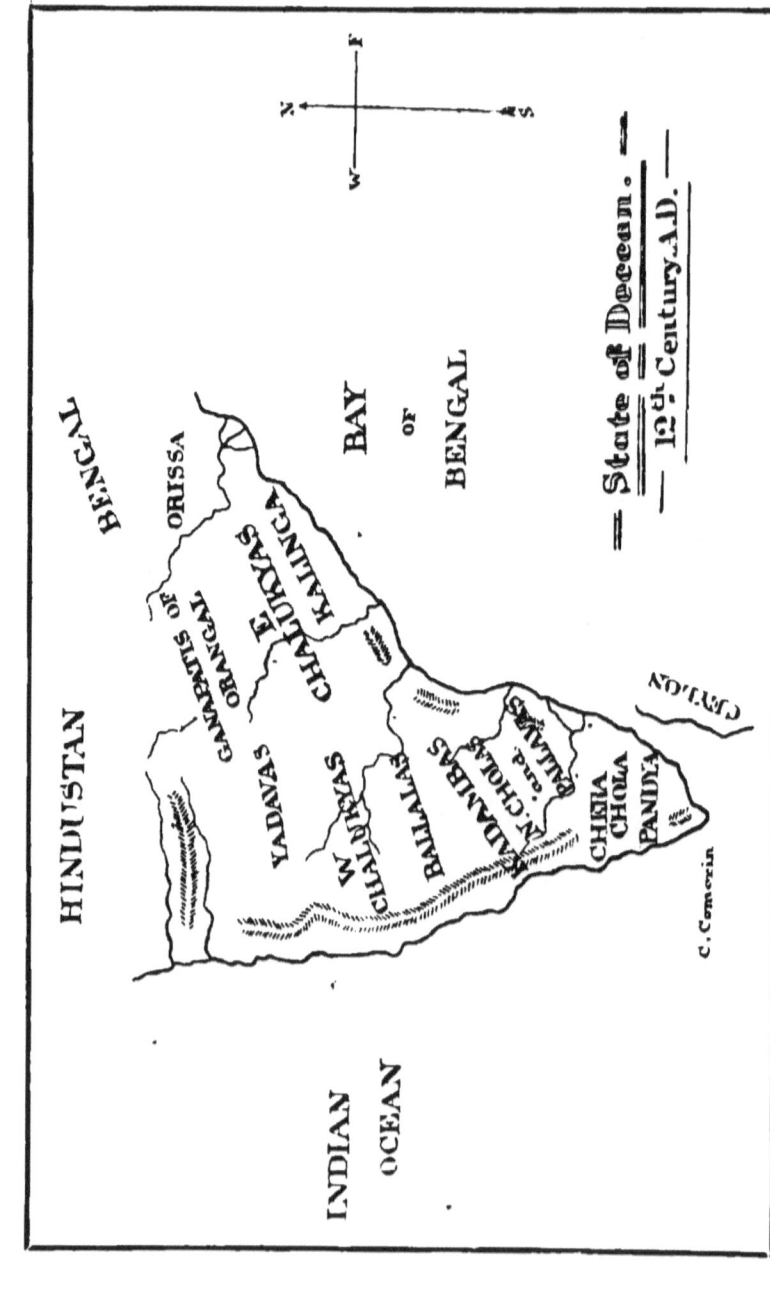

material for a record of the history of the Deccan during the time when the Mamelukes were warring in Hindustan. The usual unhistorical habit of the Hindus continued in the parts unvisited by the invaders; and the evidence of coins and inscriptions reveals little more that what Milton called "battles of kites and crows." The one point that seems clear and important is that an element of nationality was at work, and the battles were sometimes inspired by a hostility entertained by the Támils and, perhaps, other races of the Dravidians, seeking to resist the invasion of Rajputs. The annexed sketch may help to explain what is meant. It will be seen that in the extreme south the old Dravidian powers held their old places. The Pándiyan kingdom was sometimes threatened—sometimes, indeed, invaded—by the Támil rulers of the adjacent island of Ceylon. The relations between the two Támil powers, on the island and the mainland, were probably intimate: as Prakrama I., King of the Island, is said to have resided at Ramiseram, about 1160 A.D. The Cheras in the Canarese country did little worthy of record. To the south-east the Cholas were more energetic. In the central part of the Deccan (Maisur and the southern Mahratta country) was a dynasty of Jádu Rajputs* whose capital, Dorasamudra, has left traces in a Maisur village called, at the present day, Halebid. This tribe was known as that of Hoysala Ballála; and the temple of Siva, at Halebid, which is named after them, has been much admired. It is of polished stone with elaborate sculpture. The coast of "Kalinga," to the north-east, was partly under the Ganpatis of Orangal, and had been portion of the dominions of the eastern Chálukyas. The chief tribe of the Deccan Jádus held the country now known as Berar and the northern Deccan; the western Ghats and north Konkan being

---

* The Jádu, Yádava, or Yádubansi, was the tribe of the famous Sri Krishna, and is mentioned in ancient poetry.

held by the western Chálukyas whose Rájas had their court at Kalián, near Bombay, from the eleventh century of our era.*

About the middle of the following century, the eastern Chálukyas –who, like their western brethren, claimed descent from a "lunar" Rajput stock in Audh—became involved in war with the Orangal Ganpatis, who had Dravidian affinities. The Cholas—a race of pure Támil blood—absorbing the power of the Pollavas about the same time, became parties to the contest; in 119—the Ganpatis prevailed over the Chálukyas; but the northern Cholas remained masters of Kalinga till about 1228, when they too had to retire before the Ganpati advance. Nor did the western branch of the Chálukyas fare better: in 1189 they were overrun by the Ballálas, or Hoysalas, aided, perhaps, by their Jádu, or Yádava, brethren of the north. In the thirteenth century the greater part of the Deccan was divided among the Yádavas and the Ganpatis of Orangal, the Támil lines still maintaining themselves in the southern triangle, or from the coast of Coromandel to that of Malabar, and from the Kávari river to Cape Comorin.

Such is a brief summary of Deccan history up to the time when the Muslim aggressions began in that region. The Khilji Sultan at Delhi was, as has been said, a military veteran named Jalál-ud-din; and he placed complete confidence in a nephew entitled Alá-ud-din, on whom the chief command of the army was ultimately conferred. The first trouble arose in the eastern Duáb, whence the chiefs of the defeated party led a rebellious army under a nephew of the late Sultan Balban. The attempt was defeated by the Sultan's second son, about 1290, and Alá-ud-din was left in charge of Karra, as the province was then called. The next campaign was in Málwa, and was under the personal superintendence of the Sultan himself; but the result was indecisive (1292). He next pro-

* It is here that the Mitakshara digest is believed to have appeared in the reign of Vikrama VI. circ. 1075.

ceeded to the Punjab, where the Mughals were once more becoming troublesome; and it is probably to be taken as marking the humane character that war was beginning to assume, that the Sultan is recorded to have enrolled his prisoners in his own army instead of putting them to death.

Meanwhile, Alá-du-din, from his satrapy of the eastern Duáb, was watching, with contempt, his uncle's unprecedented mildness. Very different was his own idea of policy. Having obtained charge of the unfinished campaign in Málwa, he left his capital. "When he advanced from Karra," says the chronicler, "the Hindus, in alarm, descended into the ground, like ants. . . He cleared the road to Ujain of vile wretches, and caused consternation at Bhilsa." He then advanced with no more than 8,000 men, beyond the bounds of his prescribed task. The temple of Somnáth was plundered once more, and a successful invasion of the Yádava territory, in the Deccan, led to the submission of Rámachandra, their chief, who resided in the strong fortress of Deogiri. Alá-ud-din returned from his expedition laden with booty, exalted in reputation, and almost beside himself with unscrupulous ambition. His expedition, so far as Ujain, had been strictly under orders; but in going on to Kathiawár and Deogiri he had acted on his own responsibility. He now affected alarm lest he might have incurred the displeasure of his uncle, the Sultan, and insisted on the old man coming to Karra to meet him without a guard. The Sultan's true friends objected, but the Sultan himself had no room in his soldier's heart for any feeling but gratified pride and affection. He complied with every demand of his nephew, and crossed the Ganges to greet him in his camp. As he was in the embrace of the traitor he was stabbed by the by-standers, acting on previous instructions. This was in July, 1296, and Alá-ud-din immediately assumed the Sultanate. The family of Baghra became independent in Bengal, but acknowledged Delhi as the Empire.

For several years this ill-gotten Empire continued to prosper. In 1299 the Mughals advanced from Ghazni, apparently contemplating the conquest of Hindustan. They accordingly entered the Punjab once more, and advanced within a march of Delhi. The Sultan met them like a man, and intrenched himself at a place called Killi, some ten miles north of the capital. After a hot day's fighting the invaders were defeated and put to flight, but one of the Sultan's best generals was sacrficed: this was in 1298.

Alá-ud-din now became almost mad with pride; he fancied himself "a second Alexander," and in his cups proposed to establish a new religion. He undertook public works on an extravagant scale; increasing the court-yard of the Kutb Mosque at old Delhi to over 400 feet square, adding a lovely carved gateway as big as an ordinary mansion, and beginning an impossible masonry tower that was to be double the Kutb Minar in all dimensions. He so far propitiated the Muslims as to desecrate Hindu temples, and cement the mortar of his walls with Mughal blood. But to Islám itself he was disrespectful; and if he despoiled the poor he impartially disturbed the accumulations of the rich. In all these measures he showed a strange mixture of sagacity; the Hindus were to have enough to live upon; the land was to be surveyed so as to ensure the Ráyatas full half the gross produce. It is true that the usual experience of the world has pointed to nine-tenths as due allowance; but, no doubt, half a loaf is better than no bread; and Sultan Alá-ud-din may have heard some such saying. Naturally the system was far from popular. "Men looked upon a revenue officer," says a Muslim historian of the time, "as worse than a fever." Regarding his own caprices as above all law, he rarely consulted the sages of Islám. But on one occasion he asked a Kázi's opinion, only to reject the reply with scorn. There was to be no tribute, in the ordinary sense of the word; for that implied the notion of property out of which tribute should be paid. "I am but a simple soldier," said the Sultan, "and I know nothing of law: but this I do know, that no unbeliever should have more than the food to keep him alive. The revelation of the Prophet is one thing, the policy of the State another."

In business, especially in military business, this extraordinary man was uniformly successful. In 1300 he took the great Rajput fort of Ranthambor, already mentioned as the key of Málwa, the Rája and all the garrison being put to the sword. In 1303 he took possession of the almost impregnable castle of Chitore, in Mewar, and settled the country on his own peculiar principles. In the course of the next two years he so handled the Mughals, that for many years they ventured on no further incursions into Hindustan. In 1309 a force from Delhi invaded the southern regions of the country under a converted Hindu, who had risen to high military rank, by the title of Malik Kafur. The Yádava of Deogiri, now become a tributary of Delhi, gave substantial aid, but the Rája of Orangal—Pratápa Rudra II—made a gallant attempt to defend his country and capital. The first campaign turned to the loss of the allies; but in the next the Rája was driven into Orangal, where he did his best to sustain a siege. The account of the place rests on the narrative of the poet Amir Khusru. The outer wall was of earth, with a circuit of over seven miles: within this was a citadel of stone. The garrison having exhausted themselves by an unsuccessful night-sortie, the allies stormed the earthern ramparts; and on this the stone citadel surrendered at discretion. The Muslim general was politic or humane, and Pratápa Rudra was allowed to follow the example of Deogiri, and become a tributary of the Delhi State. In 1310-11 the Muslim power continued to extend over the peninsula with the slow and steady devastation of a lava flood. Dorasamudra, the Ballála capital, was taken and sacked: the kingdoms of the Cholas and Pandiyas were subdued. Not only did the Sultan adopt the new policy of reinstating all these Rájas, on condition of their paying tribute; but he took a wife from a Hindu family—that of the Rája of Gujarát. In 1312, however, the Rája of Deogiri having failed to pay the stipulated tribute, Kafur returned to the Deccan which he laid waste with fire and sword: the Yádava Rája was put to death as a traitor to the State, and Deogiri became the seat of a Muslim Government.

For one brief moment all India was "brought under one umbrella." But the Sultan was verging on old age, and he had long been an immoderate wine-bibber. He now became a victim to dropsy, and Kafur took advantage of his increasing infirmities to seclude him from the world and his family, while he himself carried on the administration in his master's name. Sanguinary orders, signed by the Sultan, were the only indications that he lived. All the strong work of the reign fell to pieces, imperial garrisons were driven out from what had been deemed subject provinces. At length it was announced that the Sultan was no more. Whether aided by treason or not, his demise took place at the beginning of 1315, and produced a momentary relief. His infant son was proclaimed, under the title of Shaháb-ud-din Umar, and Kafur appeared all powerful. Suddenly, one more of those obscure palace-revolutions took place, of whose mystery no man, then or since, could ever find the key. Kafur attempting to cause the death of Mubárak, his late master's third son, was himself slain, and the prince assumed the Sultanate, with the title of Mubárak Sháh, in March, 1316.

The young Sultan was a dissolute creature, who began where his father had ended, giving the administration over to a low-caste Hindu, and abandoning himself to a life of indulgence. This minion, Malik Khusru, in all respects a counterpart of the late Kafur, was a converted Hindu, of the low Parwári caste, but with high ability, who had made a successful campaign on the south-west coast of the Deccan, and brought back considerable booty. The closing scenes of Alá-ud-din's reign were reproduced; the favourite engrossed all power; the Sultan disappeared in April, 1321. The minister made himself Sultan, with the title of "Khusru Sháh," but he is hardly to be counted among the Muslim Kings of Delhi. Indeed he was not more than nominally a believer, and his assumption of power was a hardly-disguised Hindu movement. In fact, since Alá-ud-din orthodoxy had been rejected as a state religion.*

[For additional authorities on the subject dealt with in this chapter, see—"Sketch of the Dynasties of Southern India," by R. Sewell, Madras, 1883; Briggs' "Ferishta," London, 1829; Dowson and Elliot's "Muhamadan Historians of India," Vols. II. and III., London, 1867-77; and E. Thomas's "Chronicles of the Pathán Kings of Delhi," London, 1871.]

* On the coinage of Mubárak he is called "Supreme Pontiff" and "Khalif of God."

CHAPTER IV.

END OF THE "PATHANS."

Section 1: The House of Tughlak and invasion of Tamerlane.—Section 2: Line of Lodi and the New Mughals.—Section 3: The adventures of Babar; Social conditions of Hindustan; progress of Islám in the south.

SECTION 1.—The Gorians, the Slaves, and the next succeeding dynasties, have received from historians the name of "The Pathán Kings of Delhi;" and the name is so far useful as indicating a common origin: though, perhaps, Turkmán would have been a more exact epithet. But this foreign stock underwent considerable decay with the fall of the Khilji line; and for the next two centuries we shall have to consider the Empire of Hindustan as ruled by Sultans who, though still professing the faith of the Arabian Prophet, were natives of India, and—whether consciously or not—favourable, to some degree, to that fusion with the people of the country, of which we have already seen premonitory symptoms.

For five months after the murder of Mubárak Sháh the capital was in the hands of the followers of Khusru, who took to themselves the ladies of the royal household, and used Korans as seats, while they attended the worship of idols in the desecrated mosques of Islám. The Governor of the Punjab, Ghází Malik, himself the son of a Hindu mother, watched these proceedings with stern disapproval; but did not venture to interfere, for his eldest son, Ulagh Khán, or Juna, was residing in Delhi, an unwilling guest and hostage. At length Juna effected his escape, and hastened to his father's camp. Gházi immediately collected his veterans and marched on Delhi, gained an easy victory over the rioters, and put the usurping Khusru to death He then enquired for the heirs of the House of Khilji; but none had survived, and he was acclaimed Sultan, by the title of Ghaiás-ud-din Tughlak, 22nd August, 1321; his family or clan name being Tughlak, and the title, Ghaiás-ud-din, being assumed in honour of Sultan Balban who had borne that title, and in whose household he had been. It is a strange instance of longevity in such troublous times that his old master had been slave to Iltimsh, whose master was the conqueror of Rai Pithaura one hundred and thirty seven years before. Another vestige of the past was the grandson of Baghra Khán and great-grandson of Sultan Balban, who had succeeded his father in the government of the Eastern Provinces, in which post he was confirmed by the new Sultan.*

The Khilji line had only ruled for thirty years; but that brief period had been one of much change. The Muslim rule had been consolidated in Hindustan, and partially extended in the Deccan. The irruptions of the Mughals had apparently ceased; those northern barbarians having embraced the creed of Islám, and settled down in the kingdoms of Central Asia, or taken service as mercenaries in the Indian armies. Those Hindu chiefs who had succeeded in resistance to the Delhi Sultans were recognised as belligerent if hostile powers; the rest had entered the pale of the Empire and become feudatory princes. The bulk of the people, however oppressed, had become submissive subjects. A considerable population of native Muslims had also arisen, who—though im-

* Elphinstine erroneously states that this was Baghra himself; but Thomas has shown that he died about the end of Jalál-ud-din's reign, and was succeeded by his son Kai Kaús. The grandson's name was Baghra—hence the mistake. "Pathán Kings" p. 248

G

migrants—from force of character usually filled the higher stations of civil and military life. The Sultans and their Muslim lieutenants were beginning to hold the position of the barons and earls of England, in the almost parallel time of the Plantagenets. Consequent on this partial fusion a vernacular language was being created in Hindustan, to allow of communication among the associated classes. This tongue, appropriately known to us as "Hindustani," is the *Urdu* of the native scholars, an application of the later Prákrit of the Duáb, using, by preference, the Persian form of the Arabic character, and assimilating words from Hindi, Persian, Turkish, and any other vocabularies that may cross its path. In this power of growth lay its future fortunes; it soon began to be more than a mere *lingua franca* of oral communication, and to develop the germs of a national literature. The name "*Urdu*" is connected with the Turkish word from which we get our English "horde;" and is sufficiently indicative of the origin of the language, for it was in the Turkmán Sultan's camp that such a vernacular would first become requisite as a means of dealing between the soldiery and those who furnished their supplies. Thus, it affords an interesting example of the rule that the necessities of human intercourse must be stronger than any estrangement arising out of the pride of race, the bigotry of creed, or even the resentful feelings of subjugated nationality.

The old warrior, who had attained sovereign power in this unusually blameless fashion, was a remarkable instance of simple honesty who deserved his elevation. The offspring of a Turkmán slave by a Ját mother, he showed all the virtues which often mark a fortunate crossing of races; and he owed every step in his progress to his own good conduct. On becoming Sultan he maintained the same honourable standard, and did not allow his good fortune to disturb his habitual self-control. He did his best to reform the civil administration, impaired as it had been by years of anarchy: at the same time guarding his northern frontier, and sending his not very wise son Ulagh Khán—or Juna—to restore order in the south. The Rája of Orangal held out, and the Prince could effect but little against him. The Muslim forces invested the capital, but were unable to breach the earthern ramparts; and, being defeated by a sally of the garrison, they beat a hasty retreat. In 1323, however, the Muslims were better led, or met with better fortune. Attacking Orangal with increased numbers they captured the fortifications of the city, stormed the citadel, and carried the Rája, Pratápa Rudra, in triumph to Delhi. His son, Krishna, was allowed to succeed, but it was to a greatly reduced principality. In the following year the Sultan personally conducted an expedition to Sonárgaon (in eastern Bengal) which resisted the authority of the line of old Baghra Khán. He restored order there, and on his way back reduced and captured a rebel Rája, in Tirhut.

But his heir-apparent, Juna, was wearying for the succession. In his impatience he watched the slow, but sure, march of his father towards the capital, and frequently consulted a hermit of the sinister sect of the "Assassins." At each enquiry he named a new stage at which the Sultan was reported to have arrived; but on each occasion—" Delhi is still far "—was the only answer of the oracle. Regardless of the ties of duty and gratitude, he interpreted the dark saying by the light of his desire, and resolved to take destiny into his own keeping. At the last halting place Juna erected a wooden pavilion for the reception of his father and his brother, who had accompained the Sultan on his campaign. There was a parade of elephants when the Sultan had been conducted to his seat: Juna went down to give an order; at the next instant one of the huge beasts was driven against a projection beneath the gallery; the whole building gave way with a crash; the gallery fell to the ground. Workmen were hurried in to search among the ruins, and the body of the valiant old Sultan was found under some fallen beams, the arms extending as if he had sought to protect his boy to the last. This crime was committed in February, 1323.*

Juna succeeded to the Sultanate by the title of Muhamad Tughlak; and the manner in which he exercised his power was as singular and as unscrupulous as the manner in which he had, in anticipation of the course of nature, come to its possession. He did not prove a tyrant of the common stamp, being a man of most original character; brave and accomplished, but wholly bereft of common sense or judgment. Barni, who knew him intimately, concurs with the African Moor, Ibn Batuta, who visited India during his reign, as to his extraordinary mixture of literature without religion, and culture without humanity. Neither of these writers had any personal grievance against him; in their capacity as men of letters they experienced kind treatment at his hands. But they adduce too much evidence in notorious features of his conduct to leave any doubt as to the mischief that he caused to the country whose government he had been so impatient to seize. Having produced a famine in the country about Delhi by ill-judged and meddlesome interference, he proposed to remedy it by deporting the population to Deogiri, a thousand miles off, where he contemplated the creation of a new capital under the plausible name of Daulatábád (prosperous city), which the deserted ruins, as if in mockery, still retain. Myriads died on the way for want of proper arrangements. He then attempted to re-people the Delhi territory from other regions; but if there is one thing for which the native of India is less fit than another it is migration. Nor

* This story is referred to by Elphinstone as doubtful. It rests, however, on the authority of Ibn Batuta, who had it from an eye-witness, and who gives the name of the agent by whom the "Kiosk," as he calls it, was contrived.

was his harshness strong or methodical, like that of Balban or Alá-ud-din; nor do we read of the religious persecutions and enforced conversions, which afterwards brought ruin on Aurangzeb. He endeavoured to circulate copper tokens in place of the usual silver currency, but withdrew them at par when he found that they were unpopular. He collected a mighty host for the invasion of Persia, and then allowed it to dissolve for want of orders, and for lack of pay. He sent an expedition to cross the Himalaya into Chinese Tartary; and when it perished in the snows, punished the reserved troops who had been left behind. But he endeavoured to explain his conduct to Barni, as if he would retain an advocate to plead for him at the bar of posterity. The more he punished, he said, the more he was disobeyed; but he was resolved to carry out his plans to the end.

No wonder if the Empire suffered diminution under such a wilful guardian. In 1327 his Viceroy in the Deccan rebelled, and an expedition was sent to chastise him. The rebel took refuge with the Rája of Maisur, but the Rája gave him up for fear of consequences; and the unhappy rebel was flayed alive by order of the Sultan. In 1338 the new capital was inaugurated at Deogiri; in 1341 there was a rising in Malabar, which the Sultan attempted to quell in person; but he fell sick and returned without doing anything. Three years later a confederation of Rájas was formed, and an enormous force attacked the Muslims in the Orangal country and drove them out. This reverse was naturally followed by a general revolt in all the Muslim dependencies of the south. The Viceroy of Daulatábád—the new capital—declared himself independent. This officer was an Afghan, born however at Delhi, and in the humblest circumstances, and originally named Jáfar Khán. Under the patronage of a Brahman astrologer he rose to fortune and power; and in, 1347, headed a successful revolt by which he was enabled to become independent. He left

Daulatábád and made his capital at Kulbarga, in what is now one of the Nizam's districts, some hundred miles west of Haidarabad. In memory of his Hindu patron the successful adventurer called himself Hassan Gangu.

While these losses were going on in the Deccan, Bengal and the Punjab alike broke away from the headstrong Sultan's rule. The example being followed in Gujarát and Sindh, the fantastic despot at last bestirred himself. Desiring to chastise a Sindh Rája who had given harbour to one of the Gujarát rebels, he marched to Tatta, near Karachi, a place long famed for malaria arising from the marshes of the debouching Indus. Here he was seized by the prevailing local fever, and died on the 20th March, 1351, the most eccentric despot that ever escaped a violent end. It is related that on his deathbed he gave utterance to an impromptu stanza reflecting upon the vanity of his past career. The singular nature of the man followed him to the tomb. About four miles east of Delhi is a vast and massive group of buildings nearly four miles in circuit, faced by an artificial sheet of water, and rising grandly above a scarped rock with sloping ramparts of enormous hewn stones. In front of the principal gate of this fortified palace—which still preserves the name of the dynasty—is a mausoleum, whose leaning walls, and almost Egyptian solidity of construction, form a striking model of a warrior's tomb.* The building is connected with the palace by a viaduct across the lake, and is more than 60 feet square, with a height of over 38 feet. It contains three sepulchres, namely that of the murdered Ghazi and his two sons. In the tomb of Juna is supposed to lie buried a collection of vouchers for the pardon of the dead Sultan provided by the pious care

* The palace and tomb at Tughlakabad are the work of the first of the Tughlak Sultans—1321-3. Juna's own buildings are a small out-work near the south-east corner, and the ruins of a city and palace north-east of old Delhi, known as *Jahan Pana*.

of his successor: "I took pains," he writes, "to discover the surviving kindred of all my late Lord's victims; and having provided for them, caused them to execute deeds, duly witnessed, declaratory of their having received satisfaction; and these have been buried in a chest at the head of the late Sultan's grave, in hopes that God, of his infinite mercy, will take compassion on my departed friend."

The grateful follower who thus sought to give his predecessor letters for the throne of grace was a cousin whom the late Sultan, in default of direct issue, had educated in declared view to the succession. This fact, taken with the concurrent testimony of Ibn Batuta to Juna's accomplishments and generosity, and that of Barni to the modest humility of his manners, completes the incredible portrait of the late Sultan, and perhaps helps us to understand both the peacefulness of his end, and of the next monarch's almost unchallenged accession. On a rumour of the death of Firuz, who was with the army at Tatta, a putative son of the late Sultan was set up at Delhi; but Firuz hastening up from Sindh assumed the throne without serious difficulty. He took the title of Firuz-bin-Rajab, and his reign dates from that of the death of his predecessor, 23rd March, 1351. In his time the Muslim power decayed in Hindustan, without there arising anything to take its place. The hastily accumulated Empire of Alá-ud-din had not had time to consolidate. The earnest, but ill-regulated administration which ensued, had entirely failed in maintaining authority in the more distant parts. Of twenty-three provinces of which the empire consisted at the opening of the second Tughlak's reign, less than half were loyal at the end. And Firuz was not the man to recover the allegiance of lost provinces, or punish rebellious leaders. Being of orthodox convictions he has endeared himself to the Muslim historians; and his piety towards his predecessor is undoubted; not content with providing for the spiritual welfare of his deceased patron, he chose out the names of the best of the early Muslim rulers and caused them to be recited, before his own, in the weekly litanies. He next turned his attention to public works, not merely works of a decorative nature, but also useful—as utility was then understood. The city that he founded was upwards of six miles in length by two in average breadth, extending from the shore of the Jumna at Indrapat to the subsequent site of "Hindu Rao's house," on the north of the modern city. It comprised a palace, a chapel royal, and eight public mosques, each capable, on an average, of accomodating 10,000 worshippers; only males being provided for, this would indicate a considerable population. He also founded a city at Hissar, in Hariána; and in order to provide the citizens with good water, generously dug a canal, drawn from the Upper Jumna, and running to the west of that river, also utilising the waters of some minor streams. He built a mosque at Depálpur, on the way to Multan; he established a military outpost in the south of Gujarát at Surat, on the shore of the Gulf of Cambay; and he began to found a city at Jaunpur on the western portion of the Bihár. These points—Surat and Jaunpur—are to be noted as the probable extremes of the Empire of Firuz.* He failed in the Eastern Provinces, and he made no attempt to restore the power of the Delhi State in the Deccan or in Sindh. But within the limits of Hindustan proper the land had rest—so far, at least, as was consistent with a somewhat bigoted policy towards the Hindus. A system of bestowing *Jágirs* (fiefs) was introduced to pay the officers of the army and maintain their troops, for whom Aláun-din, Khilji, had provided money payments. A rent-charge was imposed on land traversed by royal canals, in order to provide an interest of 10 per cent. on the cost of their con-

---

* *Vide* map at page 73.

struction. The Sultan's personal income was separated from the public revenues and formed a distinct civil list; the budget of the former being fixed at a little over sixty millions of rupis, after certain irritating taxes had been remitted. But, in spite of these liberal ideals, and of the fact that his mother was the daughter of a Hindu Rána, Firuz levied the poll-tax upon unbelievers with stern severity, and even destroyed their temples. For the latter practice he had no excuse, nor did he deem excuse requisite; we know that he acted thus from his own memoirs, where he calmly mentions it as part of his discharge of duty. But toleration was not dreamt of, in the fourteenth century, either in Asia or in Europe; and we must not condemn a ruler generally wise and conscientious because he was not superior to all contemporary rulers. The memoirs, by his own hand, are otherwise indicative of high aims and earnest labour; they tell of canals, dams, bridges, tanks, as much as of mosques and palaces: and his restoration of the Kutb Minar and other edifices of his predecessors is proof of an unusual spirit of consideration and of continuity unhappily most rare among oriental potentates. The modest opening of the little chronicle is characteristic: "I am the unfortunate and pitiable Firuz-bin-Rajab, the slave of the Emperor Muhamad Sháh Tughlak." Amongst the gifts of God he reckons "a desire to erect public buildings . . . so that devout and holy persons might worship the Almighty, and remember the founder in their prayers." Among these works he enumerates many mosques, shrines, and oratories; but he likewise makes mention of an infirmary, with a staff of endowed physicians, and regular provision of food and medicine. "Here all are treated, without distinction of status or condition; and, if it be God's will, are cured."

As has been already hinted, the placid rule of this beneficent Sultan was conducive to the prosperity of Hindustan rather than to the extension of the Empire. Bengal asserted independence by sending an ambassador to Delhi, and by issuing a distinct coinage in the names of local rulers. Orissa, Telingána (Orangal), and the members of the southern Hindu confederation, interposed between Hindustan and the new Muslim power of Hassan Gangu. That successful adventurer died in peace, after an uneventful reign, in 1358; and his son, Muhamad Sháh I., reigned in his stead. To the south-west, the Canarese line of Narsingh founded the state whose capital was at Bijainagar, the first recorded monarch being Bakka, or Bakka Raya, 1350-79. The rest of the history of the South during this period will be briefly summarised hereafter.

Thus, in blended cloud and sunshine, with dominions diminished abroad, but mostly prospering at home, the years of the peaceful Firuz passed by. In 1373 he lost his son, Fatteh Muhamad, who had for many years acted as his associate in the Empire, and whose own son was afterwards to become Sultan. Another son, Zafar, was then made co-Regent; but he, too, predeceased his father. In his old age Sultan Firuz became the centre of palace intrigue; a third son—Muhamad Sháh—attempting to seize the sceptre, was routed and driven into exile; but the monarch abdicated in 1388, and before the end of the year died at a very advanced age, after a reign of thirty-seven calendar years.

The next Sultan, Ghaiás-ud-din Tughlak the Second, was the son of the deceased prince, Fatteh Khán, and assumed the government on the defeat of his uncle and the abdication of his aged grandfather. He neglected every duty; and was supplanted, before the end of the year, by Abu Bakr, son of his other uncle Zafa. The Sultan fled, but was overtaken and put to death, 31st December, 1388.

Abu Bakr was for a time supported by the courtiers and chiefs at Delhi; but his uncle Muhamad Sháh, emerging from his exile, attacked the feeble monarch with such pertinacity that, although three times beaten, he was enabled to form a party at court, by whom he was invited to Delhi and raised to the Sultanate in 1389. Next year he took captive his nephew and predecessor, who died, a prisoner, at Mirath (Meerut). Muhamad Sháh's reign was consistent with his energetic opening; he put down risings in the Duáb, and might have made substantial conquests, but his career was cut short by fever, 17th November, 1392. A momentary Sultanate of forty-five days followed; and then the throne devolved upon the younger son of Muhamad Sháh, during whose reign the Tughlak sun was to set in clouds of blood. A son of Fatteh Khán set up a claim to the Sultanate; and, for a period of three years, reigned in the city of Firuz, while Mahmud Sháh the legitimate sovereign, was shut up in Juna's walled town of Jahán Pana. This anomalous state of things was put an end to by a chief named Ikbál Khán, who ruled at Delhi in the name of the prophet Sultan. The Vazir of the empire, called Khwája Jahán, went eastward and founded Jaunpur: at the end of the fourteenth century nothing was left to Mahmud Sháh and his mayor-of-the-palace but five districts round the capital.

SECTION 2.—It was at this time that the Mughals revisited Hindustan; not, as of old, a tumultuous horde of heathen marauders, but an orderly army of orthodox Muslims, led by one of the great warriors of the world. Mention has been already made of the poet Khusru's captivity among the tribes of Mangu during the reign of Balban. From the lively description which he has recorded we gather a picture of rude barbarians—almost savages—such as may have followed Attila; Chanhgez and his sons were probably not much more civilised than their followers.

But the Amir Taimur—known to our fathers as "Tamerlane" was a different sort of "Mughal." Although affecting to trace his descent from a granddaughter of Chanhgez, he was by the father's side a Turkmán of the famous house of Birlás, who had been educated at Samarcand, the ancient capital of Sogdiana. Here he established the centre of his government, and here his sepulchre is to be seen at this day. He was a good scholar; and his autobiography, written in choice Turkish, has been praised as interesting literature by competent critics. At the age of sixty-three, after a career of unbroken conquest in Central Asia and Asia Minor, he turned his attention to the anarchic regions of Hindustan. Early in 1398 he invaded the Punjab by the usual route of Multan, routed the forces of the Sultan after an action in which he deigns to praise their behaviour, and entered the fortifications of Delhi, which were surrendered on his promise of protection, 17th December, 1398. The events of Nádir Sháh's invasion three hundred and fifty years later, were anticipated. Quarrels arising between the troops and citizens, a scene of plunder and massacre ensued: but the confusion seems to have been confined to old Delhi and Jahán Pana. Taimur himself proceeded thence to Firuzabád, where he found the Muslim population collected in and about the great mosque of Sultan Firuz (still standing); and these, on the intercession of their religious leaders, he consented to spare. He then departed to the eastward with his army. Sultan Mahmud and Ikbál Khán fled after they had lost the battle, so that they were not sharers or witnesses of these calamities. Taimur, having scoured the country from Kanauj to Jammu (north of Lahore) returned by the old route of Multan; and Mahmud—or rather his minister—resumed the old government in the desolate capital. Ikbál now openly assumed all authority; in 1400 he led an army into the Punjab in an endeavour to recover tribute, but was defeated and killed by Khizr Khán, the local governor. Mahmud was away at Kanauj at the time; but he presently returned to Delhi, where he lived ingloriously till 1412. The line of Tughlak then became extinct. A military oligarchy was at the head of affairs, under a Pathán leader called Daulat Khán, Lodi, who professed to carry on the dwindled state under the authority of the absent Taimur. But Khizr Khán marched down from the Punjab, and assaulted Daulat in Jahán Pana: the walls were scaled, or yielded; and Khizr became Sultan, 23rd March, 1414.

The dynasty of the Sáyyids—as the House of Khizr Khán was termed—held out feebly against the rising tide of disaffection and anarchy for about thirty years, during which their direct authority extended but a few miles beyond the walls of the capital, and the only advantage to the country was that the Hindus escaped persecution. The empire was at an end, Jaunpur in the east became a kingdom of some importance, as did Málwa in the south: the successor of Khizr Khán—Mubárak—attempted some assertion of authority in the north-west; and though beaten out of the Multan country by the son of the deceased Taimur, appears to have met with some success in what was then known as Katahr—the modern "Rohilkhand." He was assassinated by a party of Hindus in 1421. A grandson of the late Khizr Khán succeeded, by the title of Muhamad Farid Sháh, and dallied with the reduced duties of administration for about ten years. He was threatened by the Sultans of Jaunpur and Málwa, but saved by the interposition of the quasi-independent Viceroy of Lahore. Bin Farid died in 1443, and was succeeded by his son Alá-ud-din, who took the title of Alam Sháh, under which he speedily became a bye-word in Hindustan.*

The Viceroy of Lahore, above-mentioned, was a Pathán—or native Muslim—of the House of Lodi, by name Bahlol. Following the example formerly set by Khizr Khán, he began to threaten Delhi, on which the inefficient Sáyyad, who held that dwindled principality determined to retire to Katahr, where he ended his days in obscurity in the provincial town of

---

* The distich has been preserved;—*Badshahi Shah Alam Az Delhi ta Palam* (Palam being a village near the city.)

Badaon. Bahlol was raised to the Sultanate by a confederation of Afghan chiefs, 3rd February, 1451.

The reign of Bahlol Lodi was protracted to the unusual duration of thirty-seven years. He did not attempt any general restoration of the Empire's further limits, but he repressed the revolts of the local governors, and so prevented an increase of disintegration. As he was already in semi-independent possession of Multan, Lahore, and the Cis-Sutlej as far as Panipat, he was able, by his mere accession, to restore the whole of those provinces to the Empire. In the east he engaged in war with the usurping Sultan of Jaunpur, Husain Shah, who appears to have given the first provocation by attacking Delhi. Bahlol, after having maintained an equal strife for a quarter of a century with this opponent, at last defeated him, in 1474, when the "Eastern Sultan" was driven to take refuge in Bengal. This kingdom—for it may be justly so regarded now—was ruled by a Sultan whose name was Ala-ud-din, and his title Ali Shah; and with him Bahlol wisely forbore to meddle. He also left the Sultan of the Deccan and the Hindu Raja of Bijainagar to consolidate their power, but made some minor extensions of territory in consequence of which his empire may be taken, in the language of Elphinstone, as stretching from Delhi to the Himalaya range, with outsets in the direction of Bundelkhand. He was a man of simple habits and soldierly character; and he employed both Hindus and Mughals in his service. He died 5th December, 1488, and was handsomely buried at Delhi, where his monument is still to be seen.

His son, Nizam, succeeded, under the title of Sikandar Shah, the sub-kingdom of Jaunpur having been assigned to his brother, Barbek. The new Lodi Sultan required an acknowledgement of sovereignty which Barbek refused to give, and an army was sent to enforce the claim. Barbek had to accept a subordinate position, and the frontier of the empire was extended to Benares and even to the further limits of

Bundelkhand. In 1503 the Sultan transferred his residence to a suburb of Agra, which still bears his name. He discredited himself by a wanton destruction of Hindu temples; but the fusion of races was not to be prevented. Some, even of his own religion, remonstrated with the Sultan; the eclectic system of the Kabir Panthis became fashionable, even popular.* The reign is further remarkable as the period when the Hindus first began, generally, to study the Persian language. Sultan Sikandar died in 1517, according to Elphinstone, supported by Thomas, who takes the date from Firishta without adducing the evidence of any coin. Beale ("Oriental Biographical Dictionary") contends that this is an error, and that the true date is nearly seven years earlier—viz., 17th February, 1510.

The last King, or Sultan, of Lodi line was Ibráhim, son of Sikandar; Mr. Thomas gives the epigraphy of some of his coins, but they are undated. His reign was marked by an extraordinary variation in the relation of coin to commodities; so that, in the language of a contemporary, "gold and silver were only procurable with the greatest difficulty; and a monthly expenditure of a 100 Rs.† was considered a sign of wealth." The value of silver and gold, indeed, had begun to rise ever since the beginning of the Lodi dynasty, if not earlier; perhaps resulting from the plunder of Taimur, and the concomitant disappearance of specie in troubled times, when men are liable to be killed without an opportunity of revealing to their heirs the secret of their buried hoards. The Sultan made matters worse by accumulating the precious metals, and so increasing the demand for them. The corresponding cheapness

---

* It is on this compromise that the original founder of the Sikhs proceeded; so that early Sikhism has been viewed as a branch of Mohamadanism (*v.* Hughes's " Dict of Islám ": *in voc.*)

† *Tankas* in the text: the word *Rupi* was not introduced till some years later.

of living was much noticed; but was not altogether advantageous as the agriculturist got less for his produce, while his fiscal assessments remained the same. The earlier events of Ibráhim's reign partly resembled those of his father's time; there was the same sort of quarrel with a brother about Jaunpur, the same expedition in the trans-Jumna countries, only farther afield. The Sultan, though brave, was unpopular; and an enterprising enemy was eagerly watching his opportunity from the north-western mountains.

The new Mughals have been already noticed in the process of transition under Taimur. According to Khusru in the thirteenth century the Mughals had been under-sized, yellow, flat-faced, and filthy, speaking a monosyllabic jargon, and ignorant of the arts of life. "Turks of Kai," the poet calls them, punning on the likeness between the name of one of their tribes and the nausea inspired by their persons. What intermarriage and civilisation had made of them two hundred years later, we know from the testimony of a visitor to the chief of Mughalistan quoted by Erskine :—

"I had heard," said the holy man—for such he was, "that Yunis Khán was a Mughal, so concluded that he was beardless, with the habits of the desert. But I found a handsome man, with a fine, bushy beard; of elegant address, agreeable, and refined in words and ways, such as are hardly met except in most polished society."

This Yunis Khán was the grandfather of Záhir-ud-din Bábar, and a descendant of Chaghtai, son of Changhez Khán; his daughter being married to the great-grandson of Sháh Rukh Mirza, son and successor of the Amir Taimur. Born in Farghána—now Kokand—on 15th Feb., 1488 (the year of Taimur's invasion of India), he lived a life of adventure in Turkestan till about 1504, when he became possessed of the country now known as Afghanistán. In 1522 he had firmly consolidated his power from the passes of the Hindu Kush to

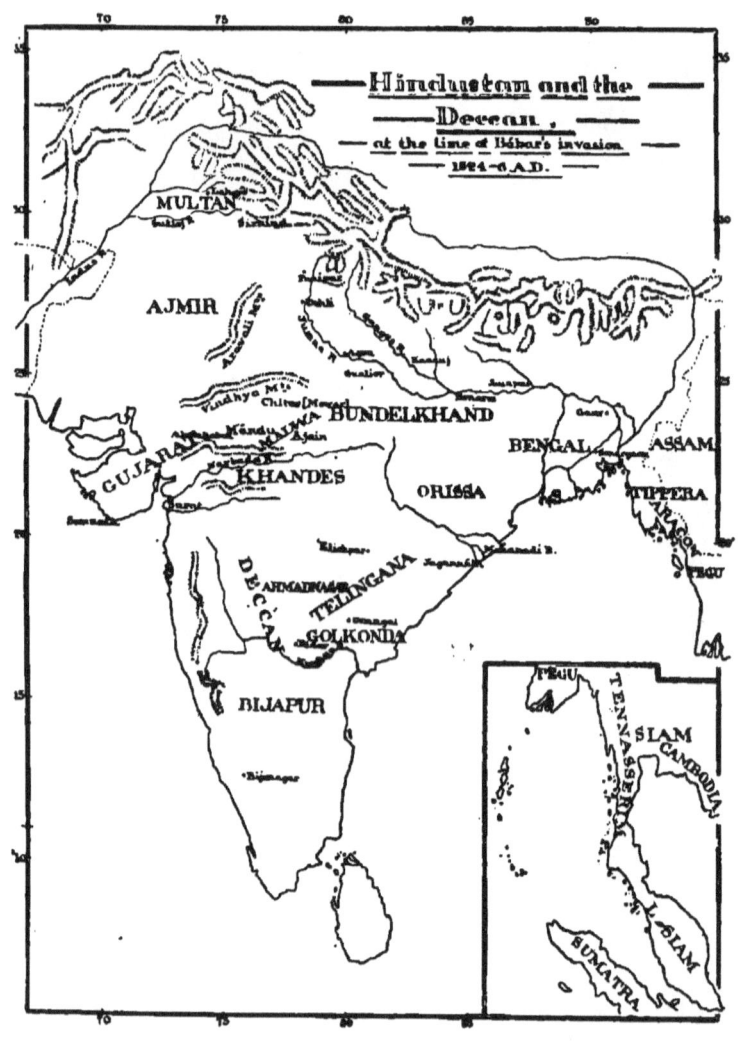

END OF THE "PATHANS."

the plain and city of Kandahar; two years later he invaded the Punjab.

Having now brought the future antagonists face to face it will be well to take a rapid survey of the condition of the prize for which they were to contend.

The nominal power of Hindustan was exercised within ever-fluctuating limits; the Sultan being ill-tempered, yet little able to cope with the turbulent ambition of the Afghán nobles. Bihár and Jaunpur were in a state of imperfect obedience, Bengal—of which the capital was sometimes near Dacca, but more usually at Guar—was a totally distinct Muslim kingdom, under the Sultan already mentioned by the name of Alá-ud-din; but he was succeeded, in 1521, by Nasrat Sháh. Gujarát —extending from the Vindhyas to Somnáth and Surat—was held by petty Rajput chiefs in subordination to a Muslim Sultan named Muzafar Shah, who was contending for the country about Mándu (the province of Málwa) with the Rána of Méwar, of which the fortified capital was Chittore. There were a few petty principalities arising in Hindustan, and the Rajputs maintained a wild autonomy south of Ajmere. In the Deccan the last of the Bahmanis (the dynasty of Hassan Gángu) were struggling against the new Muslim states which had broken off from the allegiance of their Empire, and set up, respectively, at Ahmadnagar (1490), Elichpur (1484), Bidar (1498), and Bijápur (1489). A fifth state arose on the complete overthrow of Mahmud II., the last ruler of the Bahmanis, about 1518: the capital was at Golkonda.* Further south the great Hindu kingdom of Bijainagar was still in full strength, with minor principalities—always under Hindu Rájas—in Calicut, Tanjore, and Travancore.

Such was the chaotic condition of the vast country over

---

* These Deccan States will be more fully noticed in the next section: what is now said is necessary for the understanding of the annexed map. (See also Synoptical Table, *infra*, p. 115).

which Ibráhim Lodi affected a sort of general overlordship at Agra and Delhi. But his authority was contested, even in the neighbourhood of the last-named capital; and in 1524 the Governor of Lahore—a kinsman of the Emperor, named Daulat Khán—went into revolt and invited the aid of Bábar, which was most readily afforded. Bábar had long had his eye on the Punjab, which he claimed as part of the succession of the Amir Taimur; but on arriving in the country of the Five Rivers he found that Daulat Khán was unable—perhaps also unwilling—to hand it over. A confederation of Sultan Ibráhim's officers gave him battle near Lahore, and it was not until he had defeated them in the field that he was able to occupy the city. Daulat held back, and the invaders were left to attack Deopálpore single-handed. Here, too, they were successful, and here Daulat made a show of adhesion which, however, was of little service. Daulat ultimately turned openly against the Mughals, and Bábar returned to his mountain-home, leaving Deopálpore in charge of an uncle of the Sultan who had espoused his cause. Daulat now struck in on his own account; and in Bábar's absence made himself master of all the Punjab. Bábar was unable to oppose him for the moment, being occupied in driving out an Uzbeg raid from the northern part of his dominions. That task accomplished, he returned to Lahore, subjugated Daulat, and marched on Delhi by way of Pánipat.

A lamented historian thus describes the scene:—"An extensive level tract, broken only by insignificant risings of ground; here and there the shallow soil, moistened by some scanty stream, yields a niggard growth of coarse grass, and stunted bushes. But, for the most part, one sees only the yellow-grey of the barren land. Everywhere a silent void, as if the plain were intended by Nature to be the battlefield of nations."*

Hither, on Thursday the 20th April, 1526, Sultan Ibráhim

* Court v. Noer (Prince Frederic of Schleswig-Holstein.)

gathered the hosts of Hindustan to meet the invaders. The nobles of India were arrayed in gilded armour, with hundreds of elephants bravely barded and accoutred, their tents and canopies making a field of cloth-of-gold. The day was spent in pageant and revelry. Very different was the cheer of the war-spent wanderers, who had fought their way so far from their native hills into the hot wind and the parched desert. Many of them, by their leader's frank admission, were in a state of actual trepidation approaching panic. While admitting that such feelings were unbecoming, Bábar sympathetically adds that, in the circumstances, he could not greatly blame his followers, opposed to an outnumbering host in a strange land. But the difference in the quality of the respective leaders redressed the balance. "The Emperor," so Bábar testifies, "was inexperienced and illiberal; negligent in strategy and disorderly in movement; halting without plan and fighting without forethought." Bábar, for his part, learned wisdom from difficulty, and left nothing to chance. His right was sheltered by the the walls of Pánipat: his front was protected by artillery, the guns roped together with raw hide, and covered by wagons and fascines. Behind these were ranged the musketeers with rested matchlocks, the long Afghan *jazail* which proved formidable to European troops within living memory. On the left Bábar made an earthwork guarded by abattis. In such preparations he passed the long hours. At dawn of the following day the impatient Ibrahim brought his motley hosts to the assault of the invaders, with a result that appears to us now as a foregone conclusion. On one side were the courage of despair, and something of the resources of scientific warfare; on the other side, men-at-arms of the medieval type, with crowded ranks of spearmen and archers thronging on in foolhardy disorder. The Mughal cavalry formed three divisions, two to charge the advancing enemy, and one to guard the camp. They also had their archers, who crept round the enemy's right, and galled their rear with clouds of long arrows, while the front attack was pelted from swivels in the Mughal batteries and culverins on their left centre. The nearer the Indians came to the Mughal camp the less heart they had to storm. Goaded, pressed rank on rank, unwilling to advance, unable to retreat, they suffered from their very multitude, and fell into chaos. In vain the Sultan and his chosen companion attempted to restore the battle. A courtier urged him to escape while it was yet time; but the Mughal horse were upon them, the archers were at their rear, and Ibrahim refused to make the attempt. He plunged into the melêe with his faithful followers. When all was over five thousand corpses were found heaped about their dead Sultan. The Indians lost fifteen thousand in killed alone—according to Bábar's computation—amongst them the Hindu Rája of Gwalior who had joined the Muslim Sultan in defence of their common country. Many more were cut up, or made prisoners in the pursuit; advance parties went forward and occupied Delhi and Agra. The native Muslim had been fairly overmatched, but not by a savage enemy. We hear of no further slaughter; the land simply changed masters after one supreme effort.

Section 3.—Sultan Bábar has left one of the most charming autobiographies ever written, a work which has been translated out of the original Turkish into various languages. A Persian rendering appeared during the time of Akbar, made by a Mughal noble, whom we shall presently have to notice as distinguished in public life.* The "Memoirs of Bábar" have also been translated into French by the well-known Turkish scholar, Pavet de Courteille; and an English translation of the Persian version was published by the late W. Erskine in 1826. As the "Confessions" of a medieval adven-

* A beautiful MS. of this work, with many coloured pictures, is in the Agra College Library. It was formerly the property of the Emperor Sháh Jahán, and bears his autograph on the fly-leaf.

turer the book can never fail to please, the speech being candid and the observation direct and lively. The views are those of a Broad Church Muslim, fond of fighting, wine, and pleasure, and ready to negotiate with Hindu leaders and to make use of their services. The early adventures related do not belong to our present subject; but from the beginning of the year 1526, the book is chiefly concerned with India.

On the third Friday from the date of his victory Bábar entered Agra, whither he had been preceded by the Crown Prince Humaiun Mirza. The family of the late Rája of Gwalior had come to the prince with gifts of price—amongst them the famous diamond, afterwards known as the *Koh-i-nur*, a jewel which, after bringing disaster upon many of its owners, is now in the possession of the Crown of England. Bábar treated the Gwalior family with kindness, also making provision for the household of the late Sultan Ibráhim. But neither he nor his men were greatly pleased with their hard-won conquest. "Hindustan," writes the out-spoken soldier, "is a country that has but little to recommend it." And elsewhere he tells us that, during the frightful heat of an Agra summer, the Mughals had neither food for themselves nor forage for their horses; the fields being untilled at that parched season, and the people either fled or in rebellion. The foreign troops, accustomed to a hill climate, were decimated by privation and sunstroke. Many of the officers began to murmur and to talk of leading their followers back to Kábul; but only one of them actually left, and he was put in command of the escort which took the booty thither.

Meanwhile the Gahlot Rána of Mewar—whose grandfather had conquered Málwa and Gujarát in 1440—began to add to all Bábar's other anxieties. This was the chief of Chittore, Sanga Rána, lovingly described by Colonel Tod* as decorated with no

---

* "Annals and Antiquities of Rajasthan," second edition, 2 vols. 4to, Madras, 1872. A book of endless charm from its genuine enthusiasm, but to be scrutinised in use, and carefully compared with cooler writings.

less than eighty marks of honour, in the shape of scars of wounds received from lance or sword.

This redoutable warrior advanced on Agra in the cool season of 1526-7. In their mountain fastness his ancestors had more than maintained their fame and independence. But their traditions had taught them to consider the tribes of the north as their hereditary foemen and destined supplanters in Hindustan.* So long as the Indian Patháns bore sway at Agra and Delhi, while Bábar was still only menacing them from Kábul, the Rána was fain to affect friendliness to Bábar as the enemy of his own rivals. But although he took no part in the defence of Hindustan by the Indian Muslims, he was in no mood to let other Muslims profit by their overthrow. The winter wore away in minor operations; Humaiun made a campaign in Bihár and occupied Jaunpur; Bábar was put in possession of the Fort of Gwalior. On the other side, Sanga took a fort near Delhi from one of Bábar's native allies, and collected the forces of the Rajputana states, while he was joined by some of the Lodi nobles.

Even in such circumstances each side attempted to amuse the other with negotiations, probably only intended to gain time for the maturing of preparations. It was the middle of February, 1527, before the two armies began to approach Biána, fifty miles south-west of Agra, where there was at that time a strong fort which had been surrendered to Bábar, and which he now sought to save from assault by the Rajputs; whether or no Bábar hoped to the last that the former amicable relations with Sanga might be renewed does not appear. If such was his expectation it would, in all probability, have been rudely frustrated. But the

---

* The Rána's name is sometimes translated as "Sanka." The inscription from his coinage, given by Thomas, is in the Nágri character, and equivalent to "Sangram." Sanga is given by Elphinstone, and is enough for our purpose.

solution was precipitated by an accident. One morning a young and zealous officer, in temporary command of the advanced guard, fell in with an outpost of the enemy, who charged him with 15,000 horsemen. Confusion ensued: a Yak-tail standard and several Mughal prisoners fell into the hands of the Rajputs.* Bábar, on hearing the news, hurried reinforcements to the front. The retreat of the unprosperous Mughal reconnaissance was covered, the Sultan himself bringing up some guns for the purpose.

There was evidently an end to negotiation. As at Pánipat, Bábar intrenched his camp, and made a breastwork of his wagons. Despondency and desertion broke out, and the Sultan publicly foreswore the use of wine, to which he was addicted, and swore his officers upon the Koran to conquer or to die. Nearly four weeks of inaction ensued, during which the two armies stood watching each other. It was on a Tuesday, 12th March, 1527, that Bábar, observing a movement which looked like retreat amongst the Rajputs—and probably pressed for provisions—took courage to sally from his intrenchment. The great encounter took place at Kánhwa, a march nearer to Biána, on the Saturday following. When he had arrived within four miles of the enemy's camp Bábar pushed forward with the flower of his heavy cavalry, followed by his guns. The danger dissolved on being faced; the Hindus had nothing to oppose to the fire of those new and deadly engines, and they were soon enveloped on flank and rear by well-handled squadrons. Towards evening they broke, Sanga, of the eighty wounds, sharing, if he did not lead, the flight. Owing, perhaps, to the lateness of the hour, there was little or no pursuit. A pyramid of the skulls of the slain enemies was, in Turkmán fashion, erected on the field. The country since called Alwar

* The Yak-tail standard, or *Tugh*, corresponded amongst Asiatic Turks to the "horse-tails" of which we read in the wars of the Osmanlis in Europe.

was added to the Empire, and Bábar advanced on Rajputána by way of Chandairi, south of Gwalior. This was a very populous place, with a fort of natural and artificial strength, which had once belonged to the Delhi state, and had then devolved on the Muslims of Málwa. But it had fallen into the hands of Sanga, who had entrusted it to an officer named Médini Rai, with a garrison of 4,000 "Pagans."* Bábar approached Chandairi through a wild and difficult country, felling the woods and making roads for his guns and wagons. It was the end of the year before he reached the place. After a week of open trenches the assault was delivered, the town stormed, and the garrison driven into the citadel. Here the defence was obstinate but a Beg (General) of Bábar's army found a bastion joining a part of the town wall, and effected an entry by scaling it. Another party got in by the covered way leading down from one of the gates to a watercourse at the foot of the hill. The garrison set fire to the place where their women and children were collected; and rushing out, with nothing but their swords, perished to a man, excepting a few who fell on one another's swords in Médini's quarters.

On the morning of the day which ended in this terrible scene bad news had arrived from the Eastward where a Mughal force had been expelled from Lucknow, and made to fall back on Kanauj. Bábar, who had kept back the tidings during the the fight, now communicated it to a council of his Begs.† While they were in debate another courier arrived with the compensatory news that the warlike Sanga was no more. On this it was resolved to break up from Chandairi and march eastward to support the force in that quarter, an adequate

---

* With Bábar "Pagan" means Hindu, while the Indian Muslims are "Afghans," and his own men "Turks."

† "Beg" was the title of the leaders, minor officers being called "Mir." Bábar's own title—so long as he was a mere adventurer—was the old Turkish word "Khákán."

garrison being left in the fort under the Málwa Muslim from whom it had been taken by Sanga.

Chandairi fell on a Thursday, 20th Jan., 1528. On the following Sunday the army marched, crossed the Jumna at Kinár, and proceeded at all speed to Kanauj. Just below that town they found that the Ganges, on whose bank the place stood, was lined by a large force of Indians under "Afghán" leaders. By a mixture of boldness and strategy they threw a bridge of boats across, by which Bábar passed his army over, without a battle, while his son Humaiun occupied Bihár. Bábar then returned to Agra and Gwalior, at which latter place he reaped some of the fruits of his late exertions in the submission of the late Rána Sanga's successor, who delivered the keys of the famous fort of Rinthambor.

In the beginning of 1529 bad news once more arrived from the Crown Prince Humaiun—always more distinguished by courage than by conduct. The Lodi chief, who had formerly acted with Sanga, had driven Humaiun out of Bihár, and was investing him at the foot of Chunár. The indefatigable Bábar hastened to his son's help, raising the siege of Chunár by the mere alarm of his approach, and pushing on to Gházipur by forced marches. The Muslims of Bihár were twice routed, and the province was put in charge of Muhamad Zamán Mirza, a Turkish officer of Bábar's family, while a treaty of alliance was concluded with Nasrat Sháh, Sultan of Bengal, who appears to have joined the Lodi movement at first, but to have yielded to Bábar's military superiority.

The gallant adventurer, then, had at last attained his most ambitious aims. From the Jaxartes to the Ganges, in Kabul, Delhi, Agra, and Jaunpur, he was no longer a mere leader of marauding hordes, but a veritable Bádsháh, or Emperor. Early in September, 1529, he returned to Agra once more; and one cannot but hope that he enjoyed the short interval of rest that he there found. But his health had been tried by a life of labour and hazard, begun when his years were but fourteen. During great part of the time he had drunk hard; the fierce transitions of the Indian climate tried his health. "There are neither decent houses," he complained, "nor is there good fruit, ice, or even cold water." On the approach of the winter of 1530, in the 50th year of his age, his constitution gave way. He sent for his eldest son. "Do not kill your brothers" were his last words, "but watch them with care." He died on the 26th December, and his body was transported to Kábul for interment. Over a fountain hard by he had formerly inscribed a quatrain, which may thus be expressed in English:—

> "Bright spring blooms here from day to day,
> Young girls stand by to pour out the wine;
> Enjoy them, Bábar, while you may,
> Life, once enjoyed, no more is thine."

In Bábar's unfavourable estimate of India we see some materials for a judgment of the low ebb of civilisation which had followed from centuries of Afghán bigotry and bloodshed. The inhabitants, he observes, were not well-favoured, they had no idea of the pleasures of society, no genius or power of generalisation, neither amiability, sympathetic feeling, nor that urbanity of manner which sometimes stands in place of such good qualities or conceals their absence. He also notices a universal lack of mechanical invention and of grandeur of architectural conception; and he instances shrewdly enough, so far as his observation extended, not only the want of institutions like colleges and public baths, but of such small aids to study and civilisation as are afforded by lamps and candles.

Yet, in this intellectual torpor the forces of human nature were still working, silently and in secret, for the harvest of the future; while there were many parts of India to which, even then, the criticism was unjust. The career of the Mewar

Gahlots exhibits the hardy patriotism of the Rajputs, holding their own, and more, against their Muslim neighbours of Gujarát on the one side, and Málwa on the other; and only yielding to the better organisation and more tenacious warfare of the northern invaders. In the Deccan the Bahmani Empire, founded on the ruins of the Tughlak conquest, had broken up, but only to form new Muslim kingdoms, which long continued to keep up a high standard in arts and letters. The Hindu kingdom of Bijainagar, in the extreme South, has left but little record of that sort; yet the remains of temples and palaces at Hampi—the modern name of the capital—suffice to show that there was little exaggeration in the account of the medieval traveller, César Frédéric, who said he had "seen many kings' courts, but never anything to compare with Bijainagar." Among the ruined masses of masonry are still distinguishable the remains of aqueducts and baths to counteract the pessimist complaints of Bábar; whilst arches, not generally used by the Hindus, and a wealth of sculpture, attest the skill of the people in the construction and decoration of their edifices.

Most of all ought to be noticed the advance that was going on in the dominion of mind. Under the Muslim government of Bengal, about the middle of the 14th century A.D. a man of genius had undertaken to adopt the old code of the Vedantist Mánavas to the needs of modern society by a free application of the doctrine expressed in Europe by the maxim, *Factum valet quod fieri non debuit*. The result was the *Dáyabhága*, an amended book of civil law, which has ever since prevailed in the province of Bengal Proper, and has practically given sanction to dispositions of property unknown in other regions. "Other teachers," observes a modern authority, "cite precedents, but Jimata Váhana appeals to reason. The Bengal Code is more human than ordinary Hindu law if less divine; and has caused a social progress unknown under the old system."

Nor was it only in Bengal, and in the direction of law, that progress was preparing in this apparently dark age. If ever there was a country which showed instances of the "Necessity of Atheism" * it was medieval India, enslaved by the conflicts of a monstrous pantheon. A chain of Hindu sages, Kabir (fl. 1,400), Chaitanya (a century later), and Vallabha-Swámi (who followed a few years after) were all men who—without openly discarding concrete representations of Deity—held up to popular aspiration a higher and brighter standard. Vishnu, the beneficent, and not the skull-decked Siva, was the object of their adoration. No race or caste was beyond the pale of brotherhood and the hopes of salvation. Chaitanya has himself become an idol for many of his simple admirers; but there is no doubt but that all these teachers had glimpses of something behind idolatry, the synthesis of force and energy which maintains the pillars of the universe, and, in the moral order, makes for righteousness.

In the more commonplace and material aspect of affairs the Deccan Muslims were not unprosperous during the time when their brethren in the North were undergoing so much disaster. The Hindu-loving Hassan Gangu passed away 10th February, 1358, after as eventful reign of eleven years; but his son, Muhamad Sháh, commenced as a regular Muslim conqueror, making war on his Telingána neighbours in Golkonda and Orangal, and even dictating terms of peace to the great southern power of Bijainagar. His death is dated 21st March, 1375. His successor, Majáhid Sháh, renewed the attack on Bijainagar in spite of the treaty. He was, however, repulsed, and murdered during his retreat by his father's brother, Dáud Khán, 14th April, 1378. The murderer was put to death, and succeeded by his younger brother, Mahmud, who died 20th April, 1397, after a peaceful reign. After a brief moment of

---

* The title of Shelley's crude pamphlet.

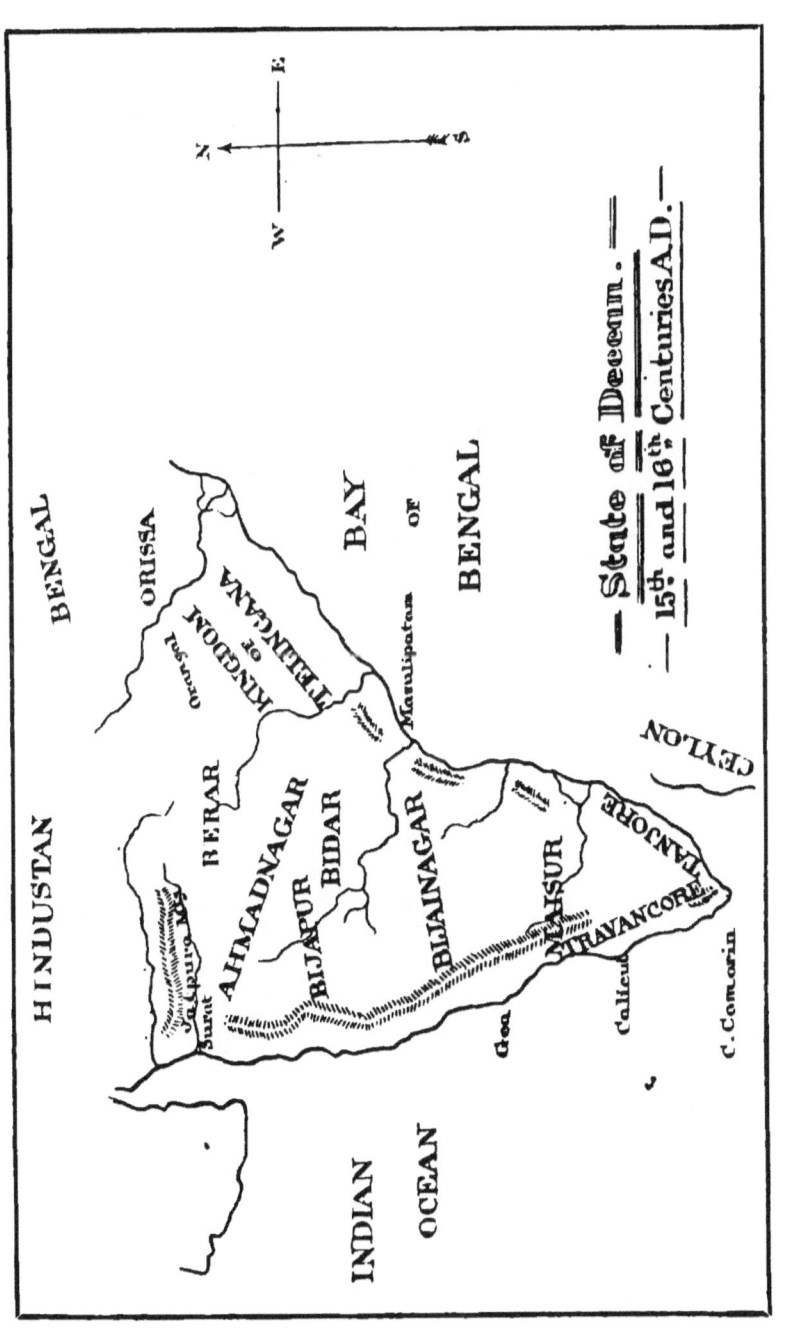

confusion Firuz, son of the murderous Dáud, obtained the masnad of Kulbarga, which he occupied for twenty-five years. A year after his accession he was attacked by Deva Rája, the Bijainagar chief; but the attack recoiled on the Rája, who was beaten back on his own capital with the loss of his son. Firuz in 1401 dictated peace under the walls of Deva's capital, and one of the terms was that he should marry the Rája's daughter. In spite of this connection, however, the war smouldered, and soon broke out again. In 1417 Firuz was defeated, and died 15th September, 1422, without having effected anything decisive in Bijainagar or settled the succession to his own territories. His brother, Ahmad Sháh, assumed the kingdom, making a fresh attack on Bijainagar, and finally overthrowing the Hindu kingdom of Telingána. He founded the city of Bidar, where he died 10th February, 1435. His son, Alá-ud-din, succeeded, and by-and-by removed the capital to Bidar. The chronic war with Bijainajar was arrested by a treaty which remained in force some years. But the Muslims were evidently bent on the overthrow of all Hindu independence in the south. Alá-ud-din died during the year 1457, and was succeeded by his son Humaiun, who reigned ingloriously for four years. He was murdered in 1461, and the kingdom remained under a Regency during the minority of his heir, Nizám Sháh. Attacked on all sides, the Regency, under the Queen-mother and her minister, Muhamad Gáwan, defended the country as well as circumstances permitted for nearly two years, when the boy Sultan died suddenly, and his brother, Muhamad Sháh II., was placed on the masnad in his eleventh year. Gáwan now adopted an agressive policy. In 1469 he took the northern sea-coast from Bijáinagar; and, two years later, marched an army into Orissa on pretence of aiding the Rája of that country against his subjects. He conquered the Kulinga country from Masulipatam to Kánchi (Conjeveram), so that the kingdom now reached its widest limit, and stretched from sea to sea. Unhappily for its future welfare, the Sultan's mind became poisoned in regard to his great minister, whom the very magnitude of his services rendered an object of suspicion. In 1481 Gáwan was put to death, and the ruin of the Government soon followed. Muhamad Sháh died 24th March, 1482, being succeeded by his son, Mahmud II. In his reign the disintegration began. Almost from the first the territory had been divided for administrative purposes into four sections; and the subsequent acquisitions of successive Sultans had not tended to unity. At the end of the fifteenth century there were no less than six sections—Kulbarga having been made into two provinces, as had also Daulatabád, Telingána, and Berár; and the kingdom which had escaped so much foreign menace soon broke up naturally into the smaller Muslim states which shared with the Hindu kingdom the whole south of India.

In 1487 Nar Singh, Rája of Bijainagar had already become master of the Pandiyan principality, and extended his boundaries to Ramisaram and the Bay of Bengal, becoming paramount throughout the Southern Triangle. In 1497 a foreign slave, named Kásim Barid, became all powerful at Court, and founded the new dynasty of Bidar. Two years later another foreigner, who had been adopted as a son by the deceased minister, Gáwan, set up at Bijápur with the title of Yusaf Adil Sháh. A converted Hindu assumed independence at Elichpur as Aimád Sháh Báhmani; and the son of Sultan Mahmud's minister, Nizám-ul-mulk, went to the northward, occupying Daulatabad. in 1499, and founding a new Muslim kingdom at Ahmadnagar. Lastly, in 1512, the governor of Telingána became the founder of a dynasty at Golkonda, under the title of (Kutb) Qutb Sháh. He took possession of Orangal. holding all the Kulinga country between the Godávari and Krishna rivers, north of the Godávari. Some of the country belonged to Kutab as lord of Orangal, and some to Orissa, where the Rajput dynasty maintained an existence of long conflict with the Bengal Muslims for another half century.

Of the condition of the people of the southern lands during the fourteenth and fifteenth centuries there is even less known than in regard to Hindustan. The worship of Siva, or Mahádeva, was the prevailing southern form of Hinduism; and the earlier type of civil law, known as the *Mitákshara*, was current among the Hindu population. Signs of fusion between them and their Muslim neighbours were notable, especially in the case of the older, or native Muslims. The immigrants by whom some of the new states were founded, professed the Persian, or Shia denomination of Islám, and were at first unfavourable to the employment and society of the Hindus. The Deccani dialect of the Hindustani language, however, became a medium of intercourse; and latterly we hear of the employment of Mahratta mercenaries; the first mention of that race, destined afterwards to have so large a sphere in Indian history. On the whole it may be concluded that the Hindus enjoyed a good deal of autonomy in every part of the peninsula; in the north, owing to the indolence of the Turkish character, and the almost equal contempt of the native Muslims; in the south, to the power of the Hindu states, the constant intermarriage of the races, and the habit of employing Hindu ministers, which more and more prevailed. The revenues generally were derived from a tithe of agricultural produce, a special tax on Hindus, which doubled their assessment, and a number of transit dues and local cesses.

[To the former authorities may be added the fourth volume of Dowson's "Elliot" and Erskine's "Life of Bábar," London, 1826; and "History of India" (same author), London, 1854.]

NOTE.—In the Fourth Chapter of Book II. of his "History of India,"* Captain Trotter has already given an account of the

---

* *History of India*. (S. P. C. K.) Second edition. London. 1889.

principal powers that were contemporary with the first Muslim Empire of Hindustan. Some additions and corrections have been gathered from works above referred to: and the general result is exhibited in the accompanying table. With a brief explanation it will be found both intelligible and useful.

In the early part of the period Bengal (proper) was divided into three parts, like Cæsar's Gaul; each portion, being named, however, not from its tribes but from its chief cities. The division of Lakhnauti was named from the capital—afterwards called Gaur—which was taken by the Khilji chief, Muhamad Bakhtyár, in 1204. The Delta was known as the Province of Sátgaon, that being the town (near the modern Hugli) which was the seat of government—while Eastern Bengal took its name from Sonárgaon, near the present town of Dacca. All these were at first held by Bakhtyár Khilji, together with the province of Bihár; but he was soon deprived of the last named and rendered a feudatory as to his possession of the rest. After this, sometimes in conjunction with Bihár, and sometimes separate, when Bihár was more directly subordinate, Bengal continued for about half a century to afford a rich prize for various Turkmán adventurers. In 1270, however, the strong hand of Sultan Balban fell upon the eastern province; Sonárgaon was taken; and the Sultan, Maghis-ud-din Tughral, was driven out, followed up, attacked, defeated, and drowned in endeavouring to escape. Balban's second son became Viceroy of Bengal, with the title of the late Sultan his father's patron. He is best known as Baghra Khán,* and he ruled the eastern province while his weak and unfortunate son Kai Kubad was pursuing his downward course in Hindustan. His other sons were both kings of Bengal in succession; and the youngest, Shams-ud-din, was in turn

* Called also Bakarra and Karra. Ibn Batuta calls him by his more formal title Nasir-ud-din (v. sup.).

succeeded by two of his own sons. After the death of the last of these Bengal was annexed to the Empire by the first Tughlak and his son Muhamad Tughlak (Juna), about 1324 to 1332. Sonárgaon had by this time broken off under a Hindu Rája: and the whole province revolted from the Empire in consequence of a successful rising of one Fakhr-uddin, who possessed himself of Sonárgaon. Ali Sháh, who was Viceroy at Lakhnauti, first attacked Fakhr with success and then rendered himself independent. Firuz Sháh Tughlak acknowledged the sovereignty of one of this line called Ikhtyar, in 1251, and Bengal remained obscure, and separated from the rest of India, until the time of Bábar.

The Hoysala Ballálas, of whom something has already been said, ruled the central Deccan until the revolt of Hassan Gangu at the end of Juna's reign (1347). They were Yádavas by origin ; and maintained an obscure independence for some time later, their looks turned southward by the pressure of Muslim power.

The gradual growth of the Hindu kingdom of Vijainagar also forwarded the decline of the Yádava Ballálas, once lords of the Deccan. Their two powerful neighbours, though they confined the Yádavas to Maisur and the south, were by no means disposed to an amicable partition of the Deccan. In 1365-6 there was a terrible war between them which ended to the advantage of Muhamad, the Bahmani. His successor again attacked Bijainagar. In 1398 the Hindu Rája retaliated; and, with varying results, the war went on till 1417. It was renewed about 1422, when an expedition was also sent to Telingána which ultimately destroyed Orangal. It was in this reign, or the next, that the capital of the Bahmani kingdom was removed to Bidar, about 1435 ; and during the reign of Muhamad Sháh II., about thirty years later, that the Bahmani kingdom received its greatest increase by the valour and ability of the great minister, Mahmud Gáwan ; and his treacherous slaughter, in 1481, proved the beginning of its ruin. The rest of its history is a series of murders, rebellions, and disasters, until in 1527 the family became extinct, and the kingdom of the Muslims in the Deccan broke up into a pentarchy.

The independence of Jaunpur and that of Gujarát, as Muslim kingdoms—are both alike ascribable to the decay of the Tughlak line of Hindustan.

I. Jaunpur never appears as a place of importance until the end of the fourteenth century, when an ambitious eunuch, formerly Vazir at Delhi, was sent there as governor. Taking advantage of the troubles caused by the weakness of the central Government he set up as "Sultan-us-Shark" (or King of the East) in 1393, with the personal title of Khwájah-i-Jahán. His adopted son Mubárak Sháh—surnamed *Karnful*—laid the foundation of a dynasty which proved a thorn in the side of the debilitated Empire for nearly a hundred years. The last of them was Husain Sháh who was reduced by Bahlol Lodis in 1478; the great mosque of Jaunpore still standing was built by this prince.

II. Gujarát was a principality made up of minor sub-divisions. The central part was under the Hindu Rájas of Anhalvára until they were overthrown by Alá-ud-din in 1297.* In 1376, Farhat-al-mulk was sent there as Governor; and Zafar Khán, being sent to take his place fourteen years later, took the opportunity of assuming independence about the time of Taimur's raid into Hindustan; his title was Muzafar Sháh, which became the hereditary title of his dynasty until the kingdom was annexed by Akbar as shown in the next chapter. The city of Surat and the peninsula of Kathiawár generally belonged to these princes and were destined to bring them into contact with the Portuguese.

The Muslim state of Málwa does not seem to have established a coinage of its own—the symbol of independence among

* This was the occasion of the romance of "Khizr and Dewal," celebrated by Amir Khusru ("Tota").

END OF THE "PATHANS." 115

Orientals—before the time of Hasám-ud-din Hushang, who founded the city of Mándu, on the right bank of the Narbada: he surrounded the place with fortifications and enriched it with a splendid mosque; and his marble tomb is still one of the sights of Mándu. His successor was his son Muhamad Sháh, in whose time the boundaries of the State extended from Rajputána on the north, to the Satpura range beyond the Narbada, and from Gujarát on the west to the borders of Bundelkhand.

The Hindu state of Mewar, or Chittore—now known as Udaipore—was ruled by the Gahlot tribe of Rajputs, and was in many respects entitled to be considered the premier principality of the northern Hindus. By reason alike of situation, and of its belonging to a specially proud and warlike tribe, it was constantly embroiled with its neighbours, Gujarát, Málwa, and the Delhi Empire, against all of whom it warred with credit, and sometimes with success. In 1275 Chittore was taken by Alá-ud-din Khilji, but recovered in the next generation. In 1419 the Rána—called Kambhaka on his coins—began a career of great success. In 1440 he defeated the combined armies of the Muslim princes of Málwa and Gujarát, and to commemorate his triumph erected the famous pillar still extant at Chittor. The third in descent from him was the famous Sangram Sinh, known in history as the Rána Sanga, who succeeded in 1509, and was still leading the Gahlot armies in the time of Bábar.

Of the Hindu kingdom of Bijainagar we need only here notice that it long continued an obscure but independent existence, favoured by the disputes of its Muslim neighbours. The Rája, at the time of Bábar's invasion of Hindustan, was a powerful ruler—Krishna Deva Ráya—whose daughter married the minister, Ráma Ráya; and he, after a disputed succession, set aside the dynasty of Nara Sinha; he lost his throne after many years (v. inf. p. 129).

[The tables referred to in this note will be found on the other side.]

SYNOPTICAL TABLE OF DYNASTIES
DOWN TO MUGHAL TIMES.

Date.	Hindustan.	Bengal.	Jaunpur.	Málwa.	Gujarát.	Dakhan.	Hoysala Bhú-lus.	Vijaynagar.	Orangal.
1193	Md. bin Sám	Bakhtyár Khán Khilji.							
1205	—	Md. Shírán Khilji.							
1205	Kutb-ud-dín Aibak.	Ali Mardán Khilji.							
1208		—							
1210	'Arám Sháh.								
1210	Shams-ud-dín Altamash.								
1211		Sultán Ghiás-ud-dín.							
1223?		—							
1226	—	Násir-ud-dín Mahmúd.					Narasinha II.		
1229	—	'Ala-ud-dín Jani.							
1229	—	Saif-ud-dín Aibak.							
1233	—	'Izz-ud-dín Tughral.							
1235	Rukn-ud-dín Fíruz Sháh I.								
1236	Sultán Itizáah.								
1239	Bahrám Sháh.	—							
1241	Alá-ud-dín Masá-ud-Sháh.	—							
1244	—	Kamr-ud-dín Tamar Khán.							
1244	—	Ikhtiyár-ud-dín.							

END OF THE "PATHANS."

Date.	Hindustan.	Bengal.	Jaunpur.	Málwa.	Gujarát.	Dakhan.	Hoysala Bilálas.	Vijaynagar.	Orangal.
1246	Násir-ud-dín Mahmúd.	—	—	—	—	—	—	—	—
1252							Somesvara. Narasinha III.		Rudramma (Q.).
1254									
1257									
1258		Jalál-ud-dín Mas'a-ud. Táj-ud-dín Arslán Khán.							
1258		Md. Arslán Khán.							
1260		Maghís-ud-dín Tughral.							
1260		—							
1265	Ghaiás-ud-dín (Balban).								
1282	—	Násir-ud-dín Mahmúd					Balála III.		
1288	Mu'izz-ud-dín Kai Kubád.	(Bughra Khán)							
1287	Jalál-ud-dín	—							
1290	Fíruz Sháh II.								
1291	—	Rukn-ud-dín.							
1295	Rukn-ud-dín Ibrahím.	—							Pratápa Rudra II.
1295	'Alá-ud-dín Md. Sháh.								
1302		Shams-ud-dín Fíruz Sháh.							
1310	—	Ghiás-ud-dín Bahádur Sháh.							
1315	Shahab-ud-dín 'Umar.								
1316	Kutb-ud-dín Mubárak Sháh.	—							
1320	Nasír-ud-dín Khusru.	—							

SYNOPTICAL TABLE (continued).

Date.	Hindustan.	Bengal.	Jaunpur.	Málwa.	Gujarát.	Dakhan.	Hoysala Bhálas.	Vijaynagar.	Orangal.
1320	Ghiás-ud-dín Tughlak Sháh.								
1324	Md. bin Tughlak.								
1332	—	Md. bin Tughlak.							
1336	—	Fakhr-ud-dín Mubárak Sháh.						Harihara.	
1341	—	Ala-ud-dín 'Alí Sháh.							
1347	—	Ikhtiyár-ud-dín.					Hasan Gongo.	Bukka.	
1350									
1351	Fírúz Sháh III.								
1358									
1375						Md. Sháh.			
1378					Farhat-ul-Mulk	Mujahid Sháh.	Muhamadan Conquest, followed	Harihari II.	
1378						Daud Sháh.			
1379						Mahmúd Sháh.			
1388									
1388	Tughlak Sháh II.								
1389	Abúbakr Sháh.				Zafar Khán.				
1390	Md. Sháh.		Kwája-í-Jahán.						
1392	Sikandar Sháh.								
1393	Mahmúd Sháh.								
1394	Nasrat Sháh.		Mubárak Sháh.			Ghiás-ud-dín.			
1397			Ibrahím Sháh.	Diláwar Khán.		Shams-ud-dín.			
1397				Hushang.		Fírúz Sháh.			
1399									
1401									
1405									
1408								Deva Ráya I.	

END OF THE "PATHANS."

Date.	Hindustan.	Bengal.	Jaunpur.	Málwa.	Gujarát.	Dakhan.	Hoysala Bilálas.	Vijaynagar.	Orangal.
1411	Daulat Khán Lodi.				Ahmad Shâh.		by Anarchy and Confusion.		
1412									
1414	Khizr Khán.								
1418								Vijaya Bhupati.	
1421	Mubárak Sháh II.							Deva Ráya II.	
1422	Muhammed Sháh.								
1433									
1434			Mahmúd Sháh.	Muhammad Mahmúd Khiljí.		Ahmad Sháh I.		Obscure.	
1435									
1440	A'am Sháh								
1442	Buhlól Lodi.								
1443					Md. Sháh.	Alá-ud-dín II.			
1451			Md. Sháh.		Kutb Sháh.				
1457			Husain Sháh.						
1457						Humayun.			
1458					Daud Sháh.				
1458					Mahmúd Sháh.				
1461			Buhlól Lodi.	Ghiás-ud-dín.					
1463						Nizam Sháh.			
1474						Md. Sháh II.		Nara Sinha.	
1482	Sikandar bin Buhlól.								
1488				Nasir-ud-dín.		Mahmúd Sháh.			
1500				Mahmúd II.					
1510					Muzaffar Sháh II.			Krishna Deva Ráya.	
1511									
1517	Ibrahím bin Sikandar.								
1518					Sikandar Sháh.	Ahmad Sháh II.			
1520					Mahmúd Sháh.	Alá-ud-dín III.			
1522					Bahádur Sháh.	Wallibullah.		Ráma Ráya.	
1525									
1525						Kalím-ullah.			

CHAPTER V.

THE MUGHAL EMPIRE; I.

Section 1: Rise of the Mughal Empire.—Section 2: Equilibrium of the Mughal Empire.—Section 3: Early European settlers and travellers in India.

SECTION 1.—The weak points of Mughal administration were noted by a very able contemporary. This was a Pathán, or native Muslim, named Farid Khán, descended from the noble Afghán tribe of "Sur." He had entered the suite of Bábar, and was in his camp before Chandairi, but soon left the service dissatisfied with the levity of the adventurers, and impressed with their incompetence for the due administration of a vast and varied Empire:—

"If fortune favour me," he said, "I can drive these Mughals back out of Hindustan; they are not our superiors in war, but we have let slip the power that we had by reason of our dissensions. Since I have been among the Mughals I have observed their conduct and found them lacking in order and discipline; while those who profess to lead them, in the pride of birth and rank, neglect the duty of supervision, and leave everything to officials in whom they blindly trust. These subordinates act corruptly in every case . . . they are led by lust of gain, and make no distinction between soldier and civilian, foe or friend."

For the present, indeed, Humaiun succeeded in peace; but the peace was of short duration. During the first few years of his reign he was engaged in campaigns against the minor Sultan of Málwa and Gujarát, which he conducted without vigour and terminated without advantage. The "Afghans"—Patháns, or native Muslims, continued to quarrel among themselves in the eastern provinces; the ostensible head of their ill-cemented confederacy was Mahmud Lodi, brother of the late Sultan Ibrahim: this chief had risen to power on the overthrow of Jalál-ud-din, Loháni, to whom Farid had attached himself on leaving the camp of Bábar; and about 1535 Mahmud possessed himself of Jaunpur. The contentions of the Indian Muslims were for the time abated, and Farid—who had hitherto been only a petty district-officer—began to prepare himself for the task of organising a permanent anti-Mughal movement, and, about this time, assumed the title of Sher Khán.

Humaiun was quick to perceive the dangerous abilities of the new Pathán leader, but slow to act upon his discovery. Amusing the Emperor with insincere negotiation, Sher Khán took possession of the fort of Chunár, near Benares; and Humaiun, confiding in his professions, turned once more to his western wars. Sher Khán's next step was to persuade Mahmud to retire to Gaur, and leave him a free hand in Bihár. In 1537 Humaiun, returning from fresh failure in Gujarát, determined to seek compensation in the eastern provinces. More than six months were wasted before Chunár, which was not won till 8th January, 1538. Meanwhile Sher Khán had gone to Gaur and driven out his nominal master, Mahmud Lodi, who repaired to the camp of Humaiun. Sher Khán now stood forth openly as the leader of the Pathán reaction; though the odds appeared heavy. On one hand was Humaiun, born to succession, chivalrous and accomplished, with the Lodi leader on his side. On the other a solitary native adventurer far from having any hered'tary right, and with no advantages but what he could derive from his own intellect and character. Yet the event proved that these were enough to turn the scale. The brother of Humaiun was in revolt at Kábul, and recruits could not join the army from that land of soldiers; the Turks and Mughals who had followed Bábar had become demoralised by twelve years of wealth and ease; the Emperor himself, with many good qualities, was a frivolous, dissipated opium-eater. On the other hand Sher Khán was full of audacity, energy, and vigilance, aware of the danger of dissension amongst his followers, and able to make of them a united body.

The result was soon apparent. In 1538 Sher Khán inflicted several minor checks on the Emperor, whose attention was at the same time distracted by news of a revolt at Agra; and who retired with such precipitation as to leave the ladies of his household in his enemy's hands. Sher Khán treated his captives nobly, and sent them to Agra unharmed. But he at the same time showed his sense of his ascendant star by assuming the further title of "Sher Sháh, Sultan-i-'Adil."*

In April, 1540, the Emperor took the field once more, and marching down the Duáb arrived at Kanauj in the early part of May. Sher Sháh, having advanced from the eastward, had taken post on the opposite bank of the Ganges; and, on hearing of the arrival of the Mughals, send a herald over to their camp, not to offer peace, but to propose terms of combat. If his Majesty preferred the Patháns should cross: if not they were ready to await his Majesty's pleasure. Humaiun scornfully replied that if "Sher Khán" would only make room he would come over and meet him: the consequence of which—doubtless foreseen by the Pathán leader—was this, that the Mughals would be left to fight after the confusion of the passage, with their backs to the river. He accordingly, with every appearance of good faith and courtesy, retired for five miles—while the Mughals crossed—and there he awaited their onslaught in a strongly intrenched position. But the Mughals had little stomach for the fray: "let us go," the men were heard to cry; "let us go and rest in our own homes." The

* Meaning:—" The just Lord."

attack was, therefore, delayed. Meantime the heat grew to a dreadful height for the luxurious foreigners; and the early rain fell with violence, flooding the camp, and swelling the volume of the Ganges already filled by the melting of the Himálaya snows. Daily surprises and skirmishes wore them out, while flushing the spirits of their antagonists. At last, on the morning of the 17th May, as if weary of the situation, both armies at the same time left their lines, under their respective chiefs. But Humaiun found no better spirit among his officers than among the men. Twenty-seven *tughs** were lowered and concealed by those whose pride it should have been to display those ensigns. "From this," naively observes one of these officers, whose narrative is here followed, "from this conduct of our officers may be imagined the conduct of the men." In spite of their artillery, in spite of threefold numbers, the Mughals could not be got to fight. "Before the enemy had let fly an arrow," pursues Haidar Mirza, "we were, virtually defeated: not a gun was fired, not a man was wounded, friend or foe." The panic-stricken men-at-arms clattered into the mud in all the vain panoply of armour-clad men and horses; the only deaths were of fugitives smothered or drowned. Never was a great host so discomfited. The Emperor was carried away in the flight, led to the river by an unknown cavalier in black, who unceremoniously seized his bridle. On the bank he found an elephant on which he was carried over. Hurrying to Agra he made but a short stay there: his mind, it was noticed, wandered; he spoke of supernatural terrors that had aided the Patháns. One of his brothers hurried on to Kábul, and so barred the direct way of escape; the luckless Humaiun was fain to depart into Multan and Sindh.

For nearly fifteen years he disappears from Indian history, during the early part of which period Sher Sháh exercised a

---

* *Vide*, note in last chapter.

beneficent dominion in Hindustan. He assumed the Empire at Delhi, 25th January, 1542, being about sixty years of age; and the rest of his brief career was devoted to the establishment of the unity which he had long ago perceived to be the great need of his country. Though a devout Muslim he never oppressed his Hindu subjects. His progresses were the cause of good to the people instead of being—as is too often the case in India—the occasions of devastation. He laboured ceaselessly for the protection of the public: "it behoves great men," he said, "to be always working." He divided the land into 116,000 fiscal unions, in each of which he placed five officials, one of whom was an Hindu accountant, and one a judicial officer, whose duty was to mediate between the servants of the crown and the members of the community. A new digest of civil and penal law was substituted for the narrow code of Islám. The lands were assessed, for one year at a time, the assessment being based on a measurement of the cultivation and an appraisement of the various crops. No official was allowed to remain in the same place for more than two years. All districts but those on the frontiers were deprived of arms. A royal highway, planted on either side with trees and patrolled by police, ran from the shores of the Bay of Bengal to the banks of the river Jehlam. Three other great roads traversed the Empire; one from Agra to Burhánpore on the border of the Deccan, a second crossed Rajputana, and a third led from Lahore to Multan: daily posts carried letters along these roads from place to place. The rural population was still sparse, and the tillage depended on a scanty supply of labour; for which reason the Government was the more urgently required to care for the comfort and content of the peasantry. Even in a hostile country the people should not be molested: "if we drive away the agriculturist," said the Sháh, "all our conquests can be of but little profit."

It is a welcome task to take note of such things as a break

in the long annals of rapine and slaughter, and we can do so without hesitation; for the acts of Sher Sháh are attested by his enemies, writing when he was dead, and when his dynasty had passed away for ever. But in the midst of his strenuous beneficence he encountered the caprice of fate which takes away a man, apparently necessary, before his work is done. Sher Sháh was besieging the fort of Kálinjar, in Bundelkhand, when he was struck by the fragment of an exploding tumbril, on 22nd May, 1545. Taken to his tent, he lay dying for two days, retaining his consciousness, and speaking of duty to the last. His body was carried to his native place, and buried in a fine mausoleum, which is still to be seen in the centre of the town of Sasseram, by the side of the "Grand Trunk Road," which the modern rulers of India have laid down on the line of his own highway.

It is the misfortune of absolute monarchy that the best rulers can never ensure a worthy successor. Sher Sháh's sovereignty was assumed by his son Salím, or Islám, Sháh, a young man apparently not ill-prepared for the post, but labouring under the usual trials of a prince born for power which he has done nothing to acquire. The old contentiousness of the Pathán nobility sprang up when the strong restraining hand was no longer there. The whole period of Salím's reign was consumed in intrigues and fruitless quarrels: and on his death in November, 1554, his son was murdered and a scene of confusion ensued. The native Muslims fell into such a state of quarrelsome imbecility that the chief command fell into the hands of a Hindu chandler named Hému.

In the meanwhile Humaiun had first wandered distractedly in Sindh, where he became the father of a more able and fortunate son. In 1543 he made his way by Herát to Persia, where he was hospitably received, but made to profess adhesion to the Shia denomination; and with the aid of Persian troops he obtained possession of Kandahar and, ultimately of Kábul, which had been held against him, by his rebellious brother Kámrán. For the next four years Humaiun held a troubled and precarious possession of Afghanistan; but in 1553 Kámrán was finally defeated and rendered incapable of further mischief by being deprived of sight; Humaiun being, perhaps, deterred from taking his brother's life by the memory of the last words of their father. And now, at last, the time seemed approaching when he could follow that father's footsteps, and become, once more, Emperor in Hindustan.

In January, 1555, accordingly, Humaiun resolved to benefit by the confusion and anarchy prevailing among the Indian Muslims; and he entered the Punjab with 15,000 mounted followers, led by an able officer, and accompanied by his young son. The Pathán nobles were in the very crisis of a family dispute, and so failed to unite for resistance; yet the force still at their disposal was not to be despised. The first encounter occurred at the passage of the Sutlej, where Humaiun's general beat back the Patháns and occupied the country immediately to the north-west of Delhi. Another Pathán army advancing to cover the capital, was opposed to the invaders' reserve, marching in parallel columns: and a second action ensued, also to the advantage of the Mughals; in this Humaiun commanded in person, and his youthful son took part; soon the former advanced on Delhi and entered the city on 23rd July, 1555. The Sur family had now but one resource left: to forget their feuds and push all their forces up from the eastward under the able guidance of their Hindu general—the chandler Hému.

Amid the uncertainties of the yet unfinished war, the long vexed and imperfectly restored Emperor was suddenly taken off by an accidental fall down a staircase. He died on 26th January, 1556, and the young Akbar was immediately acclaimed Emperor by the armies, which had now effected a junction. His guardian and principal minister was the General already mentioned, a valiant and experienced Turkmán, named Bairám Khán, a native of Badahshán, who had followed the fortunes of the late Emperor for nearly twenty years. Akbar was proclaimed at Kálanur, near Amritsir, on 15th February, and Bairám was declared his Prime Minister, alike for civil and military service.

The Hindu General, who had been conducting a successful campaign in the eastern region, now advanced on Delhi, whence he expelled the Mughals, and where he is said to have declared himself king, with the title of Rája Vikram Aditya. He then marched against the Mughals whom he found encamped upon the storied plains of Pánipat.*

The Mughal chiefs had been divided in counsel, and it had even been seriously proposed by some to carry the young Prince back to Kábul, and endeavour to postpone further operations till they could gather fresh forces for a renewed attempt. Bairám, however, overruled the proposal; and on 5th November, the decisive struggle took place. The artillery of the natives had been surprised and carried off the day before; and the bold Bairám had given a significant lesson of courage and conduct to his subordinates, by putting to death the General by whose misfortune or error Delhi had been lost, while three other officers were put under arrest. Thus stimulated, the Mughals showed no more weakness; Hému was vanquished after a stubborn conflict and brought wounded into Akbar's tent, where Bairám struck off his head: next day the victorious Mughals marched on Delhi. On arrival at the city of Sher Sháh † the young monarch received a warm welcome from the Muslim inhabitants.

---

* See description in last chapter.

† Also the scene of Humaiun's death. He was interred close by, and his noble mausoleum is famous in modern history as the last refuge of his ill-starred descendants in 1857.

The titular head of the Sur family shortly after dying, Akbar found himself, nominally, at least, lord paramount of northern India from the Himálaya to the Narbada river, and from sea to sea. But there was much to be done before the gallant boy could call himself really master of that wide and fertile land.

What may have been the condition of the people at the time of his accession, can only be inferred from the nature of his subsequent reforms. The elaborate administrative machinery of Sher Sháh must have incurred rust and decay; and the inhabitants would suffer all the more because of the few years of good government and the return of war. Again had come rapacity and negligence, and the devastations of lawless soldiers; the drums and tramplings of armed hosts, and the smoke of arson from wrecked and plundered homes. Happily for the people of Hindustan, longer times of peace were now at hand.

From the date of the accession of the boy Akbar to 1560, the empire was in an undeveloped condition. Bairám fell from power and went into rebellion; but at the end of 1560 he was pardoned, and induced to set out for the pilgrimage to Mecca; on the way, however, he was assassinated by a private enemy, 31st January, 1561. During this time the Patháns were everywhere being slowly beaten down in Bihár, the Punjab, and elsewhere.

In 1561 an expedition was sent into Málwa, where a Pathán named Báz Bahádur had affected independence, making his capital at Sárangpur, about half-way between Mau and Guna. The Mughal leader was named Adham Khán, supposed to be a natural son of the late emperor, and half-brother of Akbar the present monarch. The campaign met with success, which was however tarnished by the bastard's cruelty to some of his prisoners. The young Emperor did not take proper notice, because, as his friend and biographer afterwards observed, "The veil had not yet been taken from his eyes." Even so, Akbar issued orders that such inhumanity should not take place again; and ere long he killed with his own hand, the ruffianly half-brother who had stained his conquest, and who afterwards proceeded to murder another minister in the hall of the palace. This event is dated, by Beale, 10th May, 1562.

In the same year Akbar gave a further proof of his having begun to think for himself by marrying the daughter of Rája Bihári Mal, the Rajput ruler of Ambér (now Jaipur), whose son and brother were at the same time engaged in the Imperial service. Two taxes which pressed heavily on the Hindus were now remitted; namely, one on persons going on pilgrimage to Hindu shrines; and one the *jazia*, capitation or poll-tax, levied under Sunni law on unbelieving subjects.

After the death of the bastard, Adham Khán, other measures against the immigrant aristocracy were pursued. Their contumacy was a serious obstacle to the unity which Akbar was already seeking; and it was the work of seven years to overcome the insolence of race and teach the immigrants what was due to their fellow-subjects. In the south the Muslims were still gaining ground; in 1565 the Hindu kingdom of Bijainagar—or Kanara—fell before a temporary combination of all the Muhamadan States of the Deccan. In order to strengthen his capital, Akbar about this time began the Fort of Agra, which is still in fine preservation. In the following year he had to suppress a rebellion at Jaunpore of which the leader was one of his best foreign officers, an Uzbeg who had been honoured with the title of "Khán Zamán." Akbar's experience of the insolence of his foreign followers was now becoming so serious as to lead him to look around for native statesman and officers. Bhagwán Dás and Mán Singh, of Jaipur, have been already mentioned: a greater still was to be found in the famous Todar Mal, a man who

K

had been trained by Sher Sháh and who was now to serve Akbar in some of the most important measures of his reign.

The adhesion of the Hindus, however, was not yet complete. The Gahlot Rajputs of Méwar who had been so formidable under Rána Sanga, still defied the Mughals; and the seige of Chittore cost Akbar much loss of ease and of men, until it was finally stormed in February, 1568, much as Chandairi had been, forty years before, by his grandsire. It was during this siege that a man of letters entered Akbar's service, who was destined to influence the Emperor, both directly, and through his brother. This was Shaikh Faizi, a learned and amiable man of Arab blood; and he in his turn was to become the means of Akbar's making the acquaintance of his younger brother, Abul Fazl, destined to be a prominent minister, and also the historiographer of the reign. In this year was commenced the country-palace of Fattehpur Sikri, about twenty-one miles south-west of Agra; where, on the 31st August, 1569, the Princess of Amber brought, to complete her husband's felicity, the son (Salím) who was afterwards to succeed to the Empire. The year 1570 was passed in royal progresses, as also was the next, so that for at least twenty-four months the land had rest. In 1572 a fresh campaign was found necessary to restore order in the province of Gujarát, troubled by a new rebellion; the troops were commanded by Rája Bhagwán Dás, and his nephew Mán Singh. Next occurred an unsuccessful attempt on the famous fort of Kot Kángra in the Punjab, where a peace was patched up: and another campaign in Gujarát, where the Emperor commanded in person and was much distinguished. Todar Mal was now put in charge of the province of Gujarát. Then came a fresh outbreak of the adherents of the fallen dynasty in the eastern provinces; it was not put down till 1575.

But, while suppressing, with humane firmness, all attempts at rebellion from the followers of the late Sher Sháh, Akbar was always ready to learn in the school of that great man. The policy of Sher Sháh—it will be remembered—was to fuse his subjects into one nation, and to establish a fiscal system which should relieve the taxpayer without being injurious to the agriculturist by whom the revenue was to be paid. Availing himself of the knowledge and experience of Todar Mal, Akbar adopted this system. The land-revenue was settled on a basis equitable to the cultivator, and almost all taxation was forborne. This ideal deserves to be carefully observed for it has never since been entirely lost sight of, and has been the source of national prosperity in later days.*

Nor was Akbar's attention entirely absorbed by matters of civil administration and war. There was but little, in Hindustan of those days, corresponding with the intellectual emancipation then beginning to break forth in Europe. Nevertheless, so far as one man could affect national movements, society in Hindustan was moving. Visitors to Fattehpur are still shown a strange structure, now called *Diwán Khás*, with four galleries, and a pillar in the middle on whose capital is a central seat approached by raised pathways, one from each gallery. Here, every Thursday night, the four galleries were filled with members of various sects, while the Emperor occupied the central seat, as moderator of their controversies. "Innovators and schismatics," says an orthodox contemporary, "artfully started doubts and sophistries; and his Majesty, who only sought the truth, was thus entangled in scepticism by low associates."†

We have seen how some of the earlier Sultans had married Hindoo princesses; Akbar was the first who treated these princesses with anything like due consideration. In his household the Hindoo ladies preserved their religious observances and used their influence to incline the Emperor to toleration.

* v. inf. ch. XII.
† Badáoni.

At a later time Akbar openly lamented that he had not gone further: and he came to hate the bigoted side of his own native creed with an ardour that was not quite consistent with impartiality. But he was earnestly bent on making India, so far as he ruled it, into a united nation; and we hear from his friend and biographer, not only of debates by night at the Fattehpur Academy, but also of silent meditations in the lonely hour of dawn, when Akbar would go forth and muse "upon the problems of life and upon his own peculiar task."

It is in the same stately pleasure-house of Fattehpur that we find Akbar, on his return from Bengal in 1575, receiving the first visit of Faizi's brother, Abul Fazl, destined to influence the rest of his reign and to record something of its inner life for the instruction of posterity. The aspirant for royal favour was then only just eighteen; less of a scholar than Faizi, but far more fitted for the activities of life. For twenty-seven years he continued to be the friend and faithful servant of the Emperor: "a man," said a native contemporary, "of lofty spirit, who desired to live at peace with all men." Above all, he deserves notice as having professed the principles of toleration in government before any other public man, either in the East or West.

Events were occurring about this time in Central Asia by which Akbar's mind may have been already biassed towards a disregard of official orthodoxy: in 1575 the Osmanli Turks of the west had obtained great successes in Persia, where the Shiah sovereign who had tampered with Humaiun's faith was murdered and succeeded by a Sunni. One of this new ruler's measures was to persecute and disperse the heretical teachers who were popular throughout that country. From the days of the Arab conquest, when the old fire-worship was forbidden and persecuted, a tendency towards heterodoxy had always prevailed in Persia. The Guebres themselves clung to the naptha springs on the southern shores of the Caspian. The friars and religious mendicants, who pervaded every stratum of the community, indulged in the freest speculation: and the sectaries of Ali, the Shiahs, maintained an element of dissidence from the opinions and laws of Islám: being "distinguished by forbearance towards the professors of other creeds."* Moreover, the poets (among whom Omar Khayám is the best-known to western readers) maintained a note of free thought; and the fact that, without aid from the printing press, such writings should have braved the havoc of centuries is an indication of popular favour. All these influences were now poured into Hindustan, a new invasion carried out with the weapons of the mind. The Academy founded by the Emperor was in full work by this time; in it the reform found a favourable ground: and the result was a movement which shattered the Muslim Church in India and prepared for a long and hopeful future, never, alas! to be attained.

In the year 1577 the Muslim symbol (*Kalima*) disappeared from use in the national coinage and liturgy† the name of the Prophet was also discouraged for male infants.‡ In the meantime war still went on in the remote regions. Méwar (Udaipur) went into open revolt, and several minor chiefs of the Rajputs co-operated. Akbar gave proof of his confidence in his unifying system by sending Rajput Generals to put down their own co-religionists; but a curious anecdote of the campaign, recorded by an admiring Muslim, shows how great was still the strength of bigotry among the Muhamadans. He was present in a battle near Goganda, during the Udaipur campaign; and relates that he asked the opinion of a Muslim brother officer as to the means of avoiding injury to a Hindu contingent that was

* Muir, "Annals of the early Kaliphate," p. 452. See also "The Spirit of Islám," by S. Amir Ali; London, 1891.

† *La Allah il Allah, wa Muhamad rasal Allah*, the famous profession of orthodox Muslims ("There is no god but God; and Muhamad is God's Prophet.")

‡ The Emperor's full name was Muhamad Jálál-ud-din Akbar. After the year 1,000 A.H. the word "Muhamad" disappears from the coinage.

protecting their front. "Bah!" said the other; "Let fly in the name of God; He knows His own."

In 1578 the Emperor visited Delhi, where his father's body had been interred as mentioned in the last chapter. From thence he continued his progress to Málwa; and he took the opportunity of pacifying Méwar and Gujarát without further military operations. In 1579 a question was agitated similar to one which had been lately debated in England: namely, that of the relation of the head of the state to spiritual affairs. As king of men Akbar desired to be leader of their opinions; not exactly as khálif, or pontiff, but as founder of a mixed system in which was to be inculcated whatever good he could collect from all known creeds, from the Vedas and the Koran, from Fire-worship, Pantheism, and Latin Christianity. The consequence was that a convocation assembled in 1580, which decreed the claims of the Emperor to pronounce a final award in doctrinal controversy, subject to a saving-clause that there was to be no opposition to the Koran. The insertion of such a clause it was probably impossible to avoid; but it is doubtful if Akbar would ever have been bound by it. The system that he sought to recommend was one of eclectic Theism, equally opposed to the confident convictions of all his subjects. He only gained about a dozen adherents in his own court and family; so that, as a means of union, the system was a failure from the outset. Such things could not be carried out by any one man, however good and wise and powerful.

What the Emperor could do single-handed was to provide for the welfare of the current generation. He could not propagate his Theism without using foul means and causing hypocrisy, and from this he refrained. But in administrative measures he could at least follow the path of Sher Sháh and restore the good old times of that wise and great ruler. A census and Domesday Book were set on foot: Todar Mal was directed to proceed with his fiscal reforms. An attempt was made to call in worn coins, and to fix the value of those in circulation. The burning of Hindu widows was forbidden. Such measures could not but benefit his subjects, however powerless for permanent reform. It is only by embodying in the form of statute the needs and aspiration of the community that a government can enter into permanent organic union with the governed; and no such embodiment could take place in Hindustan at that time. The idea of law, as then conceived by the people of India, was inconsistent with legislation by any man or governing body. It is true that Sher Sháh is credited with some amount of crude legislation; but, for want of institutions and ideas it could take no root. Hindu and Muslim alike, the people believed that each class had been born under a special provision of positive injunctions, revealed by the Deity—much like what are now called "laws of Nature," in so far that they could not be altered by any authority of man. In such conditions there could be no human legislation, nor any State-enactments by which social evolution could be registered or advanced. The wisest and most benevolent reformer, in possession of the most unquestioned sovereignty, could only issue salutary ordinances, valid for the duration of his reign. And this Akbar did, to a remarkable degree.

For the next two years the Empire was at peace, and Akbar appeared to have reached the summit of human prosperity. All rival rulers had been conquered or conciliated, from one extremity of the possessions of his House to the other; except where, beyond the Indus, an ambitious brother, named Hákim, contested the authority of Akbar. The civil administration was controlled by Todar Mal; one of the late Bairám's pupils was at the head of the war department. The heads of the Muslim Church were under a cloud, and the reckless endowments of the past were resumed from mortmain. Mosques stood empty, or were used as stabling for the horses of the imperial cavalry. Jesuit missionaries appeared at court in answer to special invitation, and a small place of Christian worship was opened at Agra.

In 1581 there was a disturbance in Bengal, which was suppressed by Todar Mal, sent there on special duty. Next year the Emperor proceeded in person to the Afghán country, and drove his rebellious brother out of Kábul: he was pardoned on submission, and replaced in the government.

In 1583 the eastern provinces were again disturbed, but the disturbance was abated in the following year, the Emperor, having settled Kábul affairs, returned to Hindustan; it is probable that these Bengal troubles had been fomented by Hákim, the rebellious brother. In 1584 there was a stubborn rebellion raised by a native Muslim in Orissa, which is remarkable for having afforded an opportunity for the rise of a young Mughal officer, already mentioned as the translator of Bábar's *Memoirs*, and destined to distinction in the later military transactions of the reign. His title at this period was Khán-Mirza, and he was son to the late able and unfortunate minister, Bairám. After his father's tragic end the Emperor had taken measures for his education, and his first appearance as a general was in the third Bengal war. After serving with credit here he was sent to suppress a fresh insurrection in Gujarát; and the campaign was brought to a successful end in four months.

About this time (1585-6) came the news of the death of Hákim Mirza, the Emperor's troublesome brother. Khán Mirza returned to Gujarát, and Akbar went on to Lahore, deputing his Rajput kinsmen (Bhagwán Dás and Mán Singh) to take up the government of Kábul. Another Hindu, Rája Bir Bal, was sent in joint command with a Mughal named Zain Khan, to take possession of the hills of Bajaur, and repel the Uzbegs who were raiding in Badakshán. This led to the first great disaster of the reign; the army was cut off by the Yusafzais in their bleak passes. Bir Bal was slain, with eight thousand officers and men; Zain Khán fled on foot to the Emperor, who refused to see him. This was in February, 1586. A fresh force was sent into the mountains, under Todar Mal, supported by a flanking column, under Mán Singh, in the Khaibar; order was to some extent restored. It is to be noted that the country of these wild Muslim tribes, who are still troublesome, was thus partially pacified and held by two Hindu officers.

In 1587 Kashmir was occupied—not without hard fighting —and further operations, leading to the temporary disgrace of Mán Singh, took place in the hills between Attock and Kábul.

Early in 1589, Akbar visited Kábul, but before the end of the year had the misfortune to lose Todar Mal and Bhagwán Dás, both of whom died at the same time. The latter was no more than a brave Rajput prince; but Todar Mal has left a great name in India, not merely as a soldier, but as a statesman. "He left behind him no equal," says Abul Fazl, "whether for rectitude or administrative skill."

So far Akbar had formed and consolidated a great Empire, stretching from the Oxus to the bay of Bengal. It was natural that he should next turn his attention to the country south of the Narbada. An Imperialist army overran Berár and captured the capital Elichpur. Here they were joined by Burhán-ul-mulk, brother of the sovereign of the Nizam-Sháhi kingdom of Ahmadnagar, then the central state of the Muslim Deccan. The poet Faizi was deputed to negotiate with the emigrant prince, and to take advantage of his discontent.

This deputation took place in 1591, and at the same time, Sultan Murád, one of Akbar's sons, took possession of Gwalior and Ujain, where the Hindus had been giving trouble. In Gujarát, Khán Mirza reaped fresh laurels in a campaign against Jáni Beg, a local rebel, whom he blockaded at Tatta in Sindh. A new Pathán rising took place in Orissa, and led to oppression of the Hindu population, for whose relief an expedition was sent thither under Mán Singh, now restored to favour. News of a complete victory reached the Emperor at Lahore about the end of 1592. Khán Mirza, now promoted to the rank of Khán Khanan, had in the meantime starved Jáni Beg into submission in Sindh; the rebel was sent to court, where he obtained pardon and employment. The year was observed as being, by Muslim chronology, the thousandth from the Hegira.* The Empire was at peace; we have next to trace, on the reduced scale allowed by our limits, the effect of Akbar's military successes and civil administration.

[Authorities for this section: "Ain Akbari," by Abul Fazl, Gladwin's translation, 3 vols., Calcutta, 1783; Dowson's "Elliot," Vol. V.; "Kaisar Akbar," Von Noer, Leipsic, 1880. Also "Coins of Hindustan in the British Museum," by S. Lane-Poole, London, 1892.]

SECTION 2.—Apart from the maintenance of order by strong but humane military operations, the glory of Akbar's reign is the fusion of classes and general care for the welfare of the people. The system began in 1574-5 was at first resisted not only by open rebellion, but by the inert but obstinate bigotry and race-pride of the Muslims, whose theory was that the Hindus, who formed the bulk of the population, were fortunate if their lives were spared, and were bound to pay a special poll-tax which about doubled their fiscal contributions. This, as we have seen, was abolished by Akbar, and the employment of such a man as Todar Mal was a guarantee of fair treatment. It led, indeed, to a good deal more. Disregarding the prejudices of race and rivalry, Abul Fazl bears the warmest testimony to the virtues and abilities of his Hindu colleague. Appointed Vazir, Todar Mal preferred a humbler title, with all necessary authority. He was acquainted with all the details of administration, and his clear mind solved all difficulties. "Keeping his mind free from personal ambition, he devoted

* The Muslim year consists of lunar months, and is shorter than ours by nearly eleven days.

himself to the service of the state, and so earned an everlasting fame." The following reforms were among those due to Todar Mal :—

There was to be an accurate record of each landholder's rights and liabilities. Easy means of complaint against undue exactions were provided, with due provision for the punishment of offenders. The number of petty officials was reduced by one half. Advances of money and seed were available: arrears were remitted when remission was required. Collectors were called upon for yearly reports; and monthly returns were to be submitted to the exchequer; special narratives being required in case of special calamities, hail, flood, or drought. The collections were made four times in the year; and care had to be taken that there should be no balances outstanding at the end of that period. It is hardly too much to say that this scheme contained the germs of the successful revenue-systems of modern India.

At the same time attention was paid to the question of currency-reform. Local coinages were abolished, and imperial mints established at great centres, previous coins being called in. All establishments were paid in cash, the wasteful method of *jaigirs* and territorial assignments being discontinued. Lastly, poor-houses were opened for the relief of indigent wayfarers, and the Emperor used to visit them in person. Thus, to the north of the Narbada at least, the work of integration and good government was begun, the exertions of the administrator completing the work of the soldier, both inspired by the magnetism of an earnest and benevolent master. The next great task of Akbar was the destruction of the overweening power of the Muslim Church, but this, when effected, proved a doubtful advantage: after the great Emperor was gone his successors ruled unchecked by any organised body, and more and more scope was found for the abuses of despotism, only corrigible by the brutal remedies of regicide and rebellion.

For the present all went well. Faizi was sent to the army to negotiate with the malcontent Prince of Ahmadnagar, and to watch his relations with Ali Khán of Khándes, on the East of Gujarát, where the Sátpura range runs between the Narbada and the Tapti. On receiving the report of this mission Akbar moved from the Punjab, and began to prepare on a large scale for the conquest of the Deccan. Three armies were set on foot; the main force under the Khán Khánan—as Khán Mirza was now called—to be supported on either side by columns from Málwa and Bengal.

Such was the current of events that an extension of the empire into the southern regions was perhaps hardly to be avoided. The land there was wasted by war and misgovernment; conspiracy and assassination were the ordinary political expedients; the internal strife of Sunni and Shia almost prevented useful combinations. Once, in 1565, a momentary union of the Muslim powers overthrew Rám Rája, the Hindu prince of Kanara. Defeated at the decisive battle of Talikota, he was taken and put to death. His brother was expelled from Bijainagar, and driven into the Karnatic, where he founded minor principalities. To Akbar it may have seemed a part of his mission to bring order into the Deccan; nevertheless it might have been better for his House could he have resisted the temptation.

From the first the work was hard. Under the nominal command of one of the princes the main army advanced from Berár. Rája Ali submitted and was restored to the government of Khándes as an imperial feudatory; and the combined armies advanced to the seige of Ahmadnagar. Burhán, the fugitive of 1591, had, in the four intervening years, obtained the kingdom, and been carried off by natural death (1594): and now his infant nephew—a son of the late Sultan Ibráhim —was nominal ruler under the regency of a brave old kinswoman named Chánd Bibi, also of kin to the king of Bijápur, Ibráhim Adil II. Aided by him she opposed a vigorous resistance, personally taking part in the defence of the ramparts. Peace had to be made for fear of an attack on the Mughal rear by the confederates in the field; and towards the end of winter in 1596 the Imperialists retired from the first siege of Ahmadnagar. Some compensation for this disappointment was afforded by the cession of Kandahar, always a subject of contention between the Mughals of India and the Persian Shâh. But other troubles were at hand. The gentle and learned Faizi died at Lahore in October, 1595. Next year Akbar had his first serious illness: in the following year Murád sustained a severe defeat from the confederate armies of the Deccan, and was deprived of his command, Abul Fazl being sent to relieve him.

It was in this year that the "Ain Akbari" was published, a sort of instalment of Abul Fazl's "Imperial Gazetteer," afterwards completed in 1602. Having finished the first part of his work —which treats of the institutions and finance of the empire— Abul Fazl departed for the South, followed more slowly by Akbar himself. On 1st May, 1599, Sultan Murád died; and Salím, the crown prince, was sent against Méwar; the actual command being in the hands of Mán Singh, who was his mother's brother. Salím soon quarrelled with his uncle and retired to Allahabad, where he began to show signs of the fractious disposition by which he continued thenceforth to vex his father's government. Sultan Dányal, another of the Emperor's sons, was put in honorary charge of Khándes, while Abul Fazl went on to complete the war in the territory of the Nizám Sháhi dynasty. By the end of the year the brave Sultána, Chánd Bibi, was murdered by her own officers, and the young king a prisoner in the hands of the Mughals. Ahmadnagar was taken by storm; but the country was not thoroughly conquered for nearly forty years longer. Abul Fazl was sent for to court, but was murdered on the road, by instigation of the Crown Prince, 13th August, 1602.

The blow made Akbar reel. His sons in revolt or dying

of intemperance, his best servants removed, and his southern conquests unfinished, his fine temper began to fail, he became hasty and impatient. In 1602 a temporary reconciliation with Salim took place, and the Bijápur Sultan in the Deccan gave his adhesion to the empire. These transient gleams of returning fortune did not long sustain the Emperor's failing strength. In 1604 Sultan Dányal died—like his brother Murád before him—from the effects of drink. Akbar's health broke, and intrigues for the succession began between the supporters of the fractious Salim, encouraged by the Emperor, and the favourers of Salim's son, Sultan Khusru. The plans of the former prevailed; Khusru prepared for flight; and Akbar from his death-bed formally named Salim as his successor. He died on the night of 4-5th October, 1605, leaving an empire consolidated and peaceful north of the Narbada, though of doubtful stability beyond that river.

Enough has been said to give a general idea of this great ruler and his methods. The people had entered on a forenoon of cloudless weather, the dawn of which had been witnessed fifty years before, in the brief reign of Sher Sháh. Akbar sympathised with the Hindus, of whom Abul Fazl--no doubt reflecting his master's view—often speaks kindly, and with esteem. The cultivators and farmers were not only protected but helped. Their assessments were to be undisturbed for nineteen years—about the average of modern English and Scottish leases—but no marauding chiefs or usurping barons intercepted the payments charged upon the land in lieu of taxation.* After the twenty-fourth year of Akbar's reign the

---

* The Indian land-revenue is sometimes called "Land-tax"; it is, in fact, the very reverse. Rent must go to some one; and in so far as it goes to the state, so far the public is relieved from fiscal contribution. In fact, the salt-tax is the only item of taxation, proper, of which payment is obligatory on every inhabitant of British India. Its annual incidence is about one-fourth of a rupee.

aggregate collections of the past ten years, divided by ten, were taken as an average on which to base future demands. The total revenue, according to the *Ain*, was ten *krors* of rupees yearly, towards the end of the reign, but before the last annexations. Under the rule of Salim, who assumed the title of Jahángir before his accession, the Empire continued to feel the momentum of Akbar's rule, and fairly preserved its equipoise. Khusru fled to Lahore at first, and attempted a rebellion, which was soon suppressed, and the Prince put under restraint. A fine mausoleum of hewn stone was raised over Akbar's grave at Sikandra, mentioned above as the suburb of Agra, where Sikandar Lodi built a palace. The great system rolled on: there were twelve provinces, with an average annual revenue of twelve *krors* of rupees, over each of which was a Satrap, called originally "Nizám," or "Názim," assisted by a financial officer, whose title was Diwán. Each province, again, was subdivided into counties and fiscal unions, in the administration of which a like quality generally prevailed. Law suits of Muslims were disposed of by learned men, acting under the supervision of a Chief Justice; but Hindus had their causes heard and determined by a Brahman, who doubtless applied the Hindu law. Over all was the Emperor, who professed to hear appeals, though they were, no doubt, sifted before they came to his Majesty's court, and his judicial work may probably be taken to have been at least as symbolical as the washing of prepared paupers by the Pope at Easter; for it must not be supposed that an average Oriental ruler would submit to the irksome duty of sitting daily in open court. Indeed, in the case of Jahángir, it was much if the most ordinary duties of sovereignty could command regular attention. The celebrated diplomatic agent of James I. of England Sir Thomas Roe—who was at the court from 1614 to 1618—has left a record which shows how little justice was really done, and how much crime was committed, under the specious pretences of this reign. Neverthless, that Emperor—ill as he had often behaved in the lifetime of his great predecessor—was not without amiable qualities, and was especially attached to his able consort, the celebrated Empress, Nur Jahán. Little occurred to deserve the attention of historians: a chronic war, long continued in the Deccan, but ended for the time, in 1617, by the submission of the young Nizám Sháh and his minister, Malik Ambar; Bijápur being detached from the southern confederacy. Khusru continued under arrest, the place of heir-apparent being taken by his next brother, Sultan Khurram, who had charge of his person. Khurram was reserved and prudent; he was decorated for service in the field with the title of "Sháh Jahán," and opinion already designated him as the probable successor to the Empire, when, in 1621, Khusru suddenly died. A quarrel soon after broke out between Sháh Jahán and the Empress, who desired to secure the succession for a younger prince, Shahryár, who was her son-in-law. This prince was presently sent to endeavour to recover the town and province of Kandahar, which had been seized by the Persians: other measures of distrust towards Sháh Jahán were adopted; and in 1623 he went into declared opposition. The Emperor marched against him in person, on which Sháh Jahán, shrinking from actual conflict with his sire and sovereign, retired into Telingána and thence into Bengal, where he found safety for a time. Being threatened with a fresh pursuit the persecuted prince returned into the Deccan and sought the protection of Malik Ambar. But he was in great jeopardy in 1625, when an event occurred which for the moment effectually diverted the attention of all his enemies.

Zamánat Beg, better known by his title of Mahábat Khán (one of the Emperor's best generals, and governor of Kábul), had conducted some of the recent operations, and had now returned to the Punjab with the Emperor, and the head-quarters

THE MUGHAL EMPIRE; I.

of the army. At the height of apparent favour he incurred the displeasure of the Empress; and, in order to protect himself against anticipated arrest, he suddenly put the Emperor and Empress themselves under restraint. He surrounded them with a Rajput escort, and was marching with them towards Kabul, when they were liberated by help of the gentlemen-cadets of the bodyguard, in a stratagem planned by the Empress, and carried out at a review. Mahábat Khán fled to the Deccan, where he joined Shah Jahán; and the Emperor died in camp, 28th Oct. 1627. The Empress tried a stroke in favour of Shahryár, her son-in-law, but Sháh Jahán, hearing the news by express, hurried up with Mahábat Khán, reaching Lahore about the end of the year to find that his brother had been already put to death, and to receive the crown from the hands of Asaf-ud-daulah, the Empress's brother, and his late father's chief minister-of-state. His accession took place at Agra, and is dated 4th Feb., 1628.

Under Sháh Jahán the equilibrium of the Empire continued; the Mughal school of architecture attained its highest development, the court glittered with jewelled splendour and sumptuous festivity,* and yet the Emperor accumulated a large reserve of treasure. At the outset of the reign the rebellion of a Pathán officer named Khán Jahán Lodi, led to some alarm and trouble, especially as there seemed some fear that his course would be actively espoused by the Sultan of Ahmadnagar. The Lodi was pursued, and died fighting in Bundelkhand, 28th Jan., 1631. The Emperor resolved to make an example of Ahmadnagar; and the Sultan of Bijápur—who had long been in alliance with his neighbour—was included in the sentence. The Emperor moved down to Burhánpur, and a decisive campaign seemed at hand, when all public cares for a moment ceased at the sudden decease of the Emperor's

* It seems from the narrative of the Spanish friar Manrique that ladies joined in these pleasures unveiled.

L

loved wife, the mother of all his children. Then the Emperor determined to take the dear remains to Agra, where they were interred in a favourite garden on the Jumna side, while a mausoleum was being erected, which, after the lapse of centuries, still attracts the admiration of the world.* In 1635 the Deccan campaign was renewed, though without definite results, but Ahmadnagar was finally taken and annexed in 1637, Kandahar was surrendered to the Mughals the same year; it was soon to prove a most fatal gift. In 1639 the Rávi Canal was begun, to take water to Lahore; this has been already mentioned (CHAPTER I.) as one of the works which have been restored and extended by the British Government.

On the 10th Nov., 1643, the premier, Asaf Khán, died at Lahore in his seventy-second year; he was immensely rich, and the palace which he built, and in which he breathed his last, cost two millions of rupees. In the same year Sultan Aurangzeb, the Emperor's youngest son, asked permission to retire from the world; but his father dissuaded him. Whether the desire for retirement was insincere, or was the product of a passing cloud, it would have been better both for the Emperor and his realm if the Prince could have been taken at his word. But he was at the same time transferred from the Government of the Deccan to that of Gujarát. An invasion of Balkh was attempted, and led to three campaigns against the Uzbegs, who had intruded on that region; on the third occasion, 1646, Aurangzeb commanded, but was driven across the Hindu-Kush, and lost almost the whole of his army in 1647. Next year Kandahar was re-occupied by Persia, and was never again subdued to the Indian Empire until late in the 19th century, though thrice besieged by the armies of Sháh Jahán. The year 1648 saw the completion of new Delhi, or Shájahánabad, which had

* The lady's titles were Arzumand Banu Begam, *Mumtaz-i-Mahal*; and from the latter words her tomb is vulgarly known as the "Taj Mahal."

been ten years building. The Emperor caused his palace then to be supplied with water from an artificial channel, now completed by the British under the name of "Eastern Jumna Canal." In 1654 the revenue system of Akbar was extended into the newly-acquired provinces, south of the Narbada; and Aurangzeb was sent with an army to extend and consolidate the power of the empire in that quarter. The last vestige of the Nizám Shahi dynasty had disappeared in 1637. Then the kingdom had been formed into the *Subah,* or province, of Aurangábád. Nevertheless the kingdoms of Golkonda and of Bijápur still maintained a desperate defence; the former under the Kutb Sháhi King, Abdulla, admirably served by an able adventurer, Mir Jumla; and the latter defended by the genius of an Hindu officer, Sháhji Bhonsla, to be hereafter known as the projenitor of Sivaji, the still more celebrated Mahratta leader of the next reign, and founder of the Mahratta state. The Sultan of Golkonda having quarrelled with Mir Jumla, was haughtily directed by the Emperor to restore that minister, who had repaired to the imperial camp, and on his very natural refusal was attacked by an army under Aurangzeb in 1654. Golkonda was taken and occupied before help could arrive from Bijápur; for the present the Sultan was allowed to become tributary; and Aurangzeb next turned his armies against the kingdoms of Bidár and Bijápur in 1656. But before their conquest could be completed, events occurred in Hindustan which not only threw the Empire into confusion for the moment, but prepared for its ultimate destruction.

[To authorities cited in the former section add:—the "Itinerario" of Fra Sebastian Manrique, Rome 1653; *v.* extract given in "The Turks in India," London, 1879.

NOTE.—The following figures regarding the land revenue of the Empire during the period under review, have been taken from the best contemporary authorities.

AKBAR: about ten *krors* (one hundred millions of rupees).

JAHANGIR: about twelve *krors*, rising to seventeen at the end of the reign (Coryat and the *Bádsháhnáma*).

SHAH JAHAN: from seventeen *krors* to about twenty-two in 1647. (*Bádsháhnáma.*)

Some modern writers have adopted higher estimates, improbable in themselves, and supported chiefly by conjecture.]

SECTION 3.—While the Empire was in this condition, an element was arising which was to change the fortunes of the whole Peninsula.

Five years after that (1492), in which Columbus set sail for the west to look for India and to discover America, the Portuguese admiral, Vasco de Gama, went forth in the opposite direction. Doubling the southern point of Africa, the intrepid navigator made his way to the Malabar coast. From 1498 to 1513 Gama and his followers were engaged in hostilities with the local chief, entitled *Samuri*, or "Zamorin;" their great leader, Albuquerque having been repulsed in 1510 with great loss after a momentary success, in which the Portuguese had done a considerable amount of mischief. In spite of that repulse they returned three years later, when the Zamorin thought it best to make peace; and the Europeans were allowed to found a factory. For many years afterwards Calicut afforded a foothold to the Portuguese, from which they proceeded to make further settlements; also to establish a monopoly of the trade in Indian spices and piece goods, and to ruin the overland commerce hitherto carried on by the Venetians. But Calicut was in itself too far to the South to form a complete outlet for the produce of the Deccan, being 566 miles below Bombay; and Albuquerque, in the very crisis of the war, attacked a more important and in every way suitable place about halfway up the coast. This was Goa, in the kingdom of Bijápur, which he captured 17th Feb., 1510. Recaptured in August of the same year by the Adil Sháhi Sultan, it was once more taken by Albuquerque, 25th Nov., and has ever since continued subject to the kingdom of Portugal—except during the short period when that country itself was subject to Spain. A splendid city arose, adorned with enormous masses of masonry in the shape of churches and convents. Goa became the metropolitan see of the Catholic Church in India, and the base of proselytising operations which extended to Agra and to Pekin. In the territory around—about sixty miles long by forty miles extreme breadth—the people were found to be distributed amongst a number of self-governing communities, whose privileges were respected by the conquerors. The hills abounded in forest trees; the plains produced cocoanuts and rice; the harbour was wide and well-sheltered; and for about a hundred years the settlement enjoyed great prosperity and splendour. In 1537 it became the base of further extension; in that year was founded the port of Hugli; near the old city of Sátgaon, which had once been one of the chief towns of Bengal, but was now ruined by the change in the course of the river. Here also the European settlement prospered for a long time, though the place never attained the magnitude of Goa. When Sháh Jahán, flying before the persecutions of his step-mother, took refuge in the Gangetic province (1624), he solicited assistance from the governor of Hugli; but he was refused with contumely, and never forgot the insult. After his accession he is said to have received further provocation,* but the facts are somewhat obscure. All that is certain is that in 1631 Hugli was besieged for fourteen weeks by a great imperial army. The year was dry, and there was not enough water in the river to allow the Portuguese to employ their ships in the defence of the town. A great portion of the curtain was mined and exploded, and the Mughals stormed the breach and captured the place which the Portuguese never regained. At the same time a second European State was acquiring

* v. "Turks in India," p. 121 (some chapters of an anecdotal character, by the writer of the present history). London, 1879.

power in the East, and displacing the Portuguese in every part of India. This was the Dutch Republic, which, from the time of the temporary union of the Peninsula under Philip II., never ceased to make war on Portuguese commerce. Linschoten—whose voyages and maps were published towards the end of the 16th century—was for thirteen years in the service of the Archbishop of Goa, and availed himself of the local knowledge so procured to stimulate the ambition of his countrymen. On the last day of that century a third power appeared—chiefly desirous of trade—in the form of the English "East Indian Company," destined to found a new Indian Empire. The first capital of the company was only £72,000, but the undertaking alarmed the Hollanders who copied it two years later, with a stock eight times as large as that of the English. By the year 1605 the Dutch Company had sent out three trade fleets, and had established factories on the coast of Malabar, and founded the city of Batavia in the Island of Java. On the mainland of India the Dutch had several factories during the 17th century, of which the most important were Cannanore, south of Goa; and Chinsura, near Hugli. They contested the commercial power of Portugal with success, and waged a long and obstinate strife with the English down to the time when their Stadtholder became King of our islands (1689). Then their Indian affairs became stationary, till the taking of Chinsura by Clive, after the decisive battle of Biderra. There are now not a hundred Hollanders in all India.

The Dutch contribution to Indian history is their having weakened the Portuguese when the latter were already sinking under the effects of their own corruption. The place of the vanquished was not, however, to be taken by their conquerors. When the grasping policy of the Republic had expelled the agents of the London Company from the Spice-islands, the latter at once fell back upon the mainland: an event of which the promise and significance could not then have been perceived. The first English factory at Surat, near the mouth of the Tapti, was ceded by the Mughal governor of Gujarát in 1612; and soon afterwards a charter was obtained from the Emperor Jahángir. In 1618 a further grant of privileges was made by the same monarch to Sir Thomas Roe, whose embassy was mentioned in the last section; and a populous and wealthy city arose, with a good anchorage known as "Swally Roads." Caravans from the great cities of the interior were constantly coming to Surat, which was also a place of embarkation for Muslim pilgrims proceeding to Mecca: sea-borne trade was carried on with Arabia, the Persian Gulf, Ceylon, Sumatra, and Europe; indigo and textile fabrics, in silk and cotton, formed the chief articles of export. The Portuguese opposed the settlement in its infant days; and in 1615 the East India Company's squadron was attacked in Swally Roads by a strong Portuguese fleet, but the assailants were beaten off: an affair which redounded to the credit of the British, while it lowered the prestige of the Portuguese. The English soon got a factory at Ajmere, under imperial patronage, and must even have had agents at Agra, to judge by the evidence of gravestones in the Protestant cemetery there. In 1622 the English got possession of a Portuguese factory on the Persian Gulf, and opened an agency at Masulipatam, on the coast of the Eastern Deccan. In 1639 they founded Fort S. George at Madras, on a piece of land acquired from a Paligar, or native chief, descended from the unfortunate Rám Rája of Bijainagar. A patent was obtained from Sháh Jahán, authorising the British to trade with Pipli, a place in Orissa, of which the very ruins have perished. Five years later the English obtained further favour for their Bengal settlement from the same Emperor, through the skill and public spirit of one of their medical officers named Boughton. One result was the foundation of an English factory on the deserted site of the Portuguese settlement of Hugli, about Bengal. In 1661 King Charles II. of

England marrying the Infanta of Portugal, obtained the island of Bombay from the government of Lisbon as a portion of her dowry; the population was estimated at 10,000 souls, and the yearly revenue at a sum equivalent to £6,500. The indolent monarch took no interest in a possession so far off, and so little lucrative, and in 1668 he transferred it to the Company for a trifling quit-rent. Unwholesome and ill-defended as it was, there must have been even then conveniences attaching to Bombay, perhaps by reason of the harbour; for the chief factory on that side of India was transferred there from Surat in the course of the next few years. But these events belong to a somewhat later period than that which we are now contemplating.

During the reign of Sháh Jahán India began to attract the notice of the French government, and several distinguished travellers from France and Italy visited the country. One of the earliest was François Bernier, who went to India as agent to the famous minister Colbert in 1654. Colbert, a disciple of the astute Cardinal Mazarin, gave great attention to the maritime interests of his country; and, in corresponding with his powerful employer, Bernier gathered the materials for his famous history of the Revolutions of the Mughal Empire, published at Paris in 1670-1, to which we owe much private matter in regard to the events to be related in the following chapter. Another lively French traveller, though inferior in literary charm to Bernier, was the Baron Tavernier d'Aubonne, an engraver and a connoisseur of jewels, who travelled in India between the years 1651 and 1669; also, an Italian physician named Manucci, who was in the household of Sháh Jahán, left some interesting papers, which were somewhat boldly "edited" by Father Catrou, a French jesuit. The report of the Spanish missionary, Manrique, has been already cited.

From these authors we derive a knowledge of the relations of Sháh Jahán towards Europeans in India, which we could not have obtained from the proud and exclusive Muslim chroniclers. The wise liberality of Akbar had led to the foreign visitors receiving respectful mention from his friend and biographer, Abul Fazl; and in the narrative of Roe we find that Europeans were civilly treated by the indolent and self-indulgent Jahángir. Under Sháh Jahán a change took place. The Emperor did not exactly persecute Christians as such, but, for reasons already noted, he was personally hostile to the Portuguese. When Hugli fell in 1631 the Mughal general, Kásim Khán, not only levelled the fortifications, but destroyed the churches, and sent the priests and women of the Portuguese as prisoners to Agra, where the Court then was. They underwent great hardships on the march, and when they reached Agra the women were made slaves, and the men were put into close confinement. But this was intended as a special punishment for being subjects of Portugal; for an Italian architect, Geronimo Veronneo, who was then in the Emperor's service, preserved the lives of some of the priests, though two of them, at least, sank under their sufferings; and some years later Manrique was enabled to cause the liberation of the survivors by favour of Asaf Khán. Nor did the work of persecution stop here. While employing Verroneo and Manucci—the former of whom designed the famous "Taj," the mausoleum of the Empress—Sháh Jahán destroyed the steeple of a fine church which the Christians had been allowed to build in the previous reign, and silenced the bell which used to be audible all over the town. In a word the Portuguese underwent what Bernier was assured was "a misery and desolation not to be paralleled; a kind of Babylonian captivity." But he adds that they had, by their piratical proceedings in the bay of Bengal, brought discredit upon the Christian name. "They are thus," adds the honest Frenchman, "become a prey to their enemies, and fallen so low in the Indies, that I doubt if they will ever recover there; whereas formerly, before they had been corrupted by vice, they made all others tremble in those parts." It is also to be noticed that, although the Portuguese were more fortunate in maintaining their possessions in the neighbourhood of Goa, their conduct there was not altogether such as to raise the character of Christianity in India. A great part in the early colonisation of both Spain and Portugal was allotted to the propagation of the Cross, and the name of S. Francis Xavier will be held in unperishing honour. But unhappily, the zeal of the Portuguese missionaries was not always guided by discretion, and their dependence on the secular arm involved them in the popular hostility aroused by insolent and cruel proceedings towards the natives on the part of the civil and military officers. Moreover, not long after the death of Xavier, the Government of Lisbon established a branch of the Inquisition at Goa, which was worked by the Dominicans with characteristic and terrible rigour. To all this must be added an almost incredible amount of social corruption, among both sexes, supported by enormous and extravagant luxury during the prosperity of the settlement.

Hence we must conclude that Europeans, in the time of Shāh Jahān, presented themselves to the people of India in very varied aspects. Learned and skilful artists and savants were duly honoured and employed. Veronneo, the Italian architect, has been already named, and such was the confidence reposed in him that the Emperor gave him a credit of no less than three *krors* of rupees—considerably over a tenth of the yearly revenues of the Empire—for one building alone. A Frenchman, named Austin de Bordeaux, was employed to inlay the walls of tombs and palaces with precious stones, and—in spite of the Muslim prejudice against the representation of living forms—was permitted to affix his own portrait, as Orpheus taming the beasts, in the very throne-room of Delhi.* The missionaries who died

---

* This work was only removed when Delhi was taken in 1857; and it is still to be seen in the Indian museum at South Kensington.

at Agra were buried in handsome tombs, the inscriptions being still extant in a special cemetery, which has continued in the possession of their co-religionists to the present day. On the other hand, for the turbulent, the combative, the aggressive, there was no favour in a well-ordered Empire; though quiet traders—as the English then were—pursued their operations unmolested, and were even treated with favour. When Manrique visited the Premier, Asaf Khán, about the liberation of the Portuguese priests imprisoned at Agra, he was received with generous courtesy; his requests were granted, and he was admitted to court celebrations, and even invited to a dinner-party, where he met the Emperor, and many members of the Imperial family, female as well as male.

Of the general character of Sháh Jahán's administration the Europeans of those days give a favourable view. Thus Tavernier declares that the Emperor "reigned not so much as a king over his subjects, but rather as a father over his family." And elsewhere he speaks of him as a great ruler, "during whose reign there was such a strictness in the civil government—and particularly for the security of the highways—that there was never any occasion to put a man to death as a robber."

If we contrast this with the account given by Roe of the preceding reign, or with the state of European countries at the same, or even at a later, period, we must admit that the picture of the condition of Hindustan is very much to the credit of the Emperor Sháh Jahán.

At the moment to which we were brought by the narrative in the last section, the stability of his realm appeared still unbroken, and the sky of his prosperity without a cloud. Manucci, the Italian physician—who was then about the court at Agra—tells us that the Emperor was then about sixty years of age, fond of social pleasure, but of refined tastes and dignified demeanour. The imperial family were in seeming harmony and subordination, consisting of four sons and two daughters, all the offspring of the deceased Empress. The eldest, Dára, was a man of the school of his ancestor Akbar, accomplished and liberal, a friend to the Hindus and a liberal patron of Europeans, men of both classes being in his service; many Rajputs being in his suite besides a number of Christian engineer and artillery officers, and three priests, viz., a Neapolitan named Malpica, a Portuguese named Juxarte, and Henri Buzé, a Flemish father, who is mentioned by Bernier as having a strong influence over the Prince's mind: of the other Princes, two were Shujá and Murád, soldiers of a ruder stamp, devoted to the pleasures of their age and station. But we have already had some glimpse of Aurangzeb, the youngest; not a uniformly successful leader, but brave and calculating; who professed devotion to the strictest form of Sunni orthodoxy, while his real devotion was to his own worldly interests. Of the two Princesses the elder was Jahánárá—the Bádsháh-Begam, or Princess-Royal—very beautiful and accomplished, and warmly attached to her brother Dára; the younger, Raushanárá, was the vigilant guardian of the interests of Aurangzeb, then absent with the army of the Deccan. On the 9th April, 1656, the Emperor had the misfortune to lose by death his prime minister, Allámi Sád Ullah, the most upright man in the Empire; and from this time affairs began to go wrong. Exactly a twelvemonth later died Ali Mardán Khán, an able Persian noble, who had long served the Emperor in peace and war, and whose loss was much lamented by him. In August of the same year—1657—the Emperor became dangerously ill, and Sultan Dára assumed authority as Regent. Unfortunately the manners of this Prince were not on a level with his accomplishments; and he gave offence, not only by the latitude of his opinions, but also by arrogant ways, which offended the more worldly chiefs and courtiers. Anticipations of the Emperor's death did not conciliate regard or obedience to his representative and probable successor. Aurangzeb was treated with suspicion, attempts being made to weaken his position and influence in the Deccan, but he kept his temper, and marched slowly towards Agra in an undeclared attitude, leaving his brothers Shujá and Murád to bear the brunt of open opposition. Rája Jai Singh, of Amber, was sent by Dára to suppress the rising of Sultan Shujá, whom he completely defeated and put to flight. Shujá took refuge in the eastern provinces, of which he was Viceroy. Another Hindu General, Rája Jaswant Singh, was deputed to oppose Sultan Murád; but Aurangzeb now declared himself as a foe to the government of his elder brother; espousing the cause of Murád, in conjunction with whom he inflicted a defeat upon the Rája at Ujain; helped, as was believed, by the treachery of a Muslim noble who held a high post in the imperialist army. Jaswant Singh retired upon the fastnesses of Marwar, and the brothers continued their advance upon Agra. Dára drew out his forces at Samoghar, a march south of the place, and was defeated, after an obstinate struggle, in May, 1658; he then fled to the Punjab; and Aurangzeb took possession of his father's palace and person. From that moment the reign of Sháh Jahán was virtually at an end. After some hypocritical professions Aurangzeb deposed his father and made him and the Crown Princess close prisoners. The ex-Emperor lived for nearly eight years longer, tended to the last by his elder daughter; and died in December, 1666, in the apartments still shown as his in the fortified palace at Agra. He was buried by the side of his wife in "the Táj." His age was 74.

Aurangzeb soon undeceived the careless soldier, Sultan Murád, in whose interests he had pretended to act. Surprised in a moment of conviviality, Murád was conveyed under close arrest to Gwalior, where he was afterwards put to death for attempting to escape. Aurangzeb was crowned at Delhi, 20th August, 1659, by the title of Alamgir ("World-seizer"), and in the following month the ill-starred Dára was brought captive to the same place. He was decapitated in prison, Father Buzé attending his last moments.

This was the apparent climacteric of the dynasty. The territory directly ruled by the imperial government was bounded on the north by the Uzbeg dominions in Transoxiana—still represented by the Khanates of Khiva and Bokhára—on the South by the present confines of the Madras and Bombay Presidencies, with indirect power up to the Krishna and Tungabhadra rivers, and stretching from Puri in Orissa to Somnáth in Gujarát. From the testimony of native writers, confirmed by Bernier, it may be safely concluded that the yearly revenue at the accession of Álamgir was about twenty-four *krors*, of which about two-thirds were paid by the land; and the crown had a fluctuating income of its own besides, namely, what came from benevolences, escheats, and fines. The good financial measures of Sháh Jahán have been already glanced at. His life was sumptuous; he constructed a throne at Delhi which Tavernier—an expert in jewellery—appraised to be worth over 160,000,000 of French *livres*,* in which the Baron counted 108 rubies and 160 emeralds; embroidery of pearls and small diamonds hung from the edges of the canopy, a diamond of more than eighty carats hung from the top. The tomb of his wife was estimated—by the Emperor's own order—to cost not less than three *krors* of rupees, say, about two and a quarter millions of modern Rs.x. He built marble mosques, and halls inlaid with precious stones, at Agra and Delhi; dug two new canals, besides repairing the canal of Firuz Sháh Tughlak; and after all this expenditure left a reserve of coin and bullion which, without precious stones, was valued by the cautious Bernier at £24,000,000 of modern money. Nor had this surplus been obtained at the cost of undue exaction from the

---

* The *livre tournois* of those days was worth about fifteen pence, and three *livres tournois* = two rupees. This was the famous "Peacock-throne," despoiled by Nádir Sháh about 100 years later.

people. We have seen what Tavernier thought of Sháh Jahán's paternal rule. Bernier, who knew European countries, and who had travelled in Persia, testifies to the superior size of the Indian cities, the general cultivation of the land, and the efficiency of the police in the reign of Sháh Jahán; nor was any sign of decay apparent when the new reign began. Apart from the criminal methods that the new ruler had adopted in obtaining the Peacock-throne and all that it commanded, the omens were not unfavourable. The Emperor Álamgir was an exceptional man, with very little of the Mughal either in character or in blood. For the first years of his reign he mainly left public affairs to the tracks in which they had long been wont to run. According to the testimony of Manucci, the administration of justice was much cared for; and, although the bulk of a community may be fortunate enough to keep out of the law courts, yet there is no Eastern country in which the substitution of the King's jurisdiction for civil disorder is not a potent test of good government.

"Nothing," says the Italian doctor, "can possibly be more uniform than the judicial administration in the States of 'the Mogul.' The Viceroys, presidents of districts, chiefs of towns, all perform, in their respective spheres, the same part as that of their chief at Delhi, subject always to the imperial control." Powers of life and death were vested, he adds, in the heads of the local governors; nevertheless there were, in each province, newswriters appointed for the purpose of transmitting reports to headquarters. "Such," concludes Manucci, "are the institutions of this great empire; a state of things in which barbarism is so tempered by equity as to render the government of the Mughal empire little behind that of any other nation." Bernier, who was a great traveller, and who willingly exposed and criticised evils which he saw on his wanderings, yet finishes his work with these words:—

"Those who will a little weigh my whole story will not take

Aurangzeb for a barbarian, but for a rare genius, a great statesman and a great King."

Such was the appearance of things in the first years of the reign of Aurangzeb, or—as he should henceforth be known to us—the Emperor Àlamgir I. Nevertheless, whatever was to be the future destiny of India, it must have been apparent, to those who could see below the surface, that a new departure was at hand. The House of Taimur, or of Chaghtai as it was sometimes called (after one of the sons of Changhez Khán), usually produced easy-going warriors of liberal minds and jovial habits, fierce enough in actual war but kindly in cooler blood, and much addicted to conviviality. Àlamgir had none of this, but, it might seem, more of the Hindu character, averse to bloodshed but ruthless in the pursuit of an absorbing purpose; jealous, suspicious, and of an indefatigable turn for details. The means by which he gained his power were somewhat nefarious, yet hardly old-fashioned in the Western world of his day. As soon as he thought his power consolidated he manifested a devotion to duty, as he conceived it, which only needed the aureole of success to make it glorious. In the next chapter we shall see some of the circumstances which made success impossible.

[See list of authorities for last two sections. An account of Famine Relief in 1660 will be found in the Report of the British Commissioners, Allahabad, 1868. For information as to the first appearance of the European element, see Birdwood's *Report on Old Records*, 1891].

CHAPTER VI.

DECLINE OF THE EMPIRE.

Section 1 : Decline of the Empire.—Section 2 : The rise of the Mahratta Confederacy, and of the English Company in India.—Section 3 : The development of those powers.

SECTION I.—The abundant materials provided for the history of the reign of Sháh-Jahán fail soon after the accession of his son. Bernier, Tavernier, and Manucci, all left India about the same time, and no European observer of the same skill and industry arose to take their place. The records of contemporary Muslim observers were suppressed by the policy of the new Emperor who disliked and forbade this recourse to the bar of public opinion : Kháfi Khán, one of the best of Indian historians had to take his notes in secret,* and reserve the publication of his record till a more liberal era. It is, at the same time, clear that this historian, a most able and conscientious writer, was far from judging the Emperor as he has been since judged by European writers.

Kháfi Khán attributes much of Álamgir's ill-success to *the gentleness of his disposition* and his religious convictions. He notices, especially, that, in the 2nd year of his reign, the Emperor remitted many items of separate revenue—the octroi in towns among them. But, by reason of the impunity attending on disobedience, the orders were generally disregarded by local authorities; who pretended, indeed, to obey, but kept up the forbidden imposts for their own benefit. Thus, as he

---

*Kháfi Khán is a pen-name equivalent to " Mr. Secret"; and was probably assumed purposely with that significance.

assures us, "the order abolishing most of these imposts had no effect." The transit-duties, in particular, became so heavy that the price of goods often doubled between departure from the port or factory where they were issued and arrival at the market to which they had been consigned.

Apart from this writer's personal testimony it is difficult to get a clear notion of the period under notice. Whether from an affectation of humility or for some other reason which has not been explained, Àlamgir had the strongest objection to the history of his reign being written; insomuch that Kháfi Khán has to confess that, after the tenth year, materials were collected only with the utmost difficulty. Moreover, the provinces north of the Narbada—which formed the Empire of Hindustan Proper—had been so completely pacified and settled by his predecessors that there was but little occasion for historical record: until towards the end of the period the people of Hindustan were in the happy condition of those whose annals are a blank. And indeed, the events in the south, where the most eventful part of Àlamgir's reign was passed, present little of agreeable interest. The story is one of monotonous and vain struggle against a destiny prepared at once by the Emperor's qualities and by his defects. The ambition which led him to usurp the throne, and the attachment to Islám which urged him to exertion, were causes which gave him a certain glory, as the head of the Muslim empire, while yet they combined to make him the beginner of its ruin.

Necessarily, therefore, the period is dull and depressing; one barren of great ideas, great transactions, and great men. This much is clear, in the dearth of ordered information. The Emperor began well enough. He had a large civil and military machinery and an ample revenue: good subordinates bred by years of administrative experience on sound principles: with a contented and submissive people. Competition rapidly disappeared: Dára was executed, as a heretic; Shujá, chased out of Bengal, perished obscurely in Arakan where he had taken refuge; the two sons of Dára died—like their uncle Murád—in arrest at Gwalior. The year 1661 opened on a sovereignty which none appeared to dispute. The Emperor sought a means of strengthening his position by pardoning Rája Jaswant Singh, of Marwar (now Jodhpur), who had valiantly espoused the cause of the late Sultan Dára so long as that cause survived. He also instituted energetic measures of famine relief to meet the effects of a great drought which was afflicting Hindustan. He gave further indications of preserving the wise and humane policy of his house by marrying his eldest son, Sultan Muazzam to the daughter of a Hindu Rája.

There was, however, one source of trouble from the Hindus just coming into notice; one, apparently of no great importance, yet which it would be well to strangle in birth. This was from an obscure tribe in the eastern Deccan, where the Yádavas had once held sway, from Deogiri, over the land commanded by the western Gháts. The chief place was now Ahmadnagar, which had been incorporated in the empire; and some of the adventurous spirits of Máháráshtra had for some time sought a career further south, under the Adil-Sháhi princes of Bijápur Yusuf Sháh, who founded that dynasty, is said to have employed a chief of this race before the end of the 15th century; and in another forty years their employment had become so general at Bijápur that their language had to be adopted as the official medium of public accounts at head quarters.

In the reign of Jahángir one of their chiefs, whose name indicated a claim to Yádava ancestry, had given his daughter to the head of an immigrant family, Sháhji Bhonsla, who had risen to notice under Malik Ambar the Abyssinian champion of the Nizám Sháhi dynasty of Ahmadnagar in its last struggles. In 1636 the Bijápur ruler made peace with the Sháh Jáhán, and about the same time was joined by Sháhji Bhonsla, who had become rich and powerful as a leader of partizan horse. His Yádava wife had borne him a son, whom he named Siváji, brought up to arms and adminstration, and, on his attaining maturity, got appointed to the charge of Poona district. He soon began to withhold tribute, and seize and strengthen commanding elevations on the mountains. The connivance of the father Sháhji seems more than doubtful, since it was often to himself that was due the money embezzled by his son: but this was not observed by the authorities at Bijápur who accordingly put Sháhji under arrest, and announced their intention of holding him as a hostage for his son's behaviour. The latter kept quiet until, by intercession from Sháh Jahán, his father's release was obtained: then Siváji resumed his self-aggrandising operations, and stood forth as the declared enemy of the Bijápur government. At the beginning of Àlamgir's reign he obtained terms from that State which left him in control of the Poona district, and an army of nearly 60,000 followers. He next began to forage and plunder in the imperial dominions near Aurangabad.

While far from forseeing all that Siváji would grow to, the Emperor had seen enough of the freebooter—when commanding in the Deccan for his father Sháh-Jehán—to feel that he would be a danger to public order. He therefore sent his mother's brother, Nawáb Sháyista Khán, with what appeared an adequate force, for Siváji's immediate suppression. The Nawáb was brother to the late Minister Asaf Khan, and to the wife of Sháh Jahán whose tomb is at "The Taj"; a typical Persian, grave and politic: he led a well-appointed Mughal army out of Aurangabad, at first with good omens. But confidence begets carelessness; and the stately nobleman soon met with a reverse which not only entailed defeat but covered him with ridicule; on which he was recalled from the Deccan and relegated by his nephew to the Government of Bengal, where, he fought the Portuguese pirates and conquered Chittagong and part of Burma. The vacant command was divided between the Hindu Rájas, Jai Sinh (of Amber) and Jaswant (of Marwar). They were so far successful that they persuaded Siváji to surrender and appear at court. He arrived at a moment when the glory and urbanity of Sháh-Jahán's ceremonial were already waning. An edict for remitting the minor assessed taxes and customs levied in the last reign had been issued, and the Emperor affected the most rigid economy: in his own person and household he gave example of an almost ascetic frugality, professing to find his own subsistence by the sale of embroidered skull-caps.

In such an atmosphere the quondam outlaw found nothing that could please. To a man, in the prime of life, accustomed to command every one around him, living in the sea-breeze and the free air of the wooded mountains, there was no compensation in a life of ceremony at Delhi, from which splendour and pleasure had been alike banished, and where he was treated with no consideration. Siváji left the city in disguise, and never again trusted himself among the weariful solemnities of Mughal civilisation. These events occurred 1664-5.

The next year witnessed another important change. Rája Jai Sinh dying at his post, Sultan Muazzam was appointed, with Jaswant Sinh as his military tutor and virtual commander of the army, Viceroy of the Deccan. About this time Siváji heard of the death of his father, whereupon he assumed the title of "Rája," and began to coin money in his own name. He also attempted the formation of a navy, which became ultimately a school of pirates.

In the last month of the year 1666 the ex-Emperor Sháh Jahán died, as already mentioned, and Àlamgir seemed to have reached his highest point of success. But from that very period his bad fortunes dated. A weak-minded system of concession to Siváji in the Deccan led to the imposition of a species of blackmail on Bijápur and Golkonda, by which the freebooter laid the foundation of the Mahratta tribute or blackmail, which afterwards became so widely spread under the name of "*Chaut*." The Emperor's next mistake was to close the balcony in which his predecessors had been wont to show themselves to all classes : henceforth, the only knowledge the bulk of his subjects could have of his existence was derived from increasing taxation, or other edict, for which they might hold him responsible. One of the injudicious ordinances of this period was one imposing a five per cent. rating on the commercial transactions of Hindus, while those of the Emperor's co-religionists were only to pay half that rating. Such distinctions are keenly felt in India.

A general alienation between the government and the Hindus marks the year 1679, further provoked by illiberal fanaticism. Upon vain pretence the Emperor ordered the demolition of their temples at Multan, at Muttra, and at the specially sacred centre of Hinduism, Benares. It is at least a coincidence that the three holiest rivers of the popular faith were thus polluted at once; the Indus, celebrated in the *Veda;* the Jumna, hallowed by the Krishna legend ; and the thrice holy Ganges itself. The great temple of Keshav Rai at Muttra was demolished, and a mosque erected on the site in the early part of 1669.* The champions of the Hindus were not slow to take up the challenge. In the neighbourhood of Nárnaol, in the cis-Sutlej, four thousand families had formed an agricultural community under the name of *Satnámis*†— " Truth-famed "—from a desire to be distinguished for veracity. They bound themselves to abstain from unlawful means of gain ; to cause no gratuitous injury ; and not to submit to wrong. The scheme was meritorious, but its execution was to lead the Satnamis to their ruin. In retaliation for some acts

* *Maasir-i-Alamgiri.*

† Elphinstone gives the name as "Satnarámi," which is quite meaningless. He gives the date of rising as 1676, but it began, probably some years earlier.

of oppression by the local authorities, they occupied the town of Nárnaol, and, after expelling the royal officers, set up a government of their own. They even dared to encounter some of the forces of the state, routing the troops, and driving them nearly to Delhi. The infection spread among the Hindu yeomanry of the country, and the Emperor thought it right to take the field in person. The rebels defended themselves with much spirit, and were not finally put down for some time.

For the next few years no important events occurred in Upper India. In the Deccan, Siváji consolidated his power, never ceasing the plunder of his neighbours, but constantly improving the administration of his own country. He organised his army, employing professional officers and disciplined soldiers, paid in cash. In civil affairs he introduced reforms tending to order and good government, so that the agriculturists could pursue their useful labours in security and confidence. He ravaged Khándes and plundered Surat, where the British retired to their factory, shut the gates, and ransomed their own interests. Owing to the great and growing tendency of the Emperor to suspect the motives of his subordinates, the army was insufficiently manned, and the command divided. In 1672 Siváji for the first time closed with the Mughals in battle, cutting up a strong detachment, and forcing the imperialists to fall back on their head-quarters at Aurangábad and assume a defensive attitude which was maintained for some years. Meanwhile, the condition of Hindustan did not improve. Rája Jaswant Sinh died at his post in the Kábul country in 1678, and his family came down into Hindustan on the way to their home at Jodhpur. The religious narrowness of Alamgir prompted him to the step, alike forbidden by prudence and honour, of seeking to intercept the convoy in order that he might seize the young Rájas, and make Muslims of them. The Emperor's men came up to the caravan near Agra, and endeavoured to carry out their orders. The

Rajputs opposed them, and a few faithful retainers hurried off the lads, while the remainder of the escort covered the retreat. They fought until all were slain, but, by their act of devotion, they had given time for the fugitives to gain in safety the road to Jodhpur.

Alamgir was now passing the final stage of middle life, and had reached a period when men seldom amend either in disposition of mind or in chances of good fortune. He had ranged against his Empire two most dangerous foes; in the Deccan a united people, with an able and ambitious leader; in Hindustan the first stirrings of a Hindu revival, provoked by his own oppressive conduct. Even a Bábar or an Akbar might have found it hard to stand alone against so many and such distracting perils, but none of the jovial Mughals of those days would have got into such a position. To strike a hard blow at Siváji, and then make him their confidential servant, would have been their policy in the Deccan; to have shown impartial and sympathetic countenance to all well-intentioned Rajputs would have marked their management of Hindustan. But Alamgir had never been the man for conciliation, being unable to exercise any of his good qualities at the right time; suspicious when he should have trusted; parsimonous where expenditure was required: severe when he would have done better to show lenience; and lenient when it was necessary to be severe.

About 1680 a further error was committed, partly due to bigotry, but perhaps precipitated by want of money: namely, the imposition of the *Jazia*, or capitation-tax, on non-Muslims, from which the Hindus had been exempt since the first part of Akbar's reign. Disturbance became serious and wide; the Emperor's path was beset by protesting Brahmans; shops were closed in the very capital, so that the indispensable business of life was almost suspended. The obstinate fanatic caused the streets to be cleared by his war elephants; many lives were lost on the occasion. At the same time a pursuivant was sent to Jodhpur to bring away the idols from temples doomed to destruction. At Udaipur, in carrying out the like order, twenty of the ministers of the gods were killed. Altogether, nearly 300 Hindu shrines were thus destroyed in Rajputána alone. About this time, moved by the sorrows of his race, and yet regretting the danger that he saw coming on the country, a Rajput chief about this time addressed the Empire a spirited protest, of which a draft is said by Col. Tod to have been seen by him at Udaipur: it is translated in a work already cited.* The writer—Rána Ráj Sinh—begins by citing the Emperor's three immediate predecessors as having built up the Empire by wise liberality—by "clemency and righteousness," as the writer puts it. He then draws a bitter contrast with present doings, and pointedly asks the Emperor whether he thinks that he will please the Creator by harassing and destroying his creatures: "Do you then suppose that an artist can be pleased by the spoiling of his works?"

Nor was the Emperor able to preserve obedience in his own family. Sultan Akbar, his fourth son, who had been employed in the work of mischief, was so offended with his occupation, and so moved by pity for the Rájputs that he went into open rebellion.

About the middle of the year Álamgir had some compensation in the news of the death of Siváji, which took place at his fortress of Raigarh 5-16th June. He left a successor, his son, Sambhaji, but he inherited the power only, not the talents of his father. Akbar was expelled from Rajputána and joined Sambha; on the other hand, Sultan Muazzam, the heir-apparent, effected a temporary reconciliation between his father's government and the Rána of Udaipur, who agreed to forget the persecution of his religion. But the Emperor could not even then trust Muazzam, whose loyal conduct seems never to have wavered. He sent Ázam, his third son, to

* Tod's Rajasthan.

conduct the operations against Akbar, and summoned Muazzam to his presence to answer a charge of showing too much kindness to his erring brother.

In 1682 Akbar was led to fear that the Rajputs would want either inclination or power to support him, and he escaped to the coast with a handful of faithful companions; from thence he got away by sea, landed in the Persian Gulf, and ended his days as a refugee in Khorásán. In the following year the Emperor came to the conclusion that he could trust no one; accordingly, collecting all his resources, he departed south at the head of a mighty army, hoping to hold down the Mahrattas with one hand while he overthrew with the other the remaining Muslim states. He fell upon the latter, sending Muazzam to attack Golkonda, and employing Azam to watch Bijápur. True to his humane habits, Muazzam, after taking the capital, admitted the king to terms, again losing his father's favour by so doing. But Àlamgir temporised, observing the terms as long as it suited his purpose. After a protracted siege Bijápur fell, in 1686; the Emperor deposed the king and then proceeded in person against Golkonda. He took the city, and subverted the government for good and all about a year later. Thus the Muslim states were brought to a final end; and then the calamities of the Mughal Empire began in earnest.

Muazzam was kept in arrest for some time, and Àzam became his father's chief adviser. The land was scourged with war, famine, and pestilence. Sambha was taken and put to death; the Deccan fell into complete anarchy. The conquest of Bîjápur and of Golkonda proved worse than barren; for it only resulted in bringing the strained bark into direct contact with the rising tide of Hindu rebellion. Sambha's death was no relief: he left a disputed succession, but all parties among the Mahrattas were equally resolute in opposing the Emperor. His father's fortress of Raigarh continued to be the centre of disaffection. But his infant son, Sáhu, was taken and kept a prisoner as long as the Emperor lived.

Another Hindu tribe was now becoming dangerous. Encouraged by the absence of the Emperor, with all his best officers and men, the Játs broke out in the province of Agra, and plundered a royal convoy from Kábul, the officer in command being killed in vain defence. In reprisal the Emperor issued an edict forbidding the Hindus to use palanquins. Government seemed returning to the crude methods of Alá-ud-din Khilji. As a more efficient step, Sultan Muazzam was enlarged and sent against the Játs, with a strong force, and with a title of *Sháh Alam*, by which he was henceforth known. This was towards the end of 1691.

About this time the Mahrattas began to appear in force in the valley of the Bhima, towards Bijápur. The Emperor, on this, moved his camp to Bairámpuri, about midway between Kulbarga and Satára. In that neighbourhood he suffered a serious defeat, and was heard to express something like despair. In the Carnatic, his youngest son, Sultan Kámbaksh quarrelled with his military coadjutor, Zulfikar Khán, a connection of Nawab Shatista Khán, who held the office of *Amir-ul-Umra*. In the midst of their contentions they were surprised by a Mahratta army which they beat off with some difficulty, the Prince repairing to his father's camp. Troubles also arose with the Portuguese at Goa, and with the English at Bombay; but Kháfi Khán went on a mission to both places and by his diplomatic address settled the dispute. About the same time a little war arose between Shayista and the English in Bengal, which ended in Shayista being dismissed from his post, and the English settlement being transferred from Hugli to Calcutta (1694-9).

The Mahrattas of the west soon after this forced one imperialist army to surrender, and defeated a second in battle, capturing the elephants and baggage The jealousy of Azam against the returning favour of his elder brother rose to such a height that the former was deprived of his command and sent as governor to Kábul. Nor was Nature more kind to the Emperor, whose camp was destroyed in 1695 by a sudden flood of the Bhima, which swept away the tents, the horses, and the cattle, with 12,000 human beings. Then another imperial general was worsted and made prisoner, and the unhappy monarch could only complain that "it was useless to go on fighting when one was sure to lose."

By this time, however, Santa, the Mahratta leader, was dead, and the brave old despot was collecting all his resources for a supreme effort. In 1698 Álamgir advanced on Satára in person, and in the siege that followed he took an active part, "exposing himself as if in search of death"; the brother of the deceased Sambha was killed; the curtain of the town was breached by a mine; and at length the governor surrendered and entered the imperial service. The fall of Párli followed: but Tára Bái, widow of the deceased Rája, took up the Mahratta government and carried on the defence of her country with the energy often displayed by Indian ladies. The next few years passed in the usual beating of the air. Forts fell to costly attacks, but new forts arose; armies were dispersed, to be reassembled elsewhere; the whole Deccan was laid waste by orders of the Bái. The health of the obstinate old man began to fail. In 1704 he had a succession of fainting-fits, but he shook them off and went on with his vain endeavours. In the end of 1705 he sought a little repose at Ahmadnagar; but Ázam, who had recovered favour and employment, renewed his cabals. He had almost cleared the path to the succession: Akbar died in exile; Sháh Álam was away at Kábul, where he had taken the government in lieu of Ázam; Kámbaksh was at court; but the Emperor sent him away to Bijápur to be safe from Ázam's machinations; the latter was ordered off to Málwa, already threatened by the Mahrattas.

The end came suddenly. Alamgir died on the morning of 21st February, 1707, telling his beads and praying to the last. His death took place at Ahmadnagar, but he was buried at Aurangabad, where his tomb still stands: he had reached the great age of ninety lunar years.

During the latter part of his reign the Empire consisted—nominally at least—of no less than twenty great provinces. And the land revenue was estimated at thirty *krors*;* exclusive of other items. Elphinstone is of opinion that the new taxes produced a heavy loss to the state: the imposts may have been collected—at what cost in popular welfare and content can only be conjectured; but only a part of the money found its way to the Treasury. This was a sad descent from the palmy condition of 1670—and the Emperor's own doing; nevertheless, he should not be hastily condemned. From his own point of view he was consistent, vigilant, and determined. But his point of view was erroneous; and it is impossible not to be struck with the parallel that he presents to his European contemporary, Louis XIV. of France. The two monarchs were alike in judging matters of state from a basis of religious authority; so that the extension of a supposed holy empire was preferred to the less ostentatious duty of providing for the welfare of secular society. The imposition of the Hindu capitation-tax was an act closely resembling the revocation of the Edict of Nantes; it was so far worse that it oppressed the vast majority of the population, and caused a universal contempt of law. Political nihilism may be said to have then become the feeling of three-fourths of the Indian community.

Of the condition of the people we are left to judge from conjecture. The sturdy races of the Punjab and Hindustan maintained their self-governed townships—the "little republics" of Megasthenes—troubled doubtless by wild beasts

---

* Ramusio—"Viaggo etc," Venice, 1837. Harris "Collection of Voyages," London, 1744.

and human marauders. But the yeomen were stout of heart and provided with sharp swords and spears, well able to take their own parts, and to do a certain amount of cattle-stealing and plunder on their own accounts.

The tribunals, on the maintenance of which the Mughal government always bestowed much care, must have had no lack of occupation. Purely municipal law had not much scope; and it was an inherent vice of the system that it was unable to maintain that wholesome relation with the people that is produced by wise legislation.

Provided, by the contempt of their foreign rulers, with their own code, and able to enforce awards by an unusually strong force of public opinion, and by the terrors of excommunication, the Hindus were a law to themselves. But the correctional courts would always be active; a proverb of their own time was to the effect that "swift injustice was better than tardy justice." Even so late as the British settlement in Bengal the penal code of Islám was in full force. This system had the incurable weakness of claiming to arise out of divine revelation: as if a London magistrate were to administer *Leviticus* sentencing a man to be stoned for selling apples on a Saturday. The juristic confusion went farther. Murder, for example, was classed among torts—the next-of-kin to the deceased was master of the cause, allowed to compound with the offender for a money-payment. But statutory penalties attached to many things—such as the use of liquor—which, to modern Europeans, hardly appear at all criminal; many such were punishable by death. And not only was it more heinous to drink a glass of wine than to commit homicide, but the degree of culpability in the latter was made to depend less on the motive than on the instrument by which death was caused: thus, the man who shot another by the accidental discharge of a gun incurred a severer treatment than one who wilfully stabbed him with a bodkin.

Even the revenue administration was pervaded with this pedantry. In the translation of "The Institutes of Aurangzeb" (Àlamgir), by N. B. E. Baillie will be found an abstract of the system which, in his religious fervour, the Emperor substituted for the humane and judicious scheme of Akbar. The capitation-tax alone made a difference to a Hindu of about cent-per cent; and thus the tax was resented by the population as a duplication of their burdens no less than as a standing badge of conquest. The new system was enforced in a rescript of 1688, addressed to the provincial accountants, in which the recalcitrant are threatened with "temporal and eternal punishment."

Let a ruler, clothed with the visible attributes of power, say blankly to his subjects—"Do this, for it is my will," in the East, at least, there will be an immediate disposition to obey. But when a ruler, in evident difficulties with foreign foes and domestic disaffection, declares—as Àlamgir did—that his officers are to be guided "by the enlightened law" of a Prophet whose mission is not acknowledged, and that disobedience will meet with punishment in a Hereafter in which no one believes, the step from the sublime to the ridiculous has been almost cleared.

Accordingly, it is the testimony of a friendly contemporary, Khâfi Khán to wit, that Àlamgir's government was a universal failure. His respect for the law of Islám may have caused unpopular ordinances, it certainly weakened his hands, "so that every plan and project that he formed came to little good; and every enterprise that he undertook was long in execution and failed in the end."

[The authorities for this section have been cited in the text.]

SECTION 2.—The Mahrattas had suffered less than the Mughals by this long and desolating war. Sáhu, the son of their deceased Rája, was now twenty-one years old, having spent all but the first six years of his life as a state-prisoner at Aurangabad, but Tára Bái had ruled well and wisely in his absence. Having dismissed him to Poona, and made temporary arrangements with the Regency at Raigarh, Àzam advanced towards Hindustan at the head of the grand army of the Deccan ; but Zulfikar—who was the actual general-in-chief—disapproved of this clutch at the crown, being well aware that it was intended by the late Emperor that it should devolve on Shah Àlam. The latter came down from Kábul with the armies of the north, and took possession of Delhi and Agra, where he found the remains of the once vast accumulations of his grandfather, Sháh Jahán. In June, 1707, the armies met a few miles south of Agra ; Zulfikár led for the Pretender, the army of the north was commanded by Munáim Khán. The former was beaten ; perhaps his heart was not in the cause. Àzam and his son fell in the fight, and Zulfikar retired on Gwalior. Next day the victor assumed the Empire, under the title of Bahádur Sháh. Zulfikar was pardoned, and made paymaster-general, a post which implied the supreme headship of the military department. Munaim was created Khán Khánán, and put in charge of the ministry of the interior. Lastly, the Mahratta Rája, Sáhu, who had been already set at liberty, was allowed to assume the government at Poona, where he made preparations for opposition to Tára Bái. Sáhu's long residence at the Mughal headquarters had, however, tamed him. His first public act was to pay a visit of honour to the tomb of Àlamgir, and the rest of his active life was marked by a policy of acquiescence and civilisation. Zulfikar was titular Viceroy of the Muslim Deccan ; his lieutenant, a Pathán officer named Dáud Khán, made peace with Sáhu's government on the basis of a payment of twenty-five per cent. of the revenues. An attempt made by Sultan Kámbaksh to disturb the settlement of the Deccan ended in the defeat and death of that prince, and the Emperor's government was left free to deal with the Rajputs and other Hindu malcontents. The Emperor showed a spirit of conciliation; his mother was a Hindu*, and his own disposition was mild and humane. But the *Jaziya* was not taken off, and so the Hindus were at best but half-conciliated. The son and successor of Rája Jaswant Sinh held aloof at Jodhpur. Jai Sinh II. expelled the imperial officers from his state of Jaipur—as the Rájaship of Ambér was now called, after his new city of that name—and new forms of alienation were showing themselves nearer the capital, suggested by Rajput disaffection. The Játs, a tribe whose misbehaviour in the past reign has been already noticed, set up a chief of their own, and began an independent existence at Bhurtpore; and their kindred in Sirhind were beginning the course of ambition and fanaticism which were hereafter to distinguish the Sikh confederation in the Punjab. An eclectic theism, founded in Bengal by Kabir in the early part of the fifteenth century, had been taken up in the Punjab by a teacher named Nának. "Sikhs," *i.e.*, disciples, were to be regarded as equals without respect of caste; the *Veda* and the *Koran* were to be looked on as of equally divine authority, and a social reform was aimed at. Whether or no the Satnámis of 1670 were of this fraternity cannot be determined, that short-lived movement having been quenched in the blood of its supporters: but in 1709 it was repeated by the Sikhs, and in the same neighbourhood. Conciliating the Rajputs by timely concession, the Emperor sent an army against the Sikhs, under Muniám Khan, who returned successful, but only to die in 1711.† The Emperor moved up to Láhore, where he died in the following year (Feb. 28th, 1712), after a short but not unsuccessful reign, His eldest son tried to assume the succession; but in the general confusion he was unable to secure the person of Zulfikar, the paymaster, whom he desired to master as a hostage

---

* Said by Blochmann to have been daughter to the Rája of Kashmir.
† For an original account of the rise of Sikhism see an article by Mr. F. Pincott, in Hughes's "Dictionary of Islam," London, 1885.

for the loyalty of the army. The paymaster, decamping from Delhi, brought matters to a crisis. In a battle fought in the Punjab about the end of May, the elder sons of the late Emperor were defeated and killed. Zulfikar then began the plan, hereafter to prove so pernicious, of setting up a puppet Emperor, in whose name he might exercise the real authority; the title adopted by this prince was Jahándár Shah.*

The short reign of this and the succeeding Emperor, Farukh Siyar, are notable for accelerated demoralisation and decay; the princes themselves were nullities, who were treated as tools by the able but unscrupulous adventurers who used them and then flung them away. Zulfikar Khán was slain in the palace revolution, which proved fatal to his puppet Jahándár. In the reign of Fárukh Siyar the last of Álamgir's school of officers appeared in Mir Kamr-ud-din, son of the Turkmán minister, Firuz Jang, destined to distinction under the titles of Chin Kilich Khán, as a soldier; Asaf Jáh, as a statesman; finally, as founder of a dynasty, Nizám-ul-mulk.† Another outbreak of the Sikhs happened it 1716; it was suppressed with a severity proportioned to the difficulty attending its suppression. This was under Farukh Siyar, whose government was carried on by two noblemen of the Sáyyid tribe; Shias in creed, and much opposed by Asaf Jáh, and others of the Turkmán faction. Much suffering was endured by the people, heavily taxed by their own rulers, yet not protected against the Mahrattas, who often took whatever the imperial officials had left. Nor was there any consolation in any of the uses to which the

---

* *Jahan* is Persian for "world," and *Alam* Arabic for the same: from the death of Akbar all but two or three of his successors used one or other, in spite of the omen of the Sáyyid dynasty in 1450 (v. CHAPTER. v.).

† Under this latter title his dynasty still bears rule in the Deccan, under the new empire of Hindustan. The territory of the Nizám is nearly as large as the kingdom of Spain.

money was applied. "Muslims and Hindus," says a chronicler of the time, "united in prayers for the downfall of the government"; an unprecedented sort of fusion! In 1717 all the western provinces were under Hindu rule, except Málwa and the small parts of the coast occupied by the English and Portuguese. The people were helpless, and dependent for the simplest elements of life on the caprices of any chief or adventurer who was strong enough to hold power. The Emperor Farukh was put to death at Delhi 16th May, 1719. After two other attempts to make puppet kings, which were frustrated by their premature deaths, the Sáyyids at last hoped to find a more competent creature in Sultan Raashan Akhtar, grandson to Bahádur Sháh, who ascended the peacock throne towards the end of 1716, the last of the house of Taimur by whom that perilous seat was ever to be occupied. He took the title of Muhamad Sháh, and the early part of his reign was a kind of pause in the downward course of the Empire. "During his reign," says a Muslim writer of only a few years later, "the people enjoyed much tranquility; the Government being still respected, the honour of the state maintained, and the majesty of the throne preserved." The Mahrattas were pacified by an acknowledgment of their claim to blackmail, and were, further, vested with the independent sovereignty of the whole country from Poona to Kolhápur. The power of the Sáyyids was broken for ever, one being assassinated by an agent of the Turkmán party; the other, confronted in battle and defeated, was imprisoned for life. The head of the immigrant nobility —the Turkmán Asaf Jáh, or Chin Killich Khán—went to the Deccan and founded the Haidarabad State, which was to form a permanent barrier against Mahratta extension to the southward; he is henceforth known by the title anglicised as "The Nizám of the Deccan." He did not claim independence all at once; but having conquered the Deccan from various members of the opposite party, identified himself with those who were supporting the Emperor, and was made Grand Vazir at Delhi, the Deccan province being administered by his son. Hence arose a division, which lasted for many years, between the court-party and the country-party; the parties (as they were commonly called) of "Turán" and "Irán." The former were mostly Sunnis, of Turkmán origin, the latter either Persian Shias, or of the old Pathán stock.*

In 1724, however, the old minister departed from court, finding there an incurable levity and want of earnestness. His nephew, Kamr-ud-din Khán, succeeded him as Vazir, but the real power was exercised by Abdul Samad, the paymaster-general. Miserable was the condition of this new principality, wasted by war and neglected by those who ought to have been its protectors. But the presence of an able ruler soon effected a change. Kháfi, whose narrative ceases at this point, tells us, almost with his last words, that the cries of the desolate and oppressed had been heard in heaven; and, under the shadow of the Nizám, the Deccan was recovering her old prosperity.

The events of the next seven years are of no historical importance. The Emperor abandoned himself to a life of pleasure, though loving more the pleasures of the field than usual with self-indulgent princes. Still, all duties were ignored, disorders multiplied, officials of all sorts "stretching out the hand of rapacity and extortion upon the weaker tributaries and the wretched subjects." In the Deccan affairs were soon in a better state. Travel and traffic became safe, and the people were spared the burden of a double set of tax-gatherers. The Nizám himself could not relieve them from the *chaut*, or blackmail to the Mahrattas. But he could, and did, arrange that it should be paid to his officials in a lump with the revenue, he then accounting with the Mahratta government.

---

* The Sunnis claim to be the orthodox in Islám, clinging to the authority of tradition. The Shias regard the khalifate as hereditary in the line of Ali.

DECLINE OF THE EMPIRE.

The example of the Nizàm, so far as it involved emancipation from central control—now began to be largely followed. Churáman, chief of the Játs, held sway at Bhurtpore. Jai Sinh II. was pursuing art and science* at Jaipur; Saádal Khán, a Persian Shia, who was the head of the Irán party, had been relegated to a honourable banishment from court as Viceroy of Audh, and was founding a principality and dynasty at Lucknow; Málwa was given to a Hindu officer named Girdhar Rai, who hoped for support from his Rajput neighbours of Méwar and Márwar. Afghan adventurers were assuming power in what is now called, from one of their tribes, by the familiar name of Rohilkhand. A Brahman convert, calling himself Murshid Kuli Khán, had founded a short-lived dynasty at Maksudábád, afterwards named, after him, Murshidábád, and from this new capital ruled over Bengal, Orissa, and Bihar, an occasional gift being sent to Delhi as a symbol of feudal submission.

In 1732 the Mahrattas invaded Hindustan, and got as far as Agra. Having dislodged the Viceroy of Málwa, they partitioned that province between two of their chiefs, while the Peshwa—president of the council—received a patent as Viceroy from the imperial chancery at Delhi. This post of Peshwa was held by a Brahman named Báji Rao, who had practically set aside all superior authority, as well that of the Emperor, as that of his own native chief, the head of the house Siváji. The two great Viceroys, heads of the two great parties, the Shia Saádat and the Sunni Nizám, however, combined their forces for the defence of Islám, on which the Mahrattas retired beyond the Chambal, retaining all their conquests south of that river, including Gwalior, Ujain, and Mándu. The final treaty was signed 11th Feb., 1738, when a still greater peril was overhanging the moribund empire.

This was the invasion of Hindustan by Nádir Sháh, the

---

* He was an accomplished and ardent astronomer.

Turkmán who had usurped the throne of Persia. After an ineffectual, perhaps insincere, attempt to drive them off, the government admitted the Persians into the capital, 19th March. The Nizám, hastily recalled from the south, had been made dictator, under the title of "Vice-gerent"; but he was unable to offer any valid opposition. The old troublous time of the Mughals of Taimur seemed to have returned. On a sudden quarrel, between some of his soldiers and the townspeople, the Persian leader loosed the dogs of war upon the defenceless citizens, 120,000 of whom are said to have perished in the massacre. Then began an orderly and businesslike levy of composition. The peacock throne was stripped of its jewels: and, including the money indemnity, it was estimated that when Nádir and his followers returned to Persia they took with them plunder to the value of £142,000,000. They marched out of Delhi 14th May in good order and discipline, but leaving behind them elements of physical and moral ruin, which had hardly ceased to operate a century later in Hindustan.

It will have been observed that amongst all the disturbance and disasters of the last two generations the Mahratta power had never ceased to prosper. The strange nationality which had grown out of the ruins of Bijápur had a sap of youth rising from a tap-root deep in the traditions of the past. Like the old Hindu society, it was divided into four classes. The Brahmans contributed astuteness and business habits, while the military class, affecting Rajput descent, formed a militia always embodied; the agriculturists were called *Kunbis*, and formed a backbone of welfare as well as a reserve for defence. Lastly came a general multitude of artizans and labourers known as *Shankarjáti*, representing the fruit of mixed marriages. The king was thus regarded in the old light of a military leader, requiring Brahman guidance in affairs of state. The indolent Sáhu had been, for some years, content to carry this doctrine so far that the civil administration passed out of his hands into

DECLINE OF THE EMPIRE.

that of his cabinet or executive council, whose president was called *Peshwa*. Báji Rao, who succeeded to this post in 1720, by his foresight and ability absorbed all power in his own hands. While retaining the twofold organisation of the cavalry derived from the quasi-feudal arrangements of the defunct state of Bijápur, he reduced that force to something like the due place that it ought to hold, and established a quota of infantry which, with a proper complement of artillery, gave strength and regularity to the army. But his civil skill was perhaps inferior to his talent for military administration, or else the territory now subject to the Mahrattas was too extensive to be kept together under their system. Thus began a sub-division of the country into confederated states; but under the general presidency of the Peshwa at Poona. In 1732 the Gaikwár family became masters of Baroda, and by degrees of most of the remainder of Gujarát. About the same time the house of Holkar made its fief hereditary in southern Málwa, while that of Sindhia did the like in northern Málwa and the Gwalior country, almost up to the Chambal river. In Berár and part of the "Central Province" of our day, a similar state was founded by Rághuji Bhonsla, who carried his predatory expeditions into Orissa and Bengal.

In those provinces a quarrel had taken place among the Mughals, which, in 1740, led to the subversion of the family of Murshid Kuli and the substitution of an able Turkmán called Alá-Vardi. In 1742-51 the Berár Mahrattas repeatedly raided Bengal and reduced this Nawáb to agree to pay *chaut*, but the English factory at Calcutta escaped their ravages. It was under the panic so caused that the works of Fort William were protected with the "Mahratta ditch," never completed.

Meanwhile the encroachments of the Mahrattas to the south were impeded by the continued exertions of the Nizám. After the departure of the Persians indeed he remained some time at Delhi, in the exercise of dictatorial power; but towards the end of 1741 he once more turned his face southward, leaving the control of the Government to his eldest son, Gházi-ud-din, while he himself resumed the charge of the Deccan. About this time Báji Rao died, leaving the post of Peshwa to his son, Báláji.

In 1743 died Rája Jai Sinh II., the founder of Jaipur. He was succeeded peacefully by his son, Ishri Sinh. Saádat, the Persian died while his countrymen were at Delhi. He also, was succeeded by his son, Mansur Ali, who is known by the title of "Safdar Jang."* The Deccan was not only becoming an independent principality in the south, but was budding into minor dependencies, of which the most important was that of the Carnatic, held by a vassal called "The Náwab of Arcot:" in 1744-9 the post was held by Anwár-ud-din. In the North there was yet another Muslim state arising, in the Trans-Gangetic province of Katahr. Here a Pathán adventurer chief of the Rohilla Afgháns, had adopted a Ját lad, whom he made a Muslim under the name of Ali Muhamad. On the death of his adoptive father the young convert was received by the Rohilla clan as their leader, but in 1745 he was attacked and made prisoner by Safdar Jang, the Viceroy of Audh. Being soon after released he established himself as an independent prince at Anwala (Aoula), sixteen miles south-west of Bareilly.

While India was thus decomposing, the neighbouring countries were undergoing revolutions of which her inhabitants were doomed to feel the evil effects. In May, 1747, Nádir perished by the hands of his followers; and his Empire broke up, the southern portion—the old Gur and Ghzni—falling into the power of an Afghán chief who had seized Kandahar. This chief was originally known as Ahmad Abdáli, but he now

---

* The words mean "piercer of battle lines," and recall the supposed igin of the old French house of Talleyrand ("Taillez les rangs.")

assumed the title of Ahmad Sháh, Daurání.* In 1748, having made himself master of Kabul, he invaded the Punjab by way of Pesháwar, and marched on Delhi. For once, however, the defence was too strong for the attack. The Mughal army moved out under Sultan Ahmad, the Emperor's son, the actual generals being Safdar Jang, and the Turkmán paymaster-general; the rival parties having coalesced under the common sense of a common danger. On the 11th March an action took place in which the army of Hindustan, under the nominal command of the crown prince, was so far successful, that the invaders were glad to retire with the booty they had collected, and Delhi was saved from another sack. But the paymaster-general had been killed by a round shot; and when the news arrived at the capital the Emperor Muhamad Sháh fell from the judgment seat in a fit. He died on, or about, 16th April, 1748.

The old Nizám did not long survive him, dying at Burhánpur at a very advanced age, 19 June of the same year.† He was at first succeeded by his second son; but the wars of the succession in the Deccan must be related in a later page. We must here turn to consider another part of the old Yádava kingdom of the Deccan, which was soon to assume great importance, and to preserve it nearly till the end of the century. We have seen how the kingdom of the Hoysala Ballálas was disturbed and destroyed, and how the succeeding kingdom of Bijainagar was in turn subverted in 1565. The next Hindu principality was founded more to the South, and farther from the new Muslim's states, by one of the Paligárs, who established

---

* *Dauran* = "cycle" or "age," and the title was assumed by the Abdális out of tribal pride. They are the leading tribe of the Afgháns, now divided into several branches.

† According to Elphinstone, he died at Arcot, aged 77. There is reason for believing him to have been nearer 100; he had been in the army during Alamgir's Deccan wars.

himself at Seringapatam in 1610. His descendant, Chikka Deva (1672-1704) changed the religion of the state—which had been a form of phallic worship—and embraced the faith and ritual of Vishnu. He fought the Mahrattas with success, and reformed the system of land-holding. At his death the state extended from Bangalore on the north, to Coimbatore on the south, and yielded a revenue nearly equivalent to a million of modern money. The direct line failed under his weak grandson Dodda Krishna, and on his death a collateral named Cháma was made Rája, with whom ended the old line of Udaiyars. A period of anarchy ensued, another distant kinsman became Rája, in whose time came into notice the famous adventurer Haidar Ali, destined to make the state so prominent in later history. This famous soldier of fortune was originally an officer of police, who was born at Budikot, in the Mysore territory, in 1722. The son of a humble *employé* Haidar "Naik," as he was originally called, on the decline of the Udaiyar dynasty had risen by his abilities to the highest offices of the State. Some account of his further progress will be found later on. It will be sufficient to note here that it was at the period of which we are now treating that he first signalised himself by courage and intelligence, and obtained his first promotion.

But a new foreign element was now forcing itself into Indian politics, which it was destined to revolutionise. It has been mentioned already that the English factory on the eastern (Coromandel) coast had been transferred to Madras in 1639; about the same time that the company had obtained the settlement at Hugli, afterwards taken down the river to Calcutta, where it became known as Fort William, about 1690. These establishments were an object of jealousy to the East Indian Company of France, amalgamated out of rival undertakings in 1719. Their chief station was at Pondicherry, a place destined to a short but eventful distinction. Situated about 80 miles south of Madras, it resembled that place in having no harbour but only an open roadstead ; nevertheless, the climate was healthy, and though only founded in 1674, it soon became a strongly-fortified town with 40,000 inhabitants. In 1740 M. Dumas was Governor-General, and in the course of a successful resistance to an attack by the Mahrattas, hit upon the expedient, pregnant with future consequences, of equipping and disciplining native troops after the European method. These men were originally known as *gardes*, or "Gárdis ;" to the present day the Hindustani term is *Telinga*, a name clearly indicating the origin of the system. In English books of former days such soldiers are always called "Sepoys," a corruption of the Persian word *Sipáhi*, from *sipáh*="army."* These preparations soon came into use on a wider scale. About two years later came the fall of Sir R. Walpole, and the end of his policy of peace in England ; George II. went to war in defence of the Pragmatic Sanction ; and the French of Pondicherry presently found the opportunity to strike at their rivals on the coast. Their station was to windward of Madras during the southwest monsoon, and lay convenient for ships from the islands of Bourbon and Mauritius ; in 1744 the first-named settlement was under the successor of Dumas, the latter were ruled by an able officer of the French Royal Navy, Bertrand de la Bourdonnais.

The successor of Dumas, at Pondicherry, was a man still more able and ambitious, Joseph Dupleix. The governor of the English settlement was Mr. Morse, a mercantile man, perhaps ambitious, certainly not able. To an application from Dupleix, that the hostilities of their respective nations should not be allowed to extend to India, Morse turned a deaf ear.

---

* Compare the French "Spahi." The word "Sepoy" is so familiar to English readers as to make it seem preferable in these pages also : subject to the explanation in the text.

Dupleix, probably neither surprised nor disappointed, hurried on the repair of his fortifications, and invoked the protection of the Nawab Anwar-ud-din, both settlements being in the lieutenantcy of that officer.

The Nawáb was pleased to favour the application, and intimated to Morse that he must abstain from hostile movements. But in June, 1746, a French fleet under la Bourdonnais, appeared off the coast, beat off the British squadron, and anchored in the roads of Pondicherry: orders from the Nawábs were nearly at an end for Europeans.

Could Dupleix have kept on good terms with the Admiral, and could the frivolous government of Louis XV. have seen its way to supporting its Indian agents, the whole subsequent history of India might have been altered. At first all seemed to promise well for the French; La Bourdonnais laid siege to Fort S. George, at Madras, on the 14th Sept., 1746, and Morse surrendered a week later. After some dispute the place was made over to d'Espremesnil a member of Dupleix's council, and the Admiral went home and disappeared from the Indian scene. The Nawáb now affected indignation, and attacked d'Espremesnil in force, but was repulsed at the famous action of S. Thomé, which first showed Europeans what they could do against Asiatics.* An attack of the French on Negapatam was defeated, but a counter-attack on Pondicherry, in 1748, was gallantry repulsed, though the British fleet was commanded by Boscawen, and the land force by Stringer Lawrence. Early in the following year news arrived in India that a general peace had been concluded at Aix-la-Chapelle, 17th Oct., 1748. Up to this time the balance of success and prestige was evidently in favour of the French. Madras had to be restored under the treaty; but Dupleix stood prepared for eventualities, and might confidently reckon on the support of the Mughal powers in the Deccan and Carnatic.

* See Bernier's anticipations of 100 years earlier, in chap. xii.

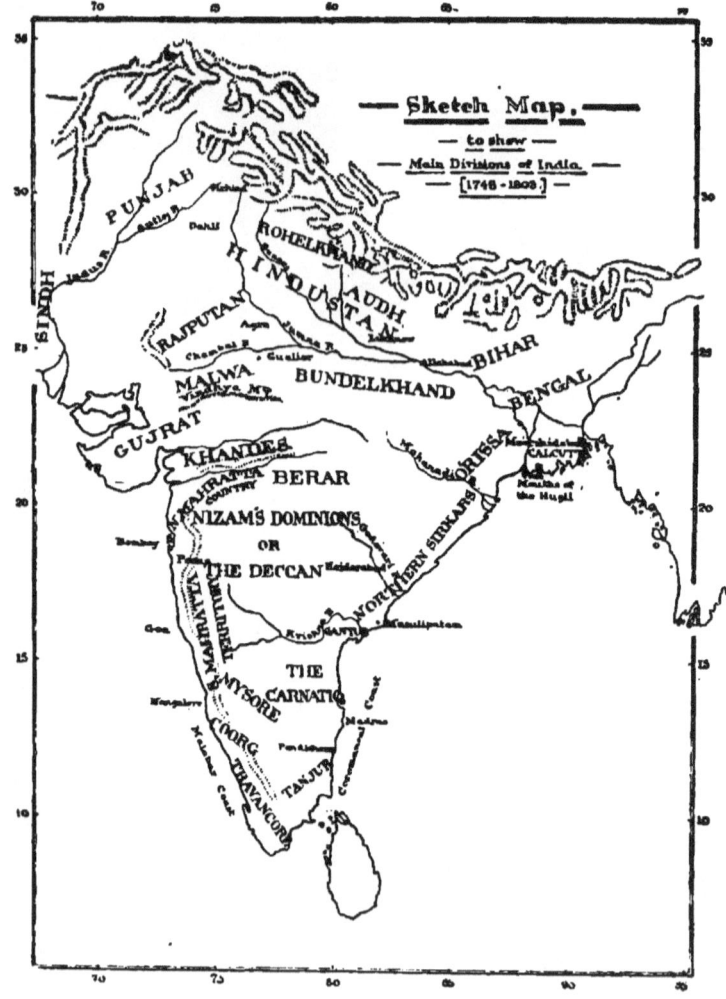

For the above section may be consulted the books already cited, also :—"History of the Mahrattas," Jas. Grant Duff, 1826; "Memoir of Central India," Sir J. Malcolm, 1820; the "Siyar-ul-mutákharin" (Eng. Trans.), Calcutta, 17—: and Col. Malleson's works : *e.g.*, "Decisive Battles of India," London, 1883 ; "History of the French in India," 1863, etc.

SECTION 3.—The narrative has now been brought up to the moment after the deaths of Muhamad Shâh and his great minister, the Nizâm of Haidarábad. In the remaining pages of the present volume we shall find the interest almost wholly diverted from Hindustan, and centred in the Deccan and Bengal. The dismantled throne of Delhi was filled by Ahmad Shâh, while the succession to the old Nizâm was fiercely disputed in the southern region. The eldest son of the deceased ruler had been for some time Vazir of the Empire at Delhi; the second —Násir Jang—was at Haidarabad, where he at once assumed the government, and obtained the support of the army; but a grandson, who was called Muzafar Jang, alleged himself to be entitled to the succession under his grandfather's will. Násir was murdered in 1750, and Muzafar became Nizâm of the Deccan, with support from the French, whose military force in the Deccan presently came under the command of a famous officer, the Marquis de Bussy. In the Carnatic a similar movement took place, Dupleix having put forward a candidate for the succession to Anwar-ud-din, who had died in 1749.

The governor of Pondicherry was thus assuming the position of arbiter—almost lord-paramount—over southern India. The British at Madras were naturally unprepared to concede the assumption : unwilling to allow the influence of their neighbours to become supreme, they adopted the cause of rival candidates, both at Arcot, the capital of the Carnatic, and at the court of the Deccan. The name of the French candidate for the Carnatic was Chanda Sahib, while the English supported the claims of Muhamad Ali. At first, however, the latter were quite overmatched. In the beginning of 1751, both the French candidates were in possession; Chanda in the Carnatic, Muzafar in the suzerain province. But, in the very hour of success, Muzafar was killed in a scuffle with some rebels, and Bussy had to bring forward a younger son of the old Nizám; his name was Salábat Jang. This prince punished the chiefs of the rebels, and assumed the post of Nizám in the middle of the year, after making over large accessions of territory to the French.

At this moment—July, 1751—the power of the governor of Pondicherry, or his influence, appeared secure through all the southern region. His nominee was ruler of the Deccan, the Nawáb of the Carnatic was his creature. The English candidate was surrounded at Trichinopoli, with no native ally but the petty Hindu state of Tanjore; and the government of Madras cowered supine in Fort S. David. The knowledge that the nations which they represented were at peace, their own purely commercial views, and their apparent lack of any commanding man of experience and capacity, were combined to cause their inactivity. Their whole forces, with the exception of about 300 British troops, were hemmed in with Muhamad Ali, by a vastly superior French force. The Peshwa, invading the Deccan in the middle of the year, was defeated by Bussy, and driven back on Poona.

It was at this juncture that the balance was suddenly turned by the appearance on the scene of an untried and untrained man, who turned out to have in his head and hand the whole destinies of India. This was Robert Clive, a member of the British Company's Civil Service, and at that moment commissary of the army. Repairing to the governor at Fort S. David, where the Presidency then was, he obtained permission to affect a diversion by marching against Arcot. Arriving before the walls on 30th Aug., he had only two hundred white troops, with eight officers—four of whom were civilians like himself—and three hundred native troops, with eight field guns; but the enemy decamped, and the British took possession of the town and fort. Following this success Clive defeated the French in two battles, and then proceeded, under Major Lawrence, to the relief of Muhamad Ali and the Rája of Tanjore in Trichinopoli. After some more fighting, the tables were turned on the French army, which was surrounded and forced to surrender, 13th June, 1752. Chanda Sahib fell into the hands of the Tanjore general, by whom he was put to death; and the British client, Muhamad Ali, became Nawáb of the Carnatic. The actual "coast," from Madras to Tanjore, with the exception of Pondicherry itself, now began to come under British influence: but the French were all-powerful at Haidarabad and Aurangabad, and had actual possession of the territory and town of Masulipatam, the sea-port, together with the country up to Cattack. Desultory fighting went on for some time, during which the fact that there was a treaty of peace between France and England barely availed to keep the Indian representatives of those nations from attacking each other's Presidency towns. But the French Company was growing weary of a contest which did no good to their dividends; and the royal government was unwilling to bear the constant strain of supplying troops and munitions of war. Thus the very grandeur of his views contained the germ of failure for Dupleix. The British were more sober, with shorter views, and so more secure of support from home. There was great ability in Dupleix, and he was often well-served—Bussy, in particular, was devoted to him—but Clive and Saunders were moderate men, content to do their day's work and leave future work to the future. Dupleix was superseded in 1754 by a new president sent out from home: this officer stopped hostilities by giving up all French acquisitions, leaving the French Company nothing but the treaty.ports on the coast.*

Bussy, however, remained with the Nizám. His presence, awing the Mahrattas, kept the Deccan fairly peaceful. For a moment that tranquility was threatened, if not disturbed, by the appearance of a most formidable competitor for the succession, in the person of Ghází-ud-din, the eldest son of the old Nizám. Advancing from Delhi; with Mahratta support, he actually got as far as Aurangabad, and a general war appeared at hand, in which Salábat and his French friends might have found it hard work to contend against the united resources of Mughals and Mahrattas. The knot was cut by fate; for Ghází died a natural death at Aurangabad in October, 1752. During these events the Bhonsla of Berar had made himself master of Orissa, while the houses of Holkar and Sindhia had completed their partition of Málwa. The army of the Gaekwar, aided by the Peshwa, had completely subverted the Mughal government in Gujarát; and the imperial government at the same time lost Rohilkhand to the Rohillas, and the Punjab to the Afgháns, while the Bangash of Farukhabad ruled nearly up to Agra. Thus the "Empire of the World" was left with no territory but the *Khálsa*, or immediate dependency, of the capital, as will be more fully shown presently.

Meanwhile the mercantile community of Calcutta was carrying on an unostentatious commercial career. The "Ghát" of "Káli" had given the name to a village on the riverside as far back a the early Muslim epoch, at least; the name occurring in Akbar's Domesday Book. When Job Charnock first came there from Hugli, the ground was covered with swampy forest,

* The dissatisfaction of the French authorities was accounted for by Dupleix having deceived them as to the state of his finances. The British government also remonstrated against being made to fight in times of peace.

infested by wild beasts, and reeking with malaria.* The first town of Calcutta clustered round the original Fort William, the site of which was abandoned after the events of 1757 to be related presently. The place had the advantage of a good anchorage for ships, which in those days were of comparatively small burden and light draft; and the old fort, completed at the time of the Bhonsla scare, was guarded on the eastern side by the river, as it would have been elsewhere had the "Ditch" been completed. In this insanitary situation, partly below the level of the sea, and surrounded more and more by filthy native villages, the Calcutta "factors" and "writers" pursued a hazardous, but often lucrative, calling. They were, for the most part, agents of the "United Company of Merchants trading to the East Indies," incorporated—as their motto ran —"*auspicio Regis et senatus Angliæ*," the act having been passed before the Scottish Union. The Company's business consisting in sending to India consignments of hardware and woollen goods, with bullion and other metals; through their agents there the return cargoes were made up of a number of eastern products: tea from China; spices from the Straits; the silks of Bhágalpur; the muslins of Eastern Bengal; and other "country produce." Could this state of things be made enduring by clear and lasting agreement with the native rulers, Calcutta might have been to India what Hong-Kong is to China, a prosperous treaty-port. Fortunately for the future fortunes of India, the primal hypothesis could not be realised: Calcutta could not be, permanently, a treaty-port, because there was no native government capable of permanently observing a treaty.

The three villages of Sutanati, Kalighát, and Gobindpur, which form the site of the present Calcutta, had been conveyed to the Company by valid patents of Àlamgir. These rights

* As late as Warren Hastings' days tigers were shot near the site of the present cathedral.—"Imperial Gazette of India," III. 247.

were confirmed, with a trading charter in addition, by the Sáyyid Ministry of 1717. But the Nawáb of that day—Murshid Kuli—contrived, in the decrepitude of the central government, to embarrass and annoy the Factory. It was not until 1742 that the Factors obtained permission from his successor, Ala Wirdi, to enclose their little territory, a semi-circle of seven miles from Chitpur on the north, to the southern boundary of the *maidán* toward Alipur. In 1752 the population was estimated at over 400,000 souls, and though such an estimate has been deemed excessive, it is certain that the prospect of gain and of protection must have tended to attract many of the inhabitants of the surrounding country, threatened by marauders, and fleeced by the officials of the Nawáb.

At length the crisis came. Alá Wirdi died in 1756, and his grandson, who succeeded, was a weak and inexperienced young man of somewhat violent temper, who assumed the title of Siráj-ud-daula. He picked a quarrel with the factors under pretence of their fortifying Calcutta against an attack which they professed to apprehend from the French of Chandernagore. His real motive was, perhaps, a dread of the consequences to his province of a repetition there of such events as had recently happened in the Carnatic: perhaps also he had exaggerated hopes of plunder from a prosperous Factory. On hearing of his hostile intentions, the Factors sent to their French and Dutch neighbours—of Chinsura and Chandernagore—to invite assistance, and prayed for succour from Fort S. George, whither the Madras Presidency had now returned. But it was in vain. Before any help could have arrived, on the 16th June, 1756, the Nawáb attacked the walls, defended only by 250 white soldiers, about as many armed citizens, and about 1,500 native matchlockmen. Drake, the President, with others of his council, took refuge on board the ships in the river, and dropped down the stream, leaving the defence to a brave civilian, named Holwell. The place was taken on the 20th, and the remaining Europeans, 146 in number, were driven at the bayonet's point into a cell in the Fort, where they had to pass the June night, without water, in a space of 20ft. square, with two small windows. The Acting-Governor, Mr. Holwell survived with some score of others, who were sent in captivity to Murshidabad; and Calcutta was given up to plunder.

When the sad news of this disaster reached Madras, the people of that Factory were in trouble of their own, in which they had been hoping for help from Bengal. The truce between them and the successors of Dupleix at Pondicherry was at first observed, but the British authorities, espousing the quarrel of the Nawáb, made war upon Mysore; and a force from Bombay, under Clive, who had lately returned from Europe, took part with the army of the Peshwa in a successful attack upon the pirates of the Malabar coast. Clive then proceeded to Madras, where difficulties with Bussy and his Nizám were fast arising. In the beginning of 1755 the latter had gone to war with Mysore, whose Rája was friendly to the French, and hostile—as we have just seen—to the British of Madras. Bussy unwillingly obeyed the command of the Nizám to join in the campaign; and the Mahrattas making claims on Mysore at the same time; in the end the Dalwai (or minister) of that State accepted Bussy's friendly mediation, and bought off the Nizám's attack. The Peshwa, being satisfied with some plunder and a share of the indemnity, was persuaded to withdraw his troops. These proceedings, however, and some other conduct of not quite acceptable kind in regard to the Nawáb of Savanore, gave umbrage to the Nizám, and encouraged the enemies of Bussy in the Durbar. The Peshwa was glad to join in the intrigue, perhaps hoping that if driven out of the Nizám's service the French officer and his followers might be willing to enter the Mahratta service. The end was that Bussy was ordered to leave the Deccan: he immediately obeyed;

but his march down the valley of the Krishna was much harassed by Mahratta horse; and he finally resolved on the bold step of turning back, establishing himself at Haidarabad, and awaiting the turn of events there. Being reinforced by Law, with a considerable column, and aided by two Mahratta chiefs whom he had succeeded in winning to his side, Bussy ultimately extricated himself from all difficulties. The Nawáb sought a reconciliation with him on the 15th August, 1756: his power seemed greater than ever; the British feared a revival of Dupleix.

It was at this moment that they heard of the crisis in Bengal (5th August). They were in the very act of sending an expedition to the Deccan to counteract Bussy, having an understanding with one of his principal opponents — the Nawáb Jáfir Ali; but their whole army was no more than 12,000 strong, of whom 2,000 only were British soldiers. War with France was known to be impending, and the French of Pondicherry were in daily expectation of reinforcements. Finally, it was determined, in council at Fort S. George, that everything must give way to the paramount duty of retrieving the disgrace and disaster of the British name and nation; a force of 900 Europeans and 1,500 Sepoys was got ready to go to Bengal in the ships of Admiral Watson's squadron; the command of the land forces was given to Clive, now a colonel in the army. The fleet sailed on the 10th October; and, after considerable difficulty, made its way up to Falta, about half-way from the mouth of the river, where they found the refugees from Calcutta, or those who had survived the exposure, encamped under Drake and Major Kilpatrick, in the ruins of an old Dutch factory. Amongst the number was a civil officer named Warren Hastings.

After the sack of Calcutta, the Nawáb had returned to Murshidabad, leaving his army in the field, under command of a kinsman, called Mir Jáfir; a Hindu named Mának Chand being governor of Calcutta, which he had done something to strengthen for purposes of defence. After receiving communications from the Council, to which he paid no heed, the Nawáb was informed that war was declared against him, a declaration which he treated with contempt. The British expedition marched up the river-bank, attended by their ships; and Mának Chand fell back on Hugli, so that Calcutta was re-occupied on 7th January, 1758. Drake was reinstated as President, the command of the land forces being retained by Clive, while Admiral Watson claimed a sort of political control over the general operations.

At this moment arrived news of the declaration of war between France and Great Britain; and the expedition was at once exposed to serious risk. Bussy's advanced post, in Ganjam, was only 200 miles distant; Chandernagore was garrisoned by 600 Europeans with a strong artillery; if the Nawáb could secure French support the task of chastising him might well exceed the means at the disposal of the British; their position in the Carnatic even might be exposed to destruction.

In this conjuncture Clive displayed a prudence which had not been shown, or indeed required, in the earlier stages of his marvellous career. It was no longer a mere question of audacity and tactics, but one demanding high qualities of diplomacy and statesmanship. The task immediately before him was to frustrate the prospect of a junction between Bussy and the Nawáb. The latter was still full of contempt for his enemies; but the mercantile men of Murshidabad were more far-seeing; amongst them being the Seths, the leading firm of bankers there; and a trader of wealth and enterprise named Amin Chand, deeply interested in the commerce of which Calcutta had, before the late troubles, held the key. These men accompanied the army which the Nawáb now led against Clive, and became the medium of his attempts at an accommodation. The Nawáb reached the outskirts of the city in the beginning of February, and took up his quarters at a garden-house, belonging to Amin Chand, within the Mahratta ditch, his army being encamped in the neighbourhood. Alarmed by a night attack, the Nawáb was persuaded to sign a treaty in which he guaranteed to the Company the privileges that had been granted them under a patent of 1717, and promised compensation for the plunder of Calcutta.

Having thus obtained at least a temporary suspension of hostilities with the Nawáb, Clive next proceeded to besiege Chandernagore, being assured that success there afforded the best hope of staving off Bussy's threatened invasion of Bengal. The consent and concurrence of Admiral Watson having been obtained, Chandernagore was attacked, both by land and river, and, after a gallant defence, captured on 23rd March. In these operations Clive had received help from an agent of Amin Chand's, named Nanda Kumar—afterwards notorious in Anglo-Indian annals.

The fall of Chandernagore appeared likely to lead to all the advantages that Clive had hoped. But it was impossible for the Nawáb to act with common judgment or to be faithful to his engagements. He took into his service a party of Frenchmen, who had escaped from Chandernagore under Law, and he continued his invitations to Bussy. He also set on foot an intrenched camp at Plassy, to cover his capital against an advance from the southward. All these things were immediately made known to Clive, through his correspondents at Murshidabad; but Bussy also heard of the fall of the French settlement in Bengal, and obtained sufficient information of the Nawáb's character to make him unwilling to listen to his overtures.

The admiral now attempted a last appeal to the fears of the Nawáb, and, on this failing, it was agreed between him and Clive that advantage should be taken of the general and growing unpopularity of the Nawáb to attempt a revolution at the capital. Mir Jáfir, husband of the Nawáb's aunt and the commander of a division in the army, had offered to aid in the deposition of Siráj-ud-daula; and negotiations were opened with him through Mr. Watts, the British officer resident at the court of Murshidabad. In the midst of this tangle of treason and counter-treason, Amin Chand suddenly proved mutinous, threatening to reveal the whole plot to the Nawáb unless the agreement with Mir Jáfir contained a clause guaranteeing him a sum equivalent to about a million sterling. The news set the council in a ferment; the lives of Watts and his associates, perhaps the whole success of the scheme, depended on Amin Chand's silence; it was determined to secure this by deceit. Two treaties were to be prepared, one on red paper, to be shown to Amin Chand as containing the clause for which he stipulated, the other, on white paper, to be the valid engagement. The Admiral refused to sign the false treaty, and his signature was recorded by another hand.* Both treaties having been signed, in his turn, by Jáfir, Amin Chand came down to Calcutta, and the plot went its course.

While these momentous but questionable operations were proceeding in Bengal, events had been proceeding in other parts of India which proved to have a bearing on the future. The hopes of the Nawáb had been sustained not only by his correspondence with Bussy, but by news from the north-west.

After the departure of Ghází-ud-din from Delhi in the end of 1750, the titular vazirate was in the hands of Safdar Jang, of Lucknow, but the actual office of minister had been undertaken by Ghází's nephew, Mir Shaháb-ud-din, a youth of but sixteen years old, but full of all manner of craft and criminal

* Not "forged," as Macaulay puts it in his "Edinburgh Review" article on Clive. Watson, though unwilling to put his hand to the false treaty, told the others that "they might do as they pleased," which Clive considered sufficient authority.—V. Elphinstone, "Rise of British Power," chap. viii.

audacity. One of his first steps was to procure the assassination of the favourite of the Emperor; this was in 1752, and a violent tumult immediately followed, raised by partizans of the country party, or Iranians, whose head was Safdar Jang. About the end of 1753 the Turanian party triumphed; Safdar Jang was driven from court after long and violent contentions, and the young Turkmán seemed master of the situation. But the Játs, supported by the Mahrattas, under Holkar, continued to trouble his repose; and, discovering that they were secretly supported by the Emperor, the audacious youth seized and deposed the futile monarch, and set on the throne a son of Jahándár Sháh—killed in 1713. He then attempted to carry on the government of the small remains of the Empire in his puppet's name. The new Emperor took the ambitious title of Álamgir II.

The dominions of Babar and Akbar and the first Álamgir were now reduced to a few districts in the immediate neighbourhood of the capital. Rajputána and Gwálior, Malwa and Gujarát, had all ceased to pay tribute; the Játs were independent, under Suraj Mall; the Farukhabád Afgháns held the Central Duáb, their kinsfolk across the Ganges lorded it in Rohilkhand. Audh and Allahabad had been formed into a principality under Safdar Jang; the condition of the eastern provinces we have seen. Elsewhere the Mahrattas were supreme, save where they were kept at bay by the English or the Nizám, or where, in the extreme south, Tanjore, Travancore, and Mysore maintained a precarious independence under native Rájas.. In the Punjab the Afgháns were paramount, though a Turkmán nobleman, named Mir Manu, professed to hold the country as Viceroy of the Emperor. On his death the new Vazir, who had taken the title of his lately-deceased uncle, Gházi-ud-din, attempted to assert his supremacy. In the beginning of 1757, however, Ahmad Abdáli came down, drove the Vazir out, and proceeded to plunder Delhi and the sur-

DECLINE OF THE EMPIRE.

rounding country. The Afghán leader took his departure in November, going into cantonments at Anupshahr, on the upper Ganges, leaving a valiant Pathán, named Najib Khán, in charge of affairs at Delhi.

Some notion of what was going on in these regions may have stimulated the ill-starred Siráj-ud-daula in his tergiversations with Clive. On the side of the Mahrattas, also, he may have entertained hopes. That enterprising community had now been, for some seventeen years, under the presiding rule of Báláji, the heads of the clans of Sindia and Holkar being their most prominent military leaders. From their partitioned fiefs in Málwa these chiefs led their horsemen wherever booty was to be obtained or territory annexed. They took service at Delhi under Gházi; and only awaited the departure of the Abdáli to make a swoop on the Punjab. One of the means adopted by Clive to frighten the Nawáb of Bengal was to inform him that the Peshwa was coming.

At last, the links of the steel net for the Nawáb of Bengal being all forged, the show of friendship was discarded. With a small but well-disciplined force Clive marched on the intrenched camp at Plassy.

[To authorities already cited the student may add Elphinstone's "Rise of British power in the East," London, 1887. Mr. Cotton, Elphinstone's last biographer, agrees with the author's own modest estimate, that he "had no talent for narration." Nevertheless, the book is based on much research among original papers and contemporary writings, and is attractive by reason of its ripe wisdom and elevated tone. All the works of Orme are important,, but scarce and bulky. Some idea of their value may be formed from Mr. Talboys Wheeler's little work, "Orme's Hindustan," Madras, 1862. Information on the siege of Calcutta by Siráj-ud-daula will be found accurately and agreeably conveyed in "Echoes from Old Calcutta," H. E. Busteed, Calcutta, 1882.]

CHAPTER VII.

THE HINDU REVIVAL AND RISE OF BRITISH POWER.

Section 1: The English settlement in Bengal, and the Hindu revival.—Section 2: The restoration of the Empire and decline of the Mahratta Confederacy.—Section 3: State of Hindustan to the first ministry of Sindia, 1784.

SECTION I.—It was the 13th June when Mr. Watts, with three subordinates, reached the camp of Clive at Katwa, having ridden the seventy miles from Murshidabad without halting. A declaration of war was at once sent to the Nawáb, and the latter replied by a letter of defiance and by marching his army to Plassy. It consisted of 15,000 cavalry, 35,000 infantry and over forty heavy guns. To oppose him Clive could only muster 800 Europeans with 2,100 sepoys, and eight field-pieces. If the Nawáb's forces were faithful and fairly led the enterprise looked ill indeed; and Clive was informed that Jáfir had been reconciled to the Nawáb, and that the plot was at an end. If he made one more march, and crossed the river, he would find himself in the presence of an overwhelming enemy. The situation was one to try the strongest nerves. Clive's first thought—unlike him as it sounds—was to write to Calcutta for instructions. He then called a council-of-war, and did not conceal his opinion that the wisest plan would be to encamp where they were and invite the help of native allies; the opinion of the officers was divided. But after the council broke up, Clive passed an hour in solitude, at the end of which he returned to the lines, and ordered an immediate advance.

About midnight of the 22-23rd the little army arrived within earshot of the enemy, and took post in a walled mango-orchard, about a mile beyond the village of Plassy, the Nawáb's army occupying the intrenchment formerly mentioned as having been constructed in the neighbourhood three months before. At eight in the morning the British advanced in line, with the river on their left. They saw on their right three divisions of the enemy, so disposed that unless they prevailed they would be surrounded with their backs to the river. In the centre of Clive's line were the Europeans, and some field-pieces were advanced on his left front. On the enemy's extreme right was a redoubt, guarded by a party of French, next came two divisions and a half, led by officers who, it was thought, might be faithful to the Nawáb; on the left came the division of Mir Jáfir, on whose fidelity no absolute dependence could be placed by either side. If he helped Clive to conquer he would be Nawáb of Bengal in the room of his master; if he thought that, even for such a stake, the game was too hazardous, he might take the British in the rear and complete their ruin. The best hope was that he would abide the event. Accordingly, after a sharp duel of artillery, in which the British were necessarily overmatched, Clive withdrew his men into the shelter of the walled orchard, from whose shelter he once more opened fire from his field-pieces. His idea probably, at that moment, was to wait in the grove till dark, and then make a night attack on the intrenchment. In the course of the forenoon, however, heavy rain fell: the British gunners kept off the effects by aid of tarpaulin, but the enemy's tumbrils were soon soaking. The Nawáb's best general then advanced to storm the position, but the British replied with a fire of grape, which laid him low with many of his men.

On hearing the news the Nawáb mounted a swift dromedary and fled in the direction of his capital, leaving the army to the charge of Mir Jáfir and his colleagues, one at least of whom was favourable to that officer's projects. They at once began a retrograde movement, with the exception of the body immediately under the command of Mir Jáfir, which showed a disposition to approach the British camp; his columns were, however, kept from advancing by the fire of a gun posted for the purpose. On the British left a hot fight now began: stimulated by the example of the handful of French, and ignorant of the ulterior designs of their chiefs, the native troops opened a steady fire upon the advancing line. While opposing them with his best tactics, Clive looked round and saw that Jáfir's division was inactive. It struck him at once that this was a sign of good-will, and that his camp and rear were safe. He at once pushed forward with all his force, dislodged the French, and stormed the intrenchment. The enemy fled in all directions; and though no pursuit was for the moment possible, a victory had been gained, which not only gave the control of immediate conditions, but is usually thought to have founded the British Indian Empire. The cost to the victors was twenty-three killed and forty-nine wounded.

Next morning Mir Jáfir presented himself, in some alarm, to tender his explanations. Clive dispelled all uneasiness by saluting him Nawáb, and the united leaders and their men marched on the capital. The wretched Siráj, attempting to escape, was brought before Jáfir, by whom (or by his son) the fugitive was put to death.

The council now shared with Clive the wages of the help given to the new Nawáb; and Clive assumed the head of the presidency, in which position he was, after some delay, confirmed by orders from home Ere long a new danger arose from the South, whence Clive had derived means for settling Bengal, and to which he was at first unable to return much assistance.

It has been seen that Bussy, though on the whole powerful at Haidarabad, had been deterred from giving help to Siráj-ud-daula in his struggle with Clive, although the declaration of

BATTLE-FIELDS OF THE CARNATIC, 1758—83.

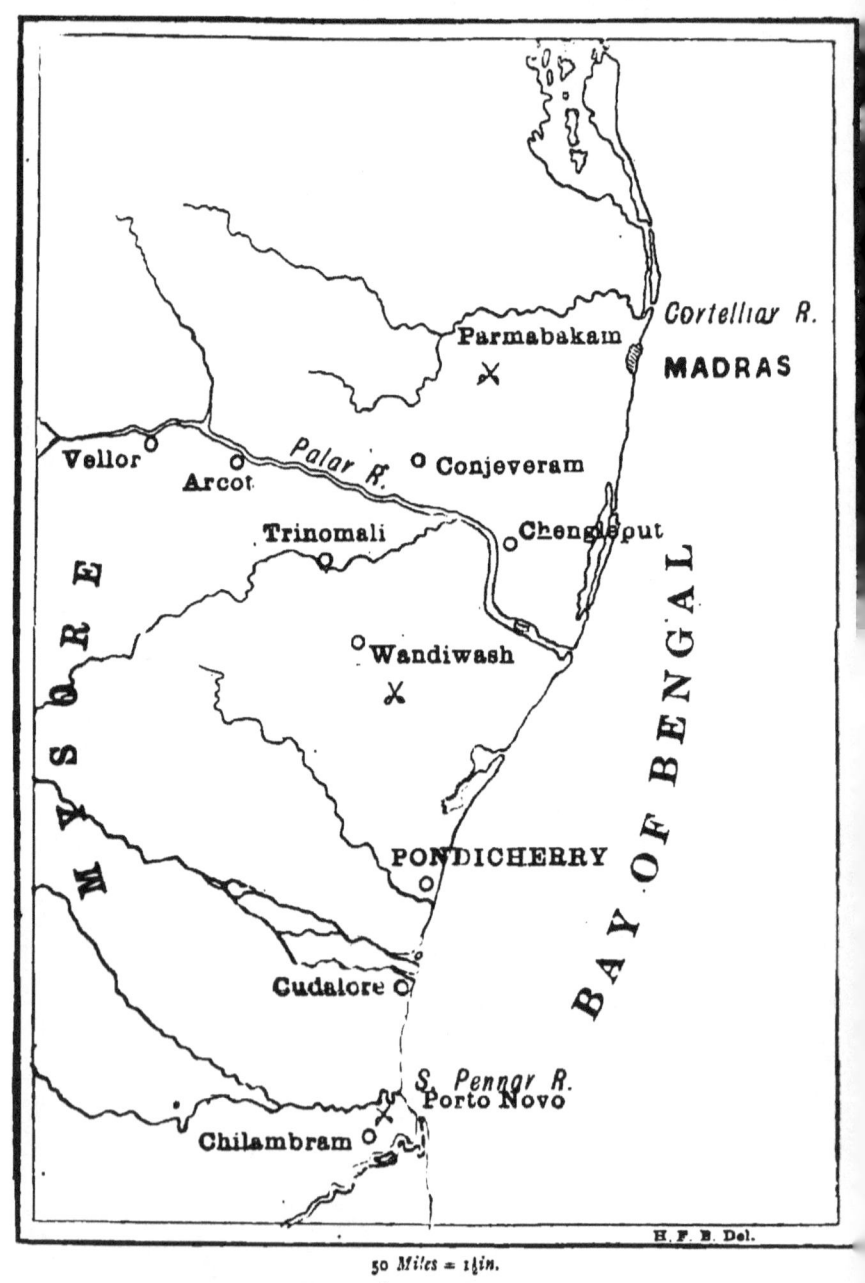

war between France and England, and Clive's attack on Chandernagore would have justified any degree of hostility. Early in 1758 Count Lally had come out from France with strong reinforcements, and had begun to threaten Madras, calling in Bussy's force from the Deccan, and tearing the diplomatic web which had taken so much time and trouble to weave.* Before leaving the Deccan, Bussy took care to place a sufficient force at Masulipatam to guard the "northern Sirkars," as the lately-acquired French province was called that lay between the Krishna and the Máhánadi rivers. Impressed with the necessity of help to his old presidency, Clive—on his own responsibility—sent all the troops that he could possibly spare to distract the attention of the French, weaken their influence in the Deccan, and—if possible—take possession of the "northern Sirkars." Such assistance was inadequate, indeed, to the apprehensions of the Madras Government; but it was more than Clive's colleagues in Bengal had been willing to grant. Owing to the great superiority of the British officer in command—Colonel Forde of the 39th Foot—it proved enough for all its objects.

Lally was an Irish refugee, a man of peculiar character—a loyal, valiant, and experienced soldier, utterly deficient in tact and temper. His lieutenant in the "northern Sirkars" was a most incompetent officer, whom Forde defeated in the field, and drove within the walls of Masulipatam, the southern point of the province. Deprived, by this disaster, of the supplies expected from the north, the French general insisted upon unstinted aid from the civilians of Pondicherry; and when it was not forthcoming treated them with the utmost harshness and insolence, and delayed his threatened attack upon Madras while he went south to extort money from the Rája of Tanjore. In

* "Le Roi et la Compagnie m'ont envoyé dans l'Inde pour en chasser les Anglais . . toute autre intérêt m'est étranger."—Lally to Bussy, 13th June, 1758 (quoted by Colebrooke).—" Rise of British Power," chap. xi.

November, 1758, he was at last enabled to march against Madras, at the head of two thousand seven hundred French foot, and five thousand Sepoys, besides cavalry and guns. Clive felt natural anxiety when the news reached Calcutta. Lally, as he observed in a letter to Pitt, then head of the Government at home, must be expecting large reinforcements from Europe and the Mauritius, or he would hardly undertake the siege of so strong a place. But Clive was not doubtful of the result, if the squadron from Bombay could but arrive in time. The French sat down on the north side of Fort S. George, 12th December, 1758. After a cannonade of nearly eight weeks, the north-east bastion was breached, but the besiegers did not deem themselves strong enough to storm. And a week later (16th February, 1759) the British transports arrived from Bombay and landed six hundred fresh troops. When the next day broke the French were beheld in full retreat, leaving thirty-three pieces of artillery behind them. The operations of Forde, to the northward, were at the same time slowly prevailing over the dangers which surrounded him, and the dilatory conduct of his only native ally. In the beginning of March his position was somewhat improved by news of the retreat of Lally from Madras; but was still anything but encouraging, since the garrison of Masulipatam was stronger than the assailants, whilst a French army and the hosts of the Nizám were reported to be advancing to the relief. On 7th April, however, the skill and courage of Forde were crowned with due success; Masulipatam was stormed without excessive loss. A few days later he was received with honour in the camp of the Nizám, who had been watching events in the neighbourhood. The "northern Sirkars" came under British influence, the Carnatic was saved. In October fresh reinforcements arrived at Madras commanded by the famous Colonel Coote of the 84th, who had been home after serving under Clive in the campaign of Plassy.

THE HINDU REVIVAL, ETC. 207

Half way between Madras and Pondicherry the French had a fortified camp on the hills of Vandivásu—the " Wandewash " of Orme. This was captured by Coote in the end of November, and in January Lally brought up all his available forces for the purpose of recovering the place. Thus the fate of the English in the Carnatic seemed once more at stake, the chief players on either side, strangely enough, being Irishmen. On the 22nd Jan., Coote made a general advance for the relief of the hill, where the French had already effected a breach in the fortifications. Lally on his side marched to the encounter, having a following of 3,500 men, more than half of whom were Frenchmen ; Coote's force was about equal in infantry, with a superiority in field guns. The French had the aid—unprecedented up to that time in India—of European cavalry. But their charge failed; the infantry of "Lorraine" were beaten back; the camp was stormed during the confusion caused by a chance explosion, and Bussy was taken prisoner. The rout became general, and the whole army must have been destroyed but for the heroic efforts of the French hussars ; the French lost 600 Europeans, including prisoners, and 24 field-pieces, besides tents, stores, and baggage. The total loss on the British side was 190 killed and wounded. Not only was Wandewash saved, but Coote was able to capture all the outlying fortresses of the French, and to threaten Pondicherry.

While these events were proceeding in the southern regions, the Mahratta confederacy had been pursuing a career of success against its neighbours in the western Deccan, and had begun to avail themselves of the retirement of the Abdáli to menace his possessions in Upper India. Incited by the audacious young Gházi, who had usurped supreme power at Delhi, two sons of Ránuji Sindia, the *jagirdár* of Upper Málwa, marched on Sukartál, the stronghold of the Pathán chief Najib. Failing here, they sent a large force across the Ganges, which drove out Najib's countrymen from whom he expected help. The Nawáb of Audh, moving against them, Najib was delivered, and Gházi-ud-din began to fear that, with the support of Sultan Ali Gauhar the crown prince, he might be deposed from power.

The present Nawáb of Audh and Shujá-ud-daula was the son and successor of Safdar Jang, who had passed away in 1754. He was young and active, and claiming to be hereditary prime minister of the Empire, was also head of the country party, to which Najib and the Patháns professed adherence. Apprehensive of the result of the junction between these chiefs, the young Turkmán called the crown prince, Sultan Ali Gauhar, into Delhi, and put him into a kind of open arrest, from which, however, he contrived to escape at the very end of the year. The Sultan reached Lucknow—after visiting Najib on the road—19 Jan, 1759.

Meanwhile the Abdáli was by no means idle. Justly regarding the young Gházi as a foe alike to good order and the interests of Islám, he encouraged Najib to opposition by promises of support. Shujá-ud-daula hastened to engage the Mahrattas in Rohil-khand from the side of Audh; they were defeated in a decisive action, and Gobind Panth, their leader, was forced to seek safety in flight, while many of his men were drowned in crossing the Ganges. One of Sindia's sons, Dattáji, was also defeated and killed in an unsuccessful raid upon the Punjab. At the same time the Peshwa was engaged nearer home in a sharp contest with the Nizám, by this time deprived of French aid. Led by his cousin, Sheodásheo Rao Bháo, the army of the Peshwa ravaged the northern Deccan and took possession of the city of Ahmadnagar, only retiring when the Nizám had consented to ransom his dominions by painful sacrifices. In the midst of all these distractions, the Abdáli came once more down upon Lahore; from thence he marched across the Lower Punjab and Sirhind, crossed into Najib's territory, in what is now the Saháranpur district, and resumed his old post at Anupshahr in the end of the rains.

The reckless stripling who held sway at Delhi had no means of meeting the storm, but he seemed to have thought that he could conjure it to pass away. Hastily calling on Suraj Mall, chief of the Bhurtpore Játs, and invoking the assistance of the Peshwa, he proceeded to murder the harmless Emperor, whom he had, himself, taken from obscurity to set upon the throne. But this crime—which was committed on the 30th Nov., 1759—so far from producing terror, only united against the Turkmán a coalition of opponents, before which he fled, and disappeared for ever from the scene of Indian politics.

About December 1st, the Abdáli arrived at Delhi. The throne was without an occupant; from the borders of Haidarabad to the frontier of the dominions of Shujá-ud-daula, there was no government but that of various lords of misrule over whom the Peshwa was lord paramount. In one respect, however, the Mahrattas were no longer barbarous; their military organisation had taken a practical ply. No longer consisting entirely of foraging spearmen and light guerilla riders, the Peshwa's army now included a regular force of well-equipped cavalry, drawing pay from the State; with a strong force of infantry and an efficient artillery, all partly imbued with French discipline. It was with such a force, flushed with recent success against the Deccan Mughals, that the Bhao moved upon Delhi. He set out from Poona with twenty thousand chosen horse; at starting he was joined by a division of infantry with fieldpieces, commanded by Ibráhim Gárdi, a soldier of the school of Bussy, who had left the sinking cause of the French. In Málwa he took up the contingents of Holkar and Sindia; and on coming farther, gathered the detachment of the Gobind Panth and the Ját army under Suraj Mall. Hopes were even entertained of the adhesion of the Nawáb Shujá-ud-daula to

P

what certainly was a Hindu combination, but might be represented as a united national movement against the foreign invader.

While these momentous omens were arising in Hindustan, the Nawáb Vazir was on the point of engaging in a remote and apparently unconnected adventure. He received the fugitive heir to the Empire with respect, and gave him letters to a kinsman of his own, Muhammad Kuli Khán, then in charge of the province of Allahabad, who willingly promised his support, as did also Kámgár Khán, the faujdar, or military governor of the adjoining division of Bihár. With this following the prince crossed the frontier into Bengal, at the close of 1759, and presently heard of the murder of his father, whereby he became entitled to call himself Emperor. He assumed the title—an ill-omened title, as we have seen—of Sháh Álam II. He confirmed Shujá as Vazir, and appointed Najib *Amir-ul-Amra*, with the titular command in chief of the armies of Hindustan. For his own part, he resolved to proceed against Mir Jáfir, whose deputy at Patna was a Hindu official, Rája Ram Narain, understood to be on bad terms with Nawáb. This officer, however, refused to acknowledge the imperial authority, and drew out his force under the walls of Patna; but he was defeated with considerable loss, including that of a detachment of sepoys under British officers, who were cut up in covering his retreat. Upon this the army of Bengal advanced and gave him battle on 15th Feb., 1760. Defeated in this action, the Emperor endeavoured to cut in between the Bengalis and their base, and endeavoured to possess himself of Murshidabad, but he was again defeated by a body of British troops on the 7th April. He then hastily retraced his steps, and being joined by M. Law and a party of Frenchmen, he resolved to lay siege to Patna. His operations, however, were interrupted by the sudden appearance of Captain Knox with a body of infantry—partly British soldiers. Muhamad Kuli had by this time returned to Allahabad, where he was killed by his cousin Shujá in a struggle for the fief there; Kámgár, who succeeded to the command of the imperialists, was taken by surprise, owing, as was supposed, to the great heat of the season, and the army was routed and driven upon Gaya. Being here joined by another local officer, Khádim Hussain, the Emperor made another dash at Patna, but was again defeated, and retired from a struggle for which his resources were insufficient. In the pursuit which was begun, the son of the Nawàb of Bengal—the same who had caused the death of Siráj-ud-daula after Plassy—was killed by lightning, and the Anglo-Bengali army retired to their cantonment at Patna. The Emperor once more encamped at Gaya.

By this time Clive had left the country, and his successor was unable to control his own Council. The moving spirits of that body were disappointed in Mir Jáfir, who was ageing fast, and beginning to display a growing indolence and an unwillingness to yield to their demands for money. They accordingly put pressure upon him to abdicate in favour of a kinsman named Mir Kásim, whom they wished him to acknowledge as heir apparent and regent of Bengal. The old man retired in dudgeon to Calcutta, hoping to make interest there for himself: and Kásim became the native ruler. On the 27th September, articles were signed by virtue of which the Company was to support him against all enemies—the Emperor included—receiving, in compensation, and for the support of their troops, the districts of Bardwan, Midnapur, and Chittagong, together with great pecuniary gifts to the civil and military chiefs.

The new Nawáb was a man of original character, of elegant manners, and singular capacity for business. His weak point was a lack of physical nerve, and even of audacity in military enterprise. But he soon showed that he had no intention of being a puppet. He disbanded the ill-disciplined troops of his predecessor, levying a body of 10,000 good soldiers with able officers to instruct them. Having made these preparations he joined the British at Patna, to defend his new possessions against the Emperor and M. Law, who were still at Gaya.

All this time the Nawàb Vazir, Shuja-ud-daula, had been deterred from supporting the movements of his sovereign by momentous events in Hindustan, on which the Hindu confederation continued to advance. Justly considering that he would be constrained to combine all the available resources of Islám if he was to oppose the enemy with success, the Abdáli left a garrison in Delhi and fell back upon Anupshahr, where he could collect the bands of Rohillas and open negociations with Shujá. It was rumoured that the Bháo intended to proclaim the Peshwa Emperor, but to leave the vazirate to its present possessor; and the prudent Najib—while acknowledging the difficulty of detaching the head of the country party—strongly urged upon the Abdáli chief the importance of doing all that was possible to defeat such a combination. He obtained the Sháh's permission to go to Audh and see the Nawáb-Vazir, and his journey ended in success. Shujá was persuaded to join the cause of Islàm; he placed his family in careful custody and repaired with Najib to Anupshahr, where he received a hearty welcome.

The Bháo, meanwhile, advanced on Delhi, and captured the fortifications without much difficulty in the last days of 1759. He also opened negociations with the Nawáb-Vazir, proposing terms which the latter forthwith loyally reported to the Najib and the Abdáli Sháh. The only practical result was that the Ját leader, Suraj Mall, lost all confidence in the enterprise, and withdrew his contingent. In these negociations the summer of 1760 wore away, but as soon as the monsoon was over the Bháo left Delhi with the purpose of overrunning the Punjab. On the 20th October he cut up an outpost of the Afgháns, and the Sháh crossed the Jumna in pursuit. On the 26th there was a collision at Sonpat; and for the next two months the army was cantoned in the town of Panipat, the Afghàns watching from the southward, where the great battlefield of Hindustan extends its desolate surface.* Constant fighting went on, generally to the disadvantage of the Mahrattas, who were at last blockaded in their lines and threatened with starvation. They therefore, on the morning of the 13th January, 1761, moved to the attack, their right covered by the cavalry, under Sindia and Holkar, their left protected by Ibráhim's Gárdis, trained Sepoys, with field-guns. The Afghán leader marched out of his camp when he heard of the approach of the Mahrattas. On his left was Najib, with a quantity of matchlock men; in the left centre, in full armour, rode the Nawáb of Audh and the Afghán Vazir, with their heavy horse; in the right centre was massed a quota of Rohilla infantry; and two brigades of Persian cavalry were opposed to Ibráhim. Sháh Pasand, the Afghán leader's chief of the staff, covered Najib's advance with a body of cuirassiers, and a further reserve was stationed a mile behind the Persians, on the right rear, under the immediate eye of the Sháh. The battle began much to the advantage of the Mahrattas. Ibráhim led on his Gárdis without firing a shot, and drove away the Persian horse; then, bringing his left shoulder forward, smote the flank of the Rohillas. The Afghán minister and Shujá, his brother Vazir, were sorely pressed by the Bháo and his immediate following; but the horsemen of Málwa were held in check by Najib, who threw up earthworks in front of his line, and kept them off with rockets and the fire of his long *jazails*.† Soon after midday, however, when the want of food was beginning to tell on the Mahrattas, the Sháh sent forward his fresh squadrons from the rear, and hurled

* V. chap. iv.
† The Afghán match-lock, carrying a ball 600 yards or more.

them on the Mahratta centre. Hastily committing the care of his family to Holkar, the Bháo plunged into the thickest of the fray; Holkar and Sindia withdrew, leaving the right exposed; the Peshwa's son was killed on his elephant; the Bháo disappeared. The rout soon became general; the head of the Sindia clan was taken fleeing, and Ibráhim fighting. The Afgháns entered the town of Panipat and made a universal slaughter. It was reckoned that 200,000 Mahrattas perished in the campaign. Soon after, the Abdáli Sháh returned to his own country, and Shujá went back to Audh charged with the protection of the House of Taimur. The Emperor's eldest son was made Regent at Delhi, with Najib for his captain general.

At first sight it seems as if the labours and losses of this campaign were not attended with very important results, but on a little reflection it will appear in fact more decisive. By the depression of the Mahratta confederacy it probably warded off an attack upon Bengal in which Shujá would have taken part, and the still struggling power of the British Company might have been overwhelmed. To the Peshwa, Balaji, the blow was final; he heard of it as he was crossing the Narbada on his way to take succour to his kinsman; and, turning his elephant's head, he hastened back to Poona, where he presently after died.

Almost on the day of the overthrow of the Mahrattas at Panipat the long duel between French and English came to an end. On the 15th January Pondicherry surrendered to Colonel Coote, and the fortifications were at once demolished under orders of the British government of Madras.

The sense of security produced by these events encouraged the filibustering government of Bengal in further adventures. Having extracted as much money as they could out of Mir Kasim, the members of the Council proceeded to quarrel with him on grounds more or less personal. Major Carnac began, indeed, a show of fighting for him against the fugitive Emperor, whom he attacked at Suán, near the town of Bihár, when the Emperor was defeated and M. Law taken prisoner. Next morning, however, the Emperor and Carnac met, and the latter alarmed the Nawáb by exaggerated marks of deference to the exiled sovereign, who offered to make the Company *Diwan* of the province. This post, which involved the whole fiscal and civil administration, was a temptation to which Vansittart, the governor, was not prepared to yield, and Carnac was ere long superseded by Coote, who had returned from the capture of Pondicherry. But he, too, carried on a system of annoyance and alarm to Mir Kasim, in which he was imitated by Mr. Ellis, chief of the factory of Patna. The great bone of contention was the privilege, claimed by everyone in the Company's service, of passing goods free of duty, transit dues being a considerable source of the Nawáb's inland revenue. 'But the favour of the Emperor was also a subject of competition among all parties, since, even in his present desperate circumstances, he was the only centre of legitimate authority in Northern India. For the present he took refuge with Shujá, the Nawáb of Audh, who was his titular Vazir. The landless sovereign lived for the next two years under Shujá's protection; but all parties kept a respectful eye upon him.

It was not very long before the Calcutta government came to an open dispute with Mir Kásim over the question of the transit duties. Vansittart, who was a moderate man, and had been brought up from Madras by Clive expressly to counteract the corruption of the Bengal Council, was ably seconded by Warren Hastings, whom we noticed in 1756 among the refugees at Fulta. Though not unambitious, Hastings was not corrupt, and was too honourable to join in the machinations of his colleagues; for which reason Vansittart deputed him to visit the Nawáb and endeavour to effect an amicable arrangement about the transit dues. As this proved an affair of difficulty in the state of the Nawáb's temper, Vansittart presently followed in person, and concluded a reasonable agreement, allowing the benefit of the Company's pass to *bonâ-fide* imports and exports, but prohibiting evasions of duty by private persons. On 28th Jan., 1763, Vansittart returned to Calcutta; and all appeared to be settled, when the impatience of the Nawáb on one side, and of Ellis on the other, frustrated all attempts of the kind. The Council decided that the governor had exceeded his authority, negatived the agreement, and authorised the use of force by Ellis in certain circumstances. The latter lost no time in precipitating a collision, and the Nawáb in return sent a body of cavalry to punish the Sepoys employed by Ellis; at the same time issuing an order remitting all transit dues, and thus putting the traffic of the British—and all British officials were then concerned in trade—upon an equal footing with the dealings of every native merchant.

This order was received as a declaration of war by Ellis and his employers, whom Vansittart and Hastings, being in a minority, were unable to counteract. Kásim, on his side, also prepared for the worst. Ellis provoked the collision which precipitated hostilities; and then attempted to escape; but was put under arrest by the infuriated Nawáb. Mr. Amyatt and some other Englishmen were murdered. The news reached Calcutta on 4th July, and it was immediately resolved to reinstate Mir Jáfir, and to proceed to extremities against Kásim. The latter had by this time a body of disciplined infantry amounting to 15,000, with a small force of vagrant Europeans under the command of a French deserter named Walter Reinhardt, but known locally as "Samru Sahib," or—in later days—General Sombre. The British force sent from Calcutta, under Major Adams—at that moment the senior officer in Bengal—was even smaller than that which fought at Plassy; but it was under a commander hardly inferior in professional ability to Clive himself; and the campaign which followed was almost as brilliant as any known in history. The first encounter was at Katwa, a few miles south of the village of Plassy, and memorable as the scene of the council of war held before the great battle. After a sharp contest, in which the Nawáb's cavalry lost its general, the enemy retreated; and next day Adams conducted Jafir back to his old palace in Murshidabad (the 23rd July). A week later they were again met by Kásim's army at the village of Gheria, not far from the old Mughal capital of Gaur. A severe action ensued, in which at first the enemy had a distinct advantage, but after four hours of hard fighting the enemy fled once more, leaving their guns and commissariat. Continuing their march on Patna, the victors found their way barred at the pass of Udwa Nála, near Rajmahal, where the hills almost touched the Ganges. Here Kásim intrenched his army for a final stand, having collected so many men that they were rumoured to number no less than 60,000. His English prisoners were detained as hostages; the unfortunate Ram Narain and other Hindus of consequence were murdered by being drowned in the river. Adams was again successful, and captured the works on 19th August, after an obstinate struggle. The Nawáb hurried to Patna with his prisoners, sending word to Adams that if he advanced they should all be put to death. The same messengers brought a letter from the brave Englishmen desiring that no consideration for their safety might retard the advance. Adams moved on, and Kásim carried out his infamous threat, employing Samru and his Sepoys to massacre Ellis and all his company—about one hundred and fifty-five persons in all. He then fled into the Audh territory. In that October Patna was taken by storm, but the gallant commander of the victorious army did not long survive his success. Major Adams died on the 16th January, 1764, as he was about to set sail for home, worn out by his glorious exertions.

Mir Kásim at first was kindly received by the Nawáb of

Audh, who was at that time in the neighbourhood of Allahabad, accompanied by the Emperor Sháh Àlam. Kásim was still reputed rich, and was followed by many good troops, including the brigade under Samru. By the request of his host he employed his force in quelling some disturbances in Bundelkhand, while Shujá and the Emperor proceeded to Benares.

The condition of affairs in Hindustan was hardly such as to inspire Sháh Àlam with any immediate hope of a restoration. The battle of Pánipat had indeed broken the Mahrattas for the present, and prevented the Hindu revival being matured under a general alliance of indigenous races. Nevertheless, there were no less than four Hindu powers whose coalition might at any time take place, and form an obstacle to the recovery of the Empire. These were: first, the Mahrattas, beaten but not destroyed; next, the proud but indolent Rájputs; third, the Jats of Bhurtpore; and, lastly, the Sikhs of the Punjab, slowly learning the secret of combination, and beginning to oppose the Afgháns with boldness and some success: one of their chiefs, Alá Sinh, having actually wrested Sirhind from the Abdáli in 1762.

Leaving the other tribes for the present, we turn to the influence of the Jats in the immediate vicinity of Delhi. Najib, whom the Abdáli had left in charge in 1761, executed his hard task with his accustomed prudence. The Mahratta administration was usually—beyond their own confines—a mere matter of collecting money; and their collectors were for the moment expelled, in consequence of the defeat of their grand army, in January, 1761. But the power of the Játs—who had escaped that disaster—became very irksome, until the trouble seemed to culminate when they obtained possession of the fortified Palace of the Emperors at Agra, whence they dominated the town and surrounding country. About the same time their chieftain, Suraj Mall, made himself master of several strong places to the south-west of Delhi, so that the capital was becoming hemmed in, and in a manner commanded, on every side save that which was open to the Sikhs. In the winter of 1763-4 the Ját chief attacked some small states on the Jumna, just bordering upon the Imperial demesne, and carried his audacity so far as to go hunting in the Park of Shádara, close to the city. Here he was encountered, with a small attendance, by some Mughal horsemen, by whom he was killed; but his son immediately assumed the chiefship at Agra, and took up a position of alliance with Holkar, and of hostility to all the friends of order.

In the meantime, great events were pending in Bengal. Shujá and the Emperor, being joined by Mir Kásim, crossed the Bihár frontier and threatened Patna, where Carnac was in a state of great uneasiness owing to the mutinous spirit of his men. Major Munro about this time taking charge from Carnac, restored discipline by measures of well-timed severity; and then awaited the cessation of the rains, when he marched against the allied Nawábs. On the 15th September, 1764, he broke up from Patna, and on the 2nd October he arrived at Baksár on the borders of Bihár and the Nawáb's territory, or, rather, that of the Rája of Benares, who was the Nawáb's tributary. By this time Kásim had left the camp, but his disciplined battalions and batteries had been engaged by Shujá, whose whole force now amounted to fifty thousand men, with field-pieces and guns of position. He was particularly strong in cavalry, including five thousand Afghán men-at-arms who had shared in the victory of Panipat. Shujá had studied the ground, which he had first occupied six months before, and where he was now so strongly posted that, if he had only waited to be attacked, he might have beaten off the comparatively small force of his assailants. The British troops were less than eleven thousand; they had some six thousand Sepoys and nine hundred native horsemen; but the Nawáb issued too confidently from his position, and was beaten after a three hours' fight, in which two thousand of his men were killed or wounded. The rout soon became complete and hopeless; two thousand more were drowned in attempting to escape, but the want of cavalry rendered pursuit impossible. Shujá fled to Allahabad, and, finding that the British continued to advance, retired to Bareilly, finally joining Malhár Rao Holkar, who had returned to the Duáb. Carnac rejoined the army with the rank of brigadier-general, Munro having left for England. The Mahrattas were driven across the Jumna, and Samru departed to seek his fortune elsewhere. The Emperor came over to the British camp, renewing his offer of the *Diwáni*, which was accepted this time. In February, 1765, Mir Jáfir died, and his son was made Nawáb; but the treaty with the Emperor which soon followed enabled the Calcutta Council to reduce his power to a nullity. The terms of the treaty—which was concluded 12th August, 1765—confirmed Shujá as Nawáb of Audh, but gave the Emperor the province of Allahabad with a charge upon the Bengal revenues amounting to two-and-a-half millions of rupees per annum, in consideration whereof the Company was granted the Diwáni of the eastern provinces, together with the districts of Benares and Ghazipur as an imperial fief. These arrangements were made by Clive, who had returned to Bengal as governor in May, 1765.

It has been usual to regard Clive's victory at Plassy as the decisive battle of British India. But it is evident that it was not comparable to the battle of Baksár. Plassy indeed may be almost said to have had no direct or immediate result beyond a palace revolution. It was Baksár which, coming after the dazzling successes of Adams, conferred upon the Company and its officers a legitimate status as servants and feudatories of the Mughal Empire and virtual masters of Bihár, Bengal, and Orissa by Imperial grant: though Orissa—as we shall see—really remained subject to the Mahrattas for many years.

It only remains to be added, in this connection, that Muhamad Raza Khán, a nobleman of Patna, was made Deputy Administrator under the Company. The new Nawáb objected, and endeavoured to procure the appointment for Nand Kumar; but the Nawáb had become so mere a cypher that his wishes were overruled at once. All non-official Europeans were at the same time ordered to wind up their affairs and leave the country; while, to guard against future danger of corruption, engagements were taken from officials not to receive money from the natives.

For the next few years the Eastern Provinces had peace, if not prosperity. Clive's intentions were noble, but it may be doubted whether anything, in either his character or previous experience, qualified him to lay the foundations of a new administrative edifice. The conditions were as unprecedented as the materials were hard to find. And Clive retired from India altogether in 1767, leaving the difficult task to even less qualified hands. "His strong will and dauntless courage," as has been observed elsewhere,* "had quelled a mutiny among his English officers and overborne all resistance within his own council. In spite of cabals around him, and a grudging support in England, he had swept away some crying abuses in the Company's service, had retrenched some wasteful outlay, and done much to atone for the corruption, violence, and blundering of the past years." But after Clive's departure the Company's affairs in Bengal fell back to something like their old disorder. What is called "Dual Government" went on in its most pernicious form, the administration being carried on by Asiatics, whom their existing conditions obliged to be selfish, while the responsibility was borne by Europeans who knew nothing of the details, and were still hankering after personal emolument. That, of course, was natural enough, seeing the example of their predecessors, and the anxiety they all felt to get back to

* "History of India," L. J. Trotter. S. P. C. K., London, 1889.

their native country with the means of enjoyment. Nor was it until some time later that the notion—now so obvious—occurred to any one in power that all reasonable expectations of this sort could be best met by an enhanced scale of pay. Thus, and thus only, could the attractions of Indian service be maintained, while its temptations for men of ordinary virtue were abolished.

In theory the Eastern Provinces consisted of three divisions, all of which were conveyed by the *firmán* of 1765. But Orissa was mainly in the hands of the collectors of Mahratta blackmail. The famine of 1770 fell on this province with great severity, as did a local dearth seven years later. The division of Orissa did not really come under British management till 1803. Of the remaining divisions Bengal was nominally ruled by the Nawáb, who was a cypher, as above mentioned. But the powers of the Company were delegated to native deputies, with whom was associated a Board of British Commissioners at head-quarters; while a number of young men of the same nation were scattered over the country under the title of "supervisors," the duty of these persons being to check the oppressions of native officials, while they guarded the interests of the Company. In other words, they were to see that proper collections were made, and that the monies were paid into the Treasury without embezzlement. But the plan proved more than dubious. The supervisors, as Warren Hastings said, were the "boys of the service and very heavy rulers of the people." The Council in Calcutta, the Board at Mushidabad, were alike unfit to keep them to their due position, the members having returned to many of the money-getting practices which Clive had endeavoured to eradicate. The control of the revenue administration was ere long removed to Calcutta, and conducted through British collectors; but the criminal jurisdiction was left in the hands of native judges, who administered Muhamadan law.

In 1770 a terrible famine fell upon Bengal, and the wrath of

Nature was added to the oppressions of man. One-third of the population of Bengal is said to have perished, and much culturable land went out of tillage. Necessarily the revenue fell off, and the Company had to pay dear for having substituted the throne for the counting-house stool. In 1772 they had to apply to the King's Government for a loan to save them from insolvency. And the conditions on which it was granted included a covenant to pay £400,000 a year to the Exchequer. A Select Committee was appointed to inquire into Indian matters and report to Parliament.

In this way the ship of State was launched in India, and went staggering through the storms of her first voyages. In judging the conduct of the British officials of the period we must bear in mind two points: political morality was not very squeamish even in English public life, and in much higher social and political spheres than theirs. From the days of Walpole to the last quarter of the century "every man had his price." And it was hardly to be supposed that young clerks would expatriate themselves to a life of danger and privation if they had not a good hope of early and handsome fortune. That is the first excuse for these men. The other is noted by Elphinstone. The gifts that they received were, generally speaking, rather of the nature of thankofferings for services already rendered than of inducements to wrong-doing. Such gifts were in the custom of the country.

In the meantime the Emperor continued to live as a pensioner at Allahabad, eagerly looking out for an opportunity of return to the palace of his ancestors. That opportunity at last arrived—as, it is said, everything does to him who can only wait. His last adviser was a Persian nobleman, Mirza Najaf Khán, who had been a client of that Muhamad Kuli who was slain at Allahabad in 1760. On that occasion he had been led to seek the protection of Clive, by whom he was recommended to the Emperor after the battle of Baksár and the consequent arrangements. The Mirza was now nominated to the charge of the district of Kora, the modern "Fatehpur," and here he found plenty of employment in the protection of the road and the general restoration of order. Other of the Imperial ministers are mentioned in the well-known *Siyar-ul-mutákharin*, but none are of historical importance.

Among the Mahrattas, also, the years that immediately followed the grant of the *Diwáni* in 1765 were uneventful. Malhár Rao Holkar did not long survive his defeat by Carnac. He died in 1765 without issue surviving; and the affairs of his state in South Málwa were ably carried on by his son's widow, the good and popular Ahalia Bai, who founded Indore, the present capital of the Holkars; the military department was entrusted to a faithful servant known as Tukaji Holkar. The Peshwa Bálaji, whose death after Panipat has been already mentioned, was succeeded by his son, Mádhava Rao, the actual power at Poona being in the hands of the young man's uncle, Rughnáth Rao, known to the English as "Ragoba." In 1769 the army of the confederacy had taken the field under Visaji Krishn, the quarter-master-general; and being joined by the Málwa contingent commenced a systematic plunder in the Ját country, and a desultory warfare ensued for a year or more. It will be remembered that Suraj Mall was now dead, and Najib was reasserting the position of the Delhi Government. At length the Mahrattas, becoming successful over the Játs, the latter were at once deserted by Samru and generally isolated. The Abdáli Sháh having retired from the Cis Satlaj, the Mahrattas profited by his absence to cross the Chambal, occupy the Bhurtpore country, and open negotiations with Najib. Their object was that they might levy black mail up to the borders of the Delhi territory without giving offence to the Muslim authorities, who might at any time bring back their Afghán sympathisers.

It was therefore to Visáji and his powerful coadjutors from Málwa that Sháh Alam now turned for aid in recovering Delhi.

Najib's good qualities were admitted on all hands, but his Patháns were rough and covetous, so that the people underwent much oppression and extortion at their hands. Their treatment, writes the author of the *Siyar*, could not be described without violating decency; nor would the description answer any purpose. "The sufferers have suffered, and what is past is past." Natural nostalgia was thus enhanced in the Sháh's mind by a sense of duty towards his people. And if Najib's presence at Delhi had acted as a hindrance it was removed very opportunely, for he died in October, 1770, leaving his estates about Saháranpur to his son, Zabita Khán, who also endeavoured to maintain himself in the government at Delhi. But Zabita was both feeble and false, and he neither carried on honest, straightforward dealings with the Mahrattas nor sought alliances elsewhere. He was accordingly attacked and chased from Delhi by the southern invaders, who, at the same time, drove the Rohillas out of the Upper Duáb, and opened negotiations with the Sháh at Allahabad.

[See Elphinstone's "Rise of British Power" (with Supplement) and Malleson's "Decisive Battles of India," also "Rulers of India" series, "W. Hastings," "Sindia," &c.]

SECTION 2.—The grant of the *Diwani* that followed the battle of Baksár had been the means of settling the affairs of Bengal and Bihár; and the offensive and defensive alliance with the Nawáb Vazir Shujá-ud-daula completed the security of those provinces. The chief interest of Anglo-Indian history was thus transferred to the south of the peninsula, where likewise the alliance of the Nizám afforded some security, and where the French ceased to cause any very serious anxiety. Nevertheless, there were two native states from whose hostility long troubles were engendered. These were the Mahrattas, still dreaming of conquest in Hindustan, and the Muslim power of Mysore, under the usurper Haidar Ali, the ablest and most persevering Asiatic enemy ever encountered by the British in India.

The first step taken by the Mahrattas, it is now easy to perceive, was one which, however alarming, was an indication that the central power of their confederacy was giving way. The arrangements for the restoration of the Emperor, Shah Álam, were conducted, not by the Peshwa's Government at Poona, so much as by two quasi-dependent chiefs. Of one of these, Tukaji Holkar, something has already been said. He represented the Regency of southern Málwa, presided over by Ahalya Bai. His colleague, who was *jágirdár*, or Lord-Lieutenant, of the northern part of Málwa, and was extending his possessions towards the Chambal, was an illegitimate son of Ránoji Sindia, who had been killed at Pánipat. Escaping from that disaster with a wound that made him lame for life, Mahádaji Sindia had assumed the leadership of the clan. He was a sworn foe of the Patháns, whom he regarded as the authors of the temporary ruin of his nation and family, while Tukaji Holkar was distinctly favourable to the party of the late Najib. When the negotiation began Tukaji was the prime mover. There is no record of the methods by which the concurrence of Sindia was obtained, but the transaction received the sanction of the Poona durbar, to which both these chiefs professed subjection; the Sháh covenanting to pay ten lakhs (one million) of rupees, and to give up to the Mahrattas the districts which had been assigned for his support by the British in 1765. To these arrangements Sindia was a consenting party.

The British Council in Calcutta, on the other hand, were not made aware of the terms; nevertheless they attempted to dissuade the Sháh from leaving their protection. The Nawáb of Audh, who, as hereditary Vazir of the empire, had every claim to be consulted, added arguments of his own. But the advice was disregarded, and the Sháh advanced up the Duáb in 1771, accompanied to the frontier of the province of Allahabad by a British detachment. His personal following was under the command of Mirza Najaf, and included a mounted bodyguard of *Ahdis*, or gentlemen cadets, and a small force of infantry called "The Red battalion," commanded by a Frenchman named Médoc, who had formerly been in Samru's Brigade. Sindia, who was resolved to make his profit out of the affair, met them about the end of the rains at Farukhábád, and accompanied the rest of the march. On the 25th December, 1771, the Emperor re-entered the city of Shahjahan, and took possession of the famous "Red Castle," or fortified Palace. Zabita fell back on the head of the Duáb, where he had several strong places in what are now the districts of Muzafarnagar and Saháranpur, besides a stronghold across the Ganges, not far from Bijnor. This fort was called Pathargarh, the town founded about it by Najib being named after its founder, Najibábád. Sindia soon persuaded the Sháh to aid his schemes of vengeance by marching against the Pathán chief; and Shujá, the Nawáb Vazir, promised co-operation in Rohilkhand, a province on which he was, perhaps, already casting a greedy glance.

The passage of the Ganges was easily effected, the river in those parts being fordable at that season of the year. The aid of the Rohillas was withheld from their brother Pathán from fear of the Nawáb Shujá; so that Zabita was obliged to fly in such haste that he left all his treasure in Pathargarh along with his family, who fell into the hands of the Emperor. But not for long; the Mahrattas appropriated the whole of the spoil, making friends with Zabita soon after, on the basis of *Beati possidentes*, but handing his women and children over to him for a further ransom.

These measures proving distasteful to Mirza Najaf, he quarrelled with his Hindu allies, who forthwith seized the palace and person of the sovereign. The Rohillas, for their part, affected to seek the protection of their powerful neighbour, the Nawáb of Audh, and concluded a treaty with him 11th July, 1772. In this they bound themselves to pay him forty lakhs of rupees on condition of his expelling the Mahrattas.* Zabita Khán was made a party to this arrangement. Sindia, remaining neutral, retired towards Jaipur, where he awaited events, supporting his army meanwhile by contributions levied from the Rajputs. Holkar, not being animated by the same vindictive feelings, took the part of Zabita, of whose share in the Rohilla treaty he was probably ignorant, and whose aid he reckoned upon during his approaching absence in his own country. But the Mirza made a firm resistance, obtaining the support of the Nawáb of Audh, and promising to renew the attack on Rohilkhand. Holkar was impatient to get back to Poona, whence news of the Peshwa's death had been received; and the upshot was that the Mirza remained in office, and a Mahratta force occupied the central Duáb, and made a raid upon the Rohillas.

The new Peshwa was desirous of shaking off the control of his uncle, the Regent, and with this view had ordered the recall of Sindia and Holkar, on whose support he had reckoned. But before they could obey the summons the unfortunate young man had followed his brother in a premature death; and Raguba made himself Peshwa, and commenced hostilities against the Muslim states to the southward, Haidarabad and Mysore. But he was promptly recalled to Poona by the intelligence that his deceased nephew's widow had borne a posthumous son, whose right to the succession was acknowledged by the durbar. He attempted force, but met with a defeat under the walls of Poona, and hurried northward in the hope of conciliating the returning armies. Raguba reached Ahalya Bai's new capital of Indore at the moment when Sindia and Holkar arrived there from Hindustan.

* "The Vuzeer shall establish the Rohillas, obliging the Mahrattas to retire, the Rohilla Sirdars to pay the Vuzeer 40 lakhs of rupis," etc. Text of Treaty, in Hamilton's "Rohillas."

Both promised their support, and they then turned into Gujarát to seek the co-operation of the Gaikwár. Their next step was to solicit help from the British Presidency of Bombay, where a desire for territorial expansion was known, or suspected to exist. Twenty-eight miles north of Bombay was the old Portuguese harbour of Bassain, now in the dominions of the Peshwa; while, nearer still, the extensive island of Salsette commanded the port of Bombay itself. The Bombay Council agreed, on condition of receiving possession of these two places, that they would furnish a force of 1,500 men to the armies under Raguba. On hearing of these negotiations the Portuguese sent a claim to Bassain and Salsette, upon which Mr. Hornby, the head of the Presidency, on his own responsibility, took summary possession of both. This took place in 1774, and was immediately followed by a breach between Raguba and the chiefs, on whose alliance he had reckoned. It is probable that Holkar's mistress, the Bai, was opposed to such dismemberment of Mahratta power. Sindia and Holkar turned upon Raguba, who fled to British protection in December of that year; and the Bombay contingent at once set out with Raguba to attack Poona.

While the Mahrattas were thus engaged in their own country, Mirza Najaf took advantage of their absence to do what might be possible to bring good government back to Hindustan; and for nearly nine years that long-disturbed country enjoyed some measure of repose. The Mahrattas, however, had not entirely withdrawn their garrisons, and they maintained friendly relations with the disaffected Patháns, with Hafiz Rahmat, Protector of Rohilkand, and with the disappointed Zábita, their connection, always intriguing for the recovery of the position once held by his deceased father. On the other hand, the Nawáb of Audh supported the Mirza—who was a Shia like himself—and kept his eye on the province that lay between his own territories and the Upper Duáb.

It has long been usual to think of the Rohillas as lawful rulers of this province, and to regard them as favourable examples of Asiatic rulers, under whom the agriculture and commerce of the country were fairly prosperous. Judging, however, from contemporary records, nothing can be more erroneous than these opinions. The Rohillas were foreign adventurers, at feud among themselves, grasping and perfidious, agreed in nothing but in misgoverning their usurped possessions and plundering the people.* The Protector showed no anxiety about the Mahratta garrisons, but the Nawáb carried out his undertaking; by the end of October, 1773, he had driven them not only out of Rohilkand, but across the Duáb and over the Jumna. He then claimed the money which had been the stipulated price of that service.

With regard to the suggestion that Shujá may have been for some time desirous of rounding off his territory at the expense of the Rohillas, we can only be guided by conjecture; there being no direct evidence. But the time and place were both favourable to selfishness; and it may well have seemed a small thing to the Nawáb Vazir that he, who had, at least, a legitimate position in the Empire, should add to the province in his charge another which was essential to its defence. For three generations, now, his house had been supporters of the tottering throne; the Rohillas were intruders of thirty years' standing. They could not defend the country from Hindu marauders, with whom indeed they were, it was strongly suspected, in collusion. So he called upon them to pay the money they had covenanted for under the late treaty; and, on this being refused, took serious measures to foreclose. It was a matter of comparative ease to obtain a patent from the chancery of Delhi for the transfer of the province; the Rohillas had been recently in rebellion, and the imperial government

* "A band of mercenary soldiers occupied Rohilcund" (Macaulay's "Clive"). See also Strachey's "Hastings and the Rohilla War."

was in the hands of Shujá's friend and deputy, Mirza Najaf. But material difficulties might well be expected, and it was against these that the Nawáb next proceeded to provide. It will be right to remember that a treaty, offensive and defensive, existed between the Nawáb and the members of the Bengal Council, who in fact owed a good deal of the prosperity of their government to that agreement. The Nawáb now called upon the Governor-General to fulfil their obligations under the treaty of 1765, which bound them to supply troops, to be paid by the Nawáb whenever he should require them.

By this time a great political change had taken place in Bengal. As the civil officers became more experienced and competent, the evils of Clive's dual government became more apparent. It had never been anything but a temporary makeshift; the Court of Directors, indeed, had fully approved its adoption in 1765, but times had since changed. The revenues of the company were falling off, and the debt was increasing; while public opinion in England was taking umbrage at the wealth of the "nabobs," those returned Anglo-Indians who came among them, like unbidden upstarts, to raise the price of "fresh eggs and rotten boroughs." The Company recorded a resolution to "stand forth as Diwán," sending out orders to Bengal accordingly; and the carrying out of the measure lay in able and willing hands. Warren Hastings—whom we last saw aiding Vansittart to protect Mir Kásim against his own temper, and that of their colleagues in council—had since those days been for some time in England, and had then come out to a post at Madras. In 1772 he received orders to proceed to Calcutta and take charge of the Presidency. He found a heavy burden awaiting him : not only was he to take over the direct collection of the revenues, but he was to hold an inquiry—if necessary a trial—into the conduct of those native officials under whom the revenues had been collected hitherto, that is Raza Khán and his associate deputy in Bihár. He was to introduce purity, pay debts, abolish deficit, and generally bring in the golden age. And for all these reforms he could only employ the existing machinery—a council whose members were the chief fosterers and beneficiaries of the old system, and in which he had only a casting vote in case of equal divisions.

To an official so pressed every expedient that an honest man could adopt must evidently have been welcome, and that was the situation of Hastings. Accordingly, the tribute paid to the Sháh was sequestered on the ground of his having himself broken the treaty by going to Delhi, contrary to the opinion and express desire of the Calcutta Council; and the districts which he had, also in violation of the spirit of the treaty, at the same time assigned to the common enemy, were now made over to the Nawáb. And when the latter proceeded to call upon the Bengal Government to equip and send to his aid troops to be maintained by him and employed against the Rohillas, the Council supported Hastings in a compliance which, because it was convenient, was not thereby rendered less obligatory. At the same time, the Home Government, acting on the report of a parliamentary committee, got an act passed—known as "The Regulating Act" —whereby the salaries of the officials were raised, the control of all political affairs was put under the Bengal Government, and the head of that Presidency was raised to the office of "Governor-General." Hastings rose at once to the responsibilities of his new dignity. His tone is already worthy of a great ruler, influenced, not coerced, by enlightened public opinion. He supplied—not without misgiving, yet with evident conviction that it was the right course—the aid demanded by the Nawáb. The brigade set out, and—a last summons to pay having been disregarded—the Rohillas were attacked in the spring of 1774. On 23rd of April they were defeated at the battle of Katra, near Bareilly; the Protector being cut in two by a round-shot.*

Mirza Najaf and the imperial troops were prevented from taking part in this campaign by troubles in Bhurtpore, whose new Rája advanced upon the capital and took Sikandrabád, and while the Mirza was engaged in chastising his insolence, Zábita broke out again in the northern Duáb. About this time (January, 1775) Shujá died, and his son, Ásaf-ud-daula, on assuming the succession, testified respect for the Court of Delhi by the transmission of a prayer for investiture, accompanied by the usual gifts. Luckily for the Sháh, the mission was in charge of a good officer, named Latáfat Khán, having command of a force of 5,000 regular sepoys and a detail of artillery. Zábita Khán, who had been negotiating with the Cis Sutlaj Sikhs, was awed by the arrival of this reinforcement, and withdrew from the districts near the capital. In the meantime the Mirza had gained such successes over the Játs that they retired to their own country, deserted by Samru, who came over to him and entered the imperial service. His original patron, Mir Kásim, was at this time living in utter destitution near Delhi, haunted continually by fears of being delivered to the British Government. He died in 1777, and his last shawl was sold to pay the funeral expenses of one who had once ruled a realm and commanded armies.

Zábita was pursued as soon as the Mirza got back from his Ját campaign; he was overtaken on his way to the Punjab, but pardoned and allowed to go back to his estates in the Upper Duáb.

* For the merits of this question the reader is referred to Mill, edited by H. H. Wilson, and the work of Sir J. Strachey ("Hastings and the Rohilla War," Oxford, 1892). When the Rohilla war was brought up as one of the charges against Hastings, Pitt, and the majority of the house, voted against the proposal, and the charge was accordingly withdrawn. See also Hamilton, "Rohillas," etc., London, 1787.'

In the meantime Raza Khán and his colleague, Rája Shatáb Rai, had been acquitted, and Nand Kumar, who had hoped to ruin them, had brought ruin on himself while engaged in forging charges of corruption against Mr. Hastings. Nand Kumar was hanged, on a conviction of forgery, 5th August, 1775, and with him disappeared the last vestige of native statesmanship in Bengal.* Opposed by Philip Francis, who hungered for the reversion of his great office, the Governor-General defended his position with dignity, and applied all the powers of his able and experienced mind to the problems before him. One of these was the rectifying of British relations with the Mahrattas, and the vindication of the Supreme Government as a paramount authority over the minor Presidencies. The Bombay Factory continued to negotiate and fight without sanction from Calcutta, in defiance of the Regulation Act; and in 1775 made a fresh treaty with Raguba, who confirmed the recent annexation of Bassain and Salsette. Colonel Keating led their sepoys to the valley of the Tapli, and fought the troops of the Poona Regency at Áras on the Bay of Cambay, 18th May, 1775; and on the 10th of the following month he drove them across the Narbada at Bhaopir near Baroch. Francis, having then a majority in Council, sent down an officer to treat with the Regency; and after some discussion terms were arrived at which were embodied in the treaty of Purandhar, which was signed on the 1st March, 1776. It annulled the engagement between Hornby and Raguba; the former's pretensions to treat being disavowed, and the latter required to disband his troops and retire on a pension. Salsette and Bassain were left to future arrangement. Hornby's Council protested against this treaty; and on the 20th August orders came out from London which, in the opinion of the Bombay authorities, virtually set aside its provisions. By

* Raza Khan was employed again, but merely as a subordinate administrator.

November Raguba was in the field again, countenanced by Hastings, and supported actively by the Council of Bombay. But the expedition proved a total failure, owing to the imbecility of General Carnac, whose record in Bengal had not prevented his re-employment in the Bombay Presidency. On the 14th January, 1779, the force was enveloped by the enemy at Wadgaon, on the mountain road leading to Poona; and Carnac feebly threw his guns into a pond, and surrendered to Sindia, who was rapidly rising to the head of Mahratta affairs.

Meanwhile a detachment of the Bengal army sent by Hastings, who had recovered his ascendency in the Calcutta Council, was crossing India to the rescue of Bombay. Colonel Goddard crossed the Narbada 2nd December, and arrived at Surat 6th February, avoiding an encounter with a body of 20,000 cavalry sent from Poona to intercept him. On 10th April, he opened negotiations with the durbar, on the basis of the abrogated treaty of Purandhar. But he dealt separately with Sindia, whose mediation at Wadgaon had been noticed and appreciated, and whom Hastings had already marked as a possible ally in the future. Goddard was careful to avoid any implication with the domestic disputes of the Mahrattas in any other direction; and no further attempt was made to force Raguba upon an unwilling community. Nevertheless Goddard positively refused to surrender the fugitive to the mercy of the durbar; and the durbar accordingly refused to make peace. Goddard reluctantly resumed hostilities. Ahmadabad, the capital of Gujarat, was stormed by his orders on 15th February, 1780, and Holkar and Sindia immediately advanced towards the British head-quarters at Baroda; and matters looked serious for Hastings, who had already on his hands the French, the Dutch, and the implacable old tyrant-warrior of Mysore, Haidar Ali.

Still, no overt act of hostility was committed by the Mahrattas; Holkar was under the influence of his colleague's stronger and more reflective mind; and that colleague was evidently beginning to reconsider the situation. Sindia dismissed the hostages whom the Bombay officers had delivered to him for the fulfilment of the convention of Wadgaon, and endeavoured to sound Goddard as to the terms that he might expect if he were to treat separately. As he was found out to be at the same time treating with the enemies of the British, no definite answer was made, and the war continued. Towards the end of 1779 it was believed that a general confederacy was begun, having for its object the expulsion of the British from India, the first, but not the last, demonstration of the want of union and collective patriotism among the native chiefs of that day. It was therefore resolved by Hastings to distract the attention of Sindia by an attack on those northern possessions to which the astute Mahratta trusted for the maintenance of his connection with Hindustan; and this was done by a march through neutral territory, and an attack on Gwalior. Gwalior, it may be remembered, was a district of the Agra province in which the Mughals had a rock-fort which was used as a sort of state-prison for political captives of high rank; and so perpendicular is the scarped sandstone, and so strong are the walls, that the veteran Coote declared in council that it would be madness to attempt its capture. But Major Popham, the officer selected by Hastings for the command of this column, was of another opinion; and, being ably seconded by Captain Bruce, surprised the Fort of Gwalior in a night-attack, without a single life being lost. The date of this memorable performance is 3rd August, 1780; and it had an immediate effect on the current of the war.

Sindia was becoming uneasy. On the one hand he was not quite prepared to shake off either alliance with Tukaji and the Holkars or his feudatory relations with the Poona Regency; on the other, he was beginning to see that he had in Hastings no common antagonist, but one whose continued hostility might be a peril to his plans. Nor was he given time for hesitation. It is true that Popham shortly after made over his charge to a senior (Colonel Carnac), who was far from being his equal in skill and daring; but Bruce remained, and by his advice a night-attack was once more hazarded. Sindia had joined his army and was, in fact, commanding in person, and recovering control of the country about Gwalior, when Bruce suddenly beat up his quarters, 24th March, 1781. The surprise was complete, and Sindia fled, losing all his tents, baggage, and elephants, but gaining a lesson which proved to him well worth the price. He at once took up the negotiations for peace with which his friends at Poona had been only dallying; and on the 13th October of the same year had the satisfaction of learning, through Colonel Muir, who had succeeded Carnac, that the Governor-General was prepared to treat on an honourable basis. Hastings restored to Sindia all that had been taken from him in the course of the war, on the sole condition of his obtaining a treaty of peace from the durbar. The immediate result was the Treaty of Salbai, by virtue of which Upper India became divided into what in modern language would be called "two spheres of influence;" and Sindia was substituted for the Peshwa as the virtual head and representative of the Mahratta nation, as of the Empire of Hindustan. The Prime Minister of the Regency, Nána Farnavis, seems to have perceived this effect of the affair, and long withheld his signature. But Sindia, whose plans were being favoured by fortune, had great objects in view to whose attainment peace with Hastings was essential. He signed as plenipotentiary, 17th May, 1782, and hastened to Hindustan, where momentous events were coming to pass.

[Authorities as for last section. See especially, Strachey: "Hastings and the Rohilla War": Oxford, 1892.]

SECTION 3.—The narrative returns to the Court of Delhi, where Mirza Najaf had just resumed his post, after defeating the Játs in the south, and driving Zábita back to his estates in the north. Ere long the Mirza, finding the Sháh inclined to withdraw his confidence, transferred his residence to the other great fortified palace of the Mughals at Agra, where he passed the next few years of his remaining life; the governor of the place being a Persian immigrant like himself—Muhamad Beg of Hamadán—a resolute soldier who had his own short part to play in local history ere long. In Audh Asaf-ud-daula, the son of the late Nawáb Vazir Shujá, was living a life of idleness, diversified by cruelty.* Sháh Álam at Delhi was sinking into inglorious repose, and allowing the local administration to fall into the uncontrolled and incapable hands of a Kashmirian favourite. In 1778, the governor of the Cis Sutlej States—the old province of Sirhind—called out the troops there to quell a rising of the Sikhs, while the Emperor took the field in person in Jaipur; and the country south-west of the capital was in charge of a converted Hindu, who had become a client of the Mirza, under the title of Najaf Kuli Khán. The Sikh rising proved very formidable; the Mughal Governor was killed in action, and the force, under the Kashmirian minister, which went out to chastise the rebels, was beaten back and only enabled to regain the shelter of the capital by the good conduct of its artillery, manned by Europeans. In the beginning of 1779, the Sikhs crossed the Jumna and ravaged the Upper Duáb, even going so far as to destroy the timber of which the country was at that time full. The Kashmiri could think of nothing but an appeal for help to Mahádaji Sindia, whose hands, indeed, were not then free, but who must have been strengthened by the application in the designs which he was already revolving in his mind. But the affair soon became

† A portrait group by Zoffany, who was then travelling in India, represents the Nawáb fighting a main of cocks with Colonel Mordaunt, the British Resident, in presence of the Hon. Mr. Wheler, of the Calcutta Council. The picture is in private hands.

urgent; already from the watchtowers of Delhi could be descried the crowds of fugitive villagers and the smoke of their burning homesteads. Suddenly the news spread that the Mirza was approaching from the direction of Agra. The futile Kashmiri went out to meet the deliverer; but was contemptuously put under arrest, while a column was sent to check the Sikhs, under Mirza Shafi, the nephew of Mirza Najaf. Coming up with the enemy under the Fort of Mirath—the " Meerut " of to-day—Shafi defeated them with heavy loss, and drove them back into their own country. Thus closed the year 1779.

Profiting by past experience, Mirza Najaf once more took up his abode at Delhi with the post of Amir-ul-Amra, leaving Muhamad Beg in charge of Agra. Samru had died there in May, 1778, more fortunate in his end than his old employer, Mir Kásim. He left a compact landed estate, given him for the support of his brigade, and the charge of both troops and land devolved upon his " Begam," a Muslim lady who had lived with him for some years past, having been originally purchased as a slave. Samru had a lawful wife, by whom he had a son, who survived him; but the wife being insane, and the son a minor, the Mirza gave his approval to the succession of the former slave-girl. In 1781 she embraced Christianity, and for the next half-century continued to reside at Sardhana in quasi-princely state, surrounded by her disciplined troops under European, or half-caste officers.

About the contemporaneous cabals and quarrels of the British officials in Calcutta, we need not greatly concern ourselves, save in so far as they affected the course of public events. It must, however, be here noted that the first results of the interference of Parliament had been anything but useful to Bengal, unless it may have been in the direction of judicial administration. But the Royal Court, however it may have had a beneficial influence in the interior of the country, was anything but an unmixed boon to the Government and people of Calcutta. Apart from the scandal inseparable from the trial and execution of Nand Kumar, the fact that the charter constituting the Court had been vaguely and unskilfully drawn both tended to damage the Court's prestige and to confuse its jurisdiction. So long as Francis had a majority, the council was ever ready to trouble the waters by fomenting quarrels of this kind—and, indeed, of every other. "We three are king," said Francis of himself and the colleagues who acted with him; and they exercised their kingly functions in the most disastrous manner, as is familiar to readers of Macaulay's celebrated essay. Even on the question of land revenue, all important as it was, now that the Company had begun to "stand forth as Diwán," the Council dared to oppose the wisdom of such an expert as the Governor-General. The majority was in favour of an immediate "permanent settlement." The Governor-General urged the need of time, and a patient examination of the assets. Baffled for the moment here, Hastings then turned to a system of subsidiary alliances, by which he hoped to secure British influence as paramount without territorial annexations. And here, too, he was opposed, for a long time with success, the more so because Francis, not content with using his power in Council, was for ever urging his views on the Court of Directors and on the Ministry at home. In 1777 two of the majority were removed by death, and though Mr. Wheler, who was sent out to the Council, became an adherent of Francis, yet so long as Barwell supported him, Hastings, by virtue of his casting vote, had the ascendant in a council of four. In the following year he began to put in operation his subsidiary scheme, and secured some influence at the Court of the Mahratta Rája of Berár, or Nagpore. In July, 1778, came news of war with France, and Hastings had to prepare for the defence of Bengal and Madras alike. The Rája of Benares was called upon to provide for the pay of troops for the frontier, and in January, 1779, as already stated above, Goddard was appointed to command the force despatched for the rescue of Bombay. In 1780 the French in the South were joined by the implacable Haidar Ali, as will be more fully shown in the next chapter; and, as if to crown the edifice of evil, Barwell was determined to leave the country. To minimise this difficulty, the Governor-General attempted to engage Francis to waive differences in face of the enemy. With the concurrence of Coote—now member of his Council—Hastings resolved to renew his demand upon the Benares Rája, on whom, in the course of 1788, he made a call for a contingent of 2,000 horse. The Rája refused, on the plea of poverty; and Hastings reduced the demand to one for half the number. Nothing but attempts to corrupt him following, Hastings set out for Calcutta in July, 1781, in the hope of vindicating the power of the Company and reducing that of the Rája. He was opposed, surrounded, and forced to take shelter at Chunar, but the brave Popham sprang to his aid, and the Rája was driven into Bundelkhand, his dominions being made over to a nephew on terms advantageous to the Company. Hastings then turned to Asaf-ud-daula for help, but the Nawáb answered that he had no money to give or lend. Property indeed there was, to the value of about twenty millions of rupees, which had been his father's, and ought to have been his, but the majority of the Council, against the wish of Hastings, had assigned it to the dowagers—the "Begams," as they were called—in 1776. This, he urged, was a method of oppression under which he ought not to suffer; could the Governor-General grant him redress, he might be able to help the Company as a loyal ally. It was a strong temptation, and to make it stronger Hastings had information that these dowagers had used some of their ill-got means in helping the late revolt in the Benares district. On the other hand, their possession, however unlawful and however ill-employed, was held under a British guarantee.

R

It was a part of this extraordinary man's character to allow no personal consideration to stand between him and what he conceived his duty. As before, in the case of the Rohillas, he probably saw that he was exposing his reputation, and giving justification to some of the detractions of his opponents. But the scales, as he held them, turned the balance on that side, and Hastings not only sanctioned, but actively supported the Nawáb's proposal. The property was taken from the dowagers with a roughness proportioned to their resistance. But that was all the mischief; the ladies received handsome pensions, and bore no malice when the affair was over.*

In the meanwhile Hastings had, literally speaking, to fight for the mastery in his council. For a moment it appeared as if all would act smoothly on the lines of the agreement under which Barwell had been allowed to depart. But ere long Francis repudiated his pledges, and it was only when he was in temporary ill-health that Hastings had a free hand—as during the Gwalior campaign. At length he determined to resume his whole power, or make an end of the struggle. He provoked Francis to a duel, and for once that illogical argument answered a reasonable purpose. Francis was not killed, but was so severely wounded as to be constrained to go home to England for the safety of his life. Hastings seemed at last to triumph.

The rest of his work consists mainly of an effective attempt to reconcile the country courts with the king's tribunal in Calcutta. The jurisdiction of the latter over the former, indeed, he could not grant; but he turned the obstacle by remodelling the Company's chief courts, and placing the Chief

---

* See documents quoted in Trotter; "Warren Hastings," Oxford, 1890. Hastings anticipated the celebrated aspiration of Danton in 1794: "Let my good name be tarnished so that my country prospers." The good old ladies sent Hastings a letter of condolence in his subsequent trouble at home.

Justice at the head of it. The Chief Justice was Sir Elijah Impey, an excellent jurist and linguist, who generously agreed to do the work without salary until his appointment should be confirmed by the Court of Directors. All the reward that these excellent public servants received consisted of calumny and persecution, but Hastings was one of those few men who build for a long permanence, and his scheme, though laid by for nearly a century, has now been at work for an entire generation, and with the happiest results. He also founded the "Asiatic Society" of Bengal, and a College, still in full operation, for the education of Muslim young men. He reformed the salt revenue so as to produce a higher revenue from lower rates, and carried out his long-cherished design of collecting material for an improved settlement of the land revenue system.

In 1782 there was a change of Government in England, Lord North being superseded by the Marquis of Rockingham. The Marquis's right-hand man was Edmund Burke, and Burke derived his inspiration on Indian subjects from Francis. Impey's recall was at once voted in Parliament, and Hastings nearly shared the same fate. Like Clive before him, Hastings adopted a high tone, and refused to remain at his post if condemned by the Court of Directors. The challenge was not taken up, and Hastings remained in office for two years more. They were years of care and trouble, though of less danger and toil than some that had preceded. At home the coalition between Fox and North brought Burke into power, and led to the passing of a new Act for the government of British India. Not, indeed, by the coalition ministry, whose bill for the purpose, after passing the Commons, was thrown out by the Lords on the king's personal intervention. But the younger Pitt—who succeeded—found India the question of the day, and passed an Act of his own on the subject in 1784; the chief feature was the reduction of the effective Directors of the

Company from twenty-one to a "secret committee" of three, who were put under a Parliamentary control. The power of the "Court of Proprietors" was also abolished.

The change of affairs might have seemed not unfavourable to the Governor-General. The king was his friend, and it seemed that the ministers were prepared to yield him full support, all-powerful as they now were, in Indian affairs.

While the British Government of India was thus feeling its way, the once mighty empire that it was replacing was in its last decline. So long as Mirza Najaf was in office, all went smoothly, if not prosperously, and the Court enjoyed a sort of sunset glow.* Besides his post at Delhi—which may have been more honourable than lucrative—the Mirza held an extensive fief of his own, the Gangetic valley from Agra to Aligarh, part of the old Ját country, and a part of Machari, the modern Alwar. He died, without issue, 26 April, 1782, leaving a high reputation among public men of that evil time, and a gap in Delhi politics that could not be filled. The succession to his office and estates was contested between his nephew—already mentioned as commanding against the Sikhs—and a henchman called Afrasyáb Khán. The Emperor was too feeble of purpose to make any definite decision of the dispute. Great excitement arose, not only in Hindustan, but in the neighbouring countries. On one side was Sindia, who had recovered Gwalior, and made peace on his own account; on the other, Hastings and his council anxious to prop the tottering Empire till there was something to take its place. First one of the competitors was assassinated, then another; Sindia drew near. At the same time the country fell under the desolation of a complete failure of the periodical rains for a period of two years.† But the Governor-General was still too hampered to

* Aftáb ("Sun") was Shah Alam's poetic name.
† The famine that ensued was long known in tradition as *Chálisa* ("The Forty"), from having commenced in 1840 Sambat.

interpose into the affairs of Hindustan, and, moreover, he was now winding up affairs in Audh previous to retiring from India.

The character of Mahadaji Sindia had impressed itself on Hastings, and he evidently thought that the best service he could render to the helpless Emperor was to facilitate his obtaining such an able minister. Hastings afterwards stated publicly that there was a time when he " would have afforded effectual assistance to Shah Àlam if power had been granted;" it is probable that he alluded to this very time, and the obstacle was opposition in the council. But he came to see that his opponents, on this occasion at least, were in the right. The Company might have justly complained if their resources —slender and precarious as they then were—had been applied to an object in which they were but indirectly interested. But, as he himself observed, he would indeed have been a madman if he had taken any steps to prevent Sindia from becoming minister of Delhi.

Afrasyáb's murder occurred in October, 1784, and Sindia, who was in the same camp beneath the walls of Agra, held an informal durbar, at which he received promises of support from all the chiefs present, Mughal and Mahratta. He then repaired to the capital, leaving Muhamad Beg in charge of Agra. On presenting himself to the Emperor, Sindia received two patents, one nominating the Peshwa—whom, though a comparatively remote and powerless puppet, Sindia always affected to serve—to the high dignity of Vice-regent of the Empire. The other, and all-essential document, was a commission to himself as deputy in the Peshwa's absence, with a grant of the provinces of Delhi and Agra subject to a monthly payment for the expenses of the Sháh and his household.

In the middle of February, 1784, Hastings set out for Audh, having in his suite a retired Captain de Boigne, whom he sent on thence with introductions to Delhi. Arrived at Benares, he found that part of the country much protected from the effects of the late famine—elsewhere distressingly visible—the exemption being ascribed to the skill and benevolence of Ráza Khán, the same who had been Deputy in Bengal nearly twenty years before. At Lucknow, where he arrived in April, he restored the balance of the State's finances, and provided for the comfort of the dowagers by procuring them part of their former estates. He was joined by the Shah's eldest son— formerly Regent in the after years of Pánipat—who had left Delhi in dudgeon at Sindia's advancement. He strongly advised the prince to make the best of the situation. And the Prince returned with M. de Boigne who carried a strong letter of recommendation from the Governor-General to Sindia. On the 4th Nov., Hastings arrived in Calcutta, where he found news of the passing of Pitt's Indian Act, which determined his already more than half-formed plan of resignation. The Government of India was henceforth to be, virtually, under control of a Parliamentary Board, and, as above said, the change might not have injured Hastings. But Mr. Pitt's speech in support of the Bill had contained thinly-veiled censure of the Governor-General, who conceived his retirement to be "both expected and desired." He willingly made over his charge to the senior Members of Council, and bade a final adieu to India 1st Feb., 1785.

This is not the place for a review of either his character or his administration. This much only need be said here.* He had found the British Empire in the East a thing of shreds and patches; he left it a harmonious whole, strong and prosperous itself, and influencing the native powers for good. And that influence he had gained without—so far as his immediate sphere went—annexing a single square mile of territory.

* *Vide* next chapter for some further observations on the subject.

The Presidency of Fort S. George had been less moderate. We will now turn to that part of India therefore, resuming the thread of our story as it was left in 1761, when Coote returned to Bengal after the capture of Pondicherry.

[Orme's book ends with the fall of Pondicherry, but the narrative will be found, to some extent at least, continued in Wilks' "Mysore," of which a reprint, in two 8vo vols., was published at Madras in 1867.]

CHAPTER VIII.

FINAL OVERTHROW OF THE FRENCH IN INDIA.

Section 1 : Haidar Ali and the first Mysore war—Section 2 : Second Mysore war and final destruction of French power in Southern India—Section 3 : First administration of Mahádaji Sindia.

SECTION 1.—There were many great administrators and leaders of men in the eighteenth century, and India was by no means without her share. Prominent among these was the adventurer already mentioned as distinguishing himself as a soldier in the Mysore service under the title of "Haidar Naik," about the middle of the century. The power of the old Hindu State had fallen into the hands of a minister called "the Dalwai," who was leading the Mysore troops in the cause of Muhamad Ali, the Nawáb favoured by the British when Trichinopoly was successfully defended against the French in 1752. It is indeed not improbable that Haidar was already imposing his strong will upon the politics of the State. Thus, when the Dalwai claimed Trichinopoly on behalf of the Mysore Government, and, on failing to obtain it, transferred his alliance to Dupleix, Haidar either learned or taught a lesson of hostility to England. In 1754 he was put in charge of the Fort of Dindigal and the surrounding district, then an important military position; four years after he got similar possession of Bangalore, the centre of the Mysore territory. These advantages, joined to the growing weakness of the Rája's Government, enabled him to throw off the last vestige of subordination; the Dalwai died, and Haidar, obtaining the suffrages of the soldiers, drove out the Mahrattas and began the substitution of a Muslim principality for the old Hindu Raj in 1760. He conciliated the French, who gave him possession of Chilambram, another commanding post on the road between Cudalore and Madras; and in 1763 captured Bednur, or Nagar, the chief place of a Hindu Rája, commanding the Malabar coast. Here he found an immense treasure, and proceeded to conquer the Zamorin of Calicut, and take Mangalore, where he established a naval arsenal. In 1766 he formally deposed the Rája of Mysore, and completed the conquest of Malabar.

This position brought him in contact with the British, who, after the fall of Dupleix and Lally, had become influential in the Carnatic, under the colour of serving the Nawáb of that province. Muhamad Ali had, at the same time, become independent of his former overlord, the Nizám, a position afterwards confirmed by *firman* from the Emperor. The Nawáb, however, proved of little more avail as a valid ruler than did his contemporaries, Jáfir and Kásim, in Bengal; and the President and Factors of Madras were compelled to take active steps for the protection of their trade. In addition to this the Nawáb had contracted the pernicious habit of borrowing money from them, and to pay his debts was obliged to ask them to rob his neighbours. The Rája of Tanjore was coerced into paying twenty-two lakhs of rupees, and made responsible for a yearly tribute.

Meanwhile, Bussy having departed, his Nizám, Salábat, had been set aside and murdered by his brother, who now held the government of the Deccan by the title of Nizám Ali, and attempted to reassert authority over the Carnatic, which he invaded early in 1763. In their own interest, no less than in that of their ostensible superior, the Nawáb, the Madras Factors were bound to prevent this; and they accordingly sent troops against the Nizám, who promptly evacuated the province.

By way of punishing this aggression and at the same time liquidating the expenses of the war, Clive after the battle of

Baksár, obtained from the Emperor, Shah Álam, a grant of the northern Sirkars, which had been cleared of the French by Forde, as already stated. The Nizám, however, mustered up courage to contest the transfer, and the Madras Government agreed to a compromise—12th November, 1766—whereby it was settled that they were to hold the Sirkars as tributary to the Nizám. At the same time they covenanted to supply him with troops in a war which he was about to wage against Haidar, in conjunction with the Poona durbar.

It was the besetting weakness of the Madras authorities of that time to emulate the bold acquisitiveness of which they had the example in the conduct of their brethren of Bengal. But they seem to have forgotten the immeasurable difference of the two Presidencies in point of ability. In Bengal Clive, Coote, Forde, Adams, and Knox were some of the best soldiers of the British army—who would have won distinction in any warfare—and their valour, joined to favouring conditions, had enabled them to make the Company masters of a wide but compact province which was self-supporting and well in hand. None of these things were forthcoming in Madras. Their best officers were but second or third-rate men; the country was broken and unconquered; their enemies obstinate and—in one instance, at least—of consummate ability. Haidar was not, indeed, unconquerable; he had heard the cries of "Har, Har, Mahdeo!" break in upon his camp when Raguba's Mahratta horsemen surprised his orgies; and had galloped across the wild and wasted country as a despairing fugitive. But he had always recovered himself; his vast treasures and his profound dissimulation had turned to friends his most dangerous enemies. He now used all his resources and united all the other powers of the south against the Madras Factors, whose own dishonesty did not prevent them being duped. In 1767 a British force was sent to oppose Haidar in the high country between Mysore and Arcot, and was beaten back by him after an encounter in the Chengam pass between the Kalráyan and Jawádi hills. Falling back on Trinomalai, they again engaged him—26th September—led by Colonel Joseph Smith, by far their best officer. The fortified hill at that place forms a strong position at the mouth of a pass, and it was bravely held by Smith until the arrival of reinforcements from Madras, when Smith in his turn became the assailant and inflicted considerable loss on Haidar. But the latter remained in the high country and sent plundering parties, who burned the suburb of Madras in which the British officials had their villas. All this time Haidar had to bear the brunt of the campaign alone; the Nizám waiting in an undecided manner until Haidar failing in an attempt to take Ambur—another rock-fort in the neighbourhood—retired on 7th December and withdrew into his own country.

If the Nizám felt any doubts as to the side which prudence counselled him to take, they were completely dispelled about the end of the year by the appearance of a British force sent from Bengal, under Colonel Peach, which entered the northern Sirkars and advanced to Orangal, the old Telinga capital of other days. A treaty was made, 23rd February, 1768, by which the tributary claims of the Nizám, and his right to British aid against Haidar, were formally confirmed; and the aid of a specified body of British sepoys, with field-guns and European officers, was promised whenever they should be required.* Not only was the Nizám thus propitiated and detached from the dreaded combination, but an insurrection kindled among the former subjects of Bednore and Calicut was fanned by Bombay and supported by the aid of 1,500 soldiers from that garrison, who seized Haidar's new port at Mangalore. This, for the time, removed the pressure upon

---

* It was the same error as that of three years before in Bengal, which indeed led to the Rohilla war in later years; a civilised government ought never to promise unconditional support to barbarians.

Madras and the Nizám's dominions. Marching across with great rapidity, Haidar sat down before Mangalore in May, 1768. The town being open to the sea, and the British commander one to whom discretion was the better part of valour, more than a thousand British troops took to their boats, leaving 240 of their sick and wounded comrades to the mercy of the Mysore adventurer.

The hatred formerly felt for the white intruders by Haidar might now have become mixed with contempt had he not found that Colonel Smith had profited by his absence to occupy the country between Madras and the elevated plateau known as the Bálághát. On the 4th August, when he got back from Malabar, he found the British army within twenty miles of Bangalore. Avoiding Smith, for whom he entertained a certain respect, he marched to attack the other British force, which lay at Budikot, Haidar's birthplace, at the foot of the Nandidrúg hill, about thirty miles north-east of Bangalore. But Smith, hearing of his movement, hastened to follow, and a junction was effected between the two British columns before any harm was done.

Haidar was now becoming anxious. So long as Smith was in command he had an opponent whom he could neither conquer nor deceive. He therefore offered terms which the British authorities at Madras might with honour have accepted. But they were as presuming now as they proved timorous in darker days; they wanted money, and the negotiations broke down on the question of tribute to their ostensible master, the Nawáb Mahamad Ali, which Haidar utterly refused to pay.

The war was consequently resumed, and the first encounter, under the walls of Malwágal—if not actually a defeat for Colonel Wood, the British commander—cost him eight officers and 229 men, in killed alone; while Haidar remained master of the fort. On the 14th November, Colonel Smith was recalled, for the time, to Madras; and Haidar twice more made an example of Wood, who was accordingly deprived of the command before the end of the year.

Haidar now resolved on carrying the war into the enemy's country. Detaching a strong force to the southward he swept all opposition before him in that direction, hemming in all the British troops of those parts at Trichinopoly. His flank thus safe-guarded, he eluded the main army, took Karúr and Erode, and marched down the right bank of the Kávari river. It was now January, 1769: the Madras Council, in alarm, sent to ask for fresh negotiations, while Smith was replaced in the chief command of the army in the field. Deceiving him by a fresh manœuvre, Haidar, with a strong flying column, advanced upon Madras, reached "the Mount" in March, and called upon the Council to halt Smith's army and send their President to his quarters to treat.

The substance of the terms which he now proceeded to dictate was this:—

All conquests made on either side during the war were to be restored to the *status quo ante*; each contracting party was to assist the other if attacked; all prisoners should be restored; the district and forts of Karúr should remain a part of Mysore—as they do indeed to this day; and the terms should be made obligatory on the Presidency of Bombay. The Madras Government was powerless; the terms indeed were better than they might have been; and the treaty was ratified on the 4th April, 1769. The first Mysore war was at an end: it had yielded no apparent results, yet sowed the seed of much future strife, and of events of long-enduring importance.

A few more words will be necessary to trace the relations between the various powers of Southern India and to show the genesis of the next struggle in which the Madras authorities became engaged with Mysore. No sooner had they concluded their agreement with Haidar than they had the explanation of the favourable terms that they had obtained from their enemy. Haidar was being called away to deal with antagonists of another cast altogether. Offended at the non-payment of blackmail, the Peshwa, Mádhu Rhadu, invaded the Mysore country with a well-appointed army in 1771, and quickly reduced a number of strong places in the eastern part of Haidar's dominions. In May the young prince's health became so seriously affected by the unwonted exposure that he was obliged to retire to Poona, making over the command to a professional leader, named Trimbak Máma, in whose hands the campaign did not languish. Haidar attempted to concentrate at Seringapatam, where he had a strongly fortified place-of-arms, but the Mahrattas inflicted a surprise which might have been ruinous to him had they not stayed their hands for the plunder of the camp. Once more the wily old chief escaped, and now he bethought himself of the late treaty with the British, which entitled him to "help when attacked." It might have been a question for casuists whether or no he had provoked the attack; but there was the text of the freshly-signed treaty. Under the influence, however, of Muhamad Ali—who was always Haidar's ill-wisher, and whose orders the Madras people professed to obey—no response was made to Haidar's call, a fresh offence which he did not fail to note for future vengeance.

Left to himself the astute adventurer lost no time in conciliating the government of Poona by a full concession of all demands, including the surrender of strong places on the frontier of the Carnatic, which brought the Mahratta garrisons in close contact with the forces of the British and of their Nawáb. So ended the year 1771. In the following year the indefatigable old ruffian sought compensation at the expense of the gallant highlanders of Coorg, a small but interesting country between the upper Kávari and the Malabar coast. There were but 100,000 of them, all told, when Haidar made his unprovoked attack, and carried off the Rája and his family, killing many of the male population in cold blood. He then set to work, slowly but systematically, to recover the places taken from him by the Mahrattas, or forfeited by him at the peace.

In 1773 the restless Raguba, a brave soldier, who only lacked the luck that waits on prudence, after the attack on the Nizám, which has been already mentioned, proceeded to check the proceedings of the audacious chief of Mysore. Haidar, however, hastened to make terms, paying, or promising a war indemnity, and agreeing to recognise Raguba as Peshwa. The subsequent doings with the Bombay Government and all that followed have been related in another place.

All this time a series of questionable transactions had been going on in the Carnatic. Urged by their evil genius, Muhamad Ali, the Nawáb, the Madras people fell upon Tanjore, whose Rája was twice plundered, in the interests of the confederates, and at last—September 1773—deposed; his country being made over to the Nawáb, but subject to all sorts of public and private claims. It was, however, restored not long after, under orders from home.

A member of the Civil Service, named Paul Benfield, one who kept the highest state and scale of living on a salary of 300 Rs. a month, preferred enormous claims on the late government of Tanjore. The Council, finding that he had no vouchers, and suspecting collusion with the Nawáb, disallowed the claim. But Benfield persuaded the members—all of whom were the Nawáb's creditors—to reconsider his case, with the result that a majority decided in favour of the claim. The Governor, Lord Pigot, opposed these proceedings, and attempted to play the part of Hastings; but the majority was too resolute, and Pigot too wanting in force and influence. Pigot was surprised during an evening drive, and taken into the Fort, where he died in captivity in April 1777.

The Court of Directors appointed Sir Thomas Rumbold, an experienced Bengal officer, to succeed Pigot; and he seems to have done his best to check the tide of extortion and misgovernment, though to his own eventual discomfiture. The next thing the majority did was to quarrel with the Nizám.

By the treaty with the Nizám, which followed Colonel Peach's operations in 1767-8, it had been agreed that the Gantur Sirkar, on the right bank of the Krishna river, should remain in the hands of the Nizám's brother, Basálat Jang, whose apanage it was, but should be made over to the Madras-Arcot confederacy on the prince's death. He had proceeded to strengthen himself in his little principality, and even to raise an efficient body of troops under French officers. These proceedings were viewed with alarm by the Nawáb and his British friends; the alarm was communicated to Calcutta, and in July 1775, Warren Hastings sent orders for the expulsion of the French troops, if necessary, by the employment of force. Basálat was afraid of the ruler of Mysore, and did not care to offend the British; but the Nizám procrastinated, and no decisive action was taken on either side.

But events were in progress at the other extremity of the globe which were soon to precipitate affairs in Southern India. In Feb. 1778, the French Government openly espoused the cause of the revolted British Colonists in North America, and war was declared which could not fail to spread to the east. In October of the same year, Pondicherry was forced to capitulate, after a respectable show of defence, and the Madras Government—always professedly that of the Nawáb of Arcot—sent a force across the country to occupy Mahé, the last remaining French station in Southern India. Haidar forbade the undertaking; nevertheless, Mahé was captured in spite of Haidar's flag, that floated over the walls, side by side with the Bourbon lilies. The rage of the old Mysore chief knew no bounds, and he resolved to have revenge for this and all other injuries—real or imaginary—at whatever risk or consequences.

His threats produced but little effect on the equal mind of Warren Hastings, who saw nothing in his enmity with which the ordinary resources of diplomacy, backed by a fair show of force on the part of the Nawáb and Madras ought not to deal. But the Nawáb and Madras had but little ability to use either force or diplomacy; Basálat, it is true, was disposed to make common cause with them, discharging his French soldiers, and allowing the Madras Government to hold Gantur on condition of a yearly rental. But the Nizám was offended at the cession of the district—which he professed to regard as part of his dominions; he forthwith took the discharged French into his own service; demanded tribute, with arrears, for the Sirkars and organised a combination with Haidar and the Poona Regency under Nána Farnavis. The latter agreed to discontinue the demand of blackmail from Mysore, and to confirm the possession of whatever territory Raguba had promised Haidar. To counteract these negotiations, Mr. Holland was sent to Haidarabad, on behalf of the Madras authorities, but he failed to mitigate the displeasure of the Nizám, and had to end by informing his Highness that the tribute for the Sirkars would not be paid.

Matters were now looking serious for Madras. The shadow of the Wadgaon convention still hung over Bombay. In Upper India Goddard's column had disappeared, plunged in the heart of an unknown and partially hostile continent. An attempt was made to avert the wrath of Haidar by sending the most respectable explanation possible. The envoy was Mr. Gray, a member of the Company's Civil Service : but the presents sent with him were both unsuitable and insufficient, and the old chief's already disturbed temper was still more irritated. He returned the presents and refused to receive the money, dismissing Gray from Seringapatam with taunts and a full enumeration of all the offences that he had received from the British at Madras since 1769. A similar attempt to mollify the indignant old chief through the agency of the venerable German missionary, Swartz, had met with no better success, a short time before.

As soon as Haidar's preparations were complete, that is towards the middle of June, 1780, he took the field and set out on his march towards the Carnatic. According to the usual computation, Haidar was now nearly 78 years of age, with a life of hard work behind him, pursued in an extreme climate, and only diversified by bouts of equally hard wine-bibbing. He was, however, still full of energy and craft, and was attended by his son, Tipu Sultan, a fierce and wilful man in the prime of life, vowed—like a modern Hannibal—to unquenchable hostility against the foes of his family. The army had been computed at 90,000, horse and foot—well-drilled and well-disciplined, and supported by a powerful artillery manned by Europeans. Of all the wars ever waged against the British in India, this is said to have had the most public sympathy; prayers were offered up in all the Mosques for its success, and —what was of at least equal value—the Commissariat was cared for by an able and influential Brahman. The force which the Madras people could oppose consisted of, British Infantry, two battalions; sepoys, four; making—with gunners —about 5,200 men, concentrated at and about the Mount. But at Gantur, 225 miles to the north, was another body of 2,800 strong, under Colonel Baillie, who was ordered to march on Conjeveram, where he would be joined by the main army under the Commander-in-Chief.

Unfortunately, neither the Commander-in-Chief nor his junior officer can have been quite an accomplished strategist or tactician. Colonel Baillie was a brave soldier, not without experience, but wanting in the initiative even when not fettered by injudicious orders; and the chief, Sir Hector Munro,

FINAL OVERTHROW OF THE FRENCH. 259

though he had won credit at Baksar fifteen years before, had yet to show whether the intervening period had added to his professional knowledge or only diminished his dash, and added to his dread of responsibility. Minor garrisons were called in, and all was made ready for the coming storm. On the 17th July, the enemy was already threading the Chengam and other passes leading from the plateau of Mysore into the lowlands of the Carnatic.

One source of anxiety the people of Madras were spared ; in spite of all Haidar's efforts, the combination had broken down. Nána Farnavis—never a fighting man—was too busy defending Poona against Goddard to have Mahratta troops to spare for the help of Mysore. The Nizám had been completely alienated by soothing messages from the Governor-General, at the same time that he learned that Haidar had sent a message to Delhi to solicit a grant of the Subadári of the Deccan, which had been for half a century in the family of Asaf Jah.

[Same authorities. See also spirited account by Malleson, "Decisive Battles of India," and Appendix to Marshman, Vol. II., where some of Jas. Mill's misstatements are exposed. See also Sir T. Rumbold's "Vindication," London, 1868.]

SECTION 2.—It was not until the 25th August that Sir Hector Munro set out for Conjeveram. The place was less than fifty miles from Madras, and had been appointed the junction for the two main bodies of the British army; but the delay in starting from Madras had enabled the enemy to occupy it, and to send on part of his army to attack Baillie coming from Gantur, and prevent the junction. Haidar then turned southwards, threatened Wandiwash, and invested Arcot. On the 29th he heard that Baillie, still on his way to Conjeveram, had encamped on the left bank of a little river, called in English books Cortelliar, a few miles north-west of of the place. Reference to the diagram will show that Baillie

S 2

was a little nearer to Conjeveram than Haidar was, but that the river formed an obstacle to his march. Disregarding this, Sir Hector directed him to join at Conjeveram, when he had already arrived within two short marches of Madras, and to march by a circuitous route. Haidar saw his opportunity, and resolved to cut in between the two British columns and dispose of them in detail. It will probably always be a question why the British commander could not have anticipated this strategy by meeting before Haidar could advance to bar the road between them. On the 3rd Sept., in any case, Haidar was masking each from the other, and by the evening of the 5th, the manœuvre was complete; but Baillie had at last found means of crossing the Cortelliar, abandoning his position to the north of the river near Parmabákam,* and writing to Munro to join him, advanced slowly.

Munro got Baillie's letter only on the 8th, and at once reinforced him by a small party, which Colonel Fletcher, with much skill, brought to his assistance through all besetments of the enemy. Baillie now staggered on for two days more, and on the morning of the 9th found himself within fourteen miles of the head-quarters of the army, at the head of 3,720 men, whom he rested during the day with the intention of completing the junction by a night march. Munro—who was detained by want of carriage, which ought to have been supplied by the Nawab, but was not—awaited Baillie in a position which he, apparently, thought needful to the protection of Madras, and where he had intrenched himself with guns of position. To add to his difficulties the rains became very heavy, the roads were flooded, and the streams and artificial watercourses suddenly began to be charged with a strong current. The force under Baillie, however, marched at nightfall, and looked forward to reaching Conjeveram by morning. Desirous of

* Perambakam of the "Imperial Gazetteer," where the latitude stated seems to be a degree too far to the E.

FINAL OVERTHROW OF THE FRENCH.

appearing in good order, Baillie halted half-way by night to give the men rest and have their accoutrements cleaned; from which may be further inferred the character of the man, if his previous dawdling was not sufficient.

But Haidar was not disposed to give them much rest, and he had the advice and aid of French officers. When the halt was over, Baillie's troops resumed their march through a road bordered by trees leading to a village on the open. Before the British column could reach the shelter of the village, it was opened upon by a fire from guns of much heavier calibre than their own six-and-three-pounder field-pieces. Then the cavalry fell on them, and soon no resource was left but to form square, and press on, hoping to be joined by Munro. But no help came; Tipu's horse numbered 25,000: there were thirty battalions of disciplined troops, independent of the French auxiliaries. At last only 300 British (whites) were left; then some of the ammunition exploded; the sepoys lost their heads, and Haidar's cavalry in the confusion entered the square. Baillie on this held out a flag of truce, and ordered his men to ground arms. The Europeans obeyed, but the panic-stricken sepoys kept up a straggling fire. The next moment every man that remained would have been massacred by the infuriated enemy, if the Frenchmen had not sternly interposed.* Out of eighty-six British officers all but sixteen were either killed or wounded; more than half the European soldiers had fallen. For the survivors remained a long and distressful captivity, but not disgrace.

That portion was reserved for the once gallant Munro. He had wandered about all that dreadful day, within earshot of the firing; his appearance would not only have saved Baillie, but forced the enemy—in all probability—to retreat. But he only strayed distractedly between Parmabákam and Con-

---

* Wilks especially names M. Pimorin, of the French army. Lally's nephew was in command.

jeveram. In the evening he learned the terrible tidings from a straggling fugitive, and returned to his camp. Such was the first battle at the place called by the British "Pollilore." No equal disaster befel them again for sixty years. Like his contemporary—to whom he had once given a lesson of courage and conduct—like General Carnac at Wadgaon a year before, Munro threw his guns into a pond, and then fell back upon Madras, pursued by the enemy.

An undue prominence may seem to have been given to this discreditable campaign of three weeks. But it had importance of two kinds. At first it gave up the whole of the Carnatic to the ravages of Haidar and his men. Villages were burned, and food and forage consumed; the men and women were commanded to migrate to Mysore; and those who delayed were massacred on their own thresholds. Its later consequences were less unhappy. Warren Hastings, on hearing of the disaster, prepared at once for its reparation. Sir T. Rumbold had gone home, in peril of his life from sickness; his successor, Whitehill, was suspended by order of the Governor-General, though "the creature," as Hastings said, "made some show of resistance." The remittances sent out for the annual "investments" on behalf of the Company were stopped, the money being devoted to the equipment of the expedition, which in three weeks from receipt of the news was ready to sail, under the veteran, Sir Eyre Coote, one of the heroes of Plassy, and the conqueror of the ill-starred Lally.

Coote reached Madras 5th Nov., 1780, and applied himself to restoring the morale of the coast army, and providing for the wants of the Commissariat. He found that, in the interval, Pondicherry had been reoccupied by the French, and Arcot just taken by Haidar. Places so near as Vellore and Chingalpat were under siege, and Wandiwash—where the brave Lieutenant Flint, with Ensign Moore for his sole white comrade, still held out—was being sorely pressed. On 17th Jan., 1781,

Coote was at last able to take measures for the relief of some of these places. The siege of Wandiwash was raised on 28th Jan., and Coote took up a position at Cudalore, where he found that a French fleet had just arrived for the protection of Pondicherry.

Coote passed a month of great anxiety, "between the devil and the deep sea," for Haidar's enormous disproportion of numbers enabled him to prevent the British foragers from obtaining provisions from the country, while the French fleet hindered supplies from reaching the camp by sea. But on 15th Feb. the fleet departed, and Coote seized the opportunity and was victualled from Madras. The antagonists now for months watched each other warily, two experienced veterans, neither of them timid, yet each unwilling to lay himself open in striking the first stroke. Coote at length made a dash at Chelambram, but was foiled, and fell back on Porto Novo, an old Portuguese settlement south of Pondicherry, where he could reckon on being supported by the British squadron, under Admiral Hughes. With only 8,000 men of all arms he waited until Haidar—whose army was about tenfold that strength—got round his position, and drew up between the British and their depôt at Cudalore.

Finding himself thus hemmed in, Coote determined to hazard a decisive blow, and on the morning of 7th July, 1781, moved on Haidar's works, turned the main position, and forced Haidar to fly, after losing one of his best lieutenants, and a number of killed and wounded, that was estimated at 10,000. The siege of Wandiwash—which had been renewed—was at once raised, and the Southern Presidency was saved from certain ruin. Haidar continued in the Carnatic for some time longer, and a great French sea officer—the Bailli de Suffrein—gained the command of the coast for a time. But Haidar never regained the position he had held after the destruction of Baillie and the retreat of Munro.

He fought a second battle on the fatal field of Pollilore in August, the results of which were not decisive, but on 27th Sept. he was utterly routed at Sholinga, in North Arcot, where he lost 5,000 men. The reign of the avaricious and mutinous Madras Council was put an end to by the appointment of a respectable military diplomatist, Lord Macartney, who at least evinced good intentions. War broke out with the Dutch, and Negapatam, their factory on the Coromandel coast, was taken. The drivelling and treacherous Nawáb was put on an allowance; the surplus revenues of the Çarnatic being taken over for five years—a prelude, as it proved, to the mediatisation of the prince, and the annexation of the province.*

Further successes followed, both on the Coromandel coast and on other sides; they were chequered by occasional misfortunes, as when a column of native troops, under Colonel Braithwaite, was surprised by Tipu Sultan, and underwent the same fate as had befallen Baillie at Pollilore. But the acute mind of the old chief of Mysore refused to take comfort from such transient gleams. The grand combination was melting away. The Nizám held aloof; Sindia was beaten down; at Poona the Nána had begun to waver; the Rája of Berar had made peace with Hastings. The country was wasted and famine-stricken, and Haidar, baffled and depressed, died 7th Dec., eighty years of age, as he was unsuccessfully besieging the fortress of Vellore.†

As soon as the news of his father's death reached Tipu he retired from Malabar, where he was engaged with a British force from Bombay, under Colonel Humberstone.‡ Coote had

* The head of the family still bears the title of Prince of Arcot, and is the premier noble of the Madras Presidency.

† The country people crowded into Madras, where for some time they perished at the rate of 1,500 a week.

‡ Haidar's remains were taken to his captial, Seringapatam, and interred in a handsome mausoleum which is still kept by the care of the British Government, which has done honour to itself by showing honour to its once cruel, but energetic enemy.

returned to Madras to die, worn-out, like his antagonist, with years of labour. On 10th April, 1783, the famous French officer, the Marquis de Bussy, landed at Cudalore, where he was presently besieged by the incompetent Stuart. But the Nána had by this time signed the treaty of Salbai, concluded on behalf of the Durbar by Sindia; and presently arrived the news of the peace concluded between France and Britain. It was then that Stuart, who had once arrested Pigot, found himself in the same predicament, being sent home under arrest by Lord Macartney. On the side of Malabar, however, the war went on for some time; and at Bednore and Mangalore British garrisons were, after a brave defence, forced to capitulate to Tipu. At last, 11th March, 1784, aided by the Nizám and the Nána, the Madras Government obtained terms which, attended though they were, by humiliating incidents, produced a cessation of the war.

Each party was heartily sick of fighting. The Governor of Madras was anxious to obtain peace and recuperation for the wasted provinces under his control. On the other hand a considerable British force, headed by Colonel Fullarton, an able and enterprising officer, was within a few marches of Tipu's capital. In concluding the treaty Macartney acted without the approval of the Governor-General; but there were 1,000 British captives to be thought of; and there were all the conquered places in the Carnatic, whose restoration formed one of the conditions of peace. Macartney was inexperienced and obstinate, but the Treaty of Mangalore was so far justified that peace was restored for a few years.

The death of Haidar was, as we have seen, immediately followed by the ratification of the Treaty of Salbai. By the end of the following June the news arrived of the peace between France and Great Britain; and Bussy retired to Pondicherry, where he presently died without having struck the blow by which he had seemed about to annihilate the imbecile Stuart.

The period is therefore to be noted as that in which the first scheme of British Indian enterprise came to completion. Commerce had hitherto been the object, as it had been in the 16th century for the Portuguese. When Warren Hastings assumed the government of Bengal in 1772, the task before him seemed to be the establishment of a sound mercantile position for the Company whose servant he was. Such small political efforts as had been hitherto made were probably intended in all sincerity for the protection of commerce. It had seemed possible to establish relations with India such as have since been formed with the Chinese Empire; treaty-ports in favouring situations, with Bengal as a larger Hong-Kong. But it was now becoming evident that for such a scheme the first requisite was wanting: to have treaty-ports there must be a native Government with which valid treaties can be made and enforced. The servants of the Company tried to do this for half a century, from the date of the mission to Delhi in 1715 to that of the grant of the Diwáni in 1765. Madras and Bombay made similar attempts, the one with Poona, the other with Arcot and Haidarabad. But all terminated in the British factories being drawn into the quarrels of their neighbours, and thence by almost imperceptible degrees, into territorial extension. This process had not escaped the notice of competent observers. Adam Smith saw, writing as far back as 1775, shortly after the passing of the Regulating Act, that Empire was coming; adding the shrewd comment:—"To found a great empire for the sole purpose of raising up a people of commerce may at first sight appear a project fit only for a nation of shopkeepers"; thus anticipating the sarcasm of Napoleon.

When the words were written Warren Hastings had become Governor-General; and a change was at hand which the great publicist understood. That change was partially due to the rivalry of France, partly to the inherent vices of all the various native administrations. Bengal could no longer support Clive's

FINAL OVERTHROW OF THE FRENCH. 267

system, the last native statesmen disappeared.* Arcot was insolvent and unfaithful; the Mahratta Confederacy was dissolving; the Nizám was not much more to be trusted than the Nawáb of Arcot, once his feudatory. The power of Mysore was still in hostile, if less formidable, hands. Sindia alone stood erect at Delhi; strong in his own transcendent skill and prudence, and in the prestige which still clung to the Imperial sovereignty of which he was the minister. Having overcome all obstacles the two ablest statesmen in the country agreed to partition it into what would now be termed "two spheres of influence."

James Mill professes to suspect something mysterious in the understanding between Hastings and Sindia; but the mystery is easy of solution.† The Empire had fallen into the hands of a competent administrator, the British having taken such portions of it as seemed sufficient for the purposes of commerce. So far there was a dominion such as Adam Smith contemplated. But it was to the interest of the British that the rest of the country should be ruled or influenced by the power most conducive to peace and order: that power was Sindia, who was recognised accordingly. Thus Hastings, one of the few British Indian rulers who never made an annexation, was yet the founder of the British power in the East.

The verdict of history on this subject was anticipated by a great advocate. In his famous defence of the printer, Stockdale, Erskine made the indirect apology of Warren Hastings. If the dominion of Britain in Bengal and the Carnatic was founded on violence it was, as he showed, madness to charge Hastings with crime merely because he had used the most

---

* Nand Kumar was hanged: Shatáb Rai retired into private life; Muhamad Raza Khán dwindled into Divisional Commissioner under the British Government of Bengal.

† Wilson's edition; vol. v., p. 15 and f. f. [Same authorities: also Wilks, "History of Mysoor," 2 Vols. Madras 1869.]

efficient means for its support, "If it be true," he urged, "that Mr. Hastings was directed to make the safety and prosperity of Bengal the first object of his attention and that—under his administration—it *has* been safe and prosperous . . . then a question may be unaccountably mixed with your consideration . . . which the Commons, as prosecutors of Mr. Hastings, should in common prudence have avoided."

SECTION 3.—After the departure of Warren Hastings the Governor-General, for the time, was a Company's servant, Mr., afterwards Sir John, Macpherson, whose chief act of importance was the occupation of Cawnpore and Anupshahr with British detachments. He also restored the Carnatic revenues to the Nawáb, who had made a temporary assignment of them in 1781, and repudiated with much spirit an attempt made from Delhi to recover the tribute of Bengal. An able and experienced man of affairs, Macpherson effected financial reforms of some moment; and, when, at the end of a year and a half, Lord Cornwallis was appointed to the permanent post, the acting Governor-General retired with a fair record, a full purse, and the honour of a baronetcy. The new ruler had not done very well in the war recently terminated in North America; but he was of unblemished character, and not an ardent politician; so that his nomination met with public approval. He landed in Calcutta, September, 1786, and found that, with the exception of the South, where Tipu was engaged in hostilities with the Nizám and the Peshwa, all was tranquil. Some war-clouds appeared upon the northern horizon, and, although the Nawáb of Audh received some financial relief by a new treaty, yet the troops were not recalled from the North-West, where the attitude of Máhádaji Sindia was still viewed with distrust. The little province of Gantur, which, on the death of his brother, had been appropriated by the Nizám, was now resumed by the British Government; and a brigade was promised to aid the

Nizám in opposing any power not in alliance with the British, Tipu's name not been included in the list. The policy of Hastings was being justified; Tipu had been recognised as a certain enemy, the chief of the Mahrattas as a desirable ally.

Meanwhile the position of Sindia at the Imperial Court was anything but secure or easy. By long-standing opposition the Nána had taught him not to lean too much on Poona; and the friendship of Tukáji was only that of an old comrade, not quite his own master, though he might begin to have views of his own. The Rajputs, proud and having old grudges against the House of Álamgir, were not the more conciliated because the head of that House was now ruled by a low-born Hindu: the Muhamadan courtiers who represented the once powerful Lords of Iran and of Turan, profited by familiar intercourse with the Emperor to foster in his mind a drowsy dream of Muslim revival; and the successors of Warren Hastings did not seem very friendly in their distant strength. To the demand which—like the Nizám in regard to the Sirkars—Sindia made for the payment of the tribute of Bengal, he had met with a stern rebuff. The Government of Mr. Macpherson caused their agent to inform him that his persistence in such claims "would be considered in the light of direct hostility," and Scindia judged it prudent to reply by "an official and solemn disavowal," both from himself and on behalf of the Emperor.*

But Sindia was indebted to Warren Hastings for what eventually proved more valuable to him than much tribute would have been. It has been related above that, before leaving the upper provinces, Hastings had sent M. de Boigne to him with a favourable introduction; and Sindia, in engaging the

* "Calcutta Gazette," 12th May, 1785. It will be borne in mind that the tribute of Bengal had been stopped by Warren Hastings, at the same time that the Allahabad province had been sequestered, in consequence of the Sháh going to Delhi contrary to the wish of the Calcutta Government.

bearer to raise and discipline a small corps of Sepoys, was, however unconsciously, laying the foundation-stone of his own future fortunes. De Boigne was a native of Savoy, who had by this time almost attained middle life, after having vainly sought advancement in many paths. Beginning life as an Ensign in the Irish Brigade of Louis XV., he had served for some years without encouragement. He then entered the service of Catherine of Russia, and was taken prisoner by the Turks in the Levant in 1770. He was sold as a slave, and is said to have been for some time employed to carry water for his Osmanli purchaser. Escaping from this trial, he made his way, overland, to India, bringing a letter from Lord Percy, on the strength of which he was granted a commission in the 6th Regiment of Madras Native Infantry. After a time he left that service and endeavoured to support himself as a fencing-master at Madras, finally going to Calcutta with a letter from Macartney to Warren Hastings. After some further adventures he now found himself the commandant of a little force resembling that once led by the deceased Samru.

Another accession to Sindia's staff was made about this time by the submission of Muhamad Beg, the Governor of Agra, 27th March, 1785. He was a Persian officer of courage and energy, and his adhesion involved the acquisition of the fortress of Akbar, a strong and central place-of-arms. Sindia's position, therefore, was improving; Tukáji Holkar was engaged in a war which the Poona Durbar had begun against Mysore, and the somewhat abrupt termination of that affair— when Tipu made terms for himself in April, 1787—did not inspire Holkar with any desire of troubling his old comrade in Hindustan. Ere long, too, he found other occupation in Bundelkhand, whither he was sent by his mistress, Ahalya Bai, to carry out the policy of the Peshwa's Government in that region. The result was the establishment of one Ali Bahádar—an illegitimate son of the late Peshwa Baji Ráo I.

as Nawáb of Banda, a position which his family continued to fill until 1857.

For these and the like services Tukaji received his reward in money assignments, which afterwards proved to harbour the germ of misunderstanding and even war, as will be shown in the proper place. For the present there was peace between the two chiefs who shared the province of Málwa. Nevertheless, Sindia felt the importance of keeping up the communication between his possessions there and his other outposts; and with that object sent Muhamed Beg to effect a settlement of an intervening district where the proud and ancient Rajput clan of Kechi Chauhans held possession of the Fort of Rághugarh.

It was about this time that Sindia made an attempt to strengthen and perpetuate his position at Delhi by strongly urging the return of the heir-apparent to the Empire—Mirza Jawan Bakht—whom we last saw at Lucknow, sueing for the support of Warren Hastings, and advised by that statesman to throw himself on the friendship of Sindia. The Prince, however, after consulting with Major Palmer, the agent of the Governor-General, felt by no means assured that he would be protected by the Calcutta Government if he went to Delhi. Perhaps he was also jealous of Sindia's power, having himself acted as Regent at Delhi in the years that immediately followed the defeat of the Mahrattas in 1761. Whatever may have been the reason, he turned a deaf ear to the invitation.

Nor did the Calcutta Government indeed, show any alacrity to intervene in Delhi politics. By Pitt's Act, provision had been made for preventing a repetition of the scandalous scenes that had so often paralysed the hands of Warren Hastings; the Governor-General was henceforth to be, virtually, supreme in his council. Cornwallis was thus a sort of Dictator in British India, under the supervision of the Prime Minister, and of his close friend, Mr. Dundas, who was the first President of the Board of Control. The views of these ministers were strongly enunciated in favour of peace and non-intervention; and Cornwallis himself, mindful of his unlucky warfare in America, had a wholesome dread of collision with the native States.* The Anglo-Indians vainly urged on their new Governor-General that "the interests of the Company were bound up in those of the Heir-apparent." The views of the Government were matured ere long :—" Many have urged the necessity of upholding the Mogul . . . but this should seem bad policy, as we should thus causelessly become obnoxious, and involve ourselves in the interest of a declining State."† The development of events was, ere very long, to show that British power had now gone too far to make such abstention safe, even if it were possible. But, for the present, Sindia had nothing to fear from British intervention.

The Prince, then, remained at Lucknow, protected, but not otherwise supported, by the Calcutta Government; and Sindia had to look about him for other means of establishing his power. One method that suggested itself to his mind was the destruction of the power of the great territorial magnates who were constantly robbing the people and rebelling against the State, from whose revenue they also alienated sums which, when added up, came to a considerable diminution. The tenures were something like the old feudal tenures of Europe; but Sindia thought—like Akbar before him—that it would be better to exact the dues in money and pay his troops himself. Most of these "Barons" were Mussulmans; but a formidable opposition was raised by one who was a Hindu, and a capable military leader, Himmat Bahádur Gosain, who revolted in Bundelkhand.

Still more serious was the feeling of the slow but valorous

* See "Cornwallis," by W. S. Seton-Kerr, in the "Rulers of India" series, pages 16-17.
† "Calcutta Gazette,' 8th March, 1787.

tribes of Rujpután. Rághugarh was taken, and the capture not only laid open the way into their country but offended their pride by the overthrow of one of their oldest and noblest clans. Punctuality was not the strong point of the Rajput character, but by the spring of 1787 they had at last formed their alliances and plans. The Kachwáhas of Jaipore, the ancient Ambér; the Gahlots of Jodhpore, once known to us as Márwar; and the Sisodias of Udaipore, famous under the older name of Méwar; collected their forces and made common cause to resist the payment of tribute by any of them, and chastise the man by whom it was demanded. Their troops numbered 100,000 horse and foot—the cavalry especially gallant soldiers—and they had 400 guns, of various kinds. Trusting to the growing disaffection of the landlords, with whose ringleader, Muhamad Beg, they had probably by this time opened communications adverse to the interests of his employer, they marched as far as Lálsaut, a small place forty-three miles east of Jaipore, where they encamped and awaited the troops of Sindia and the Empire. The latter were led by Muhamad Beg; but the fact that he was one of the threatened barons, taken with subsequent events, appears to justify the belief that he was deceiving his employers. Among the other commanders were some whose loyalty was more secure. Such as De Boigne and Rána Khán, the latter a devoted follower of Sindia ever since he saved the chief's life in the escape from Pánipat. Muhamad Beg was accompanied by a nephew like himself a Persian from Hamadán, and a gallant leader of heavy cavalry. The encounter occurred at Lálsaut, in the height of the hot season, about the end of May, 1787, and turned out ill for Sindia. After three days' fighting, in which Muhamad Beg was killed by a round shot, as he was idly looking on from an elephant's back in the rear of the line, Sindia was repulsed; on the evening of the third day, 14,000 of his infantry marched out of the lines and joined the Jaipur Rája,

T

and Ismail deserted with 1,000 horse, four battalions of foot, and six guns. The Muhamadan account of the affair is somewhat confused, but that was the upshot, though some of the best authorities* say that Muhamad Beg had gone over before he was killed; in any case, the subsequent conduct of his nephew shows that there was treachery among the Muhamadans of Sindia's so-called Imperial forces, of which the Rajput leaders were not unaware.

Sindia was also much distressed by scarcity of provisions; and his camp was subjected to nightly attacks of marauders; in fact, he was in the midst of a hostile country; so that, after a drawn battle of three days' duration, and being exposed to great losses from desertion, he judged it wisest to fall back upon the friendly territory of the Rája of Alwar, and await assistance from the Játs of Bhurtpore, who were also his allies. The Sikhs were likewise giving trouble to the North of Delhi, and he had been under the necessity of detaching a strong body of his troops to check their advance, under the command of one of his best Mahratta officers, Ambáji Inglia.

General de Boigne used afterwards to declare that this dark hour was that of Sindia's moral greatness. Sending off his heavy baggage to Gwalior, and conciliating the chief of Bhurtpore by making over to him the fortress of Dig, he lost no time in writing to Poona for reinforcements. He then sent his heavy guns into the Fort of Agra, which he put under the charge of Lakwa Dáda, one of his most trusty lieutenants. Sindia's letter to the Nána at Poona will be found in Grant Duff (III. 24) it is a manly composition, but it produced only a niggard reinforcement at the time. Meanwhile, Ambáji, hastening to his master's support, fell in with a Rajput force which put him to flight with severe loss; and Sindia took refuge in the Fort

* Grant Duff, vol. lii., Franklin's "Sháh Àlam," "Calcutta Gazette" for June, 1787. The account in the text is taken from a Persian MS. of the time.

of Gwalior, while Ismail Beg laid siege to Agra. To make matters worse, Ghulám Kádár, the son of Zábita Khán, a young man of ability and courage, but passionate to the verge of insanity, issued from his strongholds in the Upper Duáb to join the Beg in striking a blow for the cause of Islám.

While the fortunes of Sindia where at this low ebb, the heir-apparent joined himself to the Gosain leader, Himmat Bahádur, and marched with him towards the capital; while the Emperor his father,—who never knew his own best interests— opened friendly communications with the Rajputs, and received Ghulám Kadir, as Amir-ul-amra, in durbar, at Delhi. Before the end of the year, however, the small reinforcement sent by the Nána reached Sindia, who then broke up from Gwalior and advanced to attempt the relief of Agra. He was met by Ismail and Gholám Kadir near the village of Chaksana, twenty-three miles west of Agra, where his Mahratta horse were put to flight by the Muslim men-at-arms; and nothing but the steadiness of De Boigne and his European officers, prevented grave disaster. Sindia and Rána Khán then retreated to Bhurtpore where they took shelter in the fort of that place until a diversion, raised through the Sikhs, called off Ghulám to protect his northern possessions.

It was about this time, that the heir-apparent, who had reached Delhi, addressed a direct appeal to King George III. This curious state-paper reveals some of the hopes and fears that were agitating the interior circle of the court; it describes Sindia as vainly directed to "conciliate the attachment of the old nobility, and extend protection to the distressed peasantry," it classes him among the foes of the Imperial House and its allies, "the Princes and Rájas," and conjures His Majesty to "restore the royal authority, punish the rebellious, and render his name illustrious by giving repose to the people of God."

It may be readily conceived, that if Cornwallis would do

nothing there was nothing to be expected from the Government in London. But there might be help nearer at hand. The prince, therefore, endeavoured to return to Lucknow, and plead his father's cause with the Nawáb—the hereditary Vazir of the empire—while the Emperor continued his intrigues with Begam Samru, and the Rajput chiefs. In the last days of the year a mission arrived from Jodhpore—whose aged Rája, Bijai Sinh, had for years been a bitter enemy to Sindia. The envoys presented the Empire with a golden key, the emblem of the possession of Ajmere, whither they, in the name of their master, invited his majesty to repair; it was added that Partab Sinh, the ruler of Jaipore, was a party to the invitation. The Sháh accordingly set forth, in the beginning of 1788, attended by Begam Samru, with some of her disciplined battalions under command of George Thomas, an Irish adventurer who had recently entered her service.

Whilst his feeble parent was thus engaged, the Mirza met with his share of adventure on his eastward journey. Attempting to get possession of the Fort of Agra, he narrowly escaped being made a prisoner; and when he found no help from the Nawáb of Audh, he sought protection from the British at Benares, where he soon after ended his blameless but unlucky life.

The Sháh, for his part, got as far as Gokalgarh, a fortress in the Riwári country held by a contumacious "Baron" named Najaf Kuli Khán, which he thought proper to besiege. After an action with the garrison, which had sallied out to attack his camp, and in the *mêlée* being only saved by the energy of Himmat Bahádur, and the coolness of Thomas and the Begam, he forced the rebel to yield the place. But the affair gave such a shock to his nerves that he renounced the expedition and returned to Delhi, which he re-entered on 16, April, 1788.

He had only re-entered, in truth, the toils of the hunters. Begam Samru returned to Sirdhana: Sindia fell back upon

Alwar, and got beaten twice more; while Ambáji sustained another defeat from the Rajputs. But Rána Khán, who had been sent to Poona, now returned with fresh reinforcements; and in a fiercely contested battle, at the old imperial country-seat of Fatehpur-Sikri, at last drove off Ismail Beg, and raised the siege of Agra. At the same time, Sindia had the misfortune to lose the aid of De Boigne, who disapproved of the conduct of affairs and left him to go into private business at Agra. Ismail Beg was, about the time, rejoined by Ghulám Kádir, who had settled with the Sikhs; and, finding that Sindia did not molest them, the pair set out to try their fortunes at Agra.

And now began the last act of the imperial tragedy. The confederates entered the palace on 15th July, and were received as friends. Ismail Beg then formed his camp on the outskirts of the city and proceeded to levy contributions. His accomplice began a systematic plunder of the palace, ill-treating the women and children, setting up a puppet Emperor, and at length inflicting every outrage on the Emperor's family. The Emperor showed great firmness, but in vain. On 10th August, Ghulám blinded the unhappy old man and flung him into confinement. Sindia had up to this, held aloof; but was now urged to interposition, and for the next two months his troops collected on the western and southern sides of Delhi. On the 11th October Ghulám, finding that Ismail Beg had abandoned him, and that he was in danger of being invested by the forces of Rána Khán, escaped by the only opening left, and endeavoured to seek his own country and raise the Sikhs. Pursued by Rána Khán,—who had been reinforced by the troups of Málwa under Tukáji Holkar—the crazy ruffian shut himself up in the Fort of Meerut, where he attempted in vain to stand a siege. On 21st December he stole out by night, intending to make for the Cis-Sutlej States of the Sikhs; but he was captured and dragged about in triumph, until his custodians, wearied and exasperated by his abusive language, cut out his tongue, and, after other cruel mutilations, hanged him on a road-side tree. Thus, even in the depth of the great anarchy that had fallen upon Hindustan, outraged humanity exercised its rude justice.

By the unwritten traditions of the East no blind man could be a Sultan; but Sindia, who had more love of fact than of form, intended for the future to do the whole business of the state; and so felt that he might spare the Sháh the pain of open deposition. He therefore enthroned him anew, and presented anew the homage of himself and of the absent Peshwa. Nay, such was still the prestige of the imperial shadow that we are expressly told, by an observant contemporary, that Sháh Álam continued to be regarded as occupant of the throne of the House of Taimur, and that Sindia shared in the general reverence.*

But the position of Sindia was now enormously improved. Not only was the blind old Emperor's power of secret undermining destroyed, but he had discovered who were his true friends. In a poem composed by the Sháh at the time—under his literary name of Aftáb—he calls Sindia "him who is even as a son unto me;" so that one great centre of intrigue and source of danger was converted to harmlessness, if not use. Then, although no great dependence was to be placed on Ismail Beg, his interests were, for the moment at least, on Sindia's side; and the gift of Najaf Kuli's fief—that contumacious baron being now no more—not only conciliated the Mughal cavalier of fortune, but furnished him with occupation in defending his estate against the Játs and the robber tribes of the west. The temporary withdrawal of De Boigne, too, came to an end, that officer being invited to return to the service on his own terms, and remodel the army as he pleased, in preparation for future eventualities.

* " Memoire du General Comte de Boigne." Chambèri, 1829. De Boigne was still alive when this book was published; it was written by his son.

While the heart of the Mughal Empire was thus beating its last, the distant dependencies of the south were going through a singular evolution. It was becoming more and more clear that the Muslim power in Mysore was to be reckoned with, and that it was not to be bound by the mere comity of nations. Yet the proceedings of Cornwallis in regard to Tipu were so high-handed, and his means of supporting them were of such doubtful efficiency, that nothing but the gravest necessity could suffice for their justification. Reference has been already made to the letter sent by the Governor-General to the Nizám, in July, 1789, in which the help of the British was promised against enemies, amongst whom Tipu seemed to be, by implication, included. Presently came news that Tipu was promising help to the French at Pondicherry, whilst he was at the same time threatening the old Hindu principality of Travancore, whose Rája was an ally of the British.

The Presidency of Madras was then temporarily under the charge of Mr. Holland—mentioned above as an unsuccessful envoy to the Nizám. This official, when the Governor-General sent him orders to promise a conditional support to Travancore, withheld the information, and attempted to drive a special bargain for himself with Tipu. Emboldened by these feeble and discreditable proceedings, Tipu attacked Travancore on 28th Dec., 1789. Holland soon after quitted his appointment, and left for Europe, being succeeded, after a brief interval, by the Commander-in-Chief, General—afterwards Sir William—Medows.

Cornwallis now saw the necessity of action. Encouraged by a letter from Dundas, he sought the alliance of the Poona Durbar; and a tripartite treaty was concluded between the Government of India, the Mahrattas, and the Nizám (1790), providing for joint action against Tipu, and an equal partition of his territories. In February, 1790, Medows took the field; the army was no longer an affair of a few white troops with a handful of sepoys; the force under Medows comprised 15,000 of all arms, "the finest English army," wrote Cornwallis, " that had ever been assembled in India." On 25th May the whole expedition assembled on the plain of Trichinopoly the principal aide of the General being his military secretary, Colonel George Harris, of the 5th Fusiliers, hereafter to win for himself the highest distinction against the same enemy. In the meantime the ally to whose succour they were marching was showing himself worthy of their best exertions. The Rája of Travancore had only a territory of 7,000 square miles at the most, with a population of less than two millions; but he and his people possessed the courage of mountaineers. The Rája had also engaged some European officers to drill his men, and by their advice had drawn up strong lines of fortification on the north-eastern frontier of his naturally inaccessible country. Two of the forts on the coast had also been bought from the Dutch to add to the strength of the little principality from that side; and thus, when Tipu demanded their surrender, the Rája defied and beat off, with loss, the famous soldiers of Mysore. That was in 1789. Next year he was again attacked, when the tardy arrival of the British at Coimbatore drew off the attention of the invader. This was on the 23rd July, 1790, and the army obtained some successes between that date and the 21st Sept. But a detachment of cavalry was surprised by Tipu, and driven back with the loss of some of its guns, and Tipu also took some of Medows' magazines. Meanwhile the Governor-General had sent down a flanking force along the Northern Sirkars, which effected a junction with Medows, and raised his force by over 9,000 troops. The gallant Hartley, who had saved the honour of the Bombay army eleven years before, also co-operated on the Malabar coast, and in December captured one of Tipu's best officers, with over 2,000 of his men. Nevertheless, the Governor-General was far from feeling satisfied with the conduct of the war, which was bringing but a small harvest of results in proportion to the expense.* Before, indeed, he could have heard of the success of Hartley—the chief exploit of the campaign—he had set sail for Madras, where he arrived before the year was ended, and at once took up the conduct of affairs. Once more the Mysore troops laid waste the Carnatic, and Tipu re-opened his futile negotiations with the Council of Pondicherry. On 11th Feb. Cornwallis assembled his army at Vellore, and, after misleading Tipu by a series of able manœuvres, made his way into the Mysore plateau without encountering the enemy, taking Bangalore on his way, which surrendered on 21st March. So far all had prospered, and it might have been expected that the allies would now gather heart to fulfil their engagements, and take an active part in the proceedings. This, however, they failed to do; and after vainly menacing Seringapatam, Cornwallis was obliged to begin his retreat on 26 May, after destroying his siege-train, for the draught of which he had no cattle left. Some forts were taken by the British; on the other hand, Coimbatore was battered to the ground by Tipu, the remains of the garrison being taken away captive. So far Cornwallis had done no better than Medows, if as well. In the following year, however, the allied forces made a show of exertion; the Mahrattas, in particular, took some places, and plundered parts of the Mysore country, but the objects of the British Government seemed no nearer of attainment. Nevertheless, the prestige of that Government was to some extent maintained, and even increased, by the pertinacity with which the army occupied the country on the north-east of Mysore, and reduced the frontier castles.

At length, in Jan., 1792, Cornwallis felt at liberty to make a great forward movement. The army had been reinforced, and was now in great strength, and the commissariat had been thoroughly organised. The camp of Tipu was assaulted, the

* Authorities chiefly quoted in text.

Governor-General being wounded, while Tipu was forced to fly, and evacuate all his posts north of the Kávari river. On the 5th Feb. Cornwallis stood before the walls of the outworks on that side, with 20,000 good troops and a powerful siege-train. The works being taken in a night attack, though not without heavy loss, the Sultan judged it prudent to ask for terms. An agreement was made, by which some territory was ceded, and money penalty paid, and the Sultan's two eldest sons were delivered up to the British Governor-General, as hostages for the fulfilment of the conditions. Travancore was saved; the adjoining highland principality of Coorg was restored to its hereditary chieftain; and each of the treacherous and useless allies was rewarded with a slice of the forfeited territory, enough being retained by the British to round off the territories of Madras, and—for the first time—give interior possessions to the little Presidency of Bombay.

[See authorities already cited. Also Malleson's "Seringapatam, past and present," Madras, 1876: Michaud; "Progrès et Chute de l'Empire de Mysore"; 2 vols., Paris, 1801-9: and Marshman; "History of India," 3 vols., London, 1867, a most useful summary.]

CHAPTER IX.

THE END OF THE ANARCHY.

Section 1: Cornwallis as a Reformer—Section 2: Sindia's Second Administration—Section 3: Wars in the Deccan and Destruction of Tipu.

SECTION 1.—Thus far Cornwallis had been carrying the work of Warren Hastings to a necessary, if not always intentional conclusion. The treaty of Salbai, followed by the treaty of Mangalore, was in appearance, a peaceful settlement; yet the result had been an increase of British influence, which soon led to further expansion. All the military policy of the period was thus shaped. In civil affairs also the mark of the last Governor but one was plainly impressed; and although, in this department, some deviation was made, the change was not always of unquestioned benefit. The institutions of Cornwallis were, it cannot be doubted, due to a genuine benevolence. But their wisdom was not equally certain, for they were sudden and rapid rather than due to natural evolution. What Pitt and Dundas ordered, in pursuance of the recommendations of the Governor-General, was, it must be admitted, wanting in full knowledge, and tainted by the preconceived opinion—from which no British statesman of that day could be wholly free—that the measure of reform was the interest of the master-country. Hence things from which Hastings would have shrunk—the permanent settlement of the land, the exclusion of natives from all posts of honour and authority, the renewal of the Company's commercial privileges and illusive responsibility; while the King's Cabinet and the British Parliament assumed the actual management of those political and military proceedings which grew out of the necessities of the trade.

How completely the preference of British interests, real or supposed, must have affected these arrangements may be seen very clearly by anyone who examines the state-papers of the time. Thus, to take one example, Cornwallis closes his famous minute on the Land Revenue of Bengal by the remark that the real value of the Bengal Presidency consists in the degree to which it is able to "furnish a large annual investment" for Europe and and China. We shall observe this—which may be called the commercial fallacy—pervading all the reforms of the day.*

First, then, let us briefly consider the legislation on land tenures, ending in what has been since known as "The Permanent Settlement." It has often been said that Cornwallis was a blind Englishman, who could find nothing to surpass the usages of his native land, and who sought to advance Bengal by giving the people what he conceived to be the benefit of the quasi-feudal system of landlord and tenant. But in point of fact that was by no means the sole peculiarity of the Bengal "Settlement," nor was it invented by Cornwallis; the Revenue Board of ten years before having already recognised the agents in possession as holding a vested interest in the estates, and having laid down the lines of the new system by a series of tentative agreements. In 1786 the Court of Directors had sent out instructions that the revenue should be henceforth fixed for ten years; and added, that if it was found to work well, then the assessment should be confirmed in perpetuity. Before carrying out these orders Cornwallis judged a further enquiry requisite. The result was perplexing; for while, on the one hand, the subject appeared wrapped in impenetrable darkness, on the other the experts, headed by Mr. Shore, an old-standing member of the Board, maintained that the "Ryots," as the tenants were called, had clear and distinct rights which

* "Letter to Dundas," quoted by S. Karr; "Cornwallis," p. 76.

were deserving of patient consideration. The rights of the "Zemindar," or collecting agent, might have arisen by prescription and in the decay of the Mughal Empire; but those of the ryot were of a different kind, amounting to a sort of ownership which was both more ancient and more absolute. When the field of enquiry was afterwards enlarged, and when competent observers went into the matter, in the Upper Provinces, it turned out that Shore was perfectly right; in fact, a proprietorship of this kind was, in the ancient usage of the country, held by associations (often of one blood) who recognised that they were liable to pay the surplus produce to the representatives of the community, agents, farmers, or grantees, while they took care that the definition of "surplus" should be as favourable as possible to themselves. Thus, so long as they paid something in that way, they held themselves entitled to do what they liked with the land, and to defend their possession against all interference from without. If the State were strong, its collectors, or its assignees took the entire net produce, like Alá-ud-din Khiljì,* leaving the agriculturists no more than what would enable them to live and to carry on the cultivation. If, on the contrary, the State was feeble, the associated villagers would, either by their own united strength, or under the protection of some "Baron," withhold all but the very smallest payment of quit-rent. And all these middlemen, agents, assignees, or usurping Barons, in all times and conditions, kept such portion of the collections in their own hands as circumstances might permit. In Bengal alone this system had undergone a further change, and hence had arisen a special state of things, which, if it increased the difficulty of laying down just principles, made it easier to conclude an ill-considered adjustment. In Bengal, the village associations had broken down from the feeble character of the people and the ease with which they could be oppressed and superseded

* v. supra Chap, iii.

by reason of their distance from the centre of government. And not only so, but the long continuance of war, pestilence, and famine, had diminished the numbers of the labourers so much, that, as in Europe after the "Black Death," the employers of labour had in their turn become the weaker party in the new contractual system which was arising under the British. The middlemen could and did crush the village fraternities; but they could get no money out of the land without cultivators. In European countries the dearth of men during the latter half of the fourteenth century led to a rise of wages; in Bengal, where wage-labour was not the rule, the like course led to indulgent treatment and coaxing of the agriculturist.

Thus, when once it had been reported to the King's ministers in London that immediate measures must be taken to create a valuable property in the land, it occurred to everyone that this interest ought to be permanently vested in the Zemindars who alone possessed the means for locating tenants and developing the resources of the country, while from them alone the surplus produce might most certainly and conveniently continue to reach the Treasury. They had the ear of the local authorities, too; and when the reports of these latter came before Pitt and Dundas, the minds of those statesmen were already predisposed in favour of so tangible and easily intelligible a tenure.

Nevertheless, as is now everywhere seen, these Zemindars were not in any sense proprietors, and such rights as might have come to them by prescription or mistake, would certainly prove adverse to the occupants as soon as ever these latter should become sufficiently numerous to be led to compete with one another for land. There were, (indeed there still are) in Bengal, occupants whose generic title, *Khudkásht*,* preserved the memory of times, when the peasant proprietors from whom

---

* The word is a Persian compound meaning "one's own cultivation," or "the cultivation of one's own land." (v. "Platts' Hind. Dict.," p. 495.)

they derived their origin were "cultivators of their own land." For a picturesque description of the position of these men, the reader may be referred to Mr. Seton Karr's book already quoted.* Such men are still to be found; but it did not occur to Pitt or Dundas, any more than to Shore or Cornwallis, that the solution of the vexed questions of Indian landowning might be looked for in that direction; it was not suspected that, in point of fact, these men were the "allodial" proprietors of Bengal.

It is not to be supposed that Cornwallis intended to sacrifice the interests of the ryots, however imperfectly he may have understood them, to the creation of a class of landlords on the English footing. His intention, clearly enough expressed in previous correspondence as in subsequent legislation, was that the ryots should be protected. But they were to be protected as tenants having rights of litigation, with courts of law provided to see that the terms of their leases were duly observed and to guard them against illegal exactions. It was an attempt to enforce contract rather than one to maintain status.

Thus prepared and safeguarded the measure was enjoined on Cornwallis, with his complete concurrence, and announced to the public of Bengal in the official organ† in a sort of essay or leading article, in which the merits of the question were discussed. And a fiscal system "which varies with each variation of the real rent of the land and . . . with the improvement or decline of its cultivation" was condemned on the ground of the superior encouragement to improvement given or promised by "a permanent settlement." A perpetual assessment was accordingly offered to all existing possessors, on the basis of the last decennial valuation; and they were enjoined to avoid oppression of the ryots, whom, for the moment, it was also their own interest to conciliate. It was left for later

* "Cornwallis" (Rulers of India). Oxford, 1890.
† "Calcutta Gazette," 9th May, 1793.

times to show how much more instructive is practical experience than theory that is not exhaustive. It was not perceived in 1793, that the improvements of which Bengal husbandry was in need were such as should be either effected by the officers of the State or by the cultivating occupants freed from dread of unauthorised enhancements and illegal cesses. In parts of India since settled, where the State, in the interest of the general tax-paying community, keeps an eye on the unearned increment, the officials have an interest in the promotion of drainage, canals, roads, and all kinds of aids to agriculture that demand skill and capital. And the cultivating occupants, on the other hand, make their modest improvements—manuring, petty-irrigation, and so forth, so long as they know that the result will not be an enhancement of their rent. But the middlemen did not see the reason why they should trouble themselves with such things. Drought very seldom falls on Bengal; and consequently a kind of slovenly fertility usually prevails, and the spontaneous liberality of nature yields enough for the primary wants of a dense population. But the estates are deeply charged with mortgages and with layers of subinfeudation: the people are in a backward condition; and on the rare occasions when famine does visit them there is no social machinery for its resistance, and the people die like autumn-leaves. In a journal of travels by a native of Bengal, published in the second half of the 19th century, nothing is more often noticed by the writer than the contrast between the prosperity of Hindustan and the backward state of the Lower Provinces.* He also notices the unfitness of direct taxation as a fiscal instrument in India. Following a misleading analogy Englishmen sometimes speak of the Indian

* "Trips and Tours." Reprinted from the "Weekly Englishman." Calcutta, 1866. The writer expresses his particular surprise at 1, the women being clothed; 2, the land being all cultivated; 3, the existence of numerous towns. Simple signs of welfare!

Land Revenue as "the land tax." But it is in reality no tax, rather the reverse of a tax. "So far as this source goes," said James Mill, before a parliamentary committee, "*the people remain untaxed.* The wants of Government are supplied without any drain upon the produce of any man's labour or of any man's capital." The merits and demerits of the Permanent Settlement have been tersely summoned up by an eloquent writer, who is at the same time one of the most experienced and distinguished of the older school of Bengal Civil Servants :—

"Cornwallis had only the experience and the legacies of failure to guide him. Pressed for ways and means, and anxious for reform in more departments than one, he committed himself to a policy which—in regard to the three interested parties, the Zemindar, the Ryot, and the Ruling Power—assured the welfare of the first, somewhat postponed the claims of the second, and sacrificed the increment of the third."*
It must be added that the third, according to modern ideals, only represents the people; and that, on this view, to bind his successors for all time to abstain from giving any relief to the tax-payer by participating in the progress of cultivation, or apportioning the demand on land to changes in the value of money, was hardly the work of a consummate statesman.

In any case more precautions ought to have been taken to protect "the claims of the Ryot." To leave the poorer party in a contract to sue against the extortions of the richer was little short of a mockery, unless the law was most clearly laid down, and unless the means of enforcing its provisions were extremely cheap and efficient. Neither of these conditions was fulfilled. The status, the liabilities, the rights, of the various classes of tenants were not defined; and it required stringent legislation, at different times during the succeeding century, before the omission could be rectified. The Zemindars found themselves in the position of the French *Seigneurs*

* Seton-Karr; *ut-sup.*

before the Revolution. It was not only in the direction of greedy enhancement and capricious eviction that the rural population suffered. The Zemindars practised all sorts of exaction; taking fees from buyers and sellers, in transit and at fairs; and claiming dues on transactions such as marriages in their families, in which the tenants could have no concern. Moreover, they were often absentees, not unfrequently, in the course of time, mercantile men in Calcutta, who never went near their estates, and who drew their revenue through agents or —what was perhaps worse—through mortgagees, farmers, or sub-farmers.

The Courts, through whose mediation alone the tenantry could hope to get remedy for these burdens, obtained much attention. Cornwallis reformed the Civil Service of Bengal, raising the salaries of Collectors and Judges, whom he placed under the control of higher Courts, both Divisional and, finally, at the Presidency. Hitherto a good deal of the judicial administration had been in the hands of native officials. This had not worked well; and the reform, naturally, swung round to the opposite extreme. The control and the responsibility rested with Englishmen, imperfectly acquainted with the conditions of the people: while the real work, carried on in actual contact with the people, was left to be done by a multitude of Asiatics, in the receipt of the most miserable salaries.

The last important measure for which this administration could be held answerable was the complete transfer of all political power to the Board of Control, while the semblance of Government and the commerce of the East were left as before in the hands of the Company. In consultation with the Governor-General, Dundas proposed this policy, which was originally defined by the "Declaratory Act" of 1788, confirmed by the Charter of 1793. The views of Cornwallis were honourable; he looked on the consultative voice left to the Court of Directors as likely to be useful in shaping the choice of high officials and the policy that they were to pursue; he believed that the patronage which the Court still retained, the nomination of the "writers" and "cadets" sent out to recruit the civil and military services, would be safer in their hands than in those of politicians; and he honestly thought that to open the commerce would be to flood India with lawless adventurers. But the progress of events has shown that these dangers were exaggerated, and capable of prevention by measures more worthy of a civilised community. On the other hand, it was not then perceived that the ostensible authority left to the Court was a screen to avert responsibility from the government of the Board of Control with whom—in practice—Parliament seldom interfered, while the commercial usefulness of the Company had almost come to an end.

In February of the year from which the "Regulations" of Lord Cornwallis date, the revolutionary Convention of France declared war against Great Britain. On receipt of the news the Governor-General directed the preparation of a force for the capture of Pondicherry; and, at the end of August, set sail for Madras, intending to take the command of the expedition. But his voyage was delayed so long that when he arrived at Madras he found that Pondicherry had been besieged by Colonel Braithwaite, and had capitulated about 15th September. The other French settlements were evacuated at the same time; and on the 10th October, 1793, Cornwallis sailed from Madras, arriving in England after an unusually quick passage of 115 days. He was made a marquess for his services; and his tenure of office is to be noted as a period of great change, and a preparation for still greater.

The rest of India enjoyed the benefit of the arrangement, or understanding, between Sindia and Hastings; except that Tipu's dominions were reduced, but not his fanaticism or his longing for revenge. The knowledge of this had made Cornwallis anxious. Without any disturbance of the general tranquility he devoted some part of his short stay at Madras, before laying down his office, to the securing of an understanding with the other parties to the treaty concluded, in 1790, with the Nizám and the Court of Poona. Sindia had somewhat officiously sought to interpose, but Cornwallis preferred to adhere to the old lines of diplomacy, and treat with the Durbar direct. In 1793 he clenched the matter by the offer of a supplemental treaty, in which he would have bound his allies to act together, with candour and moderation, in future cases of dispute. The proposal suited the Nizám, against whom the Mahrattas had some pressing claims; but the Nána, though desirous of a friendly understanding, was unable to see his way to a written guarantee; and it may be that the influence of Sindia, who was then at Poona, was exerted in the same direction. A marked feature of the time is presented by the rivalry between these two ambitious men, as will be more fully explained in the next section.

[In addition to works already cited especial reference is advised to Harington: "Analysis of Bengal Laws and Regulations," 3 vols., folio, Calcutta, 1805-17. An able sketch of Cornwallis's revenue policy will be found in Trotter's "History of India," published for the S.P.C.K. (2nd ed., 1890).]

SECTION 2.—It has been already mentioned that Sindia was a military jágirdar—or "baron"—of the Mahratta Empire. The Nána was the Brahman Minister of the Peshwa, who had become hereditary President of the Mahratta Confederacy, whereas Sindia was only one of several provincial feudatories, who, in the manner common to Eastern Empires, had made themselves independent in fact, while still professing to recognise a sort of legitimacy in the titular overlords. The descendant of Siváji still held his faded sovereignty at Satára; and at each vacancy at Poona the new Peshwa sought investiture at his hands; but the Satára Rája was, otherwise, a mere lay-figure in politics, and his usurping deputy at Poona was little better; his authority being in its turn usurped by others, professing to be only subordinate ministers. At the time that we have now reached, the Peshwa was Mádhu Ráo Naráyan, born 1774, when Raguba was aiming at the office : and as the power of the latter declined, the minister by whom the child's cause was espoused became ever more and more powerful. This was the official known in books as "Nána Farnavis," his real name was Janardhan Bálaji, and he had been on the campaign that ended so disastrously in 1761. But he belonged to the Brahman tribe, and was a "man-of-the-pen," with neither taste nor training for war. Scandal credited him with the paternity of the boy so opportunely brought forward in opposition to the claims of Raguba; and on the ultimate ruin of the latter the Nána became practically administrator at Poona, and claimant of all the indeterminate authority of the infant Peshwa. The Confederacy was at that time still coherent, in theory at least, and consisted of four great states besides the original Mahratta country—or territory of Baglana—directly subject to the Poona Government. These four States were as follows :—

1.—GUJARAT, or the State of the Gaikwar; lands scattered over the western region, from the frontiers of Málwa to the Arabian Sea, inclusive of the great Peninsula of Kathiawár, at the extremity of the Gulf of Cutch. The chief town was Ahmadabad.

2.—SOUTHERN MALWA, the Holkar State, ruled by Ahalya Bai, widow of the founder's son; her capital was Indore, which she built about 1770.

3.—NORTHERN MALWA, including Gwalior. This was the local nucleus of Sindia's power; the capitals being Ujain and Gwalior.

4.—BERAR, or the State of the Bhonslá; comprising the modern "Central Provinces," with Orissa. The capital was at Nagpore.

It will thus be seen that, had the rulers been united, there was a Mahratta Empire extending from sea to sea, and from the banks of the Tungabhadra to those of the Jumna. Kolhapore, on the Malabar coast, and Tanjore on the extreme south of the Coromandel, were also smaller Mahratta States, each under a chief of the family of Siváji. But the condition of unity was lacking.

It was, however, one of the constantly pursued aims of Mahádaji Sindia to recognise the Durbar, or Cabinet of Regency, of the Minor Peshwa, and to act as umpire in Poona politics, whilst, as Mayor of the Palace at Delhi, he ruled in Hindustan. This plan, which furnishes a clue to a great part of the events between 1775 and 1794, brought Sindia and the Nána into contact, sometimes into opposition. The jovial nature and frank manners of Sindia contrasted with the ascetic stiffness of his rival; but in point of astuteness there was not much difference; and neither was much disposed for an open rupture. Thus, when Sindia was in his deepest trouble, in 1787, we have seen that the Nána and Holkar came to his support, and that he was, with their aid, able to resume his place at the headquarters of the Empire. The late revolution at Delhi, although not undertaken on his behalf, had improved his prospects immensely. In Muhamad Beg and Ghulám Kádir had perished the two leaders of Muslim opposition whom he had most reason to fear; Ismail, who remained, was inferior in ability, and was for the present well-disposed. De Boigne had accepted the task of remodelling the army, and had made a good beginning by the quiet sagacity with which he checked a show of disaffection. The force originally raised—which had been steady and useful in the late Rajput campaign, though too small to turn the scales of battle—was without a brigadier, and had not been paid for eight months, a state of affairs which made them mutinous. Sindia did not like to reason with armed disputants, and was for charging the sepoys with an overwhelming body of horsemen, but De Boigne persuaded the chief to adopt more humane measures; and on obtaining leave to take his own course, adopted such a mixture of justice, tact, and firmness that he kept the bulk of the men while getting rid of ringleaders and dangerous characters. Recruits were then sought among the same manly races as contributed to form the British army of Bengal; and in a few months some sixteen battalions were ready for service, with a quantity of field guns, Mughal horse, and irregular spearsmen. Many of the native princes were raising troops of the kind about the same time. We have already seen European officers serving under the Nizám's brother and under the Rája of Travancore; the Nizám, as we shall presently see, had a large force under a good French general. But Sindia's "new model," led by De Boigne under the white cross of Savoy, was distinguished over all, perfect in discipline and never beaten.

Its value was soon put to proof. The proud but unpunctual Rajputs had hung back while Sindia's affairs were at their ebb, but now, when the tide had turned, they resolved on trying their luck once more. Ismail Beg was easily persuaded to give up his fief in Riwári, where he found life too quiet for his taste; and he had the less objection to cross swords again with the Mahrattas that a general expectation prevailed that the Afgháns would soon come down from their mountains and make common cause with their Muslim brethren in the Deccan.

To confront this combination Sindia made all speed with his preparations. Besides the "new model" brigade, which was prepared the quicker because the non-commissioned officers were all old soldiers out of the legion lately disbanded for mutiny, Sindia had some troops of the ordinary character, whom he put under the charge of two good and true Mahratta officers: Gopál Ráo, and Lakwa Dáda, distinguished for his defence of Agra in the late troubles. Ismail, on the other hand, was well supported; his infantry was not equal to De Boigne's, but his heavy cavalry, composed of Persians and Afghans, disbanded after earlier wars, but still ready for any service that promised pay and plunder, was a formidable force, just suited to the character of the Beg. In March De Boigne left the cantonments near Mathra (Muttra), and set out to attack the Beg before he could effect a junction with the Rajputs. A cloud of Mahratta horsemen screened his movements and watched those of the enemy, who was found on 10th May, encamped at Pátan, in a rocky tract between Gwalior and Ajmere. De Boigne, having a strong brigade of infantry and fifty guns, intrenched himself and blockaded the place for some weeks. At last, 19th June, Ismail Beg resolved on a sortie, the Kachwáha Rajputs from Jaipore having managed to reach the scene, and appearing ready to fall on De Boigne's flank and rear, so as to expose him to two fires, Unfortunately for the Beg, Sindia's money and diplomacy had been at work, and the Rajputs remained inactive. In vain the mailed squadrons with clash of arms and rattle of kettle-drums thundered down the hill upon the raw levies; the squares kept their cool blood, the enemy's saddles were fast emptied, the cavaliers fell back, and, as evening fell, De Boigne deployed his men, advanced in line, drove back the last fragments of resistance, and took the works by storm. Ismail's loss in the day's fighting included 100 guns, 50 elephants, and all his luggage. On the morrow his infantry came over to the conquerors, while he himself, with the wreck of his cavalry, galloped hard until he reached the city of Jaipore. Holkar had arrived, and might have taken up the pursuit, but was perhaps more usefully employed in keeping back the Rajputs. The "Calcutta Gazette" (22nd July) gives De Boigne's modest account of the action; his officers and men, he says, behaved well, and his brigade lost 120 killed and 472 wounded. It was a spirited little affair, which showed that the new force was already tempered for its work; and it augured ill for the medieval system of warfare now about to try conclusions with scientific battle.

In August, De Boigne received instructions to call Bijai Sinh to account for having abetted the revolt of the Beg. This, it should be observed, was a more serious task than hoodwinking the Kachwáhas of Jaipore, not nearly so warlike a race, and much more exposed in their fertile country, open at all seasons to attacks from Delhi. But Bijai and his Rahtors lived in a remote and barren district far to the west; Márwar, or the "Land of Death," having, as outwork and chief seat of state and pleasure, the fair lake and plateau of Ajmere on the eastern side of the Aravali hills. Hither came De Boigne on 21st August to punish Bijai for a long course of insult and injury from the day when he, at that very city, murdered Jai Apa Sindhia about the middle of the century. De Boigne easily occupied the city of Ajmere, but was delayed by the great natural strength of the fort of Táragarh which towers above, on a mountain nearly three thousand feet high. While contemplating the chances of storming this eagle's nest, De Boigne received news that the old Rája had set out from Jodhpore and was advancing to the relief. He accordingly left 2,700 men to guard the siege-works, and marched down the Jodhpore road, coming upon the Rahtor camp about half-way, at a place called Merta, standing on high ground, with the town-wall covering its rear. The spot was of evil omen for Bijai, for it was here that, after murdering Jai Apa at Ajmere he had been caught and crushed by the united forces of the Mahrattas in 1754. It was the afternoon of the 9th September, and De Boigne, overruling the impatience of the Mahratta officers, gave his men some hours of rest. The night was passed by the Rahtors in revel; and while sleeping off its effects their camp was surprised at dawn by Colonel de Rohan with three of De Boigne's best battalions. The Rahtor cavalry quickly armed and mounted. The attack was beaten off, and a headlong charge dispersed the horsemen of the Mahrattas. But the Rahtors were powerless against the disciplined squares of De Boigne's infantry and their field-pieces loaded with grape.* Four thousand saddles, it is said, were emptied as they rode back. The squares then deployed, as at Pátan, and advanced in line; and the whole camp, artillery and munitions, were in their possession soon after 10 a.m. The retreat of the Rája and his men was covered by the remains of the cavalry. But Táragarh, the citadel of Ajmere, presently capitulated, and Bijai soon made peace with De Boigne, who entered Jodhpore on 18th November, 1790. The Rána of Udaipore next submitted, and, so far as native resistance went, Sindia was absolute in Hindustan. He now authorised De Boigne to augment the force by raising two more brigades; bringing the disciplined corps to a total strength of 18,000; and he assigned for guarantee of pay a territory extending from Muttra to Delhi, and northward to Bulandshahr, with a yearly revenue of two and a quarter million rupees.

In 1791 Sindia proferred his help as above said, to Cornwallis, to be employed against Tipu; and was equally surprised and disappointed to find that his offer was courteously declined, while at the same time his rival, the Nána, was allowed to contribute a contingent of the Poona army. This was a service of no great advantage in the field, but most useful in the temporary retreat of the British, and amply recompensed in the following year. About this time came a renewed rumour of Afghán invasion. It had long been known that Tipu—who had already sent an embassy to the Court of Louis XVI., was chafing under the partition of his territory. And it now came out that he was in correspondence with Zamán Sháh, grandson

---

* The invention of this formation of infantry against horse has been attributed to General de Boigne.

of the famous Ahmad Abdáli, the victor of Pánipat.* The prospect of a new combination of the Muslims alarmed Sindia, who contemplated a counter-stroke by attacking the Nawáb of Audh to prevent all chance of his imitating the policy of his late father in 1761. But the movement was repressed by Cornwallis with stern menace. Confident of his ability to keep the feeble and frivolous Asaf-ud-daula in check, the Governor-General caused Sindia to be notified that the Nawáb was the ally of the British, and that they would resent any injury done to him or to the people of his province.

Thus circumscribed, and almost isolated, Sindia determined to leave his possessions in Hindustan to the care of De Boigne and his Mahratta colleagues, while he proceeded to Poona to counteract the designs of the Nána and make himself master of the politics of the confederacy.

By this time (1792) the cohesion of the Mahratta States was worn almost to a thread; and it may well have seemed to Sindia that events were approaching which would call for all his resources. Gujarát, indeed, was quiet; and the authority of the Peshwa and his durbar was acknowledged by the Gaikwar. But the other states were far from being equally submissive. In what are now the Central provinces and Orissa, the Bhonslá Rája of Nagpore had established a power which was all but independent of Poona. Under the title of Rája of Berár Raghuji II. had extended the power of the state at the expense of the Nizám, and had maintained the independent alliance with the British which had been begun during his minority by his uncle, the Regent. As to the state of Indore, its loyalty, both towards the Poona Durbar and towards Sindia, had been maintained as long as Ahalya Bai retained power;

* Two draft letters, from Tipu to the Sháh, were found at Seringapatam some years later, which appear to be of this date. They contained a complete project for an invasion of Hindustan, in which the Mysore army was to co-operate.

but she was now old and worn out with religious austerities, while Tukáji Holkar, long her faithful servant, was beginning to show a spirit of dissatisfaction, and a tendency to redress what he deemed his grievances by acting on his account. As a counterpoise to Sindia, of whom he was becoming very jealous, he now raised a force in imitation of that formed by De Boigne, and placed in command a Breton officer of long-standing Indian experience, the Chevalier du Drenec, formerly a subaltern of M. Law. If the help of the Nána had been sometimes grudgingly bestowed, such backwardness might easily be turned into hostility should Holkar succeed in obtaining power at Poona. As will presently appear, these perils were by no means imaginary, and came to a serious height when the reins of Sindia's chariot dropped into less skilful hands.

Sindia therefore proceeded to Poona, announcing that he was sent by the Emperor, Sháh Álam, with gifts and honours for the young Peshwa, Mádhu Rao II. He reached Poona on the 11th June, 1792, and pitched his camp in the grounds of the British Residency: on the 20th-22nd, the ceremony took place, the powerful visitor presenting himself in humble guise and affecting the character of a menial servant.

Meanwhile, Holkar profited by Sindia's absence to strike at his power in Hindustan. Opening a correspondence with Ismail Beg, whom he urged to attack Delhi, he forced a rupture with Gopal Rao, by demanding an immediate adjustment of the accounts of prize taken in former joint expeditions. De Boigne sent his best subordinate, Colonel Perron, into Riwári, where the Beg was preparing for revolt in communication with the widow of his predecessor, Najaf Kuli; this was a sister of the infamous Ghulám Kádir, who lived at Kanaund, on the border of the great desert that extends from the confines of Hariana, to the valley of the Indus; and she readily accepted the concurrence of the Beg. The sandy soil formed a natural protection against attack, being both deficient in water and difficult to pass for guns and wheel carriage. The spirited Pathán lady defied Perron's summons, and Ismail attacked him with the old vigour. But the lady was killed by a shell, and the garrison forced the Beg to surrender, when he was taken to Agra and kept a prisoner in the fort there till his death.*

De Boigne had reserved for himself a more formidable antagonist. He brought Holkar to bay, as the latter was advancing to relieve Kanaund, and crossing a spur of the Aravalli range. Holkar had a good force of Mahratta cavalry, and his new legion consisting of four battalions, whom he posted on the crest of the pass with thirty-eight guns in battery. The post was naturally difficult of approach, and Holkar protected it with his horsemen. But nothing could resist an infantry like De Boigne's; the column, 9,000 strong, with field guns, pressed on with sturdy valour; trees on each side impeded Holkar's charges; the pass was stormed and defended with equal determination, till Colonel du Drenec, left almost the sole survivor of his legion, surrendered with all his guns. Holkar fell back on Málwa, where he consoled himself by sacking Sindia's capital of Ujain. The date of this action—which De Boigne considered the most severe he ever fought—was 30th September, 1792, two months after the Poona reception.

Sindia remained at Poona, whence he made a tentative move to see if he could recover the tribute of Bengal from the British, whom he believed to be just then in a mood of penitent moderation. But he showed no ill-temper when he found that he had miscalculated, and that his demand was met with the same stern repudiation by Cornwallis, as had already been

---

* The Beg was not closely confined, but lived in a comfortable house inside the Delhi gate, on high, well-ventilated ground, whence there are fine views of the river, the Taj, and the surrounding country. It is known as the house of Dán Sáh Ját.

given to a similar claim by Macpherson seven years earlier. Whatever may be thought of the abstract justice or legality of this attitude in 1785, Sindia might have felt sure that it would not now be abandoned. He had no desire to add to his cares by a rupture with the British, having had more than a taste of their fighting qualities, and been specially warned against such a quarrel by De Boigne. He accordingly hastened to disclaim the Delhi newswriter who had been used as the touchstone of his essay, assuring the Government of Bengal that he quite acknowledged British supremacy in that part of the Empire, and confined his ambition to the task of maintaining the imperial authority "in those territories which still remained under its direct administration."

Sindia's manly attentions and genial ways made a favourable impression on the mind of the young Peshwa Madhu Ráo, just entering on his 19th year, and brooding somewhat sadly under the ascetic manners and austere control of his guardian, the Nána. It may be doubted, indeed, whether the visitor obtained any practical ascendency in the councils of the durbar, which was, at that very time, chafing at the very secondary part that Mahratta power had been made to play during the Mysore war, and, therefore, declined to join the triple alliance proposed to them by Cornwallis. Nevertheless, as months went on in which constant intercourse with the one was followed by the gradual estrangement of the other, the Nána began to despond. He, whether sincerely or not, tendered his resignation to the Peshwa, and announced an intention of retiring to end his days as a religious recluse at Benares.

When Sindia heard of this, his first impulse was to suspect mischief. He did not believe in the Nána's professed intentions; rather reading in them a design dangerous to himself. He therefore at once sent orders to De Boigne to despatch to him at Poona a body of 10,000 of the disciplined troops under Perron; men whose backs no enemy had ever seen, and whose native barbarism had—in the words of a contemporary observer—been "submitted to the discipline and to the civilisation of European armies."* A serious crisis appeared to be imminent. The hostile intrigues of the Nána—"The Indian Machiavel"—were supported by the open enmity of Holkar, and by the scarcely less manifest ill-feeling of the Conservative party at Poona, who viewed Sindia's prosperity with jealous eyes, and disapproved of his readiness to adopt foreign agents and foreign methods.

The clouds were dispelled—for the moment—by the sudden and mysterious death of Mahádaji Sindia, which happened on 12th February, 1794. In Mahratta records the cause assigned was fever; but the event was too opportune not to be imputed to treachery; and the story believed in Hindustan was that the chief had been waylaid by assassins who were driven off, but not until they had inflicted hurts from the effect of which Sindia died the next day.† He left behind him an unfinished work and a great reputation. When he first appeared on the scene in Hindustan, the country was a welter of anarchy, while the Deccan was full of contending interests and elements of purposeless strife. At his death a beginning of order had been made. The best army in the country had been cured of its bad habits, and made into a serviceable engine. At Aligarh, and further north, at Sirdhana, beginnings of civil order had been made by General de Boigne and Begam Samru: the British influence was stealing upward from Benares. In the south the Mahratta confederacy was at peace within itself, and its good understanding with the British had brought about a temporary balance of power with Mysore and the Nizám. And much of this—though it may now seem little better than

* "The Bengal Journal," 18 September, 1790.
† So related in the "Tarikh-i-Muzafari": a Persian MS. History of good repute, mentioned favourably in Dowson's "Elliot," vol. viii., to which we owe much of our knowledge of the affairs of Hindustan at that period.

a compromise with disorder—was a distinct inroad into the general anarchy that followed the invasion of Nádir Sháh, and was in great part due to the bold sagacity and moderation of Sindia. He thus merits the description given to him by a high modern authority as "a statesman and soldier of almost unsurpassed ability."* Before his death he declared his desire that his power should be assumed by his grand-nephew, Daulat Ráo; and it is a proof that his will was respected when we find this lad of fifteen, without any lawful adoption, obeyed as heir to such great power and dignity.

A signal confirmation of this estimate of the deceased chief is to be seen in the confusion that followed his disappearance. For a while the strong experienced hand of De Boigne kept matters straight in Upper India. Rumours of a threatened Afghán invasion continued indeed to prevail. Taimur Sháh—the son of the famous Abdáli—died in June, 1793, leaving the government of Kandahar and Kabul to his son Zámán Sháh: but domestic troubles—and perhaps some fear of the growing power of the Sikhs—kept him quiet for the time.† A sketch of the earlier relations between the Sikhs and Afgháns will be found in the monograph, by Sir Lepel Griffin, in the "Rulers of India" series, beginning at p. 73.‡ There it is stated that Ahmad Sháh attempted to conciliate the warlike horsemen of the Punjab, though without much success; and it seems now—on looking back from the vantage ground of later experience—that their hatred of Islám and their power of military combination must have proved a bulwark against any repetition of northern incursion. But these things were not then so clear. And, indeed, the ease with which a brilliant European

* "Imperial Gazetteer," v. 230.
† This was noted in the "Calcutta Gazette" of 28 May, 1795. For the next few years eyes of fear or hope continued to be turned in this direction from every part of India.
‡ "Ranjit Singh," by Sir Lepel Griffin, K.C.S.I., Oxford, 1892.

adventurer of that period kept the Sikhs in check—even carrying the war into their own country—may well have given rise to a low opinion of their power in war.

This remarkable man was named George Thomas; but the part which he performed was too obscure and too much of the nature of episode to justify a detailed account of his doings here. Still, his career should be noted as an instance of what unaided energy was able to conceive and partly carry out in the India of those days. We had a glimpse of him in the Emperor's futile expedition of the spring of 1788, when he saved the camp in the sortie of Najaf Kuli's garrison at Gokalgarh. Since that date he had left the service of Begam Samru, and entered on the business of a soldier-of-fortune on his own account, offering the services of himself, and a small body of men whom he had disciplined, to any local chief who might be disposed to employ them, for pay and plunder. Thomas was then at Anupshahr, the quarters of the British brigade of observation, on the upper Ganges. The position was central to the political geography of those days; with Rohilkhand to the east, the central Duáb to the south, and to the west, Delhi. On the north-west and north, lay the tracts —called "The fifty-two Parganas"—which had been inherited by the late Ghulám Kádir (as grandson of Najib and son of Zábita) but which, since the revolution of 1788, had been in Mahratta hands. This fertile and temperate region, comprising the modern district of Saharanpore, at the foot of the great mountain chain, with the Ganges on one hand and the Jumna on the other, had long been a temptation to the Sikhs on the right bank of the last named river; and Sindia had put it in charge of an energetic officer, Apa Khandi Ráo, by whom Thomas was engaged, in the latter part of 1792; and commissioned to raise a small force in addition to his usual following. The first employment of the corps was the establishment of the Apa's power in Mewát, a stony plateau lying between

Delhi and Alwar, occupied by lawless tribes. The news of Sindia's death arrived before the expedition had got to work. Before the end of the year 1794, however, Thomas had made sufficient progress to be able to canton his little legion in Tijára, the chief town of the district, about fifty-five miles south-west of Delhi. While here he received an offer of employment in Sindia's army, which he declined, and soon after had the opportunity of saving his former employer, Begam Samru, who was undergoing captivity and danger from her own men at Sardhana. Dashing across country he reached Sardhana—a distance of 100 miles—and appeared before the mutineers accompanied by his mounted bodyguard; when by audacity, eloquence, and the expenditure of a large sum of money—which was never repaid—he obtained the release and restoration of the Begam. Before the end of 1795 Thomas was employed against the Cis-Sutlej Sikhs, who had invaded Saharanpore, whence he expelled them, at the same time expressing the opinion that, for want of unity, they would never become formidable. The forecast was natural. Thomas could not know that forty miles beyond Lahore a boy had lately come forward as head of the Shukarcharia clan, who was destined to weld those wild warriors into one of the most formidable military powers of the East.*

SECTION 3.—While these seeds of the future were germinating in Upper India, British influence was extending in the southern regions. The Mahratta Empire had so very nearly supplanted that of the Mughals, as a general centre and unifier of the Peninsula, that it might have seemed doubtful, in the failure of Islám, whether Sindia—had he but been ten years younger—might not have carried out the Hindu revival to a complete conquest. With one foot resting on the base of the

---

* Ranjit Sinh, born and bred at Gujránwála, and in 1795 about fifteen years old, had become chief by the death of his father. "Imperial Gazetteer," and Griffin, as above.

THE END OF THE ANARCHY. 307

Himalaya, and the other on the shore of Palk's passage, the arch of Mahratta power already spanned the Peninsula. But the sudden death of Mahádaji Sindia loosened the keystone, and the decay of the abutments soon followed. The Irish adventurer and the Sikh marauder fought in Saharanpore; at the other extremity the principality founded in Tanjore by the brother of the great Siváji, was becoming a British dependency. A similar lot had fallen to the bold and patriotic chief of Travancore; while no maritime outlet now remained to Tipu Sultan except Mangalore, taken by that chieftain in 1783, and left somewhat imprudently in his possession by subsequent treaties.

Half-way between Tanjore and Travancore lay all that was left of Tipu's territories, and he, at least, was by no means prepared to be mediatised. Nor, indeed, was Tipu what in the East would be deemed a bad ruler. Inferior in strategic and political ability he was—as most men must have been—when compared with his father; and he had grievous faults of character and temper, being passionate, revengeful, and fanatical. But he was brave, sober, industrious, and—if one only conceded the principle that the ideal of sovereignty was a theocracy with an earthly Sultan for Viceregent—Tipu was no mean example of that kind of tyrant. On the principle of Louis XIV. he styled himself "Khudadád Sarkár" (the God-sent State.) To hate those whom he considered the enemies of Heaven was with him a duty none the less incumbent because it happened to be pleasant. The British were the worst, being enemies of himself besides being unbelievers. The Mahratta Durbar was in much the same predicament; and the Nizám—Muslim though he was—had joined the infidels in attacking the Sultan of Mysore, and partitioning his dominions.

It was upon the last that the flood of his evil temper seemed about to break loose. Profiting by the death of Mahádaji he procured the assent of the Poona Durbar, by whom an attack on the part of the Nizám had just come into expectation. But Mr. Shore, of Bengal—who had been created a baronet, and had succeeded Cornwallis as Governor-General—was adverse; and the triple alliance was dissolved for want of one strong mind to keep it in force. Tipu, moreover, could not, at the last moment, bring himself to join the Mahrattas in making war on a Muslim; and the Nizám was left to contend with the unbelievers on terms that would have been far from unequal but for his own effete imbecility. It must be said, in his excuse, that he was far advanced in years, being a son of the old minister of Álamgir, the famous Ásaf Jáh. But he had in his service an excellent French officer, who, if supported, or even left alone, might have sufficed for his defence.

Michel Raymond had come from France as a merchant, and on the capture of Pondicherry in 1778, took service in the French corps employed by Haidar. On the arrival of Bussy, in 1783, Raymond became aide-de-camp to that General, and on his death, two years later, entered the service of the Nizám's brother, Basálat Jang, afterwards passing into that of the Nizám himself. He now adopted a plan very similar to that of De Boigne, in the North; forming battalions of native infantry under European officers. By the time of which we are now treating there were no less than twenty of these corps, and the officers, to the number of 124, were of European blood. On the 10th March, 1795, the army of the Nizám, in which this division was included, marching from Bidar, came in contact with the troops of the Peshwa, near the foot of the Purandhar pass, within two marches of Poona. Could they but prevail the capital of the Peshwa was at their mercy. The trained infantry of the Mahrattas was about equal in number to the division of Raymond on the opposite side, including ten of De Boigne's veterans, under Perron; there was an immense force of Mahratta cavalry; the troops of Gujarát and

THE END OF THE ANARCHY.

Berár were there, and the horsemen of Sindia and Holkar ; and the Mahrattas also appear to have had a preponderance in heavy guns, which were placed in position on the slope of the hills. The battle took place on the 12th March, and began by a decided advantage gained by the Muslim cavalry, which broke and rolled up the Mahratta right. On their left the battalions of Raymond advanced steadily, in spite of a disconcerting shower of rockets and the fire of the guns on the hill-side. The Muslim horsemen, however, fled before the tempest, on which the Nizám recalled the infantry under Raymond and fled with his cavalry. Raymond retreated in good order, but the day was lost. The aged Prince, whose nerve was gone, and who —after the fashion of most Asiatics—trusted nothing but his cavalry, sought refuge in the Fort of Kardlá, from which the battle takes its name in history. Next day he was cannonaded, and soon forced to capitulate ; and it might have seemed as if the Mahratta confederacy was going to recover its empire in India.

As events turned out, however, this was not only the last triumph of their arms, but the last occasion on which the great standard of their empire ever floated over a united Mahratta army. Annoyed at what he conceived his desertion by the British, the Nizám at first turned his eyes towards an alliance with the French Republic, then at war with England ; dismissing, in the month of June, the British battalions which had been sent to his aid by the Governor-General, Sir J. Shore. But they were soon after recalled, and though the arrangement by which the district of Cuddapa was assigned for the support of Raymond's force was not cancelled, Shore allowed the battalions to remain.

These precautions proved superfluous. At the very moment of success, when all the Mahratta States appeared ready to combine for the mastery of Southern India, the ambitious designs of the Nána were shattered in one night. His ward, the Peshwa Madhu Ráo II., weary of the part that he was made to play, dashed himself from the roof of his palace, and died two days later, 24th October, 1795. His death was followed by a period of inextricable confusion, in which, after a year of intrigue and tergiversation on the part of the Nána, of the new Sindia, Daulat Ráo, and of most of the other Mahratta grandees, a treaty of peace was concluded with the Nizám, 8th October, 1796; and with the help of the Haidarabad army the son of the once turbulent Raguba was made Peshwa, by the title of Báji Ráo. A strange turn of the wheel of fortune, by which the dotard who, to save himself from utter ruin, had to make a humiliating surrender in the middle of one year, became disposer of the throne of his enemies before the end of the next. Baji Ráo was installed as Peshwa on 4th December, the last—as it proved—who ever held the proud Presidentship of the United States of Maharáshtra.

If the Nána expected advantage from his share in this transaction a bitter disappointment was at hand for that most selfish of politicians. The new Peshwa was a man—as his after conduct was to demonstrate—who knew not one honourable feeling. His first step, on obtaining power, was to instigate Sindia to seize and imprison the Nána; the next, to set on his brother, Amrit Ráo, to assassinate Sindia, after causing the latter to sack the capital, which went through the horrors of war at the hands of its own rulers. Sindia owed his life to the irresolution of his enemy the Peshwa.

While the western capital was the scene of these events, the British Governor-General was having his share of trouble in Calcutta, and it was such as to excuse his unwillingness to undertake military adventures. This arose out of discontents among the European officers of the Company's army, whose privileges had been curtailed at the very time when—in order to compensate for loss of private trade—the pay of the civil officials had been largely increased. The military officers were the inheritors of bad traditions; so far back as 1766, when Clive had been forced to use very stern measures to suppress a combination among their predecessors, having a similar origin. But there was no Clive in Bengal in the year 1796, and the mutinous attitude which had been threatening for two years now assumed the character of formal demands, with which Shore and his advisers judged it prudent to comply. Dundas, in his indignation, would have sent Cornwallis back to Bengal to deal with the matter as a soldier should; but the Court of Directors supporting Shore, a compromise followed, by which the officers obtained all their demands, and more.

In the course of 1796 further trouble arose from the growing weakness of the administration in Audh. Sir J. Shore proceeding to Lucknow, attempted to rouse the attention of the Nawáb Asaf-ud-daula, but found it impossible to make any impression on his mind or create an idea of duty. On the 21st September, 1797, the Nawáb died, and was succeeded by Vazir Ali, of whom the "Calcutta Gazette" was happy to report that he was "a youth of about eighteen, of a very promising disposition." A salute was fired from the ramparts of Fort William in honour of Vazir Ali's accession; but the smoke from the guns had scarcely blended with the surrounding air before rumours arrived which ill agreed with this official optimism. We must bear in mind that existing arrangements were at this time liable to constant peril from combinations of Muslim powers inviting the aid of the Afgháns to the overthrow of the Mahrattas; and that not only did the British desire to support the existing state of things; but since Salbai the Mahrattas had, on the whole, been their best friends. Regarding the British as a Hindu power, by reason of this alliance, Vazir Ali was likely, it appeared, to join such a combination of Islám. Shore who had left Lucknow, was also informed that Vazir Ali's parentage was more than doubtful.

He therefore returned, held an inquiry, and pronounced against Ali Vazir's claim to the succession, which he conferred upon a brother of the late Nawáb, named Sáádat Ali. Vazir was sent into British territory ; where he, unfortunately, gave way to his temper, and murdered Mr. Cherry, the Resident at Benares.

Sáádat Ali obtained peaceable possession of Lucknow 21st January, 1798: his fort of Allahabad was made over to the British, and he became responsible for the permanent maintenance of a body of their troops numbering 10,000. The number of the Nawáb's troops was strictly limited, and he was not to negotiate with any foreign state. This was called a subsidiary alliance, but it came very little short of a total abolition of the independence of Audh.

Meanwhile the Sultan of Mysore struggled in the gathering toils. In the beginning of the year 1797 there were about sixty Frenchmen, ill-educated rogues for the most part, harboured in Seringapatam, who formed a Jacobin club, after the original had long since been overthrown in Paris. They held meetings, called Tipu " Citizen Sultan," and planted a tree of liberty in front of his palace while his guns thundered a salute. We are not, however, left to imagine that the Sultan and his ministers were dupes. On the contrary, the records found in Seringapatam a year and a half later, are enough to show that the subject was suspiciously viewed and anxiously discussed.

"Your Highness is not ignorant," wrote Mir Yusaf, of the Revenue Department, "that it is the custom of the French to promise much, but to perform little." On which the Sultan remarks, "If the theatre of war were in France would not the *Khudadád Sarkár* do all in his power to assist? and surely the Frenchmen cannot do less. No doubt a close connection will cost us something; but, on the other hand, an alliance with adventurers, who wander about with their houses on their backs, is a delicate affair." In this dilemma the "God-sent

State"—as Tipu called himself—would do best to send to Mauritius Ripaud, a French Corsair who had taken the lead amongst the Seringapatam Jacobins, with two envoys bearing letters to the Governor. Accordingly the Muslim envoys set out from Mangalore on board of Citizen Ripaud's brig, and reached Mauritius after a voyage in which, as they recorded, they underwent much suffering from sickness and from the discourteous treatment of the captain. Nor did they do much when they arrived. General Malartic, indeed, who then governed the island, received them kindly; but he was without authority to pledge the alliance of the Republic. All that he felt empowered to do was to call for volunteers; and about fifty officers, artificers, and soldiers embarked with the envoys on their return voyage, the whole commanded by Colonel Chappuis with a naval colleague named Dubuc. By the same opportunity Citizen Ripaud, transmitting his report to the Sultan, took occasion to warn his highness against General Raymond of the Nizám's service, whom he denounced as neither an admirer of the Jacobins nor a well-wisher to the Sultan. The little expedition reached Mangalore in May 1798. Dubuc was sent as an envoy to the Directory at Paris; and Colonel Chappuis and his followers proceeded to Seringapatam.

By that time Raymond was no longer a factor in Deccan politics; he died 25th March, the very day on which Sir John Shore left India; the temporary government falling, by routine into the hands of Sir Alured Clarke, Commander-in-chief of the army. But in less than two months a ruler landed in Calcutta who was to alter all existing designs and to give a new ply to the whole course of British Indian politics. This was a brilliant Irish nobleman, the Earl of Mornington, a friend of Pitt and Dundas; full of zeal against France, and with an insatiable capacity for labour.

The state of India was now becoming such as to tax all the resources of the British Government, which had attained a position where it was almost equally hazardous to stand still, to retreat, or to advance. The Afgháns had marched from Pesháwar, with the avowed intention of invading Hindustan.* The Mahratta Confederacy was torn with dissensions, the treacherous Peshwa now intriguing with Sindia, now restoring to power the aged and discredited Nána. General de Boigne, the steady friend of order, had retired, leaving his post and influence to be wielded by Perron, a good soldier but a feeble politician. The young French hero who had just driven the Austrians out of Italy was occupying Egypt and opening communiciations with the Sultan of Mysore. With the British fleet hardly yet purged of mutiny, and Ireland on the verge of rebellion, the Ministry at home could do no more than trust India to the wisdom and energy of the Governor-General.

The problem before Mornington was most grave. The policy of his immediate predecessors, Warren Hastings and Cornwallis, had been to meet the difficulties of their position by temporary expedients for balancing the country powers against each other, and to conjure the spectre of Islámite combination without allowing Audh and the Nizám to be swallowed up in a universal Hindu revival. To Lord Mornington the continuance of such a policy appeared impossible in the present condition of affairs.

One danger indeed passed away. Instigated by a mission from Shore, the Persian army had invaded the western parts of Afghanistán, while the Sikhs met the army of Zamán Sháh with unexpected firmness. After a furious battle near Amritsir the Sháh retired on Lahore, which he made over to Ranjit Sinh, to be held as a fief of the Afghán Empire; and he retired to his own country in the beginning of 1799; destined—as it after-

---

* From Tipu's papers we learn that he believed that the Sháh had reached Delhi.

wards proved—to return no more till after many years he came as a fugitive dependent on the unkind hospitality of his former feudatory.

But the danger from the hostility of the French remained in full force. Perron commanded some 40,000 good troops in Hindustan; the successor of Raymond had an almost equal army in Haidarabad, of which about 14,000 were good infantry under European officers; the mission of Tipu to the Mauritius became known by the publication of Malartic's call for volunteers. The first step of the new Governor-General was to propose a fresh treaty for the acceptance of the Nizám, embodying a clause for the disbandment of the force under French officers and their replacement by a body of British sepoys; the Nizám received the proposal with much hesitation; but acting on the advice of an able Minister he ultimately signed the treaty. A simultaneous step was to propose a subsidiary alliance to the Peshwa, by whom it was for the present declined, but with an oral assurance of support, which was not fulfilled. It now remained to carry out the disbanding of the Nizám's French army, which was effected with the good luck that awaits the audacity of competent men. The men were disbanded, by the British contingent, without effusion of blood in September 1798; the French officers being sent to Europe. This valuable service was greatly due to the firmness and tact of Captain John Malcolm, afterwards distinguished in many fields of duty.

About this time died Tukáji Holkar, who had, by the death of his Mistress, become head of the State of Indore, but had ceased, for some time past, to take any very active part in external politics. His place was assumed by an illegitimate son, Jaswant Ráo, afterwards a sore trouble to the British, but at first chiefly notable for his opposition to Daulat Ráo Sindia, and its important consequences. It must be confessed that this young chief—Sindia—had chiefly himself to blame for the troubles that he was enduring, He posed as the swordsman of the Peshwa—who did not want him—rather than as vicegerent of the Empire where he might have been very useful; at the same time his behaviour at Poona was habitually insolent and sometimes violently hostile; he plundered the bazaars, confined or killed public men, and persecuted the ladies of his predecessor's household. When Tukáji died Daulat Ráo stirred up feud and murder in the Holkar clan; and he gradually became associated with low ruffians, of all creeds and classes, in a way to signalise himself as a public and universal nuisance.

But the Governor-General did not at first view Sindia as a pressing danger. It was the Malartic proclamation which stirred him to action; and the first enemy, to be attacked—if possible—neutralized and isolated, was the Sultan of Mysore. He it was in whose interest General Malartic had made the proclamation; and he it was who, if the Directory should embrace his cause, would be the most earnest ally of any force which General Bonaparte might send to India from Egypt.

When Lord Mornington took up the office of Governor-General the government of Madras was temporarily in the hands of the Commander-in-Chief—General Harris—the same whom we formerly saw as staff-officer to General Medows. His Chief Secretary was Mr. Webbe, an able and honourable member of the Civil Services. To these officers Mornington addressed himself in the middle of 1798, forwarding a copy of the proclamation, and directing them to prepare for eventualities, should Tipu not make haste to disavow the proceedings of the Mauritius government. They replied in a manner which showed the difficulties of the situation, especially the deficiency of carriage and of cash. But Tipu made no such disavowal as the Governor-General required, and he accordingly directed Harris to make ready an army for the attack of Seringapatam. In vain Webbe pointed out the difficulties and dangers of "a premature attack"; while Harris declared that no army—even for defence—could be ready before "the monsoon in October. At the same time, however, he loyally set to work to accelerate the execution of Mornington's orders.

The obstacles were all that had been stated. Even in Calcutta—when Shore had left a deficit—money could not be procured at a lower rate of interest than twelve per cent.; at Madras the twelve per cent paper was at a discount. In point of carriage there was nothing but the small, half-wild cattle of the country, procured by force from the agriculturists. The Sultan, on the other hand, had his money ready, his treasury full, a standing army, and a train of excellent oxen and willing drivers: it was not impossible that he might take the initiative and burst on the Carnatic as his father had done in 1780. On the whole, however, up to the middle of July at least, the Governor-General did not despair of "renewing the efficacy of our alliances and obtaining satisfaction from Tipu without a war"[*]; in the very hope of doing which, nevertheless, lay the need for strenuous preparation. In connection with these designs Mornington urgently pushed the negotiations at Haidarabad and Poona; and, if no very active aid was received from those Courts, their neutrality at least averted complications. On the 21st August the permanent governorship of Madras was taken over by Lord Clive, son of the victor of Plassy; and the Commander-in-Chief, set free for professional duties, did his best to remedy the serious evils which had been allowed to grow up in the military administration of Madras. The Governor-General bore testimony, both privately and in official records, to Harris's energy and zeal, noting that the latter—by no means a wealthy man—had undertaken "to be responsible in his private funds for the sum required to put the troops in

[*] See letter to Harris, of 15th July, in Lushington's "Life of Lord Harris." p. 135

motion." This most generous and patriotic offer completely silenced all opposition.*

The troops immediately in question were those required to disarm and break up the French sepoys at Haidarabad, which was justly thought an important step in the attack on Tipu. From that quarter the danger daily diminished; while the spirit of the British at Madras as surely rose, and the opposition to the vigorous policy of the Governor-General gradually ceased. Tipu neither attacked the Carnatic nor showed any desire to submit—did not even answer the communications of the British Government, which accordingly assembled the Madras army at Vellore, a column of Bombay troops being at the same time ordered to co-operate from the western coast. The Governor-General at the same time came down from Calcutta and took up his post at Madras to watch and control operations. General Harris reached Vellore on 27th January, 1799, and at once assumed command of the army, the largest and best equipped that had ever acted under the orders of the Madras Government. It consisted of 21,649 men, about one-fourth of whom were Europeans, 160 field-pieces, and forty siege-guns. Among the leaders of infantry were General David Baird, and Colonel Arthur Wellesley—brother to the Governor-General, and destined to be conqueror of an abler if not more rancorous enemy than Tipu; the cavalry was under General Floyd, two of his subordinate officers being Colonel—afterwards Sir John—Sherbrooke, and Stapleton Cotton—afterwards Lord Combermere.—The Bombay column, under General Stuart, marched at the same time from Malabar.

After fighting their way up, against attempts on the part of the enemy to repeat the tactics which had once been so successful against Sir Hector Munro, the main bodies of the Madras and Bombay armies appeared before the Sultan's

* Lushington, *ut. sup.*, p. 163, correcting one of James Mill's hasty and numerous inaccuracies.

capital in the beginning of April. There was but little time to spare, for the south-western monsoon was at hand; the delay of a day might entail disaster. On the night of 6th April, Baird was sent on a reconnaissance which was to a great extent unsuccessful. Next night the 33rd Foot endeavoured to surprise the fortified grove of Sultanpeta—south-west of the City—under the command of Colonel Wellesley. The future Duke of Wellington was completely unsuccessful, and came back to the General's tent before daybreak, professing ignorance of the situation of his men. But the attack being renewed on the 6th by daylight, and supported by a strong body of cavalry, was at length perfectly successful. The grove and village were occupied: Colonel Shawe was posted a little further to the north, and the parallel completed against the western angle of the fort, which was at the same time raked by the guns of the Bombay column on the other side of the Cávari. Up to this time the confidence of the Sultan had been sustained by his French assistants and the predictions of his astrologers; he now showed a disposition to treat, but his negotations being marked by duplicity and procrastination, the siege operations were not suspended: so that by the 30th the batteries were all at work; and the wall showed a practicable breach on the 3rd May. Next day a column of 4,500 men advanced to the assault under Baird, supported by a reserve under Wellesley. They set forth at one p.m., Harris observing to Malcolm that they must succeed or perish. "Success," said the General, "is necessary to our existence." The forlorn hope consisted entirely of Europeans, supported by two subaltern's parties; the one under Lieutenant Lawrence of the 77th Foot, father of men destined to become famous in history; the other under Lieutenant Keene, of the 9th Madras Regiment, whose son is the writer of the present narrative.*

* Keene was Harris's nephew, afterwards the Rev. Professor Keene, a distinguished Arabic and Persian Scholar (v. "Dicty. of National Biography," Vol. XXX.)

The French officers conveyed the information of the assault to the Sultan, who was taking his mid-day meal in the north bastion. Hastily ordering up his troops he took a rifle and sallied forth to meet the assailants. But it was too late: the British forces were already in possession of the place. The Sultan presently fell, fighting to the last, at the very gate of his palace. There his body was afterwards found, under a heap of corpses, and was honoured by the victors with a solemn funeral attended by his sons. His remains were laid by the side of his father, in the Lál Bágh, at the eastern end of the island; and his epitaph, still preserved, tells that he died "a martyr to Islám." The French officers were well treated and sent to Europe; and the sons of the Sultan were assigned pensions—one of them living to become an honoured member of Calcutta society down to the middle of the 19th century.

The victory was only just gained in time. That night the rain fell in torrents, the Cávari rose, and the trenches were filled with water. "Had we not got into the town when we did," wrote one of the officers, "we must have raised the siege, spiked the guns, left all our tents and baggage, and fled without food, through a country that had been ravaged."

The Hindu Rája was fetched from captivity and placed upon the *masnad*, the limits of his territory being curtailed so as to round off the possessions of the Nizám and the Carnatic. The latter was still under the titular rule of the Nawáb; but the result of the war was, in effect, to complete the constitution of the Madras section of the British Empire as it exists at the present day, and to give the British possession of every port on the Indian coasts. It was, indeed, still more; for it fixed the attention of the Eastern world. The Nizám, whose cavalry was present (and ready to have joined the enemy in case of failure) became the ally of England as his successors have ever since been. The Mahratta leaders were intimidated if not wholly reduced to good conduct; and the designs of the French on India sustained a check from which they never really recovered. The fall of Tipu Sultan did for the south of India more than the victory of Baksar had done for Bengal; and may indeed be justly regarded as the foundation of the great pacification of India which has followed the assertion of British supremacy. The Governor-General wrote to Pitt that he expected either to be hanged or rewarded, undertaking to be satisfied in either case; for to him, he said, *an English gallows seemed better than an Indian throne.* He received, in fact, the thanks of Parliament and an Irish Marquessate. General Harris—whose deeds were effaced by those of the Governor-General—obtained no acknowledgement of his service until 1813, when he was created a Peer by the Prince Regent.

[In addition to authorities previously cited, see "Wellesley Despatches" and "Life of Lord Harris," by the Right Hon. S. R. Lushington, (second edition), London, 1845. Also Article on the siege of Seringapatam in "Calcutta Review" for April 1892.]

CHAPTER X.

WARS OF WELLESLEY.

Section 1 : Condition of Hindustan in 1799-1802—Section 2 : Condition of Mahratta Empire at the same date—Section 3 : The conquests of Lord Wellesley.

SECTION I.—The Marquess of Wellesley, as he now became, had—like all human beings—the defects of his qualities. His great mind was of the stuff of which conquerors are made, and his ambition was not unmixed with egotism. His Irish title he called "a gilded potato": we have had a glimpse of his neglect of subordinates—however indispensable they may have been to success—in his neglect of Harris; his great, unselfish, brother he was heard to designate "that hero of my own making." But in a career such as he was now engaged in some self-confidence was excusable—nay, essential to success. For good or for evil, the government of Great Britain was now compromised. Most of the native powers had been disabled; and it was but a question of time and of fortune, whether India was to fall back into anarchy or to become a complete dependency of the British Empire. Time and fortune were on the side of Britain; though there was much yet to be done before that question could be finally decided. The power of Daulat Rao Sindia was still erect in Hindustan, where Lakwa Dáda—once the brave defender of Agra—was now ruling as his lieutenant. Perron held quasi-sovereignty at Aligarh with his disciplined brigades. The rest of the army was under the command of Rája Ambáji, a trusted veteran. Sindia himself remained at Poona, attempting, in his crooked way, to exercise predominating influence over the equally treacherous Peshwa; the Nána was sinking under the weight of years and anxieties; Jaswant Ráo Holkar was restoring his resources and preparing to counteract the aims of Sindia.

In such circumstances the French general seemed to have an almost clear field in Hindustan. As a subordinate he had been well esteemed; but he was without mental training, and unfit for supreme power. For the moment, indeed, he had no difficulties to contend with but what might be of his own creation. Thomas, like himself, had been a "blue-jacket;" but there is no reason to suppose that the British ex-seaman would have interfered with Perron, if Perron did not interfere with him. For the time Thomas confined his operations to the westward, where the brother of the late Ghulám Kádir—whose title was "Muin-ud-din," but who was more commonly known as Bhanbu Khán—had been living for the past seven or eight years in exile, and hoping to recover the family possessions by help of the Sikhs. His grandfather, Najib-ud-daula, had held, it may be remembered, the country on both sides of the Upper Ganges, Najibabad, Sukertal, Muzafarnagar and Saharanpur, the "Fifty-two Parganas," and the last incursion of the Afgháns had also been attributed to his instigation; for he, too, was of Afghán, or Pathán blood, and anxious for a repetition of the campaign of 1761. Perron, as the servant of a Mahratta State, was, of course, opposed to all such movements; the fifty-two Parganas were—as we noticed in the last chapter—held by a Mahratta chief, named Apa Khándi; and Thomas, in defending them for the Apa, was fighting for Sindia and his French general. He had, as already related, little difficulty in disposing of Bhanbu Khán and the Sikhs; but the real danger began for him when that affair was over. By way of protecting himself he retired, after the Apa's death in 1796, to Jajhar, on the borders of Jaipore; and ultimately made for himself a little principality in Hariána, between that territory and the possessions of the Cis-Sutlej Sikhs. He then transferred his head-quarters to Hánsi where he established a mint and foundry, and began to collect a force for the conquest of the Punjab. He went on to take forcible possession of all the strong places in the neighbourhood; and by the beginning of 1799 had established his authority over the greater part of Hariána.

On the other side of the Jumna Perron was falling into bad odour with his Mahratta colleagues, whose natural jealousy he aggravated by unconciliatory demeanour. In August, 1798 he found one of these officers at Delhi exciting the blind old Sháh Álam to a hostile attitude; and Perron thought himself obliged to take the extreme step of sending a strong force thither under a French colonel, named Pedron, who seems to have been a good and able man. Pedron contrived to spare the aged Emperor the humiliation of a bombardment, and to obtain access to the palace by moral suasion, backed with bribery; Colonel Drugeon with a trustworthy garrison was then left in charge of the place. Scarcely had this been accomplished when another Mahratta chief revolted at Agra, requiring the presence of the general in person. He took a siege-train with him, but did not become master of the fort until April, 1799. In the meantime serious trouble arose, both in the Gwalior territory and in Rajputan; in which latter country Lakwa Dáda had to deal with a fresh combination of the Rájas of Jaipur and Jodhpur. Ambáji went to the rescue with field-artillery and a brigade of regulars under Du Drenec, who had left Holkar and taken the command under Daulat Rao Sindia. It was the old story of tribute claimed by Sindia's officers on behalf of the Emperor, refused by the Rajputs on the ground of their independence of the Mahrattas. The armies met at Sanganir—a few miles from the city of Jaipore—and were fairly matched in point of numbers, the Rajputs having more cavalry, but no regular infantry. A choice body of 10,000 heavy horse charged the brigade of Du Drenec in the most reckless style. Heedless of the fire of grape-shot and musketry which laid low 1,500 of their foremost rank, they rode through the brigade and trampled it into the sand. Du Drenec himself was almost the sole survivor.* But the time had gone by for the triumphs of horse over foot: there were still enough good musketeers left in the Mahratta ranks for discipline to assert its power; in all the rest of the field the Rajputs were repulsed, and this one action decided the campaign in favour of Sindia's army.

But a new trouble ensued; the victorious Dáda espousing the cause of the ladies of his late master's family, whom Daulat Ráo was persecuting, raised the standard of revolt in Central India. He occupied the country south-east of Gwalior, where his late comrade, the Rája Ambáji, was sent to suppress him and a petty local chief, who had joined him, from Datia in Bundelkhand. Ere long, Perron, hearing complaints of harshness towards European officers on the part of Ambáji, resolved to go in person: he arrived in December 1799, and assumed command of the army. On the 5th January, 1800, an action was fought at Bijaigarh, and the enemy were driven into their intrenchments. Having a considerable force of cavalry, with sixteen guns and a corps of regulars under Colonel Tone, a brave and able Irish officer, the Dáda made a respectable resistance.† But the works were stormed on 5th May; the Datia Rája was killed; Tone was allowed to depart and take service with Holkar; and the Dáda retired to a place of pilgrimage in the Udaipore State, where he died.

---

* For a graphic account of this romantic feat of arms see Fraser's " Memoirs of Jas. Skinner," given from Skinner's personal observation (vol. i., p. 147.)

† Colonel Tone was brother to the celebrated Wolfe Tone; he met with a soldier's death in 1801.

While Perron was thus engaged, George Thomas had made use of his leisure to build up his power at Hansi. Having some of the love of order which a man would be likely to pick up as a warrant-officer on board a man-of-war, he contrived to collect a population in a country long desolated by Afgháns, Sikhs, and Mahrattas, but by no means deficient in natural fertility. Here he restored the fortifications, coined money, cast guns, and established a factory of ammunition and small arms; prudently resolving to prepare for attack and defence, but purposing to confine his operations—so far as he might—to the western side of the river Jumna.

The revenues of his estates sufficed for his workshops and military forces; which comprised three battalions of infantry, fourteen guns, and a *khás risála*, or bodyguard, of Rohilla horse. With these followers he made some inroads on the Jaipore country, in which he displayed his usual vigour and intelligence; and after some more such forays, he at length set forth on his long meditated campaign against the Sikhs. This was at the opening of the year 1800; Thomas was engaged seven months in the expedition. He returned with a considerable booty and the position—as he said—of " Dictator in all the countries south of the Sutlej."

Thomas was now at his highest; with a little more aid from fortune he might have turned the scales and even altered the whole subsequent course of Indian history. Perron was losing ground everywhere, and Sindia was hard pressed by the superior energy and warlike ability of Jaswant Ráo Holkar, and by the faithlessness of Báji Ráo. It seemed to Thomas that the new vigor which Lord Wellesley was infusing into Deccan politics might be displayed, to the advantage of the British nation, in Hindustan. He therefore opened a communication with the Calcutta Government through a friend, Captain E. W. White, to whom he entrusted the offer of any services that might be desired by the Governor-General. If directed to advance he would occupy the Punjab, placing himself under the orders of the British Commander-in-Chief. In this plan, he added, he had nothing in view but the welfare of his king and his country. "I shall be sorry," he wrote, "to have my conquests fall to the Mahrattas; I wish to give them to my king." Wellesley was to invade and conquer in those regions ere long; but the time was not quite come; for the next twelve months his attention would be absorbed by southern affairs. But that an adoption of the proposals would have averted some loss and suffering, and that, with the help of Thomas, the conquests of 1803 might have been anticipated—with the sparing of valuable lives—may be taken for a certainity. An intelligent Englishman, then serving under Perron, who afterwards had personal experience of what Thomas could do as a soldier, recorded the opinion that it would have been feasible at that moment to persuade Sindia to discharge Perron, and put the British seaman in his place. This, he says, would have rallied all his brother officers of British blood to the cause of Sindia as an ally of their country, and French influence would have been destroyed in Hindustan. Other conditions were tending in the same direction: Bonaparte having by this time left Egypt in the pursuit of his ambitious projects in Europe. The invasion of India overland, which that wonderful man had concerted with the Czar Paul had collapsed; and all things were favourable to an anti-Gallican move in Upper India, such as the Governor-General had long meditated, and such as—in effect—he carried out two years later. It seems therefore impossible to deny the adventurous seaman credit for an unusual amount of political foresight; but his diplomacy was wanting in luck—and luck is generally another name for prudence. Thomas next turned to Holkar, who had overrun Málwa and was now being threatened by a force under a Dutch officer in Sindia's service, named John Hessing. After some indecisive skirmishing Hessing retired under the walls of Ujain—Sindia's chief place in north Málwa; and here he was caught in the open by Holkar. Breaking the Dutchman's line by a skilful employment of superior artillery, Holkar pierced through the gaps with all his horsemen. A frightful carnage ensued: of the European officers in Sindia's service seven were cut down in the defence of their guns, and three more were taken prisoners. Hessing owed his escape to the speed of his charger. This battle was fought in June 1801, and Thomas endeavoured to avail himself of Holkar's success to keep Perron in check, while he renewed his attack upon the Punjab.

But Perron's resources were too great. He sent a fresh force into Málwa, under Colonel Sutherland, who brought Holkar to bay at Indore. In the action that ensued the army of Holkar was beaten, and the chief had to suffer the loss of his capital and ninety-eight guns. At the same time Perron took advantage of the absence of Thomas to enter his territory, and the adventurer was compelled to return when he had nearly reached Lahore, and undertake the defence of Hariana. It is not certain that, even then, the French General was absolutely bent on the ruin of Thomas, though it must be admitted that he had plenty of provocation. But it is a fact that he invited his audacious rival to a personal interview, where the offer of a post in Sindia's service was renewed: Thomas was, however, called upon to assume a position of distinct subordination, to surrender his estates, and march with four battalions to reinforce the expedition against Holkar. This Thomas declined; he objected to serve under a Frenchman; he suspected Sindia; he was unwilling to serve against Holkar with whom he was still in friendly correspondence. It is hard to say whether his refusal was in accord with the dictates of prudence, which was not the adventurer's strongest point; but it is impossible to avoid sympathy with his motives. The decision was, in point of fact, his ruin: he retired to Hansi, where he was presently called on to oppose a strong detachment of Perron's army under Major Bourquin. The result of the campaign was inevitable : corruption alienated his best Asiatic subordinate ; the Cis Sutlej Sikhs gladly sought their revenge by joining the combination against their old enemy ; the Begam Samru ungratefully sent a corps to join in crushing her old servant and deliverer. After a spirited defence in which he displayed all his wonted audacity Thomas was compelled to surrender on 1st January, 1802. He was permitted to depart to his old asylum, the British cantonment, at Anupshahr, whence he proceeded towards Calcutta by river, in company with Major Francklin, his future biographer. But his strength was broken, and he died on the way, leaving a name which deserves to live in history.

His fall may be taken as marking the end of the great anarchy of Hindustan, a state of things which alone admitted of such a singular career. A few notices of the miserable condition of the country at that time will be found in the concluding pages of this volume ; and some further remarks by native eye-witnesses may be seen in the eighth volume of Dowson's "Elliot." In such an epoch the people disappears, and all that catches the eye is the conduct of bold ambitious spirits to whose prominence the times were naturally favourable ; while their biographies afford our only knowledge of events. Mirza Najaf Khán, Mahádaji Sindia, Haidar Ali, stand out like castellated crags above the wasted plains. And the Tipperary boatswain—perhaps descended from one of Cromwell's Ironsides—rose, as these did, but with less advantage at starting.*

* Some curious facts about Thomas have been collected by the present writer, in an article in the "Calcutta Review."

He completely preserved his British *feelings*, though he had almost lost the use of the English language : he was at one time adopted into a Hindu family. His coinage bore the superscription of the Mughal Empire—as did, for a long time after, the coinage of the Company—but he stamped it with a T.

Perron, for the moment, was now supreme. His income has been reckoned at sixty thousand rupees a month, and his army consisted of three brigades, each composed of ten battalions amongst whom were many of De Boigne's veterans; two hundred heavy cavalry, and fifty guns manned by European bombadiers and native gunners, were attached to each brigade, the cavalry being probably only needed to protect the artillery, as the Mahratta leaders had a vast body of horse independent of the regulars. The brigadiers and the commandants of battalions and companies, were either Europeans or country-born men of European origin. But Perron was by no means equal to his great position. We have had glimpses of his relations towards some of his native colleagues. With the Europeans he was not much more popular; although the officers of British blood were by no means the least forward in action, he showed a marked preference for his own countrymen. We shall find presently that such preference—however, natural—was of no service to him. Many of the sons of British fathers proved faithful to the last; some of his French protégés, in the words of one of his officers, " repaid his unjust favour with ingratitude." The same authority (L. F. Smith), asserts that " while only four non-British officers were killed in twenty years of war, fifteen British officers fell in the same space of time." By the end of the year 1800, however, Perron's position seemed to defy all hostility. He had brought all Hindustan under subjection, and every native ruler from the Narbada to the Sutlej, regarded him as paramount after the overthrow of Holkar and George Thomas. His self-control gave way under so much prosperity. Instead of being as De Boigne called him—a good, plain, honest soldier, he began to affect quasi-royal state, to listen to parasites, and to neglect straightforward merit.*

* Abridged from the narrative of James Skinner, who was then in the service. [I. 188].

On 10th November, 1799, General Bonaparte, having returned from Egypt, assumed the newly-constituted office of First Consul of the French Republic. Inflated by success, the Franco-Mahratta Dictator sent M. Descartes as an envoy to seek his alliance; but it is not apparent that any immediate result followed. France was somewhat exhausted by a seven years' war; and the great genius of the man who had now possessed himself of the control of the nation felt the necessity of gaining a breathing time for the restoration of civil order and institutions. It was then that he wrote his celebrated letter to the King of Great Britain; and though the reply that he received from Lord Grenville must have appeared to him cold and even arrogant, he did not allow his temper to get the better of his prudence. After the resignation of Pitt, in 1801, the negociations for peace were renewed; the Czar Paul was murdered; and the French were expelled from Egypt. The time was becoming unfavourable for any concerted attempt on British power in India. 'It is true that Pitt was no longer ostensible director of British politics; but other considerations prevailed. The preliminaries of peace were adjusted in London: six months later the formal treaty was signed at Amiens, 27th March, 1802.

It must not be supposed that Lord Wellesley's neglect of George Thomas in 1800, and the need that he felt for a clear and strongly defined action in southern politics, altogether distracted the attention of that great statesman from other parts of India. His master mind embraced all parts of the vast and distracted peninsula. Mahratta influence in Tanjore was entirely destroyed at this time, the Rája being, by a high-handed but almost inevitable stroke, sequestrated from a post which he had long abused; and an amiable young member of the family was recognised as titular prince, on a handsome allowance. The case of the Carnatic remained to be dealt with. It will be remembered that the Madras Government—

with the exception of the land about Fort St. George, and a few scattered jagirs—did not profess to have the rule of the country, but only to act as the subjects and servants of the Nawáb, the same Muhamad Ali that their predecessors had enthroned at Arcot in the days of the French War. He died in 1795, after a troubled reign of nearly fifty years; and was succeeded by his son, a weak and indolent man, surrounded by parasities and eaten up by creditors. The army that Harris had led to the conquest of Tipu was, in name, the Nawáb's army; but its expenses had to be paid by the British; and when the war was over a correspondence was found among Tipu's papers which showed that the Nawáb had been encouraging the resistance of that public enemy. Other letters, too, came out, from which it appeared that the Nawáb was at the same time sending despatches to the British Government in London, unknown to the local authorities, and in a spirit of hostility to them. All these were indeed matters not at first understood; yet there was quite enough to lead the Governor-General to call on the Nawáb to conclude an arrangement, already proposed to him by the Government of Madras, whereby some mortgaged districts, on which he persisted in making unlawful charges, should be assigned to the Company in liquidation of his debts and subsidy. A treaty already existed—dating from Cornwallis's time—by virtue of which the Carnatic could be taken over, in certain circumstances, and on certain terms. Fortified by instructions from the Court of Directors, Wellesley now sternly reminded the Nawáb, of his obligations, but expressed his reluctance to proceed to extremes. Then came the discovery of the Nawáb's correspondence with Tipu, as already stated. The cup was now full; the Nawáb avoided deposition by a timely demise; but his successor was only recognised on condition of a new treaty, by which the whole of the civil and military power of the state was assumed by the British. (1801).

So much for the South. In Hindustan the most pressing

duties then seemed the maintenance of Audh, as a bulwark to Bengal, and the protection of Upper India, generally against a fresh incursion of the Afghán. The relations of Persia, too, had acquired new importance from the proximity of the Russian advance, and the known connection between the Czar and the First Consul. In 1800 an embassy laden with splendid gifts and friendly overtures, was sent to the Court of Teheran, under John Malcolm, the officer whom we have already met with at Haidarabad, and at the siege of Seringapatam. The objects of the mission were to all appearance, fully attained; and no more was heard of invasion from Russian or Afghán. In Audh a new treaty was obtained, in November, 1801, from Sáádat Ali, Shore's Nawáb: under this agreement British administration was introduced into the lower Duáb and Rohilkhand : the British, on their part, guaranteeing the remaining dominions of the Nawáb-Vazir.

Wellesley had thus created the Madras Presidency, and the eastern half of the "North-West," so called by reason of the situation of the "Ceded Provinces," to the rest of the territory subject to the Government of Bengal. It may here be noted that—although these districts have since grown into a distinct Government—the civil servants there are still supposed to belong to the "Bengal Civil Service," and the Commander-in-Chief of Bengal still commands the army far beyond their limits : so that the Punjab itself is garrisoned, in part at least, by the "Bengal Army."

In regard to the young officers of the former service Wellesley attempted a grand reform. A college was founded in Calcutta, for the instruction of the young men intended for administrative control, opened, and for some time visited by his Excellency in person, and distinguished by the number of good, and often famous, public men whom it trained.* But the

* Among the names on the Calendar of the time are those of Elphinstone, Metcalfe, Jenkins, Hamilton, Bayley, and others who rose, at last, to real distinction. ["Primitiæ Orientales." Calcutta 1803-4.]

Court of Directors—jealous of its few remaining powers—nipped the project in the bud, and established a college of their own, at Haileybury, near Hertford. Irritated at this and other instances of interference the imperious Marquess tendered his resignation in 1802. By the friendly meditation of the King's Ministers the Directors were induced to make a sort of apology to the masterful Satrap, who then consented to remain in office till the end of 1803.

[Most of the books cited recently are still recommended, including Malleson's "Last French Struggles," and Fraser's "Memoirs of Skinner." Louis Ferdinand Smith's "Rise, Progress, and Termination of the Regular Corps," is the work of a clever comrade. Calcutta, N.D..* See also Francklin's "Military Memoir of George Thomas," 4to. Calcutta, 1803.]

SECTION 2.—With the possible exception of himself no one could have foreseen what Lord Wellesley was preparing when he agreed to remain in India another twelvemonth. Inconsistent as it seems with the irritability shown by the Governor-General's resignation there was, perhaps, a sense in his mind that if he remained in office he could bring his policy to grander issue than any other ruler. Having tamed, by war or negotiation, all the surrounding or intervening powers, he was now face to face with the dissolving confederacy of the Mahrattas; an adroit use of whose dissensions might realise the visions of ascendency, if not of Empire.†

In order to understand the methods by which the Governor-General proceeded in his attempt to substitute British for Mahratta arbitrament and to shift the centre of Indian gravity from Poona to Calcutta, it will be needful to look a little more closely at the relations of the Mahratta chiefs to one another. We have already seen something of these; the tendency of the

* Smith's book was reprinted in London, 1805, and there is a copy at the India Office.

† v. extract from the "Annual Register," in the next section.

Berár State to claim independence; the inherent, though often concealed, opposition of the two clans who divided the possession of Málwa. The Berár State was often ready—for its own purposes—to ally itself with the Calcutta Government. During the life of Mahádaji a similar disposition had been shown in Málwa, where the elder Sindia accepted the support of the British while the Holkars were kept from troubling by the wisdom of Ahalya Bai and her faithful henchman. But by the time of which we are now treating both Tukáji and his venerable mistress were dead; and the family of Holkar was torn by violent competition and animosity. It was admitted, indeed, that Tukáji had become head of the clan, and that his power was something heritable in his family. But who was the rightful heir, or by what considerations ought the succession to be regulated?—these were points whose adjustment might well prove difficult among those crudely selfish people. Tukáji Holkar had left two sons, born in wedlock, whose names were Kashi Ráo, and Malhar Ráo, neither being of much capacity. But their bastard half-brother, Jaswant Rao, though wild and lawless, had acquired in his neglected youth a hardness of temper which inspired him with very high hopes. The legitimate brothers soon quarrelled; and on the death of Nàna Farnavis in 1800 Sindia came forward, as chief adviser of the Mahratta Empire, with an armed arbitration. The force under Malhar Ráo was attacked and defeated by Sindia. Malhar lost his life, and Jaswant—who had supported him—fled from the field; but, after various adventures, appeared in the Narbada valley as the champion of Khandi Ráo Malhar's son. Du Drenec had no belief in the adventure and left the Holkar service for that of Sindia; but Jaswant Ráo engaged other European officers, and rallied to his side a number of the speculative soldiers of the time, notably Amir Khán, the famous leader of Pathán marauders. He had now begun to form the definite design of becoming master of the State of

Indore, or South Málwa, with an outlook towards the direction of affairs at Poona. It was in pursuance of this scheme that he entered on the course of hostility which began by the successful engagement with Hessing at Ujain, in June, 1801, described in the last section. The military resources of Daulat Ráo Sindia were too vast to be seriously shaken by one defeat; and on 14th October being reinforced from several quarters, including 14 battalions of De Boigne's veterans under Colonel Sutherland, Sindia inflicted on the Holkars a severe defeat when they had advanced within a mile of Poona.

Wellesley judged the moment favourable for a renewal of his proposals for a defensive alliance. It was true that the Holkars were, for the moment, driven off; but Sindia remained, with his villainous henchman and father-in-law, Sherji Ráo; and the Peshwa's power was so reduced and circumscribed that in his despair he was almost ready to surrender at discretion. On the 20th November of the same year, he notified to Colonel Barry Close, the Governor-General's able and resolute agent, his readiness to accept a part of the conditions on which British support had been tendered—what were Wellesley's wishes he was but too well aware. Not only did the Governor-General desire to be constituted protector of the Mahratta Empire and arbiter of its affairs, but he wished for one of those "subsidiary alliances" whereby a British army was to be quartered on the Poona State with certain specified districts assigned for its support, and an engagement to employ no other Europeans. Whether we are to call it patriotism, pride, or ambition, there was a feeling amongst the Mahrattas of great aversion towards the idea of their states becoming dependencies of the foreigners, as had been the fate of the Nizám and the Nawáb Vazir. So the Peshwa proposed a compromise: Europeans not belonging to a nation at war with England might be retained—so he pleaded—and if the Governor-General lent him a few battalions of sepoys his Highness the Peshwa would see to their pay, but would not part with any portion of Mahratta territory. Of these modified offers the Governor-General did not think immediate notice necessary, preferring to await the development of events which he hoped might be such as to induce a more submissive frame of mind in Báji Ráo. Six or seven months, however, went by during which the Peshwa made no sign; and in the meanwhile considerations—connected with the general politics of the British Empire—had arisen to dispose the Governor-General to make fresh overtures.

The peace of Amiens had been characterised by Sheridan as an arrangement of which everyone was glad but no one proud. It soon appeared that it was also one to which it would not be easy to bind the haughty aristocracy which had then the conduct of British affairs. The Tories had never concealed their hostility to the First Consul as enemy of legitimacy and swordsman of the Republic; the Whigs generally objected to him on the opposite ground that he was a Cæsar who was bent on stifling the infant liberties of his country.* It soon appeared too likely that the treaty would, in effect, be little more than a temporary armistice. The British Ministry—scenting a design to renew the French occupation of Egypt—refused to loose their hold of Malta, which they had engaged to restore to the Knights of S. John; and when Admiral Linois arrived at Pondicherry to receive the stipulated restoration of the French possessions in India he was put off with excuses and had to depart without effecting the purpose of his mission. The British Cabinet continued its armaments in Europe; and Wellesley—in spite of the disobedience of Admiral Rainier commanding the Indian squadron—went on with all possible preparations against the

* Sir Francis Burdett refused to be presented to Napoleon; Mr. Fox attended a *levée* at the Tuileries, but hardly answered a word to Napoleon's courteous and flattering address.

renewal of hostilities. While yet uncertain whether or no his resignation had been accepted at home, he wrote to General Lake, the Commander-in-Chief, to the effect that the forces must be reduced in obedience to orders from London; but that, even so, preparation should be made for not very remote exertion: "it is indispensable to our safety in India," he said, "that we should be prepared to meet any future crisis of war with unembarrassed resources." * In a similar spirit he rebuked the Admiral for failing to act against the island of Mauritius, so useful to the French as a place of arms in Eastern seas. His assertion of general authority was supported by the king's government in the following year; but in the meanwhile the chance had gone by; and the corsairs of Mauritius continued to prey on the Company's commerce for nearly a decade longer.

In connection with these high-handed displays of patriotic energy—Wellesley proceeded to press his offers on the reluctant Báji Ráo ; offers which he professed to regard as no less advantageous to one side than to the other. These proposals, modified as far as the Governor-General thought feasible, were presented to the Peshwa in July, 1802. His Highness took no direct notice of the overture; but one of his ministers paid a visit to Colonel Close, in the course of which the ultimatum was reached that, before any other negotiation could be entertained, it would be absolutely essential for his Highness to pledge himself to the acceptance of the same subsidiary terms as those which governed the "defensive alliance with the State of Haidarabad."† Unable to bring themselves to do this, the Peshwa and Ministers turned to Sindia, in hopes of being by him defended against Jaswant Ráo.

At the begining of September, when the rainy season was showing signs of cessation, the army of Sindia—under the general command of Sheodasheo Ráo—took post at Paithan,

* Second despatch of 8th Feb., 1802, *W.D.* II., 625.
† Intercepted despatch of 12th April, 1804, paras. 18—20.

in the Godavari valley, while columns under Holkar's orders were converging to attack Poona. The Holkar party continued to be represented, however, at the Peshwa's Court, and to urge upon his Highness the conclusion of an arrangement opposed to the views and interests of Sindia whom Jaswant Ráo considered himself quite able to resist. He asked that his elder half-brother, Káshi, should be removed from the charge of Indore for which he was obviously unfit, while he—Jaswant—should administer the State on behalf of his nephew, Khandi, who was kept in confinement by Sindia. As the Peshwa knew that this meant a rupture with the latter, of whose power and violence he had but too much experience, he hesitated in his replies, and Jaswant advanced on the capital. Sindia's general on this broke up his camp, and crossed the river Godavari; while Báji Ráo and many of the richer citizens prepared to removed their families and property from Poona. It was felt on all sides that the brave and skilful leader of cavalry was not to be disregarded.

The opportunity so long awaited by Wellesley seemed, even now, to linger strangely. On 20th September the Peshwa made one further attempt at evasion and sent to the Resident a fresh proposal. The "auxiliary force" should remain in British territory, ready at all times for any service that the Peshwa might require; the British Government should abjure in perpetuity all interference in Mahratta politics or between his Highness and the Nizám; his Highness might employ such Europeans—of whatever nationality—as might not be personally hostile or obnoxious to the Company; conditions which not only modified but defeated every principle that the Government of Calcutta had in view in offering its alliance. The overtures were accordingly rejected, and the armies continued, like two black storm-clouds, to approach each other. An encounter on the 8th October showed the coming tempest; Sindia's army lost a quantity of guns and and baggage; and

Báji Ráo sent his women with all his jewels to a strong hill-fort. After the affair of the 8th, Sindia's general continued his advance, and came in contact with the van of Holkar's army on the 25th October, 1802, about ten miles from the city. The brigade of De Boigne's old force were under Colonel Dawes, an officer of British extraction, and the Peshwa's body-guard furnished a small but choice body of heavy cavalry. On the other side Holkar had three brigades of infantry, each under a good British officer; Jaswant himself, clad in complete steel, led the cavalry. At first the loyal valour of the bodyguard swept everything before them, till Jaswant Ráo came up with the reserve cavalry and retrieved the honour of his horsemen. The British officers on both sides fought with the tenacity of their race; hand-to-hand and foot-to-foot, with push of bayonet their faithful followers contended, until Holkar and his men-at-arms, returning from the pursuit of the bodyguard, cut down the artillery men at their guns, killed most of Sindia's Europeans and broke in pieces the ill-supported and out-numbered foot. Colonel Dawes was killed on one side, Major Harding—commanding one of Holkar's brigades—fell on the other; Jaswant Ráo, in spite of his armour was wounded in two places. This was the first time that any of De Boigne's men ever succumbed; but there were only four battalions of them against fourteen; they could not conquer, but they died.

Meanwhile the consternation in Poona was extreme. The inhabitants who could escape made haste to do so, on the road to their places of refuge they were robbed with insult by bands of highwaymen. The fields were abandoned by the husbandmen, the half-ripened crops being cut and carried.*

* From Colonel Close's report, cited in the intercepted despatch obtained from France and published by Stockdale, 1805. (791 paragraphs, reporting the political transactions of the year 1803, dated 12th April, 1804.)

The submission of the mean and unscrupulous ruler of Poona was now complete, all pride and patriotism having vanished from that abject breast. The British Resident on receiving his prayer for protection sent to Bombay, Haidarabad, and Madras for troops. These orders were, without delay, comfirmed by the Government at Calcutta, while Jaswant Ráo, on his part, pushed on his revolutionary projects.

For the present the object of all these anxieties was only anxious to put as great a distance as he could between himself and his capital which he abandoned in hot haste, retiring at one gate as the victor entered by the other. Colonel Close, after warning Holkar and his friends that nothing could be settled but by the sanction of the Governor-General, withdrew from Poona at the end of November, reaching Bombay on the 3rd of the following month. The Peshwa sent word, from the sea-coast, that he sought an asylum at the hands of the Government of Bombay; and, so soon as the approval of the Governor-General could be obtained, a ship was sent for the accomodation of his Highness, who landed at Basain a few days later.

It should here be mentioned that, even before the battle, the Peshwa had given Close a letter signed with his own private seal, in which he undertook to take into his pay the desired number of British sepoys; to assign to them a cantonment in his own territory with land to the value of 26 lakhs of rupees per annum; and to conclude a defensive alliance with the Company on the basis of that which had been made with the Nizám. In accordance with this seemingly absolute surrender the Governor-General wrote to Close, 16th November, 1802, expressing his satisfaction at his Highness' determination, and promising to exert all the resources of the British power in India for the re-establishment of the Peshwa's authority. The Resident was further charged to take the first favourable opportunity of reducing the agreement to the form of a treaty in which all the principles so long vainly urged upon his Highness should be formally and definitely included.

And now that opportunity had indeed arrived, in its most golden aspect: while British troops, from two separate quarters were converging to neutralise the possibility of valid interference, either from Holkar or from Sindia, the Peshwa was a voluntary refugee in a British station, his nerves still trembling with the din of a lost battle, not knowing what was to become of him, unless he could purchase the protection of this formidable power that had been so long pursuing him with its unwelcome friendship.

The despatch of 16th November reached Close on 6th December; and he lost no time in seeking a conference with the Minister in attendance on the Peshwa. The meeting took place on the 8th December; when the Resident conveyed to the Minister an assurance that no more delay or equivocation would be tolerated; and that any failure on the part of his Highness to conclude a treaty on the terms already determined would be met by ulterior measures, amongst which would be a demand for payment of all the expenses incurred on the Peshwa's behalf.

On the 16th the fugitive President of the Mahratta Confederacy arrived at Basain, where he was waited on by Colonel Close with a draft-treaty. Báji Ráo tried to produce a discussion, but Close was not to be put off. And so at last on the 31st, the Peshwa admitted him to another audience, at which he gave up all further opposition; and the treaty was, then and there, "concluded and exchanged."*

This therefore—the last day of the year 1802—is to be regarded as the third great date in the history of the British in India. The battle of Baksar had given them Bengal, and the

* Intercepted despatch, par 75.

subordination of Audh; the fall of Tipu gave them the Presidency of Madras and the submission of the Nizám; by the treaty of Basain they obtained the Presidency of Bombay, and decided the question whether or no the predatory and quarrelsome Mahratta Confederacy was to be supreme in the great peninsula. It did even more, more perhaps than could at the moment come into contemplation; for it opened the path to the wide and fertile regions of Hindustan, and to the prevalence of peace and order in a long distracted land. In the language of General Arthur Wellesley—the future Duke of Wellington—"the treaty of Basain and the measures adopted in consequence afforded the best prospect of preserving the peace of India; and to have adopted any other measures would have rendered war with the whole Mahratta nation more than probable." It is true that war did ensue: but it was not with the whole Confederacy; hence it was shorter, easier, and less devastating than it would otherwise have been; and when it was over there was no hostile power left within the whole borders of India.

It was not to be expected that such a decisive step towards sovereignty should fail to alarm and annoy those with whose projects it interfered. The first to feel this was Daulat Ráo Sindia, who is said to have complained that the treaty had "taken the turban off his head." The subsequent conduct of this chief certainly warrants the inference that he must have been deeply committed to projects and hopes which the treaty of Basain thwarted. Yet there was no ground of complaint that he could venture to allege. The interference of the British for the Peshwa's restoration had been solicited by Sindia himself; and the records are there to show that the treaty was not conceived or carried out in any spirit of hostility to that chief.[*] He was not only party, personally, to the initiatory negotiations

* v. "Selections from Wellington Despatches," S. Owen, Oxford, 1880.

but his Vakil* was aware of the whole transaction. The principles which Wellesley laid down were too reasonable to be openly denounced by any one making the least pretence of being friendly, and the fact that the columns from Madras and Haidarabad continued to converge towards the country of the Peshwa was a special reason why objections should be circumspect. Holkar, indeed, began to open negotiations with the Court of Haidarabad, but these the Nizám loyally reported. Sindia, with better prospect of immediate success, sent an envoy to Nagpore, where the Raja of Berár was already engaged in warlike preparations, and openly expressed his dissatisfaction with the submission of the Peshwa.

The troops from Madras and Haidarabad were now united, and on the 26th March encamped at Purinda (famous for the abortive treaty of 1776) where they were presently joined by a third column, brought up from Mysore by General Wellesley, who assumed full military and political charge of the operations. Jaswant Ráo, on hearing of the arrival of the British in his neighbourhood, retired from Poona, leaving the charge of affairs there in the hands of Amrit Ráo, the Peshwa's brother, with whom he was, for the time, in combination. A general expectation prevailed that this governor intended to sack the city and set fire to it before evacuating, but General Wellesley made such speed that any design of the sort was frustrated. Hurrying up the troops of the Peshwa from the westward, Wellesley set off from camp on the night of the 19th April with the British troopers of his army, and made his way, over sixty miles of rugged country, by the line of the "little Bhor Ghát"—a most difficult pass in those days—arriving in Poona the next day. He and his dragoons were received as deliverers by the citizens, who at once evinced their confidence by returning to the city and resuming their usual avocations.

* Agent: It is the custom of feudatory chiefs and princes to be represented at Court by permanent ministers, or agents, who are called Vakils.

Sindia was at Ujain when he heard the news of the defeat of his general at Poona; but on the 13th December, 1802, the Governor-General received a letter from him, giving the information that he should set out for Poona, where he hoped that the British Government, in accordance with the treaty of Salbai, would concur with him in supporting the authority of the Peshwa. On the 9th of January, 1803, the same chief was officially informed of the conclusion of the treaty of Basain, and expressed his satisfaction, though in a somewhat guarded manner, and his intention to await the arrival of Colonel Collins, then on his way to join the camp, before deciding on the steps which he should take for the objects common to the two states. This last missive appeared to the Governor-General suggestive of a desire to take the place lately sought by Holkar, and so to oust the British Government from that influence in Poona politics which it had been endeavouring to obtain ever since 1799.

On 1st March, 1803, Collins waited on Sindia at Burhánpur, and informed him that the Government of Calcutta was prepared to conclude with him an alliance similar to that just concluded with the Peshwa; and, as nothing decisive occurred for the next ten days, the matter was again brought to Sindia's notice; the British Agent adding that the Governor-General was sincerely desirous of reconciling him with Holkar, and of pacifying the whole of the Deccan. The resentment of Sindia now came to light. At an interview on the 16th March his Agent informed Collins that Sindia was astonished that he had not been informed in time of the intention to conclude a separate treaty with the Peshwa, and that he must consult with that ruler before giving a decisive answer. The Governor-General's remarks on this were high and haughty, but Collins, in a personal interview with the chief—24th March—conveyed the purport without offence; indeed, while never wavering from a position of due firmness, he acted throughout with the greatest tact and courtesy; and Sindia, on this occasion made an oral admission that he had no grievance against the British Government. But his subordinates were less reticent, and one of them, in a conversation of 18th April, showed his master's state of mind by bluntly asking Collins if the British really desired to take the turban from Sindia's head?

From these negotiations it may be inferred that Sindia was becoming by this time determined to pick a quarrel. There was nothing in the treaty of Salbai—to which he frequently referred—that could give him a claim to impose a veto on any further agreements between his suzerain and the British Government. The negotiations between them had been going on openly for above two years, during which he had made no objection. After the battle of Poona he had expressed his satisfaction at the action of the Governor-General. After the conclusion of the treaty he had at first expressed acquiescence. But, it appears that between the months of January and March he and Perron had made up their differences. At the same time he could not fail to perceive that the British columns continued to advance; and he found that he was expected to make a treaty similar to that accepted by the Peshwa, one article of which would have deprived him of all the European officers of his army. Turbulent, self-willed, and utterly unscrupulous, it could hardly be expected that he should not endeavour to hold aloof from an alliance proffered on these terms. Yet Wellesley could hardly believe that, even with the aid of the Rája of Berár, with whom he was reported to have opened a correspondence, Sindia would dare to incur the risk of a conflict with the power that had overthrown the Sultan of Mysore. Nevertheless, the Governor-General thought that the time had come when a categorical explanation of Sindia's intentions ought to be demanded; at the same time it was to be suggested to that chief that a substantial proof of his pacific designs would be afforded by his withdrawing his troops to Hindustan.

Lastly, on 3rd June, Wellesley sent instructions to Collins which may be regarded as containing an ultimatum. For they conveyed an intimation which may be summed-up in the following three clauses:—

1. If Sindia marched with his army to Poona it would be taken for a declaration of war;
2. If Sindia attacked the Nizám he would be repelled by every means in the power of the British Government;
3. But the Governor-General was prepared, either to make Sindia a party to the treaty of Basain, or to conclude with him a separate alliance.

At the same time the Governor-General sent a letter to Sindia, direct, in which, recapitulating what he had said through Collins, he entered into friendly arguments, explaining the grounds of his present action and his firm determination to carry out the treaty with all due consideration for the interests of Sindia, and of all the other vassal states of the Mahratta empire, of which the Peshwa was the head. A similar letter was transmitted to the Rája of Berár, warning him against any combination hostile to the British or their allies; to which was added this representation:—Either the State of Berár was a vassal State of the Mahratta Empire, in which case the Rája had no right to question the power of his superior to make any alliance that might seem proper; or the State of Berár was independent, and in that case had nothing to do with the affair. The letter ended by the offer of a similar alliance with Berár, with the proviso that the refusal of that offer would in no way affect the friendly feelings entertained by the British Government towards the Berár State, but that any attempt to interfere with the treaty of Basain would lead to war.

It is, of course, impossible to say that the British Government was actuated by none but the avowed motives in these proceedings. As has been already noted, the position was full of grave anxiety. The tranistory nature of the peace of

Amiens was evidently forseen; the refusal to surrender the French possessions in India is sufficient proof of that. Perron was known to be full of hostility, and the strength of his position was also known, and even exaggerated: at one moment Wellesley regarded the General as a French potentate virtually independent of Sindia in Hindustan: on the other hand the rejection of Thomas's overtures, coupled with the absence of all mention of a conquest of Hindustan in the Governor-General's public correspondence so far ought to be accepted as considerable evidence that the attitude adopted towards Sindia was only due to the ostensible facts. Sindia and his immediate predecessor had made agreements with the British by which the vassal States of the Mahratta Confederacy were clearly estopped from objecting to similar steps being taken by their acknowledged overlord; for whatever they could do *à fortiori*—could be done by him. It was clearly dangerous, if not impossible, to allow a feudatory to dictate to his lord in such a case. A masterly summary of the whole political complications, by which Lord Wellesley was at this time beset will be found in his brother's "Memorandum," given as an introduction to the "Selections" of Mr. Sidney Owen.

The relation of General Perron towards the final determination adopted by Sindia in this momentous crisis must always be somewhat obscure. In March, in consequence of a letter received from Perron, the Governor-General regarded him as prepared to leave the service of Sindia; and Skinner informed his biographer that there had been a quarrel between Perron and his employer at Ujain, which had led to the resignation of that officer in the beginning of the year.* But either the resignation was not accepted or was soon afterwards withdrawn; for Skinner—who was then serving in the army—adds that Perron, about this time, drew up a plan for a combined attack

* "Intercepted Despatch," par. 488. See also "Wellesley Despatches," III. 63.

on the British power. From the same source we gather that the resources at the disposal of the allies were formidable. Sindia and the Berár Rája between them could count on the services of a hundred thousand irregular troops, of whom half consisted of good cavalry. There were not less than forty thousand regulars—infantry and gunners—staunch and steady men under European officers. Sindia alone had more than three hundred pieces of good artillery. Of three hundred Christian officers all but about forty were French.

On the 6th July, 1803, Wellesley received from England an intimation that war with France would soon be renewed; and two days later, in writing privately to General Lake, at Cawnpore, he revealed the larger scheme that this intelligence opened to his mind. He admitted that he had come to the consideration that "the reduction of Sindia's power on the north-west frontier of Hindustan was an important object in proportion to the probability of a war with France ;" a view which he reinforced, in an official form, ten days later. Before the end of that month the die was cast : the Governor-General writing to Collins, stated that the reasons given by the Confederates—Sindia and Berár—for the non-withdrawal of their troops were so clearly illusory, that he must order him to leave Sindia's camp at once. On the 15th July, further justification of hostilities was received from a fresh quarter. The Collector of Moradabad, nearly a month before, had sent off a letter enclosing a communication that he had received from a man already mentioned in this narrative—Bhanbu Khán, brother of the late Ghulám Kadir, who had managed to get back to his ancient family seat at Najibabad in Rohilkhand—annexed was a circular, received from Perron in Sindia's name, in which the chiefs of Hindustan were invited to rise against "that unprincipled race, the English," and to give their cordial co-operation to General Perron. A month earlier similar missives had been received from the Collector of Allahabad, addressed to chiefs in Bundelkhand.

A memorandum found at Pondicherry about this time gives some support to the apparent paradox that a campaign in the neighbourhood of Delhi, was an essential part of the defence of Dover: and it is quite possible that the French Government would have created a diversion of British resources by co-operating with Perron, but for the breaking out of the terrible negro revolt at S. Domingo which called forth all the available means of the First Consul for maritime enterprise. So strangely, even at that period, could the affairs of one part of our planet affect the fortunes of another. This paper is signed by a Lieutenant Lefébre, but appears to have been based on information supplied by Perron for submission to the First Consul. The purport of it is that the aged and blind Emperor, Sháh Álam—then a prisoner in the custody of one of Perron's colonels—should be recognised and supported as a protégé of the French Republic. "The English Company," it was added, "by its ignominious treatment of the Great Moghul, has forfeited its rights as Diwan of the Empire." This flimsy attempt to veil an unprovoked aggression under the worn-out mantle of the extinct Empire of the House of Bábar, was thus no more, in reality, than a feeble endeavour to repeat the defeated policy of five years ago at Seringapatam. But it seems to have contributed to the feeling of the British authorities against the French officers in Sindia's service, and the determination to extirpate them from Indian limits at whatever cost.

Sindia and the Rája of Berár met at Malharpur, a village on the Nizám's border, 4th June; and, as was but natural in the circumstances, pursued a long course of shuffling, in the apparent hope of persuading the British authorities to withdraw their troops. But Arthur Wellesley—who had received full political powers from his brother—refused to listen to anything, or move a man, until the confederates had set the example; and at last, after a display of the utmost patience and perserverance, Colonel Collins was obliged to carry out his conditional instructions by leaving Sindia's camp. This step—which took place on 3rd August—was the virtual commencement of the war: and the Governor-General must be acquitted of precipitation and cannot be charged with undue fettering of his agents. For five months there had been little room for doubt as to Daulat Ráo's hostile feelings: yet up to the date of his meeting with the Bhonslá—as the Berár Rája was called—both the Marquess and his brother professed to hope for a peaceful settlement. And it is quite possible that such an end might have been compassed: for Daulat Ráo had quite enough intelligence to know the strength of the British, and had twice appeared on the verge of acquiescence. But the Bhonslá was a barbarian who had seen nothing of the British, either as politicians or as soldiers. And, after all the arguments that could be urged upon him, the case was one of those in which there is something to be said on either side. The Bhonslá therefore—knowing nothing of the law of nations, or the feudal system—replied that, by the unwritten customs of the Mahrattas, one chief—even were he the highest—could not compromise the Confederation without the consent of the whole of the States of which that Confederation was composed; and in so saying he may well have spoken in good faith.

Sindia, however, had few other friends. He had all the faults that are to be usually found in young men brought up with great expectations. His precedessor had been turbulent and vindictive in his earlier days; but always self-restrained and prudent, with affable ways and a faithful nature by which he made friends and kept them. But Daulat Ráo was cruel by caprice and full of insincerity. He was suspicious, moreover of those by whom he was served; and his servants were, for the most part ready to desert and betray him if their own interests seemed to require such courses.

It was the office of statesmanship to profit by this unpopularity; accordingly, so soon as Sindia—whether persuaded by the Bhonslá of Berár, or by the gasconading General Perron—showed that he had chosen the alternative of war, the Governor-General sought every opportunity of undermining the enemy in every quarter. Bhanbu Khán, of Najibabad, was thanked for his communication and promised a reward. Negotiations were opened with Himmat Bahádur—leader of Gosains, or fighting friars—who commanded for Sindia in Bundelkhand, and had written to the Collector of Allahabad. The bloodthirsty and grasping Sherji—Sindia's father-in-law—attempted to make terms for himself. The correspondence with Perron was renewed, and messages were sent to the poor old Emperor, neither of which had an apparent good result, though both brought benefit a little later. Lastly, a proclamation was addressed to all British subjects serving Sindia—either as officers or soldiers—in which they were clearly notified of two things: those who left Sindia before the fighting began should have employment or pensions, or be provided for in other ways; and those who remained should be regarded as guilty of high treason. Perron, it should be noted to his credit, declared that it was his intention to remain with his employer until he should be formally dismissed and relieved by a successor; which probably means that he did not much like the responsibility of his position, and was hoping to hand it over to Ambáji, who was spoken of as coming to take charge in Hindustan. The Emperor also made a show of refusal, directing Lake to fall back, and threatening to take the field in person if he did not obey. But, at the same time, an Agent of the Emperor's came to the camp privately, and explained that the manifesto had been dictated by the French officers at Delhi. As for the officers and men, the proclamation acted variously in various cases. The sepoys, who had been taken into the service from the Company's, when the armies of the latter had been reduced in number, had often left their families in Bihar or in Audh; and—regarding these as a sort of hostages—now hurried home in hundreds. Of the British-born officers, some had been deserted by their fathers and brought up by their native mothers and their mothers' kinsfolk. Such men had no regard for England or unwillingness to fight against her; as we may judge by the case of Skinner, who—though afterwards Colonel and Companion of the Bath—was at this time little more than a Hindu spearman: he had lived, he used to relate, as a Rajput, and had as profound an ignorance and dislike of his father's country as any Hindu of them all; he sincerely desired, he said, to strike a blow for Sindia and to prove his loyalty to the salt that he had eaten for eight years. The educated English, Scots, or Irish had, no doubt, more intelligence and greater patriotism; and nothing was easier for the Frenchmen than to persuade the General to class them all in a lump as unworthy of trust. Of these latter—the French—we have seen that L. F. Smith taxes them with ingratitude; and it seems certain that Louis Bourquin, commandant of the 1st brigade, did about this time get up a conspiracy against the General at Delhi; and in the course of his proceedings robbed Perron's banker of a large sum of money, reduced the men of the 2nd brigade, and blockaded the Emperor and Colonel Drugeon in the palace. At the same time he wrote to the native officers of the cavalry which were with Perron at Aligarh, and offered them rewards if they would arrest or assassinate the General. On all sides there was enough to tax a stronger mind than that of the ex-ship carpenter.

In the Deccan, meanwhile, some obstacles had retarded the due activity of the troops. The old Nizám had been sinking and his ministers had made his condition an excuse for inertness. But he died on the 8th August, and was succeeded as

"Subáhdár of the Deccan" by his eldest son, Sikandar Jáh. This nobleman made great show of submission, but it soon transpired that his officials—who were presumed to know their master's wishes—were withholding supplies and refusing to open the gates of their fenced cities for the accommodation of British troops wishing to halt on the line of march. All the diplomatic pressure that could be applied by the Wellesleys through their Agent at Haidarabad, was exerted before these difficulties could be removed. General Wellesley then immediately crossed the Nizám's border and laid siege to the famous fortress of Ahmadnagar, which capitulated at once—12th August.

Sindia was in great strength in the neighbourhood; besides the numerous cavalry of the Bhonslá, and his own, he had four brigades of regulars, horse, foot, and artillery, with the best part of Begam Samru's contingent; all under Christian officers. If, in Hindustan, the regular army had been somewhat unduly depleted, yet Perron had three brigades and 8,000 good cavalry, while Du Drenec was marching to his assistance from Ujain. The force with which Lake was marching against him from Cawnpore was not much more than 10,000 strong of all arms, of which only one battalion of foot and three cavalry regiments were Europeans. About 3,500 men were at the same time assembled at Allahabad for operations in Bundelkhand; 5,216 were got ready to invade the Bhonslá's province of Orissa by way of Jagannáth and Katak: and General Wellesley was to open the campaign in the Deccan with nearly 17,000 men, to meet the main strength of the confederate chiefs. A force nearly equal to that of Lake, in the north, was kept in reserve in the Carnatic; altogether the British forces amounted to 55,000 men, but scattered over a vast surface. Lake left Cawnpore, with the bulk of his small force, 7th August, and the Governor-General's final orders reached him on the 16th. If the country were with Perron, and if his white officers were staunch, he had, in troops and places of strength, the means of offering a substantial resistance. Major Smith is of opinion that he desired to do his duty, and Skinner seems to have thought the same as Smith. It was hoped that the Rohillas would rise to neutralise the brigade of observation at Anupshahr, and that Ambáji would get in Lake's rear from Bundelkhand; Holkar was to overrun Bihár and Bengal; the Bhonslá co-operating from Nagpore. The firmness of the army under Sindia in the Deccan might be depended on, for Sindia had provoked the quarrel, and might be said to be almost fighting for his life.

Such, then, was the ostensible outlook and position of the combatants at the beginning of August, 1803. But the European leader on one side was weakened, almost bewildered, with a sense of isolation and betrayal; on the other was the Marquess of Wellesley, faithfully served and obeyed by his brother Arthur, and by General Gerard Lake, officers implicitly trusted by their followers, and never accustomed to regard with excess of anxiety either the numbers or the skill of their opponents; wont to strike hard and to tell the truth to friend and foe.

Perron's hopes, as we have seen, depended upon the promptitude and solidarity with which his forces might be expected to act. Each of the three brigades ostensibly serving under his orders comprised ten regiments, or battalions, of foot, in which the commands were largely held by officers of European blood and training; each had forty field-pieces, with a contingent of Mughal horse, such as won the battle at Pánipat, and averted the worse consequences of defeat at Baksar. There was also a considerable amount of light troops, horse and foot. The fort of Aligarh, near Köel—where Perron resided—was held, with a good garrison, by Colonel Pédron, a member of the General's family and a resolute, well-conducted soldier. The 2nd and 3rd brigades were at Delhi, behind strong walls, and with a fortified palace for citadel. But, unfortunately for

Perron, the officer in command there was his declared enemy, the incapable but unscrupulous Bourquin. To make his position still worse he had now to face the open defection of his British officers.

He did all that was possible for a man of narrow intelligence, in a trying situation. Sending orders to his banker at Delhi to open an unlimited credit for the defence of the place, he despatched a body of cavalry under Captain Fleury, one of his best French officers, to get in rear of Lake's march and harass it to the best of his ability. He then drew out the remainder of his force—consisting chiefly of cavalry—in front of Aligarh, and it was then that he became aware of the disaffection among his subordinates.

For this, indeed, he could not have been altogether unprepared. Two years earlier a scene had taken place at Hansi, which might have opened his eyes to the feelings of those gentlemen. After Thomas had surrendered to Bourquin, the fallen adventurer was dining at their mess, when the Colonel proposed "Success to the undertakings of General Perron:" Thomas passionately refused the toast, and the British officers turned down their empty glasses. And now, on the eve of action, two of them, Captains Stewart and Carnegie, came to Perron (having by that time probably heard of the Governor-General's proclamation of the 20th), and told him that they could not serve against their fellow-countrymen. Perron affected to be taken by surprise, but he indignantly gave orders for their immediate dismissal, including that of seven other officers of British blood who were then in his camp.

This affair occurred on the 28th August. Next day, General Lake appearing with his dragoons, who were accompanied —according to the custom then existing in the Anglo-Indian Army—by six-pounder pieces, called "Galloper Guns"; a sort of precursor of modern horse artillery. The Mughal horse were soon thrown into confusion; and Skinner, who was on the ground—and at that time far from sympathising with the British—seized the occasion to try to get himself exempted from the order of dismissal. Seeing the General pass with some horsemen he ran up, seized the bridle, and renewed the offer of his services. "Ah! no," cried Perron, "it is all over: these fellows have behaved badly: go over to the British." And he rode off, calling as he went; "good-bye, M. Skinner: no trust, no trust."

In this distracted manner disappears from the war the cause of so much anxiety. Perron quitted his camp, retiring in good order to Háthras, a strong place between Aligarh and Agra; leaving instructions with Pédron to defend the fort at Aligarh to the last extremity. But he received at Hátras confirmation of the appointment of Ambáji to take over the command in Hindustan; and he felt that he could now retire with honour from the service of an ungrateful master. Accordingly, on the 6th of September, General Lake received an express from him demanding leave to repair to Lucknow, across the Company's territory, escorted by his *khás risála*, or mounted bodyguard. The permission willingly accorded, Perron went to Lucknow, where he was received with all the respect due to his rank; and, in company with Fleury and an aide-de-camp, proceeded, with the sanction of the British Government, to Chandernagore. Ultimately he returned to France, where he took his place in society, and made good marriages for his two daughters.*

Before Lake was aware of the submission of Perron, he was joined by his infantry, and found before him the task of reducing the fort of Aligarh. But the details of the campaign, together with that of General Wellesley in the South, must be the subject of another section.

[The books recommended for study in connection with this

* One to a Rochefoucauld, the other to a Montesquieu (Bingham's "Letters of Napoleon," II. 130).

section will be found cited, in the text and margin, or at the end of the preceding.]

Section 3.—Our story must still concern itself chiefly with diplomatic and military struggles: for we have come to a new departure, and have to see how the Marquess Wellesley forced the dominions of Akbar into the reluctant hands of "the cheesemongers of Leadenhall Street," as he described his honourable masters. Some perception of the direction that his policy might be expected to take was already revealing itself to keen observers. Thus, in the "Annual Register" for 1803, a bold writer observed that the real object of the Marquess was, evidently "to fix on an extensive and solid basis the *paramount power* and authority of the British Government in the East." This was indeed plain speaking: for the writer could not have been aware of any war then pending in India, unless it was that between Sindia and Jaswant Ráo, in which the British did not seem then to have any particular concern. But, shortly after the Marquess had consented to postpone his resignation, a shuffle of the cards took place, which altered the future aspect of the game. Sindia—egged on, as appeared later, by Holkar, and perhaps also by Perron—entered into close alliance with the Rája of Nagpore or Berár, whose territories extended from the border of Bagtana to the Bay of Bengal, and who, on the strength of his Bhonslá pedigree, had a vague claim to be the head of the Mahrattas.

In vain did the Marquess point out to these chiefs that they had nothing to complain of, both having signified their approval of the Treaty of Basain; in vain did he offer to both a similar defensive, or "subsidiary" alliance. With the sagacity of an experienced pilot he foresaw that their silence and their combination alike portended mischief. He accordingly took his measures, in the spring of the year, and made all possible preparation for the coming tempest.

On the 22nd July, Mr. Mercer was sent to Bundelkhand

to treat with Himat Bahádur, who shared the administration of that province with the Muslim descendant of the late Peshwa, Báji Ráo I.; already mentioned in this narrative. Himat offered his alliance for the promise of a fief in the Duáb; and as he was a good soldier with a body of stout Gosains—the famous fighting friars—at his back, it was held prudent to accept his terms. At the same time the Rána of Gohad was invited to use his influence with the Játs to hem in Sindia's forces on the right bank of the Jumna : the Rájas of Jaipore and Jodhpore being likewise moved to the same purpose. Similar invitations were addressed to the Begam Samru, who held lands, on military tenure, both at Sardhana in the Upper Duáb, and on the opposite side of the Jumna above Delhi. This remarkable woman was of Arab ancestry, and had been bought as a slave by the late Walter Reinhardt—Sombre or "Samru." She embraced the Romish form of Christianity, and she had succeeded to Samru's command and possessions at his death (1782). Accordingly, she is usually regarded as his widow—though she could never have been lawfully wedded, seeing that Samru had a wife who, though out of her mind, survived him many years. But the Begam was a person of sense and spirit; and the people on her estates were peaceful if not exactly prosperous. For all these objects political powers, accompanied by general directions, were given to the Commander-in-Chief, who was also furnished with instructions for the protection and conciliation of the inhabitants of the invaded districts—all of which were duly and successfully carried into effect. The people in those districts were in general oppressed by the local chiefs who had acquired a spurious authority either by purchasing farms of the land-revenue, or by acquiring grants of a superior tenure in return for which they were expected to maintain troops. These lees of the quasi-feudal system of the old Empire long continued to poison the social system; and some details as to the resulting condition of the country will be found in our 12th chapter (Section 3). Perron had been of course supreme; but beyond collecting the revenue he took little share in the administration; and the revenue seems to have been collected at the point of the bayonet, if we may judge from the fact that a whole brigade of regular infantry was kept, for fiscal uses, at Sikandrabad, near Bulandshahr. In addition to the negotiations above mentioned, overtures were held out to the Rája of Patiála, and to the Sikh chiefs of Sirhind.

Not only were these negotiations generally successful, but other states—Udaipore and Kota—sent in their envoys with offers of alliance. The relations with Ambáji, indeed, continued unsatisfactory; and the town and fort of Gwalior—which he had promised to cede—were only obtained by a mixture of force and conciliation employed towards the Governor. The Begam Samru, however, came over, not only politically but personally, having herself carried to the tent of General Lake in a palanquin. At the same time she recalled her battalions that were serving under Sindia in the South. The Sikhs proved entirely friendly; and the young Rája of Lahore—Ranjit Sinh—sent an envoy to offer the Cis-Sutlej districts to the British, and to propose a defensive alliance. Both these results came in sight later on.

Meanwhile, the army marched slowly up through a country far from hostile, their camp being thronged—as Thorn informs us—by every description of male and female visitor.

Sindia now began to show an unmistakable distrust of Perron; and Rája Ambáji, who had moved from Bundelkhand to Gwalior, wavering, had Sindia but known it, was appointed "Subahdár of Hindustan." Ordered to take charge from Perron at the first prospect of war, he marched slowly through the country between Bundelkhand and Agra, so that Perron did not hear of his supersession until the first week in September.

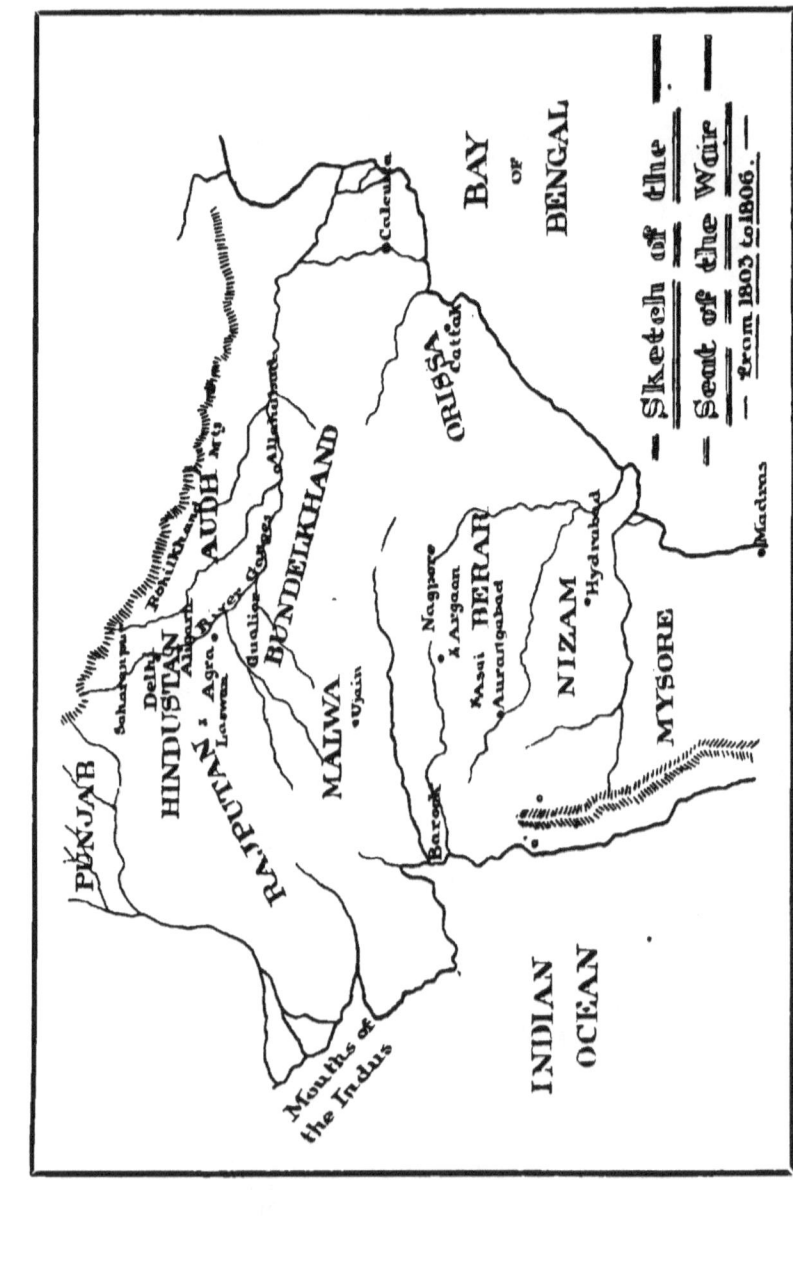

By that time General Lake's patience was exhausted. Becoming convinced that the enemy was only amusing him with negotiations the better to carry on warlike preparations, and finding that Fleury was operating—not without success—in his rear, Lake resolved upon assaulting the Fort of Aligarh before the final measures for its defence could be completed. The place was strong by virtue of situation, surrounded by marshes and a wide and deep moat (*b*), with a narrow causeway (*c*), leading to the 1st gate. At the end of the causeway was a bridge covered by a strong traverse with three guns (B), turning sharp to the left was the main gate (A), opening on a road round the base of a strong barbican (D), surrounded with its own ditch and manned by sharp-shooters; a door (E) at the end of this road opened on another bridge over the great moat, at the end of which was yet another door (F). Again moving sharp to the left, the road led under the rampart of the Inner Fort (A) to an interior gate (G), which opened into the heart of the works (*a*).

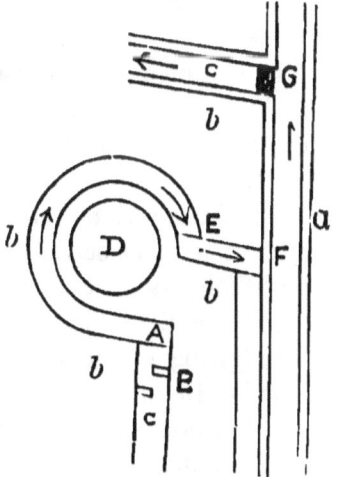

Such was the place that Lake —with a full knowledge that the commandant had received orders to hold it to the last, and suspecting that the approaches were being mined—had resolved to capture. The storming-party consisted of four companies of the 76th foot, six battalions of sepoys, and a detail of artillery with two twelve-pound guns. The party was to be guided by one of the discharged European officers, named Lucan, who was well-acquainted with the peculiar character of the approaches. Setting out two hours after midnight under command of Colonel Monson, they took the traversed bridge, and blew open the main gate with the fire of a twelve pounder; five officers being killed and Colonel Monson, the leader, wounded during the operation. The stormers then advanced to the second and third gates, which were easily forced; but when they reached the last gate it was found too strong to be opened by any amount of firing. As the troops were all this time exposed to the marksmen in the barbican, great loss continued to be endured until Major McLeod of the 76th, succeeding in opening a small door in the side of the gate, admitted his men. The resistance soon ceased; and the want of the usual sally-port told against the garrison, of which a considerable portion fell in trying to escape. Colonel Pédron was made prisoner, with about 2,000 of his men. This brilliant feat of arms cost the British 260 killed and wounded, the gallant 76th alone losing seventy-three officers and men.

The rest of Lake's campaign was fought in the same fearless old fashion; there was a resistance of mercenaries, true to their salt, but deprived—very much by their own suspicions—of the light and leading of their European instructors; against them was hurled a body of troops, smaller and no braver than themselves, but to which a few hundreds of British soldiers gave the requisite determination, the whole being led by the daring British gentlemen of that time. But, before giving consideration to a few essential details of the events in Hindustan, let us turn to other quarters.

In addition to the blows aimed at the confederates in Central India, it was deemed of the first necessity to take armed possession of Bundelkhand, which had been ceded by the treaty of Basain. And this country—if not held by the British or their allies—would leave a door open from northern Berár into the lower Duáb. Himat Bahadur, as has been shown, was willing to submit, for a consideration; and he did, in fact, join the British column, which left Allahabad for that service.

under Colonel Powell. This officer was soon after joined by Colonel Shepherd, of the Mahratta service, followed by a brigade 10,000 strong and a small complement of Mughal horse and native artillery. But the proceedings were opposed by the Nawáb of Banda, Shamsher Bahadur, the Muslim offshoot of Báji Ráo I. already mentioned. An obstinate battle was fought—though without much loss on either side—and the usual attempt at negotiation ensued; but the peaceable tendencies of the Nawáb were greatly forwarded by the capitulation of Kalpi, after a short cannonade—4th December, 1803. On the 18th January, 1804, the Nawáb finally came into the British camp; and his possessions—as then guaranteed—remained in his family till 1858. Another place, to be painfully notorious during the troubles of the Mutiny, was now reduced to submission; the local ruler of Jhánsi acknowledging British sovereignty.

On the same day as that on which Lake encountered Perron under the walls of Aligarh—August 29th—Arthur Wellesley arrived at Aurangabad, having with him one regiment of dragoons and three of native cavalry, 1,731 sabres in all; two battalions of British foot and six of sepoys, a total of 7,000 bayonets; two "companies," batteries, of European artillery, and some native sappers and gun lascars; together with a brigade of Mysore horse, making about 12,500 men in all, besides a small contingent of light cavalry contributed by the Peshwa. A few days before, the confederate chiefs had slipped past the other British force—Colonel Stevenson's—and crossed the Ajanta Pass into the Berar territory: they were apparently in difficulties about supplies. The object of the British was above all to bring them to action; but it was also deemed necessary to keep them either from advancing on Poona, or from ravaging the country of the Nizám. As they were now being driven to subsist in a country friendly to them, they also began to desire an engagement; and Sindia, probably pushed on by his European officers, judged the moment propitious for attacking General Wellesley before he was able to effect a junction with Colonel Stevenson's column. On the 23rd September the General heard that Sindia's camp was only six miles away, and he accordingly determined to take the initiative and fall upon the enemy without waiting for the attack, or for the arrival of his colleague. Leaving his camp under a strong guard he at once advanced; and on ascending a hill beheld the camp of the enemy on the plain beneath, near the junction of two small streams, of which the southern—called the Kaitna - ran between them and himself, while their rear rested on the bank of the northern affluent—the Jua—and was sheltered by the fortified village of Asai. It was now an hour past mid-day, and the army had marched twenty miles. But Wellesley moved his battalions to the right, covered by all his cavalry. His effective force consisted of about 5,000 men of all arms, the enemy's infantry alone being about double that strength, with the brigades of Pohlmann and Dupont, 8,400 good infantry, and 2,000 men of the Samru contingent, who, however, remained in camp to guard the baggage; the guns were nearly sixty, and the cavalry was very numerous.* Having found a ford where the guns could pass, the General crossed the Kaitna and wheeled to his right. The enemy were driven back till they reformed parallel with the Jua; and the 74th Foot, getting between their left and the village, were nearly annihilated by artillery and charges of horse before the cavalry could come up and save the residue. The enemy's horse—with this exception—kept at a distance; and the infantry was at last put to flight and driven over the northern stream. But the British had suffered severely. One-third of the little army was either killed

* The Begam Samru's infantry was under the command of Colonel Saleur, a respectable French officer; the reason of their being left in the rear was, probably, that the Begam was known to be in negotiation with Lake in the North.

or wounded; the 74th alone lost eleven officers killed and six wounded, with 400 non-commissioned officers and privates. The General's orderly-trooper was killed at his side, and his own horse was shot under him; so that—seeing what great events were to turn upon his after-life—his escape may be called "providential"; the rather that, of the ten officers of his personal staff, only two escaped. The enemy left 1,200 bodies on the field; and lost besides their guns, camp, stores, and ammunition, and seven standards.

Next evening the General was joined by Colonel Stevenson; and he remained in the neighbourhood of the pass to guard the Nizám's country, while the other column moved into Berár.*

On both the western and eastern coasts of their country the confederates were equally overcome. On the 29th August Colonel Woodington gallantly stormed Baroch, at the mouth of the Narbada river, and proceeded to occupy Champanir, a district belonging to Sindia, on the frontier of Gujarát. In the following month an expedition under Colonel Harcourt, military secretary to the Governor-General, occupied Cuttack (Katak), the central district of the province of Orissa, and advanced to support the armies of the centre.

While the confederates were reeling under these blows and making abortive and insincere attempts to negotiate with General Wellesley, the war proceeded, both in the northern Deccan and in Hindustan. After securing the fort of Aligarh, Lake marched towards Delhi; and on the morning of 11th September received news that Bourquin had left the town in great

---

* A spirited account of the battle, with an excellent sketch-plan, will be found in Colebrooke's "Life of Mountstuart Elphinstone," vol i., p 63. The future Governor of Bombay and historian was then a young Civil officer, attached to General Wellesley's staff. He was by his side during the battle, and the General complimented him by saying "he ought to have been a soldier.'

strength and was marching down towards him. Bourquin, it may be remembered, was the officer who, having with some difficulty overcome the brave but unlucky George Thomas, had engaged in conspiracy against Perron, his own superior. He was now to meet still more formidable antagonists. On arriving at his next halt—six miles from Delhi—Lake found Bourquin at the head of sixteen battalions of regular infantry, with 6,000 cavalry and a strong artillery, in all 19,000 good troops. They opened a searching fire upon the British cavalry, which had to stand exposed for a whole hour awaiting the arrival of the infantry. At length Lake—after his own charger had been killed—executed a retrograde movement, which the enemy mistook for a retreat, and hurried out of their batteries with vociferous cries of triumph. By this time the British infantry had joined their mounted comrades, and the whole line presently advanced, led by the Commander-in-Chief in person. Charging the enemy with fixed bayonets, the infantry line drove them from the guns. The line then broke quickly into columns of companies, through which the British horsemen poured with their galloper guns, scattering the enemy in all directions. They are said to have lost 3,000 men, and the victors obtained possession of sixty-eight guns, with a quantity of ammunition and some treasure. By special invitation of the Emperor Lake entered Delhi on the 14th, when Bourquin and four of his European officers surrendered as prisoners of war. On the following day Lake proceeded to the palace, conducted by Mirza Akbar, the son of the fallen Emperor, and found the representative of all that splendid line, blind and necessitous, awaiting him in faded pomp. But the gladness of the long lines of crowded spectators through which the elephants pursued their slow and stately progress, testified to the emotions aroused at the deliverance of the citizens from Mahratta domineering and the insolence of low-bred Europeans.

These events—as the Governor-General affirmed—secured to the British the possession of the Duáb, and paralysed the French influence; while the people of the country, noting the valour, humanity, and justice of the officers and men, unhesitatingly accepted the change of masters. The Emperor's name would still, the Marquess hoped and believed, possess its old prestige; and his first care would be to provide a suitable establishment for the aged sovereign, so happily restored to his ancestral position. No treaty was to be made, but "a connection would be established, on permanent principles, between the Royal House of Timur and the British power in India."* The Commander-in-Chief was created *Khán Daurán*, which—as he was informed—was the second title in the Empire, the first being reserved for Sindia. The Emperor ultimately received a monthly allowance of 90,000 Rs. besides the revenues of the city and the district of Delhi, the same being administered by a British Resident.

Some more work, however, remained for the army in Hindustan; whilst in the Deccan, also, the confederates sought for a little longer to stave off the inevitable. Let us turn first to the latter struggle, as it came to an earlier and more important end.

When Colonel Stevenson left Arthur Wellesley near Ajunta, he proceeded eastward in pursuit of the confederates; but Sindia had lost all desire for fighting, and the war was maintained by the Bhonslá alone. On the 16th October, Burhánpur —an old Mughal capital, with walls—capitulated, as did, five days later, the almost impregnable hill-fort of Asir, close by. On 28th November—being joined by the General—Stevenson had the satisfaction of bringing his men into contact with the

---

* v. "Notes relative to the late transactions in the Mahratta Empire," by the Governor-General, Fort William, Dec., 15, 1803. See also "The Governor-General in Council to the Secret Committee," June 2, 1805.—["Wellesley Despatches," iv., p. 553.]

enemy, consisting chiefly of the army of Berár, under command of Venkáji Bhonslá, the Rája's brother, who, in ignorance of Wellesley's arrival, desired to prevent Stevenson from besieging Gáwilgarh. His cavalry charged with great bravery, particularly a body of fair-complexioned Muslims from the north; some of the sepoy battalions were driven back, but the cavalry restored the fight; near 400 of the Persian horse were found dead where they had charged; as night fell the broken forces fled, being pursued with loss by the British cavalry by the light of the moon. This action takes its name from the village of Argaon, between Akola and Elichpore, and was followed by a half-hearted submission on the part of Daulat Ráo Sindia, who was by this time beginning to foresee the total breakdown of his defence in Hindustan. On the 15th December Stevenson took Gáwilgarh; and the Bhonslá made haste to follow the example of his confederate and sue for peace, but with more earnestness.

In the instructions received from his brother, at the beginning of the troubles, General Wellesley had been ordered to push on war with all possible vigour, if war should appear needful; but he was also empowered to open negotiations for peace whenever the confederates, or either of them, should withdraw from active resistance, or give other convincing proof of a sincere desire of accommodation with the British Government and its allies. Accordingly, ever since the end of November, the General had been in oral communication with an envoy rom the Bhonslá, in which he met all subterfuges, evasions, and pretensions, with skill and firmness, yet without deviating from the courtesy due to a defeated enemy. On the 16th— the day after the fall of Gáwilgarh—the envoy made his final appearance, empowered by his employer to concede all the General's terms, and the treaty was signed on both sides next day at Dewálgaon, in the Ajunta hills. By this instrument the Rája was to give up the vague claims that he professed to derive from his Bhonslá pedigree, by virtue of which he pretended to a hereditary superiority to all Mahrattas; he was to recognise the Company's possessions in Orissa, and those of the Nizám in North Berár; he was to abstain from demanding *chaut*—the Mahratta blackmail—from all and sundry; in return for all which concessions the British would leave him in possession of Nagpore, and restore whatever forts and dependent districts had been taken from him during the war. During all the preliminary negotiations the General was assisted in interpretation and copying by Mountstuart Elphinstone and John Malcolm. The three young officers acquitted themselves well, and acted with the entire approval of the Governor-General throughout, particularly in "separating the interests of Sindia, Berár, and Holkar."*

Nevertheless, with Holkar there was, for the present, no war, and consequently no necessity for negotiation. With Sindia it was different, that chief had been more or less delusively treating ever since 10th November, and trying in his indirect way to discover the intentions of the British General without compromising himself. When, however, the General refused to treat with any one who did not produce credentials, proper powers were exhibited by Sindia's agents on 21st November. But nothing conclusive was done so long as Sindia arrogated to himself the power of negotiating for the Bhonslá. On the 8th December Sindia's envoys had a long discussion with the General in his tent, which was terminated by a plain intimation that Sindia could not be allowed to treat for the Bhonslá—unless, indeed, duly empowered by that chief to do so. After the Bhonslá had made his separate treaty, however, that pretence could no longer be maintained; accordingly, on the 23rd December—just a week after the conclusion of the treaty of Dewálgaon—

---

* v. Despatch of 11th December, 1803, par. 7. At the close of the war Elphinstone was sent to Nagpore and Malcolm to Sindia, as Agents to the Governor-General.

Sindia's chief minister, the famous Wital Panth, came to the General's camp, and the negotiations took an earnest and practical turn. The proceedings are worth attentive study. The "Talleyrand of India"—as Wital was called by the British officers—showed the most consummate diplomatic skill, while the future national hero of Britain displayed all the upright tenacity which was to distinguish the whole of his illustrious career. Article by article the preliminaries of the treaty were discussed, and all reasonable pleas of the envoy fully considered, and if possible conceded; due exception being made of any agreements which might be entered into by the Commander-in-Chief or the Governor-General. On the 30th December the treaty was concluded at the camp of Anjangaon, near Elichpore.

That treaty having been abrogated by the misconduct of Sindia not long after, it is not necessary to enter into its details. Every disposition was shown to preserve and protect the rights of Sindia as a feudatory and landholder; but he was required to resign all pretensions to power in Hindustan, and to promise never again to employ in his service subjects of any European State at war with Great Britain. This last clause he adopted with alacrity, volunteering the statement that he "had not the smallest desire ever to see the face of a Frenchman again"; and this part of his engagements he, for the rest of his otherwise faithless career, faithfully fulfilled.

The events which precipitated this sudden surrender on the part of Sindia now require brief notice. It will perhaps be remembered that besides the fortified palace of Shahjahan at Delhi there had been an older castle, built by the great Akbar, at Agra, about 140 miles lower down the river Jumna. After ceasing to be a royal residence it had undergone a number of vicissitudes: held by the Játs, then by Mirza Najaf, defended by Lakwa Dáda, and at last held for Sindia as vice-gerent of the empire. It was now garrisoned by some new levies and by 3 battalions of the 5th brigade, commanded by Colonel Sutherland; the governor of the fort being Colonel Hessing, whom we saw defeated and driven to headlong flight by Jaswant Ráo Holkar, at Ujáin.

Having made over charge of the city and palace of Delhi to Lieut. Colonel D. Ochterlony, General Lake marched for Agra on the 24th September. A detachment of four cavalry regiments, and three and a half battalions of sepoys had been posted at Muttra, on the right bank of the river, under command of Colonel Vandeleur of the 8th dragoons. Here came the Chevalier Du Drenec, accompanied by Major Smith and another officer, to surrender to Vandeleur. On 2nd October the detachment joined the main body and followed the Commander-in-chief to besiege the town and fort of Agra, where they arrived on the afternoon of the 4th. A summons to surrender met with no reply; and it became known that the luckless sepoys of the enemy, not knowing who was to be trusted, had imprisoned Hessing and Sutherland and were preparing a brave but unskilful defence. A force of seven battalions, with twenty-six guns, was collected outside the fort; being either men of the brigade lately brought up from the Deccan by Du Drenec, or the men of the 2nd and 3rd escaped from Delhi: or perhaps both. The walled town was taken, after a severe action, on the 10th; and a week later the garrison liberated their European officers and, by their mediation, obtained a capitulation. Stores, guns, and twenty-four *lakhs* of treasure rewarded the captors.

But even now all was not over. Rája Ambáji, whose name has so often occurred in these pages—had, as we have seen, been negotiating with Lord Wellesley on his own account: so much so that in the month of October it was believed that he proposed "to shake off his fidelity to Sindia and put himself under the protection of the British government—upon certain conditions.* But the conditions were not fulfilled; and Ambáji

* "Intercepted despatches," par. 526.

slowly continued his way to take the command vacated by Perron. By the end of the month he had reached a place called Náswári —the Laswaree of the despatches—about midway between Alwar and Agra. His force consisted of seventeen battalions of regulars, seventy-one guns of good pattern and finish, and nearly 5,000 cavalry. The infantry was made up of the battalions of du Drenec and the remains of the Delhi garrison.*
Hearing of the approach of his force, Lake marched against it; and pushing on at the head of the cavalry, as his custom was, came in sight of the enemy encampedon a plain, at the foot of the Mewát hills and protected on the northern side by a stream, about sunrise of the 1st November. Two thoughts instantly presented themselves to his mind; the enemy's guns must be taken, and his retreat to the hills must be cut off. The troops with Lake amounted to less than three thousand horsemen, of whom seven hundred or eight hundred were Europeans; the force of the enemy we have seen. But the Commander-in-Chief was of the good old school of Clive and Coote, who thought that nothing was so promising against Asiatics as a straightforward thrust. The stream was the chord of an arc formed by the hills to the north; and Lake lost no time in dashing through it at the head of his cavalry, and flinging himself upon the hostile line extending from Naswari, on the bank, to Mahlpore about the centre of the plain. Three times did Lake and his burly dragoons ride through the high grass, charge through the enemy's guns and break the line of infantry. Colonel Vandeleur, of the 8th, was killed; the horses and men were wearied, the guns could not be brought away. The enemy's right now fell back so as to form in front of Mahlpore, with their line nearly striking the stream at a right angle. A cessation of action then ensued, during which the British infantry came up and were halted for breakfast. During this interval the ever-unstable Ambáji endeavoured to make terms,

* General Lake to Governor-General. d. 2nd November.

but nothing came of it; and the action was resumed about noon. Never had the forces of a native State fought so well, never did British troops behave with a more steady valour. The horse of the Commander-in-chief was shot under him, his son was severely wounded while furnishing his father with a fresh charger; another officer commanding a dragoon regiment was killed; General Ware's head was taken off by a round-shot. Amid the carnage and tumult Lake preserved his coolness, and watched all parts of the field. His left horse and foot marching up the river, turned upon the enemy's right; two cavalry brigades cut in between their left and the hills; Ambáji dismounting from his elephant fled from the field on a swift horse. Still the men fought on, and it was not until the last gun had been captured, and seven thousand bodies stretched upon the ground that their cavalry—after sustaining repeated charges from their dragoons—drew off, leaving about two thousand infantry prisoners in the hands of the conquerors. The British loss included thirteen officers and one hundred and sixty soldiers and non-commissioned killed; the wounded exceeded six hundred and fifty.

An eminent modern historian* considers this brilliant action to have been the turning point of the war. It is, nevertheless, to be borne in mind that Argaon was not fought for nearly four weeks after Laswáree, while another month elapsed before the preliminaries of peace were fixed. However influential therefore the battle may have been in aiding the dispositions of Sindia, the battle of Laswáree can hardly be considered decisive; especially when we observe that the so-called "treaty" of Anjangaon was in effect only a temporary truce, and was not perhaps intended by Sindia to be anything else.

While the wounds of his State were still raw, indeed, and before its ruin had been repaired, Sindia was fairly quiet; and even brought to light some communications from Jaswant Ráo,

* Colonel G. B. Malleson, "Decisive Battles," ed. 1883, pp. 292-3.

in which that unscrupulous adventurer attempted to make him a catspaw in a new campaign.

The additional twelvemonth for which Lord Wellesley had consented to serve had now gone by, and a glorious period it had been. But he still continued in office; and the rest of his incumbency was destined to be chequered by a certain amount of varied fortune, disasters occurring which were caused by the restless spirit of Jaswant Ráo Holkar, and against which probably no precautions on the part of the British government could have altogether availed. The Mahratta chief was a man of variable mood—indeed he eventually died insane—but he was an excellent partizan leader, and was animated by a hatred of the foreign pioneers of order equal to that formerly displayed by Haidar Ali of Mysore. But, inasmuch as these episodes were but of short duration and had but little effect on the fortunes of the country, we must be content with giving them a somewhat cursory notice.

It was towards the end of the year, and after the conclusion of the treaty of Anjangaon, that Jaswant Ráo moved up from Málwa, and approached the territories of the Rajputs. He had lately murdered three of his European officers, and was discovered to be sending letters to various chiefs in Hindustan, instigating them to rise against the British Government. There was no lack of friendly representation on the part of Lake, but there was an obstacle to anything like a good understanding in that Lord Wellesley found it his duty to lay down a principle in the conduct of negotiations that Jaswant could not admit. He was told that he could not be treated as the head of the Indore State without detriment to the rights of his legitimate brother, Káshi Ráo: and if this decision did not exactly imply that the British Government would take part with Káshi, yet it involved a determination not to recognise any claim to *chaut* or tribute from allied States on the part of Jaswant; and that determination had to be made known. This was done on the

29th January, 1804, when Jaswant was called on to take away his troops and cease from demanding tribute in Hindustan. A year of trouble followed the refusal of this demand. Jaswant professed to think that the success of the British in the late war had been only due to their artillery; and that, when it came to a question of personal prowess, the Mahratta lance and the Mughal sword would certainly prevail. In March he sent in extravagant proposals, which he strove to enforce by equally extravagant threats. His movements as leader of a large cavalry force were also stimulated by the state of his own country and the neighbouring districts to the south, where a three-years drought had deepened into famine. In April, under these various motives, Jaswant took possession of Ajmere and threatened the lands of the Jaipore Rája. Lake, under sanction of the Governor-General, gladly took up the challenge of the freebooter and gave him the opportunity to make good his vaunts. Poetry and romance have thrown a certain aureole about the "Pindári"; but in reality Jaswant and his ally, Amir Khán, were but ordinary marauders without even the vulgar virtues of their calling, as was soon demonstrated by Lake. If they brought up guns their guns, were taken; if they attacked a distinct officer, he defended himself successfully with a handful of jail guards and messengers.* The armour-plated horsemen were overthrown or put to flight; the light cavalry could not always outmarch the British dragoons; the chiefs only saved themselves by the most headlong galloping. Holkar was overtaken at Farukhabad, his camp completely surprised, and himself glad to escape without striking a blow; Amir Khán, on another occasion, left behind him his palanquin and a complete suit of armour. The result was that the marauders were kept in such perpetual motion and such constant alarm that they never had time to plunder, barely to collect supplies for themselves and forage for their horses.

* Moradabad, Fatehgarh, Mainpuri were so defended.

In Central India alone they seemed for a moment to have some chance. Colonel the Hon. W. Monson was detached for the protection of Rajputan, in an unpropitious season, and with an insufficient force. Entangled in a wild and wasted region, deserted by most of his allies, and all his native horse, he struggled on for three months, and at last brought the miserable remnant of his column to Lake, at Agra, 31st September.

About six weeks later Holkar was emboldened by this success to besiege Delhi. Colonel Ochterlony at once sent to Colonel Burn, commanding at Saharanpore, who hastened to his assistance with a battalion of sepoys and some irregular infantry. For ten days the British officers, devotedly served by their native infantry and their few gunners, defended the wide range of rotten ramparts against an army of twenty thousand men, till relieved on the 15th October by the timely arrival of the Commander-in-Chief. On being chased out of the Duáb, Jaswant sought refuge in the Ját principality of Bhurtpore, where his army was defeated, with the loss of seventy-eight guns, on the 13th November, at Dig; on which occasion Monson, who took command on General Fraser being disabled by a wound,* had the satisfaction of recovering some of the guns and wagons which he had lost in the summer.

Lake (created a viscount for his services), lost no time in coming up with reinforcements. On arrival he took command of the forces, and assaulted the fort of Dig, which—though belonging to the Rája of Bhurtpore, a professed ally—had fired on the British troops during the battle. The place was taken by storm; this success emboldened Lake to besiege Bhurtpore itself; and he dispersed the followers of Holkar and Amir Khán, who endeavoured to drive him off, but the siege itself

---

* Of this he subsequently died, and was buried at Muttra, where his monument was to be seen a few years ago.

never prospered. The fortifications were strong, the ditch was wide and deep. Four resolute assaults were driven back, the stormers hopeless and reeling with slaughter. Lake found that the place was not to be rushed like Aligarh and Dig, but his spirit did not fail; and, sending for his battering train, he was preparing for a formal siege, when the Rája, weary and anxious, hastily, sent in proposals of peace. The proceedings of Jaswant Ráo still called for attention, and the Home Government was known to be desirous of a pause in the forward movement. The Rája was accordingly admitted to terms, and the army broke up from Bhurtpore on 21st April 1805.

The failure of this siege, coming after Monson's retreat, showed that British generals were not infallible; and the discovery encouraged Sindia to raise his head. Generals Lake and Wellesley, as it turned out, had offered him different terms about Gwalior; and, when the chief claimed the benefit of the more favourable, the Governor-General--in spite of energetic protests from his brother and Malcolm, the Resident—treated Sindia with oppressive severity, and deprived him of both Gwalior and Gohad.* Sirji Ráo, Sindia's evil genius (of whom mention has been made more than once above) urged his master and son-in-law to resistance; by his advice the camp of the Resident was plundered, and an advance made on the Chambal with a large force under the command of the veteran Ambáji; while the British Resident was placed in a kind of honourable arrest. Lake, however, strongly remonstrated; Holkar and other possible allies held aloof; and, finally, Sindia made his submission. Amid these cares and anxieties, and with his unfinished policy hanging—so to speak—in fragments, Lord Wellesley was suddenly relieved of his duties by the appearance of Lord Cornwallis, who had

* The latter is now the small Ját principality known as the Ránaship of Dholpore.

undertaken the office of Governor-General a second time, at the earnest desire of the Court of Directors, and who landed in Calcutta on the 29th July.*

It is, of course, quite easy to blame the whole "forward policy," and to criticise every measure by whose aid it was carried out. Equally simple, on the other side, is the roseate picture of national strength and glory that English historians have often been content to draw. Both extremes will be avoided if we will only let Lord Wellesley speak for himself, and see what it was that he undertook to do, and what—after it was done—he believed himself to have accomplished. The nature of the task which the Marquess conceived to be before him towards the end of 1802 is well put by the memorandum —already cited—that opens the volume of Mr. Owen's "Selections from the Wellington Despatches." His conception of what, afterwards, had been done appears in his Appendix A ("Notes," Part III.), and his despatch in council, dated June 2nd, 1805. It will be fair to infer from these documents that the conquest of India was not the object of Wellesley's wars. He speaks of "Our alacrity to resist aggression and to punish all the Principals and Accomplices of unjust attacks . . . on a Government uniting moderation with energy . . . and equally determined to respect the just rights of other States, and to maintain its own." There is more to the same purport, making it evident that, while seeking out influence by way of treaties, often imposed at the bayonet's point, the Government of Calcutta did not conceive itself to be conquering the people of India, who, indeed, did not, as a rule, make any resistance. Therefore, their laws, creeds, and customs were to remain in force; and no new taxation appears to have been contemplated. "The throne of Delhi" was to be protected; but the British were placed under no obligation to consider the

* The dissatisfaction of the Company was shared by Castlereagh and Pitt.

political rights or claims of the Emperor, or any "question connected with the future exercise of the imperial prerogative and authority."

[Consult "Notes Relative to the Late Transactions," Dec. 15, 1803; also Parts II. III. of the same, Fort William, 1804. Thorn's "War in India," London, 1818, is a straightforward narrative, with good plans of battles, in most of which the author took part as a cavalry officer. It only remains to be added that the important political narrative cited as the "Intercepted Despatch," is a paper of unequalled value. Captured by the French at sea, it was published, in a French translation, in the *Moniteur* of June 5, 1805. A re-translation into English appeared in London (Stockdale, 1805).]

CHAPTER XI.

THE EVE OF EMPIRE.

Section 1 : Non-intervention, in two shapes — Section 2 : Internal administration under Lord Minto — Section 3: Revenue, Justice, Public Debt.

SECTION 1.—In later days it has become so customary to regard India as a mere dependency of the British Empire that it may seem strange to think that, at the opening of the nineteenth century the country was still a fortuitous aggregate of disconnected Asiatic powers which most Englishmen who thought of the matter at all were inclined to respect and maintain. Not only was conquest deprecated by Pitt, Dundas, Castlereagh, and Canning; but even Wellesley's able brother, who did so much for his ambitious schemes, shrank from the the idea of rapid advance: while Munro—perhaps the ablest of Anglo-Indian statesmen—recorded a strong protest against the "subsidiary system." One of his expressed objections was "its inevitable tendency to bring every native State . . . . under the exclusive dominion of the British Government." It was by this school considered questionable whether such a change was to be desired, either in the interests of the natives or of the people of Great Britain. "One effect of such a conquest," so Munro urged with prophetic judgment, "would be that the Indian army . . . would gradually lose its military habits and discipline . . . to feel its own strength and. . . to turn it against its European masters."* Another objection to Wellesley's system, abundantly illustrated by later events, was its tendency to support and protect evil and negligent native rulers who would otherwise have been kept within some bounds by dread of popular indignation. A prince of that sort was able to combine the practice of all but the very extreme of Asiatic oppression and misrule with the immunity of a European guarantee. This was painfully exemplified in the ultimate course of affairs in Audh ; where the complaints of the people were as much neglected as the remonstrances of the protecting British, until annexation appeared the only remedy. But annexation was an almost equal evil; because—as Elphinstone and Munro were never weary of pointing out—wherever direct British administration was introduced, the higher posts were always given to Europeans, and the freedom from domestic oppression was "purchased by the sacrifice of independence, of national character, and of whatever renders a people respectable." (Munro). In this choice of evils it was natural that Cornwallis, and those at whose earnest request he resumed the office of Governor-General, should have endeavoured to check the rapid progress of the Wellesley system. Within little more than five years the capital of the Muslim dynasty of Mysore had been stormed and the Sultan killed : the whole of the Carnatic and the southern region generally were in the hands of the British or their feudatories. The Nizám's army had been dissolved and himself reduced to the portion of a more or less obedient vassal. The Peshwa had been subdued if not tamed : the Bombay Presidency had been founded : the British were directly administering Hindustan by European Commissioners and District-Officers. But nothing had been done to give the people an

* Elphinstone, at the time of the mutiny, drew the attention of a correspondent to this minute as something marvellous (v. Arbuthnot's " Sir T. Munro," 115-31. Madras, 1886,)

amount of welfare at all proportioned to the extension of the power of their new masters. The inhabitants of the newly-acquired territories found that they had changed the creed and colour of their administrators but not the comfort of their lives; while those of the older provinces did not perceive any corresponding advantages from the extension of the sphere of rule. Nothing was done for education or for the employment of natives: taxation was as heavy as before and much more rigorously enforced. The increase of the military establishments produced a strain on the finances which time, indeed, might ultimately relieve but which was, for the present, all but intolerable.

Meanwhile Holkar was unconquered, and Sindia only half conciliated. The first question was how to set up a mode of living, with regard to those chiefs, which should allow the British territories a moment of repose. Now, this was a severe test of the scheme of moderation which, in modern language, would be perhaps termed "masterly inactivity." For Holkar and Sindia by no means represented indolent old fashioned States, only anxious to be left in unaspiring apathy: on the contrary they were the chiefs of a bustling and predatory community who could not be brought within a scheme of peace without the most severe repression. It was therefore most unfortunate that the well-intentioned counsels of Cornwallis and his employers should have been exposed to such an ordeal on their earliest application. Methods that might have succeeded with Audh, or with Udaipore, were sure to prove worse than useless with predetermined freebooters. Cornwallis did not spare himself; old and infirm as he was, he set out for the Upper Provinces, announcing to the Home-Government his intention to terminate the present troubles by firm but conciliatory negotiation. And to this end he sent orders to Lord Lake to desist not only from aggressive acts but even from all military operations. The detailed plan of the Governor-

General, so far as can be ascertained from the scanty materials on record in this part of his papers, was to discontinue the extension of the subsidiary system and to return to what Warren Hastings had intended when framing the treaty of Salbai in 1782: he was ready to make alliances with Holkar and Sindia on a footing of equality; to confirm the territories they still held and even to cede them some more; and to refrain from defensive treaties with powers inside of their spheres of influence. He expressed his desire to inspire native rulers with confidence, so that (each in his appointed circle), all might pursue the welfare of their subjects, leaving the British Government to do the same.

This benevolent policy would have taxed the mind of the experienced veteran by whom it was conceived. In conception it was attractive: nevertheless, at least as applied to Jaswant Holkar and Daulat Sindia, it seemed to have the one incurable fault of being impossible. How far such a man as Cornwallis a seasoned soldier and statesman, accustomed to affairs on the grand scale and strong in the sympathy and support of the heads of the Government in London, might have rectified this we cannot say. He might (as Lord Moira did afterwards) have, by-and-by, seen the error of applying a system of order to these lords of misrule; and, in so doing, might have persuaded his employers at home to give him a free hand for their repression. But unhappily, Cornwallis did not live to learn: for he sank under the cares and fatigues of his position, dying at Ghazipore, on his way up country; 5th October, 1805. His successor was a distinguished civil officer whom the Court of Directors had long desired to advance, Sir George Barlow. Under Wellesley he had been known as an assiduous advocate and instrument of the forward policy; being an official of the kind called "zealous" and "loyal"; one to whom zeal meant unquestioning obedience of orders, and whose loyalty was of the strictly personal sort. Under a convert of this class the new system was in no danger of neglect. Dangerous concessions misled foes and friends alike: to the one they involved dereliction, to the other they assumed the character of timidity and licence for plunder and outrage. The veteran Commander-in-Chief denounced the course in vain, and at last indignantly threw up his policital powers. Two years followed, years of inactivity that was anything but masterly. Lake's indignation is not wonderful when it is borne in mind that the policy indicated to him included "the divesting ourselves of all rights to the exercise of interference with the doings of every State beyond the Jumna." The veteran knew, and repeatedly pointed out, that the Jumna was no military frontier; being in its northern course, a fordable stream--the reader will remember that Ahmad Sháh, the Abdáli, crossed it with horse, foot, and artillery in October, 1760;—and he also knew at what cost the treaties had been won which gave the rights that it was now proposed to surrender. Whatever might be the faults of the subsidiary system, it was neither prudent nor honourable to leave the Rajputs to be plundered by such men as Jaswant and Amir Khán; and engagements to abstain from all action in the regions held by such leaders was only to invite their ravages and those of all the disbanded soldiers and mounted gang-robbers that they might see fit to harbour.

Something, however, the Commander-in-Chief effected; Sindia, having shaken off his infamous father-in-law, Sherji Ráo, was persuaded to release the British Resident, Mr. Jenkins, and to enter into a preliminary negotiation. The pay of the army was in arrears, the finances of Calcutta having been left in such a state by Wellesley that the most pressing needs of the Government were only met by extraordinary expedients. Nevertheless, backed by the energy and skill of Malcolm, Lake was able to take the field and pursue Holkar, who had marched into the Punjab. In the last month of the year a treaty supplementing that of Anjangaon was concluded with Sindia's agent, who had accompanied the army. This engagement was signed at Amritsir, on the 5th December, and provided that the Chambal river should, generally, form the boundary between the Company's territory and those of Sindia; the Rajput States being left under the protection of that Chief. Sindia engaged to dismiss Sherji Ráo for ever from his councils, and was, as a matter of friendly consideration, allowed to hold the town and territory of Gwalior. Sindia was also to keep Gohad as far as the Chambal, on the northern bank of which the small principality of Dholpore was made over to the Ját chieftain from whom Gohad was taken. At the same time Ranjit Sinh, the Rája of Lahore, was induced to promise to give no support to Jaswant Ráo Holkar, whose camp was not far off; and the freebooter, thus isolated, was obliged to accept the terms offered him by Lake and Malcolm. Jaswant Holkar, as is most likely, had no intention of being bound by these terms; in any case they showed him how far he would be able to do mischief with impunity.

Lake's idea seems to have been to allot to the State, at that moment represented by Jaswant, a sphere resembling that already assigned to Sindia: the latter had to respect Hindustan north of the lower Chambal, say from Kota to Dholpore; the northern boundary of the former was to be the chain called "Bundi Hills," traversing the Duáb between the Banás and Upper Chambal. This ill-chosen frontier, however, might not have left Jaswant free to work his will on the Rajput land from Udaipore to Jaipore; and the Rajput Princes of that land were allies to whose protection the British Government stood pledged. Such as it was, that covenant was concluded— also at Amritsir—on 5th January, 1806; but before long Sir G. Barlow's Government had added a supplemental article. By this the clause restricting Holkar's influence to the south of the Bundi Hills was abrogated, and the States of the Rajputs, allies of the British Company as they were, became exposed to the rapacity of Jaswant and Amir Khán. It was on this occasion that Lord Lake forswore politics and resolved to confine himself, henceforth, to the work of a soldier.

Lake returned to the Duáb by a route somewhat divergent from that which he had taken in advancing to Amritsir, and went into cantonments before the end of February at Delhi. Here a variety of military spectacles and festive entertainments took place, in which part was taken by the Begam Samru. This famous woman continued, for more than a quarter of a century, to reside at her little town of Sardhana; which was half-way between the Mughal capital and the military station of Meerut. Here she built a Catholic Church and a handsome mansion for her own dwelling; and here she exercised a hospitality which will be found duly acknowledged by Bishop Heber and other contemporary travellers. At Delhi the blind old Sháh was sinking under the burden of years and sufferings, now somewhat alleviated by the benevolence of the Calcutta Government; the administration being under the local resident, Mr. Seton. The fallen monarch, nevertheless, was far from satisfied; the great indolence and weakness of his character had increased with age; and it was found necessary to restrict his direct authority to the precincts of the palace, leaving the revenues of the Delhi territory to be collected by the British administrators, who paid a monthly stipend for the maintenance of the Sháh and his household. The Sháh died in December, 1806; his successor—who bore the once-glorious name of Akbar—was described by Ochterlony as "imbecility personified—weak, proud, and in the highest degree rapacious and avaricious." His weakness and avarice ultimately combined to keep the question of sovereignty dormant for half a century, and then it came up—as most neglected obligations do—for settlement with compound interest.* Akbar Sháh's pretensions, and the

---

* For a statement of the difficulties attending the position of the ex-Emperor and his relations to the British, see Kaye's "Metcalfe," pp. 149, f.f.

way in which they were dealt with, will be mentioned presently.

Meanwhile Jaswant Ráo was slowly returning, by a parallel route, to Málwa, subsisting his bands and those of his associate, Amir Khán, by the plunder of the Rajputs. The States of these unfortunate, but imprudent chiefs, were in a condition which prevented them from uniting for general defence against the Mahrattas in the manner of twenty years before. In 1787—as we have seen—they had organised a war against Mahádaji Sindia in which, though ultimately defeated by De Boigne, they had been able to command some degree of respect. In the present instance, though the power of Sindia was too much broken to be very formidable, they had still enemies against whom their most united efforts could not have been more than sufficient. Unfortunately they were not only disunited but opposed in deadly strife. The Chiefs of Bundi and Kota were attacked and plundered in detail; the Rána of Mewar held apart in the fancied security of the Udaipore fastnesses. The Rájas of Márwar, of Jodhpore, and of Jaipore, who were at open war, bid against each other for the help of the marauders; all hope of British mediation or protection being frustrated by the inexorable obstinancy with which Barlow adhered to his non-intervention policy. The consequence was that Holkar and Amir Khán feigned a quarrel, and the one harried Márwar, while the other—while affecting to take no part in the quarrel—left Jaipore to its fate. Amir Khán then changed sides and murdered Siwái Singh, the Jodhpore Rajá's hostile kinsman; while Sindia, recovering his spirits, took a hand in the game, and extorted an exhorbitant ransom from Jaipore. Then the remote and haughty Mahárana of Méwar (Chitore or Udaipore) was attacked and plundered. Still Barlow looked on and made no sign.

In some other parts of India, however, the policy was not pursued with complete consistency. Thus, alike in the Nizám's dominions and in Audh, the subsidiary system was carried out, to an almost minutely vexatious extent. In Nágpore even, where no subsidiary alliance had ever been accepted, the Bhonslá Rája received unexpected support. In Gujarát the authority of the Gaikwar was strengthened, as against the recalcitrant feudatories of Kathiwár and Katch; while the civil administration of the principality itself was ably reformed by Major Walker, the benevolent and judicious British Resident.

All the more discreditable, in the eyes of all India, appeared the desertion of the ancient Houses of Rajpután who were, unquestionaly, allies of the Company, and one, at least, of whom had lately done good service. Jaswant Ráo naturally attributed Barlow's reserve to fear of himself; and his insolence swelled to frenzy. Raised to the head of the Indore State by the opportune deaths of his brother and nephew, the lawful heirs, he set no bounds to his audacity but such as arose from his growing habits of self-indulgence. The deaths of the heirs were attributed to his machinations, though no proof was ever forthcoming; and he now gave himself sovereign airs, and drank to excess daily. He also made extravagant demands upon the Company, which even Barlow's Government could not entertain.

While northern India was in this alarming state, an event was occurring in the Carnatic which, though of less actual importance, caused a far greater anxiety among the British officials. It has been already mentioned that the sons of Tipu, on the death of the Sultan and the subversion of his power, had been sent to reside on pensions at Vellore. This was an ancient but strong fortress, which had held out for two years against all the resources of Haidar Ali—1780-82—and was considered as safe a place of confinement as any in India. But the sepoys of the Madras army who formed the bulk of the garrison were, by the time of which we are treating, demoralised by a long peace, and irritated by some new regulations as to uniform; and in this state of feeling appeared open to temptation on the susceptible point of religion. Persuaded by the Mysore princes that the changes in their costume were a preparation for their conversion to Christianity, the native soldiers in Vellore were easily and entirely seduced from their allegiance. Before daylight on the 10th July, 1806, they took their arms and amunition; and surrounding the barracks of the British troops, poured volley after volley, through the windows, on the unarmed sleepers. The princes then supplied them with a banquet, and the tiger-standard of Tipu was hoisted on the flag-staff. But Colonel Rollo Gillespie on hearing of the affair, hastened up from Arcot at the head of some cavalry, blew open the gates with his galloper-guns, slew nearly 500 of the mutineers, and took the princes prisoners. They were deported to Calcutta; and on the news reaching London, the Commander of the Madras army and the Governor, Lord William Bentinck, were at once recalled. At the same time Barlow's nomination to Bengal was cancelled; and, after some controversy, Lord Minto, the President of the Board of Control, was sent out as Governor-General.

Minto landed in Calcutta on July 20th, 1807, and at once took over charge from Barlow, who became senior member of Council, but was ere long consoled by the Governorship of Madras.*

It is due to Barlow, whose bad qualities, or bad fortune, pursued him to his new scene of action, to note that Minto's opinion of his predecessor—though recorded in the confidence of a private letter—was not wholly unfavourable. While noticing the coldness of his manner and his consequent want of popularity, the Governor-General bears testimony to his

* In these days of youthful Governors dwelling in comfortable quarters on the mountain tops there seems something monstrous in the notion of men of nearly sixty beginning their Indian career in such a place as Calcutta. Minto's early letters show that he was almost appalled at the heat. The Council sate from 10 a.m. to 3 p.m. twice a week.

devotion to his public duties, his sincere and honourable character.

Minto commenced his career with a strong feeling of the old danger from France and what may be called the keynote of his policy. From his correspondence we get the notion of a manly benevolent character, which makes us all the more inclined to regret that he had not more leisure to attend to the internal affairs of India, and the welfare of the people. His first task, however, was of a local nature, and one which seemed likely to re-open the question of non-intervention, that "metaphysical term" which, in the cynical language of Talleyrand "seems to mean much the same as intervention." A portion of the Bundela country had come into the Company's possession in 1803, by means already mentioned; but the country was covered with forts, some of great strength, and held by chiefs of lawless habits, and given to causeless quarrelling, so that an amount of tumult and insecurity arose, which seemed imperatively to demand repression. On the views of the Government becoming known most of these chiefs submitted to the arbitrament of British officers, and a species of order was restored. Two possessors of hill-fastnesses, however, still held out; a brigand-chief named Lakshman Dáwa, in Ajaigarh, and Daryao Sinh, who held Kalinjar. There was also a military adventurer, named Gopal Sinh, who had usurped the small territory left, after many vicisitudes, to the family of the former Rája, Chattar Sál. The country, generally, is wild, and is traversed by no less than three chains of hills, in one of which are situated the two strong places above named, on almost inaccessible scarps. In the days of which we are speaking the total number of these hill-forts was reckoned at one hundred and fifty. The hills of Bundelkhand are low and stony, covered with shrub-jungle, and the heaven is hot above, and the black soil below yawns with mephitic fissures. But Minto rightly thought that impregnable forts, and intolerable climate were things that a rising power like the British in India could not afford to recognise. Lakshman held Ajaigarh on terms which he declined to fulfil, and when called on to surrender flatly refused.* Colonel Martindell proceeded against this rebel early in 1809, taking on the way an outpost which cost him a loss of 143 killed and wounded. The fort is 1,744 feet above sea level, and the granite rock on which it stands is scarped all round to a height of fifty feet, encircled by a stone rampart. After some time had been wasted in vain parley, fire was opened and the rampart breached in two places; on which the Commandant surrendered, (13th February) and Lakshman, who escaped for the moment, was taken eventually and placed under surveillance near Calcutta, in the enjoyment of a small pension. The fort was made over to a descendant of the former lords. Lakshman's family were treated kindly, but were all destroyed by a male member in whose charge they had been placed, who ended by destroying himself. Proceedings were next commenced against Gopal, who went into the forest and assumed openly the character of a bandit. Aided by the remarkably malarious climate he long eluded pursuit, and even plundered the peaceful citizens of Tirohán, within sight of a British cantonment, which he burned to the ground, while the troops were looking for him elsewhere. At last, after several fights from which when worsted he always managed to escape, he was hunted down in the Ságar country, and gave himself up on the promise of pardon. Emulating the wise and humane policy of the great Akbar, Minto took the bold rebel into favour and bestowed upon him estates which are still, it is believed, in the possession of his family. To complete

---

* See his candid enumeration of his offences in Wilson I., App. iv. "I have behaved," he concludes "in an unparalleled, ungrateful, and rebellious manner. . . . The grossest ingratitude and faithlessness appear against me. . . . All the inhabitants, great and small, are wishing every moment to be my last."

this part of the story of Bundelkhand it need only be added that the famous fortress of Kálinjar, the scene of Sher Sháh's death, in 1554, was invested by the force under Martindell in the beginning of the year 1812; it is on an isolated rock 900 feet high, and was at that time provided with strong loop-holed walls and seven gates, one opening on another. Invested on the 19th January, it resisted an attempt at escalade on February 1st, when the Commandant, seeing that the resolution of the British troops would ultimately prevail, surrendered on terms. The fortifications of Kálinjar have been long since dismantled. No further trouble was experienced in the pacification of the country, but an expedition was sent against the neighbouring chief of Rewa, who had actively aided the rebellion, and a treaty was imposed upon him in October 1812.

Affairs in other quarters—still farther across the Jumna—took Minto far beyond the bounds of Barlow. That upholder of non-intervention had inherited, from the Wellesley days, the nominal command of a tract near Delhi—but on the other side of the river—of which we had a glimpse when noticing the career of George Thomas. When that gallant adventurer succumbed to the enmity of General Perron, the province of Hariána became the spoil of a series of marauders, the last of whom was ruined by Holkar, in 1806, on his return from the Punjab. The Resident at Delhi consequently took the management of the little province into his own hands; and for the next fifty years it continued to form a part of what was known as "the Delhi territory." At first there was some trouble with the Bhattis, a turbulent tribe of Rajput blood, but Muslims by creed, who, under a chief called Khán Bahádur, attempted to oppose the peaceable settlement. He was accordingly called upon to obey the Regulations as introduced by the Assistant Resident—Hon. E. Gardner—and, on persisting in rebellion and plunder, was attacked and expelled from the district. But a large body of the clansmen threw themselves into the town of Bhiwáni where they stood a short siege, conducted by a brigade of foot and artillery under Colonel Ball. The place was breached and stormed, the rebels losing 1,000 men, while the Company's troops lost 132 killed and wounded. The assessment of the revenue and the cessation of marauding expeditions followed; and the country speedily attained an average level of agricultural prosperity.

But this apparently domestic difficulty immediately led to a fresh task. By undertaking the settlement of Hariána, British administration was brought into actual contact with the Cis-Sutlej Sikhs, who occupied a debateable land between the Company's territory and the country directly subject to Ranjit Sinh, the Rája of Lahore, whom we lately saw receiving a visit from Lord Lake. Soon after the departure of Lake and his army, Ranjit had interposed in the quarrels of the local chiefs of this region, which interposition led the latter to invoke the protection of the British: hearing of their application Ranjit on his part also wrote a letter to the Governor-General, in which he proposed that his authority should be recognised up to the Jumna. Minto on this sent Mr. Charles (afterwards Lord) Metcalfe, at the head of a friendly mission to the camp of the Punjab ruler; who received the mission amicably; though he by no means desisted from his aggressions, but seized Ambála and began to levy tribute from the petty Rájas of the neighbourhood.

It is difficult at this distance of time to say what were the determining motives that caused Minto so much alarm at these proceedings. On first hearing of them he recorded an opinion that Ranjit might possibly be threatened with a declaration of war. (Oct. 1808). The fact was that the Government still had the fear of a possible French invasion; while strong rumour pointed to an alliance between the Punjab ruler and the still partially unconquered ruler of Bhurtpore. If Lake had had his own way in 1806 Ludhiána would have been then made the frontier station of the British army; and although on this, as on many another point, Lake's views had been abandoned by Barlow, and the veteran Commander had now left the country, the opinion stood on record, and doubtless received due weight. So Minto resolved that the maintenance of the Sikh chiefs of the Cis-Sutlej was a matter to be dealt with "upon grounds of immediate policy rather than upon any abstract principles;" and—once more—an instance was afforded of Talleyrand's remark. The object in view could not be obtained by a merely passive attitude. "A consequence of our refusing our assent to Runjeet's proposal," Minto had to admit, "must be the necessity of our affording open and immediate protection to the Sikhs, and employing a military force for that purpose." This was non-intervention, perhaps, but it looked very much "the same as intervention." In any case communications to that effect were at once forwarded, both to Ranjit and to the Envoy who—though young in years—displayed through all that troublous time the qualities which marked the great men of Wellesley's school: coolness, good-humour, and inflexible resolution. At first the Punjabi Potentate was, not unnaturally, much excited; but the Governor-General was firm, and his firmness was ably seconded by his youthful agent. He humoured the Rája, caroused with him, but never let go of his object. Towards the end of the year, having followed Ranjit to the sacred city of Amritsir, Metcalfe addressed him a straightforward letter in which he plainly, though politely, stated the ultimatum of his Government: Ranjit must restore all the places, that he had taken, and withdraw his army to the right bank of the Sutlej, if he desired to preserve the friendship of the British. Delay of course ensued; Ranjit left Amritsir for Lahore, whither he was promptly followed by the pertinacious Envoy; his ministers endeavoured to amuse Metcalfe by dwelling upon the peculiar character of their master; but in vain: Metcalfe would not allow the plea, and insisted on an immediate answer, which, nevertheless, was still delayed. Weary of subterfuge the Envoy at last ordered the advance of a British force from Delhi. Another meeting then occurred on December 22nd; and still nothing definite could be got from Ranjit. Yet the end was none the less approaching: little by little, the Rája began to give way: alarmed by the news that Colonel Ochterlony, the brave defender of Delhi, was really advancing on the Sutlej he recalled his garrison from Ambála on January 6th, and proceeded to Amritsir accompanied by the Envoy, to whom he made plenty of oral promises, but gave no treaty. A last attempt to shake Metcalfe's firmness was tried by means of an apparently accidental collision between a body of armed fanatics and the men of the Envoy's escort. Led by their European commanding officer the sepoys repelled the attack, routing a vastly superior body of men by force of skill and discipline: and the lesson was not without effect on the observant mind of the soldier-chief. Meanwhile Ochterlony reached Ludhiána; another force left Delhi in support: and finally the desired treaty was concluded on April 25th, 1809. Whatever may be thought of the consistency or morality of Minto's policy, it is impossible to avoid seeing the great advantages that flowed from the tenacity with which it was carried out; when once formed, one of the shortest in expression, the treaty was one of the longest in duration. For the next thirty years it was faithfully observed on both sides. The chiefs of the Cis-Sutlej were upheld in the exercise of all just rights, no tribute being imposed upon them. Some acts of Sovereignty have, from time to time been found necessary on the part of the British Government; and friction has occasionally resulted. But the general condition of the country has been one of little-interrupted peace; and the paramount power has, in time of trouble had few more faithful allies than some of the Cis-Sutlej States.

While these transactions were cementing the Punjab to the British Indian system, an abortive attempt to carry out the same policy towards the rulers of Afghanistán and Persia was being conducted, under Lord Minto's directions, by two more of the rising political officers of the day—Mountstuart Elphinstone and John Malcolm. These missions, however, were (from various incidents) so ineffectual that a full account of them would be out of place in a short work like the present. Elphinstone's mission got no farther than Pesháwar, where the negotiation with which he was charged broke down. It must always be taken as part of the French scare; but even so, one can hardly understand why Minto and his councillors should expect the Afgháns to protect British interests for no corresponding advantage to themselves. The Amir—or Sháh as he was called—was courteous, and the envoy obtained a good deal of information about what was then an unknown land: but the danger of domestic strife was imminent; and the Sháh wanted assistance which the Envoy was not authorised to give. So Elphinstone came back; and Sháh Shuja was not long afterwards driven out of this stony kingdom by his brother, and never again wore its crown of thorns till a brief and tragic hour thirty years later.

The exact extent of the peril cannot now be known under fear of which Minto took these steps. We can only suppose that something was known in London with regard to far-reaching aims of Napoleon, while not much was known to any European statesmen of the obstacles that would beset an invader having first to conquer Russia as a preliminary to the invasion of India. All that need here be noted is that, in May, 1807, on the very eve of the battle of Friedland, General Gardane had been despatched to Teheran with instructions from the French Emperor to enquire what assistance Persia would give to a French army moving on India. "But the General's mission does not end there," pursued the instructions of Napoleon: "he is also to communicate with the Mahrattas and learn exactly what support the expedition would receive in India." We cannot be surprised to find British statesmen taking violent alarm in such circumstances as these, nor at Minto being for a renewal of Malcolm's influence over the Sháh of Persia which had been so happily exerted in 1800. But this time Malcolm was less fortunate: when he landed in Persia he found Gardane in high favour and a message awaiting himself, in which the Sháh refused to receive him and forbade his advancing to Teheran. Malcolm retired, breathing defiance; and almost persuaded Minto to order a hostile landing on the shores of the Gulf. Then came the news of the famous meeting of the Emperors on the Niemen-raft: and the menace seemed to be multiplied. The project of a friendly mission—renewed in Calcutta—began to be conceived, in London also; and presently an amused world saw Malcolm at Teheran, courting Fateh Ali Sháh on one side, while the Envoy from St. James's was wooing him from the other. The only effect of this comedy on the fortunes of India was that her finances were made answerable for all its cost: the expenses of the royal embassy being charged to the Indian Government no less than those of the mission sent by that Government itself. But the Peninsular war began to absorb the military resources of France; while the Russians retired from the Georgian frontier; and the Sháh consented to a treaty with the Court of St. James's with which Minto was obliged to be content.

The only farther exemplification of "non-intervention" that marked this period arose out of Amir Khán's attempts upon Nágpore, already mentioned: the Pathán freebooter being sternly warned off, retired from the land of the Bhonslá.

In 1811 Charles Metcalfe, as a well-earned reward for his able conduct at the Court of Ranjit Sinh, found himself officiating as Resident at Delhi with the "Great Moghul,"—Mr. Seton having obtained other employment. The palace was still full of crime and intrigue; and the Sháh most tenacious of the fragments of authority yet remaining in his hands, and very desirous of an increase of the eleemosynary stipend from the Government, which he called "his tribute." He endeavoured to obtain the mediation of the Nawáb of Audh; and was entangled, by a wily Hindu, in a sham mission to Calcutta. All ended well at last: the Sháh's eyes were opened and his lips closed by Metcalfe's firmness.

The only other internal trouble of the time arose from the turbulence of the Diwán of Travancore, which was not abated without some military operations. The State was sequestered for a time, but the Rája's authority was ultimately restored.

[Authorities for matter dealt with in this Section are Ross's "Cornwallis Correspondence"; "Lord Minto in India," by Lady Minto; Kaye's "Metcalfe"; and Basáwan Lál's "Memoir of Amir Khán," translated by H. T. Prinsep; also Wilson, Vol. I. (being Vol. VI. of the "History" by Mill and Wilson.]

SECTION 2.—While these events had been proceeding in the north, the Madras Presidency was exposed to a tempest of which Minto said that it was as great a danger as "the British Empire, in all its parts, was ever exposed to." We have already seen how near the sepoys had been brought to a general mutiny in 1806; the quarrels of the Governor with the Commander-in-Chief now led to the revolt of a thousand European officers and to positive acts of civil war, enough— had it continued—to set all India in a blaze. The quarrel between Barlow and General Hay Macdowall arose out of the irritation of the General at what he construed as official neglect. After the recall of Sir John Cradock, on account of the outbreak at Vellore, the Court of Directors had issued orders that the Commanders-in-Chief at the minor Presidencies should not have seats in the Executive Council. With that order—so far as Madras was concerned—Barlow was, of course, obliged to comply: but it still rested with his discretion to show the new Commander the courtesy of consultation, at least on military questions. This course, unhappily, was not adopted; the soldier's pride burst into flame: he resigned his post and embarked in a ship bound for Europe, having first recorded an intemperate order. On January 31st, 1809, Barlow retaliated by suspending the Adjutant-General and his deputy—by whom the order was issued—on the ground that the General had been guilty of sedition, and that they were his abettors. All this—which would in itself have been little more than a deplorable incident—was aggravated by the fact that the officers of the Native Army had grievances which they had long and vainly urged upon the local Government, and by the personal unpopularity of Barlow, who had scarcely emerged from a dispute with his civil subordinates in which an odour of scandal had been stirred.

The actual struggle was precipitated by a fresh order from the Government of Madras, in which four officers of rank were suspended, four removed from their commands, and four more superseded. This severity was not justified by any public trial or inquiry, but was founded upon information derived —in a somewhat underhand way—from clerks, and insufficient (if it had been proved) to establish any serious violation of discipline. As soon as the order was known the whole army was in confusion. From Jálna, beyond the Godávari, from Haidarabad, the capital of the Nizam's dominions, came peremptory demands for the restoration of the officers, several of whom had distinguished and recent service to cite; a joint movement on Madras was threatened if the demand should not be granted. At Masulipatam the Company's European regiment—whose men had a grievance of their own—put their Colonel under arrest, espoused the cause of the mutinous officers, and opened a correspondence with their brethren at

Haidarabad. The officers in garrison at Seringapatam, defying the orders of the Resident at the adjoining capital of Mysore, drove out the handful of King's troops, shut the gates, and invited succour from the neighbouring stations. A body of sepoys, under misleading statements from their officers, attempted to join them, but were dispersed with carnage by a loyal force of cavalry under Colonel Gibbs: civil war had begun, and threatened to become universal throughout the province.

Amid these portents the civil rulers exhibited an honourable firmness. Barlow insisted upon a "test" being submitted to all the officers of the army in which they should, by their signatures, declare their readiness to obey his orders; and Lord Minto, however he might privately deplore any mistakes that the Madras Government might have made, felt bound to issue an order indicative of entire support. He did more; his order was issued at the end of May: and when it seemed likely to have no good effect he set sail for Madras and took up the case in person. The knowledge of his firm but just character, and the sense of the awful nature of the alternative, combined to change the resolve of the officers: though, unwilling to humble themselves to Barlow, they joined in a letter of penitence and submission to the Governor-General. On September 25th, a general order announced to the army Lord Minto's reprobation of the officers' conduct, and his determination to vindicate the claims of discipline, but with all due consideration for legality and justice. In place of the secret and arbitrary proceedings of the Madras Government, courts-martial sat on a few of the ringleaders, four of whom were cashiered and others permitted to retire. Finally, Barlow was recalled by the Court of Directors, and the exclusion of the Commander-in-Chief from the Council was repealed. All the removed officers were ultimately pardoned by the Court of Directors and restored to the service of the Company.

India was now settling down. Jaswant Ráo had drunk himself into hopeless insanity, in which state the once formidable freebooter died, a chained maniac; the affairs of his principality were assumed by his widow, Tulsi Bái, who administered them, mainly, by the agency of his old client Amir Khán: and the unprincipled but not imprudent Pathán had been by that time taught by experience that a firmer hand was at the helm in Calcutta and that he must abstain from depredation. But elsewhere the habits engendered by half a century of anarchy could not be suddenly eradicated; and the growing prosperity of Bengal attracted the attention of robbers as formidable as the Pindáris themselves. Organised gangs of banditti levied contributions up to thirty miles from Barrackpore; and it was not until special orders had been framed, special magistrates appointed, and some of the most prominent gang-leaders hanged, that an impression could be made upon the proceedings, so discreditable to a civilised government, of the Bengal dacoits.

On a larger scale, and in a more distant sphere, the property of Indian subjects was still more in need of protection. The want of harmony between Mornington and the Admiral commanding the eastern squadron in 1799 had interfered to prevent the capture of the "French Islands" at that time, and the expedition had been ultimately diverted to Egypt. Since then the islands had continued to harbour corsairs, like Surcouf and Lemême, who had plundered Indian commerce to the extent—as was calculated—of about two millions sterling.* The island of Bourbon—now Réunion—lying between Mauritius and Madagascar, and measuring 38 miles by 28 miles, was captured by Colonel Keating in a few hours, early in 1810; but an attack on the larger island was defeated with the loss of five British frigates taken by the brave

---

* Six Indiamen were captured in 1809.

Duperré. This, however, was almost the last disaster to British enterprise of which the Mauritius was to be the scene. It happened on August 23rd ; but the possession of Bourbon now afforded a station for the British ships; and a blockade, only partially successful, was applied to Mauritius, the capture of that island being a part of Minto's scheme. The skill and energy of the French captains enabled them ere long to break the blockade; on the 12th September they fought another action in which they forced a British frigate to strike, and actually captured the vessel carrying the Commander of the British expedition, General Abercombie; this vessel however, was retaken the same day. Early in the following month a fleet of warships and transports assembled at Rodriguez; and on the 29th November a force of nearly 12,000 men was landed on the shores of the Mauritius. The Governor, General Decaen, though much outnumbered, offered a respectable defence for the night; next day an advance on Port Louis was made, in which the invaders suffered as much from the heat as from the enemy. On the 31st there was a further advance and a brief action in which two British officers were killed, but the enemy's guns were taken. On the 1st December, Port Louis being surrounded, and threatened by an irresisitible superiority of force, General Decaen demanded and obtained an honourable capitulation : and the island has ever since remained a British possession, though in the enjoyment of French law. The sister island was restored to France in 1815.

Although these measures were eventually justified by orders from home, they had been undertaken by Minto in anticipation and upon his own responsibilty ; being—as he thought —warranted by the disgrace and damage suffered from the French possession of the islands, and by the flourishing state of Indian finances. In reporting the result to London he dwelt with pardonable complacency, on the "perfect tranquility which was maintained (in India) during the absence of so large a body of troops." This afforded—as he said—proof of a favourable state of political security. It also encouraged the Governor-General to carry out an enterprise he had for some time contemplated, whereby the influence of the French and their corsairs in eastern seas was completely and finally annulled. The conquest of Java had little, if any effect, upon the evolution of India; but it was the greatest and most glorious effort ever made by the Government of the country, beyond its own limits; and, as such, is deserving of record in Indian history.

It is well known that the possessions of Holland had come under the dominion of France, at the time we are now contemplating, and Napoleon seems to have governed them through Dutch officers. But Marshal D'Aendels, the officer in charge of Java and its dependencies, was unpopular with his own countrymen, no less than with the natives; being a man of strong passions and overbearing character. While Minto was at Madras a small expedition (sent from that Presidency in October, 1800), had landed at Amboyna, and forced a capitulation on the Governor, who retired to Java, and was at once shot by order of D'Aendels. The Madras force cruised about the Straits for six months, taking a number of small places; while Napoleon replaced D'Aendels by a less ferocious and more popular officer, General Janssen, and sent out reinforcements to Java, raising the garrison to 17,000 troops—European and native—the greater part posted in a strong position about eight miles from Batavia, the chief town. The British Fleet, consisting—with transports—of no less than eighty-one sail, arrived off the coast of Java 30th July, and landed on 4th August, 1811; the Governor-General being present in person, and the land-forces—consisting of 6,000 British and 6,000 Indian soldiers under the general command of Sir Samuel Auchmuty. Batavia was occupied on the 7th, and on the 10th, possession was taken of Weltevreeden, an unfortified cantonment. Janssen, meanwhile, was intrenched at Fort Cornelis —the place already mentioned—strong both by nature and art, and protected on both sides by rivers. The daring Gillespie, the same who had relieved Vellore in 1806, was in command of the front attack, supported on the right by Colonel Macleod, and aided by a diversion in the enemy's rear to be attempted by a small mixed force under Major Yule. Gillespie's advance arrived before dawn on the 26th, and found the bridge still standing; without awaiting the rest of the column he crossed and stormed; the rear force soon came up; Macleod carried the work on the enemy's left, though at the cost of his own life; the enemy fled and were chased ten miles; 6,000 prisoners were taken, inclusive of the men newly-arrived from France. The British loss was near on 900 killed and wounded. On the 16th September Auchmuty came up with Janssen near Samarang and defeated him again; the same evening he signed a treaty of surrender; the soldiers and officers became prisoners-of-war, and the British reserved full discretion as to the civil administration. Colonel Gillespie remained in command of the troops for some time, during which he continued to distinguish himself by his reckless energy; and the government of the island was intrusted to Mr. (afterwards Sir Stamford) Raffles, who proved a most successful administrator; and also an incomparable authority upon the island.* It was, however, restored to the Dutch after the fall of Napoleon.

For these services Minto admitted that he expected rewards. Returning to Bengal in October, he turned to domestic matters, in some of which he was destined to meet with almost more serious trouble than in his military operations. His

* "The History of Java." Two vols., 4to. London: 1817. For an excellent civilian's account of the expedition, see Minto's Letters. He bears warm testimony to the conduct and character of the unfortunate Janssen.

first anxiety was caused by the letters from England which he found awaiting his arrival; not only did the despatches contain no recognition of the services on which he justly prided himself—connected with the Madras mutiny and the conquest of Mauritius—but his private letters led him to apprehend that he might be called on to adopt a posture of defence. To this feeling was now added a sense that he had acted against orders in regard to Java. In conquering that island, indeed, he had acted in accordance with instructions; but his humane reluctance to leave the Dutch colonists without protection against the natives had caused him to make provision for the civil and military administration there, which contravened a distinct direction to leave the colony to its own resources. Such things, viewed by unfriendly eyes, might be misrepresented. The attention of the people of Great Britain was at that time so much absorbed by great foreign transactions, and by trouble and distress at home, that it might well be in the power of hostile Ministers to make the remote Governor of British India suffer for conduct really deserving of high praise and reward. The Peninsular war was at its crisis; active hostilities were waging with the United States; a Prime Minister had been assassinated amid symptoms of popular sympathy; the Regent was attempting, with the aid of his favourite, the Earl of Moira, to put the Liberal party in the wrong, and carry on the Government through the agency of men like Sidmouth, Eldon, and Liverpool. The discussion of the Company's charter was at hand, the enemies of Barlow were stirring, and their cause was espoused by some of the Whigs, and, notably, by the "Edinburgh Review." Minto might well expect to be made the Jonah of the tempest.

Nor were troubles wanting of a more immediate nature. The evils of the subsidiary system were coming to a head in Audh, where the continual demands of the Nawáb for the aid of British bayonets in support of the farmers of the land-revenue, were met by the Resident—Major Baillie—by demands for a more humane and regular assessment. Baillie was earnestly instructed to adopt a tone of respect and moderation towards the incompetent ruler; but moderation and respect only led to equivocation and delay, the usual resource of Asiatics in such conditions.

On another side the Pindaris were increasing in audacious rapacity. Secure under the non-intervention policy, they had taken up their quarters in Nimár, an almost inaccessible fastness of woods and hills between the upper waters of the Tapti and Narbada rivers. Here they were covered by Málwa on one side, where Amir Khán favoured them with all the resources of Holkar's territory, added to his own newly-created principality of Sironj and Tonk; on the other side the Pindaris derived immunity from the independent power of Nágpore, where the Bhonslá still repudiated all attempts to bring his State into the subsidiary system. Thus protected, the freebooters had been encouraged to extend their depredations into the Company's territories; and, in 1812, they were threatening to plunder the wealthy British city of Mirzapore. The approach of troops averted this calamity; and a measure of temporary salvation was obtained for the western frontier by treaties, in which the chiefs of Tehri and Rewa undertook to close their passes, while a cordon of troops was—as a further protection—aligned upon the British side, and extended to Midnapore on the sea-coast.

The Audh trouble also was for the time staved off by expostulation and warning. Friendly arrangements were, at the same time, made with the Peshwa and the Nizám, by which those rulers might, it was hoped, be enabled to manage their affairs without calling upon the British forces. But Minto must have felt that all these measures were little more than palliatives; and that the time for more vigorous action could not be very distant. In his present uncertainty as to support from home, and with the burden of labour and increasing years beginning to tell upon him, he may, perhaps, have been content if he found himself able to adjourn the evil day.

Meanwhile, it was necessary to make provision for the expenses of the late military operations and to maintain at least an equilibrium in the finances. The subject will be treated in another place; for the present it need only be considered in its bearing on public tranquility. One of the expedients—adopted as far back as 1810—for effecting financial reform had been the assessment of a police-rate upon inhabited houses in towns;* and a great ferment had arisen in Benares in consequence. The people shut up their houses, abandoned all their business, and assembled in multitudes outside the town. An attempt was even made to march on Calcutta, but all means, appliances, and supplies were wanting; so that, when the crowd had made one march, their number thinned off and the rest accepted the advice of the Rája and went home, trusting their cause to a petition. The translation given in the Appendix to Wilson's 1st Vol. gives the grounds of their objections: they may be thought rather curious than interesting, being chiefly the expression of alarm at novelty and a vague idea that Governments ought to be possessed of some inexhaustible reserves of treasure out of which to provide for the discharge of the primary duty of public protection. The end, however, appeared to justify the means. So far as the holy city was affected the tax was repealed (Reg. VIII. of 1812); and when, in the ensuing year, it was applied to Dacca, Patna, and Murshidabad, care was taken to put both assessment and expenditure in the hands of a municipal committee (Reg. VIII. of 1813).

Nor was the close of Minto's administration free from

* Reg. XV. of 1810; notable as the first—and not most promising—effort in the direction of local finance, subsequently adopted with such good results in India.

trouble arising out of the religious zeal of his own countrymen. At the Danish settlement of Serampore, just opposite the Governor-General's suburban retreat, the Baptist Missionaries had set up a paper-factory, a printing-press, and a school; by which instrumentality they hoped to be able to propagate a knowledge of the Christain Scriptures. Unhappily they could not find a method of diffusing their own opinions without impugning those of their neighbours; and their press not only produced Bibles, but also pamphlets of a controversial kind in which attacks were made on the beliefs of Hindus and Muslims. Such publications alarmed the Government, already rendered especially sensitive by the recent affair at Vellore. One of these works was even pronounced "scurrilous." On this being brought to his notice, Minto called on the missionaries to use more caution in their proceedings and utterances, inviting them to remove their printing works from Serampore and establish themselves in Calcutta, where they would be more directly under the control of the British Government. The good missionaries replied by pointing out that the proposed transfer of their business and plant would cause them great inconvenience and expense, which they represented as unnecessary, promising that no further publications should be issued before being submitted for approval of the Government In this the worthy men may have appeared to display the wisdom of the serpent, inasmuch as their plan had an obvious tendency to make the Government answerable for their future teaching and to give their publications, henceforward, the character (or semblance at least) of State authority. Be this as it may, the compromise was accepted by the Government. Dr. Carey, the head of the mission,—whose linguistic acquirements were of a very high repute—was also made Professor of Sanscrit in the College of Fort William. Towards the end of Lord Minto's administration some missionaries who had gone out to Calcutta without a license from the Court of Directors were ordered to be sent home; but this was the constant practice, and was done about the same time to a member of Minto's own household. Personally, he always befriended the missionaries. He also spoke warmly of the translation of the Christian Scriptures in addressing the College of Fort William, as visitor.

That Institution, although curtailed of some of its original splendour, still continued—then, and for long after—to be a seat of oriental learning, where young civil officers could learn the native tongues, and where learned natives could meet with some encouragement to pursue and make public their useful labours. A number of important and valuable works on legal and linguistic subjects issued from the College-press, in the years 1808-9 and 1810: followed by works of Eastern poets and prose-writers, reproduced in a more permanent form than their original manuscript. Finally, it should be recorded that —for the first time since Warren Hastings—a sincere attempt was made for the support and encouragement of purely indigenous learning. The abstract sciences were found to be decayed, the circle of study contracted, many valuable works disused, in some instances lost. This alarming growth of ignorance was tending to deprive the people of the means of culture and self-development; it even tended greatly to obstruct the measures taken for their better government. For all these reasons Minto resolved to add to the resources of the College of Benares, and to improve its management, while he recommended the foundation of new Hindu and Muhamadan Colleges in various great centres.

Minto's enlightened care for letters failed to please the friends of missions, whose view of his proceedings is thus reflected in a local organ of more than thirty years later:—

"Having succeeded to his heart's content in crushing the efforts of Christian evangelists, he next directed his attention to the heathenish institutions which owed their origin and support to . . . some of his predecessors . . . And not only so, but his purpose consentaneously tended to add to their number at the expense of the State."*

Some time in 1812, Minto had intimated to the Court of Directors a desire to be relieved about the beginning of 1814. Somewhat to his surprise he suddenly learned that he was to be anticipated in this project by the unmerited measure of dismissal from office. The Directors hastened to explain that this was due to no displeasure or want of appreciation of "his eminent services": Lord Moira had rendered himself useful to the Prince Regent, and the Prince Regent could think of no better way to reward Lord Moira's usefulness. There was truly much ungraciousness in the way in which this good and distinguished man was treated: but, when all is said, it was more a question of manner than of anything else. The contemplated career of Minto was only curtailed by six months, at the most; and the Ministry, by recommending him for an earldom, showed—as he good-temperedly noted—that his recall had no connection with his conduct. Some of the most eminent members of the Court protested against the measure, alike on public and on personal grounds: and Minto received the thanks of Parliament: but the influence of the Crown was strong in those days; and the Court of Directors, with their political existence trembling in the scales of fate, could not afford to act with any extreme show of independence. Minto, on the other hand, had certainly been somewhat autocratic. He had deviated from the Cornwallis policy, which Barlow had so zealously obeyed; and he had made conquests abroad which, while annihilating the power and influence of France in the East, had ended in causing embarrassment to Great Britain. In the following section we must consider, as fully as our space will

* "Calcutta Review," Vol. III. "The expense of the State" was furnished—be it remembered—by the Hindus and Muhamadans. *Tantae ne animis cœlestibus irœ?*

permit, how far this bold course had been harmonised with the due regard to the welfare of the people, and the prudent management of the national affairs which are so important as elements of that welfare.

[The authorities to be consulted are those already cited. The case of the missionaries is stated in many pamphlets of the time, preserved at the India Office; also in the 2nd Vol. of the "History of India," by J. C. Marshman, the son of one the body.]

SECTION 3.—Next to the due protection of the frontiers against foreign aggressions—for which Minto had so boldly and skilfully provided—the greatest need of the Indian populations was a sound state of the finances, and an efficient administration of justice. It can hardly be affirmed that Minto left his mark equally well on these departments. Finance, in that day even more than now, included the whole rural economy of the greater portion of the men, women and children, from sea to sea, and from the snows of the Alpine border to the peak of Comorin. As for justice, it was a part of the administration which had been so long neglected that its establishment on a national and honest basis was a primary need for the national evolution.

Taking "finance" in its broadest sense, we may regard it as implying more than the mere administration of the public money, which is a matter of high technical skill chiefly interesting to experts; the work also includes the raising of that money; and the details of this branch touch every person in the country. In Minto's time the land-revenue made over 70 per cent. of the whole resources of the State. Even now—when fiscal resources have so greatly developed—it forms nearly a half: and millions of the population pay nothing else, except the duty on the salt they consume. If we examine the fiscal condition of the chief nations of the world we shall be struck with a remarkable law; viz: that the burden of taxation in a country is usually in direct ratio to the degree of freedom or self-government, which may, from this point of view, be correctly called the dearest thing in the world. Thus, the money voted in one Parliament of William and Mary was far greater than all that was extorted by Charles I.; and to come to our own times, the rate of incidence per head in the modern world is greatest in the United States, in Great Britain and her self-governed colonies, and in the French Republic; while it is lightest in Russia, Turkey, and British India. The reason is perhaps obvious; but with that question we can have here no concern, so far at least as European countries go: in India—especially in the early decades of the 19th century—the cause was plain enough: namely, ignorance. The financiers of Calcutta at that time neither knew how to tax the subjects so recently brought under the sway of the Company, nor had they much temptation to make the experiment: the case of Benares, lately mentioned, was a severe and stern warning. It was the more essential that they should do their best to acquaint themselves with the principles and practice of the land-revenue which was not merely the sheet-anchor, but almost the whole motive-power of the ship. They early perceived that the traditionary law of India gave them the right of claiming as much of the produce as they could appropriate without starving the agriculturalists or provoking a general insurrection. But they had great difficulty in discovering who was the person to whom to look for this share. Hence the discussions so keenly urged from the time of Hastings to that of Cornwallis—the best part of twenty years—as to who was the owner of the land in India? The question may seem to us equally easy and unnecessary; in a country of anarchy and fist-right, the landholder is he who can hold the land. In Bengal the land had got to be held by a set of agents, originally strong local proprietors on their own account, appointed to collect from their poorer neighbours, by an indolent or imbecile government; and allowed to intercept a portion, theoretically appraised at 10 per cent. as a remuneration for their exertions. It was in this class that Philip Francis and Shore persisted in finding the proprietary right; and it was to this class that Pitt and Dundas instructed the not reluctant Cornwallis to confide the administration of the several economies of Bengal. They were to be the feudal baronage of India, managing and improving, taking up waste land, and improving what was already under cultivation.

By Minto's time it was becoming clear that these expectations had been too sanguine. Already an able school of reformers was arising in the Madras Presidency which was questioning the ownership of Zemindars and Poligars, and putting forward claims on behalf of the Ryot, or actual cultivator. Here, they said, was the true landlord to be sought: not among the agents or farmers, to whom the rulers of provinces might have found it convenient to intrust the work of collection, not even in the State itself, which had only a vested right limited, if not by law, then by custom and necessity.

Such were the opposite points from which the ownership of land was viewed in Bengal and Madras. Bombay was still too backward, too small, and too recently acquired, to take a part in the fray; and it may be assumed that the revenue there was taken in any way that it could be got, without much speculation. There, as elsewhere, if no formal settlement had been made, the idea was to get as much for the State as might be possible after the actual cultivator's necessary expenses had been met, including the price of seed and replacement of exhausted stock. This was, in fact, a percentage on net produce: the precarious salvage of anarchy.

But Bengal, Madras, and Bombay by no means made up the whole of British India, even in those days. There were, in the newly-acquired districts, tracts as large as the British islands in which the Muslim had held direct sway almost ever since the days when the Normans conquered England. Was the same state of things to be looked for as under the Mahratta Desmukhs, the Tamil Rájas, the Poligars of the Balaghat, or the Zemindars of Bengal? We know now, that it was not; but the labours of the historian and the jurist had to be joined to the researches of the statesman and the investigations of the administrator, before a conclusion could be reached.

The fact which slowly emerged, and on which all the more successful land-revenue officers have—consciously or unconsciously—had to proceed, is that which may be best stated in the language of the late Sir H. S. Maine. *Status* was nine-tenths of the law, *contract* only the residue. Wherever—as in Bengal and parts of Madras—rich barons had made what in feudal times were called "fiefs," the cultivating proprietors passed from their old allodial status to that of "villains" or copyhold, tenants; still—where they were able—clinging to a heritable and transferable right and claiming not to be liable to eviction except on certain extreme grounds. Such was the condition of those variously known as sub-proprietors, hereditary occupants, and the like. But they could not be dealt with, directly at least, without sweeping measures against the superior holders, who had acquired the right to collect and to deduct their commission from the collections they were making; and who had thus acquired something of the position of what, in a corresponding social stage of Europe, were called "tenants-in-chief." Nevertheless, the very name they bore ought to have told Minto and his councillor of the mistake made by Shore and Cornwallis: for the title Zemindar (*Zamin*—"land," *dár*—"holder for management") no more implied property absolute in the soil than *Tahsildar*, or *Mamlatdar*, other titles of office which still obtain, with no ambiguity or misconception. Hence—as already observed—permanency, though a fault, was not the only fault of the Bengal settlement; it also erred by ignoring, and almost obliterating, the older and more genuine status of the cultivating occupant.

Thus, when Messrs. Cox and Tucker were sent to make preparation for the extension of this settlement in the "Ceded and Conquered" (now the North-West) Provinces, it did not take them a twelvemonth to discover traces, not only of allodial ownership in this class, but they also discovered that the status of the great "proprietors" was more official than proprietary, and that the cultivating occupants had elements of true ownership which they commonly exercised as members of a joint-association, or—as Europeans might say—Commune. The existence of these Communes in many widely distinct regions has long since become a common-place of the subject, and has been often regarded as an archaic institution of the Aryan race. But, inasmuch as it has been found among populations of non-Aryan descent, it may be safer to regard it as a form of agriculture incidental to human society in a certain stage of its evolution.

However, this may be, there it was, in Hindustan, and indeed in many other parts of India. It may be inferred that it arose from the original clearance of forest-land by a father and his sons; or—in some cases which are known—from the conquest of aborigines by an immigrant tribe or family. In both instances—especially the latter—clients and serfs would be retained to aid in the cultivation, and thus would arise another class of cultivators; more like our "labourers," but paid not in wages, but in allotments of land.

Thus, then, three well-marked classes emerged on the view of the Commissioners. These were:—

First.—The Grantees, or usurping Barons; of whom Mr. Tucker observed that they were "hereditary administrators of the revenue, with a beneficial interest in the land."

Second.—The cultivating occupants, who were either members of a commune with many elements of proprietary right;

or were, at least, holders of a heritable and transferable occupancy under certain definite—or definable—conditions; and,

Third.—Non-proprietary labourers, holding allotments as tenants-at-will; very apt, however, to wander if not well treated.

This state of things was also traceable in many parts of the Madras Presidency; and it was the opinion of Lord William Bentinck, when Governor there, that the rights of the first class were too vague to form a claim on their behalf to be recognised as the contracting parties with the Government. He accordingly proposed to settle with the second; as advised by Colonel Read, and his able follower Munro. This measure was soon after frustrated for the moment by Barlow, Bentinck's successor, who ordered the introduction of the Bengal system. Zemindars were to be formed, or created, and a "permanent settlement" concluded with them.

For the North-West Provinces a similar policy was ordered by Minto, in contravention of the report of the Commissioners, who urged—amongst other objections—that the right of contracting with the Government demanded judicial inquiry: and that at least twenty-five per cent. of the culturable land was still lying waste and unappropriated. The people were indifferent, where not positively hostile, to the principle of permanence; the claims of the village-communities were also beginning to attract the notice of the best observers. The Bengal system, too, was beginning to show signs of weakness: in the twenty years since 1793 so many estates had been sold that the old noblesse, whom it had been intended to preserve, were almost gone. Finally the sufferings of the Bengal ryots, under enhancement and illegal exaction, were already such as to call for legislative interference.

All these considerations combined to move the authorities in London; and in 1813 orders came out from the Court of

Directors—doubtless inspired by the Board of Control, which led to the adjournment of the introduction of the Bengal into the North-West Province. .

Nor was the ryot system of Read and Munro to be applied to these provinces. After Barlow's recall that system had, through the zeal and intelligence of Munro, been finally adopted in a great part of the territory subordinate to the Government of Madras. But in Hindustan the village-system found an equally strenuous and able advocate in Metcalfe; and, in July, 1813, such strong and reasonable objections to the "ryotwári settlement" were sent home that this system was also postponed, pending further inquiry.

The immediate results were not of unmixed advantage to the people. Hasty settlements were made as we learn from the highest authority.* The estimates on which these were based were conjectural; the accounts of the estates were notoriously incorrect; by reason of the prevailing ignorance, undue influence fell into the hands of the native officials, who used it for the purpose of misrepresentation and corrupt practice.. Such was the condition of this fundamental matter when Minto resigned his office. In Bengal the future of the people was compromised; in Madras a benevolent conviction had obliterated the village system and reduced the rural aristocracy: in Hindustan the communes narrowly escaped extinction, and were submerged by a crowd of speculators.

In regard to the administration of justice, again, no very great advance was made. The old system of the Hindus had turned, ultimately, upon the action of the village elders, the headman and four assessors, curiously resembling the old English "Reeve-and-four." The reforms introduced by Warren Hastings and Cornwallis had given rise to a regular chain of courts, one hearing appeals from another; and a great deal of litigation had arisen necessarily favourable to

* Letter from Holt Mackenzie quoted by Wilson, Book I. chap. VII.

lawyers and their more wealthy clients. Arrears accumulated: more European officers were appointed—at a ruinous cost—the use of native agency was universally decried. The bulk of the people was thus virtually excluded from legal remedy while the forces of the State were employed to debar the lower classes from taking the law into their own hands. In Madras and Bombay some attempt was made to improve this state of things by local legislation—for which these Presidencies received powers in 1807—but it cannot be said that any profound insight into the subject was revealed, either there or in the provinces more directly subject to the Governor-General. The administration of penal law was not much better. The civil judges were also magistrates: the Muhamadan law was followed—except in respect of some punishments, such as mutilation—which were abolished. Work accumulated to such an extent that in one district alone there are said to have been at one moment 1,500 persons awaiting trial in the lock-up.

Act III., of 1812 was aimed at this abuse; but it did not provide any increase of the staff, and was therefore a mere palliative and almost a sham.

Next to warlike undertakings it was in State finance that Minto's chief successes took place. The decline in which this important branch of affairs had been left by Wellesley received but little amelioration in the short and feeble administration of Barlow. But Minto, while conducting the great and successful military operations mentioned above, did not neglect this department of his duty. By increased receipts from Bengal, by new taxes in Madras, and by reduction of interest on the public debt, Minto converted a deficit into a handsome surplus. Taking the rupee at its then value, the revenue in 1807-8 came to a total of £15,670,000, and the expenditure —inclusive of interest on debt—to £15,979,000. In 1813-14 the revenue amounted to £17,228,000 and the expenditure to no more than £15,575,000.

It is to be feared, however, that these exertions of the Government—however admirable—were not of much benefit to the people of India; for the whole of the money was sent home to London by positive order of the Court of Directors, at that time more than usually pressed for resources.

On 4th October, 1813, Lord Moira landed in Calcutta and took charge from Minto. His administration marks a new departure in the affairs of British India: and it was accompanied by a radical change in the powers and attributes of the Company he was supposed to serve.

[Consult—if possible—the celebrated "Fifth Report" of the Select Committee; also Wilson, as already cited, and Marshman, Vol. II. on the period. Wilson's statement is especially able, and shows wide research.]

CHAPTER XII.

REVIEW OF THE FOREGOING.

Section 1 : Hindustan during first Muslim period (1193-1398)—Section 2 : Under Mughal Empire (1586-1748)—Section 3 : End of pre-British period.

SECTION I.—There are not wanting in various parts of history instances of the existence of an apparent limit to the duration of a dynasty or political system left to the ordinary laws of nature, and not cut short by war. Thus, in the Roman Empire, the democratic absolutism devised by Augustus, B.C. 30 came to an end by the death of M. Aurelius, A.D. 180. The famous Khalifate of Bagdad—founded A.D, 754—ran its bright course till 964, when it proved unable to hold its own against Nicephorus Phocas, and ceased to exist as an Empire : though not entirely extirpated for nearly three more centuries. The contemporaneous empire of the Karlings in Western Europe lasted from its foundation in 752, to the usurpation of Hugh Capet on the virtual exhaustion of the Imperial Line, in 956. In England the foreign monarchy founded by William the Conqueror, came to a natural end with the death of Henry III. and the appearance of elected Deputies in Parliament, 1060-1272. In modern France the Bourbon monarchy lasted from the accession of Henry IV. (1589) to the death of Louis XVI in 1793. Turning again to England, if we take the " Petition of Right" as the beginning of the Government by King, Lords, and Commons, we shall find that it was worn-

REVIEW OF THE FOREGOING. 421

out, and came to an end in 1832, when the influence of the Lords in Parliament was destroyed, and the Crown became little more than an ornament on the summit of the political fabric. From such instances we might feel tempted to infer that—be the reason what it may—the ordinary vitality of a dynasty or constitution is not good for more than seven generations; though in many cases that limit may not be reached, or even approximated.

This duration was at least twice made good in Indian History. The Turkmán or purely foreign government, which lasted from the invasion of Muhamad Guri, or Bin Sám, to the flight of the feeble Abdulla in 1378, was often broken by palace revolutions, but never changed in its character, or effect, upon the people, until it had spent all its force, and the Empire of the "Lord of the World" extended, according to the doggrel quoted in CHAPTER IV., p. 93, for about six miles from his house-door. The Mughal Empire, founded by Bábar in 1526, was quite worn-out before the death of Muhamad Sháh, (1748): "the Seal," as a native historian says, "of the House of Taimur."

Of the condition of the people during the earlier, or Turkmán, period in Hindustan, we have little exact information. When the storm first began to gather upon the Northern hilltops, the Hindus were in a state of considerable culture and prosperity. They still possessed, in the Veda and the writings of its early commentators, a supposed basis of law, the apparent finality and shortcoming of which were reconciled to the wants of a growing society by something savouring of legal fiction: that is to say, the religious schools and orders developed the Canon, *pro re natâ*, by help of new precepts which appeared in the guise of supplementary tradition. Thus the law preserved the austere dignity of regulations for human conduct, arising out of a sort of cosmic necessity. The Gods and the Hindus being what they were, such-and-such principles were of eternal obligation: but their written record was not intended to be complete ; and details were to be dealt with, from time to time if they arose by the wisdom and inspiration residing in the bosom of the sages. It was a sort of Common-Law tempered by the Bench.

Of law, thus conceived and depending for sanction chiefly on the opinion of an acquiescent public, a formal digest appeared—probably in the Deccan—towards the end of the 11th century of the Christian era, when the Muslims of Ghazni had already gained the Punjab and were threatening the whole of Hindustan. This is the *Mitakshara* itself a birth from the school of Yájnavalkya and Manu, contemplating the ancient social framework. The old Aryan religious thought is still seen playing round normal ideas, or domestic habits, and taking an active part in the rules of the tribe and the family ; the *patria potestas*—as in ancient Rome, with the worship of the *Pitris* (ancestral manes) which in both systems formed the *sacra* of the *gens*—forming the basis of right and duty. Status is everything, contract is barely recognised. The performance of funeral rites is necessary to the repose of the dead and to the heir-ship of the surviving son, who required to hold the estate in order to meet what was a primary charge upon it. Out of this proceeded the continuity of families and tribes ; and its guarantee was provided for by the rules of adoption with the curious ceremony of the *Srádh*, originally a sort of All-Souls' day where the kindred entertained their dead, like Ulysses in the Odyssey. The ancient codes provide for the frame of suits : the archaic tribunal was a committee of the village elders ; and the procedure opened by a distraint of the defendant's cattle, by which device the burden of action and of proof was shifted from him who complained of wrong to him who was presumed to be the wrong-doer. The estimated value of the cattle became the stake, or sum-in-suit, and the losing party either forfeited his cattle or their price, according to the Court's decision.

REVIEW OF THE FOREGOING.

The classification of later and more scientific times did not go the length of furnishing distinct provinces for property according as it was real or personal. The distinction—so far as any existed—was drawn between property acquired from ancestors and property acquired by a man's own exertions. The rules for the devolution and transfer of these two classes differed from each other, as did from both those relating to the paraphernalia or peculiar chattels of married women.

The land in each village was held entirely, or for the most part, on common tenure: either the cultivation was by joint labour and expenditure, when the proceeds were brought into a general account for sharing profit and loss; or there was annual partition of land, so that each might cultivate his share separately. As strangers began to intrude, and ideas of individual ownership to be realised, a mixed method arose, and partitions became permanent. Indeed, some such system continues to be the typical township-constitution in the Punjab and parts of Hindustan down to the present day.

These customs and institutions, while giving to Hindu-life a certain tenacious strength, have kept it on a low evolutional level; and, in conjunction with the system of Caste, tended to give invaders the full benefit of the rule: *Divide et impera*.

Another result had been to develop the practice of particular arts and crafts, in particular races and situations. Architecture—the art which so largely affects and interprets men's thoughts in regard to private and public life; the comfort of men's lives and the splendour of their religious worship—became with the Hindus almost wholly a matter of decoration; their temples and palaces, starting from wooden structures and caves hewn out of the living rock, ignored the resources of the arch and covered only narrow and obscure spaces; while decoration, unconnected with construction and straying beyond the limits of taste, until it was pursued as an end, for its own sake alone, became grotesque; the sport of a wild polytheism.

But the Hindu workman remained; the patient skilful workman. To him has been given, more than to most other men, to be content with a seat on the lap of mother earth, and the tepid fanning of his native air; while his chisel plays over wood or stone, tracing the lines laid down for him; for so he earns his daily bread, with many holidays, and a happy ignorance of art-canons or vast designs; and when death comes to him he meets it with indifference, letting the unfinished pattern fall from his failing hand into that of his son long since trained for the office.

So far as our knowledge goes, the Turkman conquerors long viewed these things with stolid indifference. Those of the Hindus who resisted them did it without union and were beaten in detail. If they renewed resistance after conquest they were regarded as rebels, and scourged with fire and sword. If not, they received a contemptuous toleration which admitted of their being employed in services for which the rude invaders were unfit. The sculptures—nay, the very forms—of the early Saracen architecture of Delhi and Ajmere show the hand of the Hindu artificer; and the coins of the early kings tell the same tale in the character of their inscriptions, and in the bulls and mounted horses which had been common under the Hindu Rájas, but which no Muslim engraver would ever design. The risings of the "Rais and Ránas," and the frightful slaughter inflicted on them and their followers—when they did not submit—form but an incidental part of the story of the later kings of Delhi of the "Slave" line; and it is under Sultan Balban—who virtually ended that line—that the rude engraving of animals and the use of Hindu letters cease upon the coins.

It was, however, Alá-ud-din, the second of the Khilji Kings, who accentuated the distinction between the Hindus and Muslims, no longer as conquered and conquerors but as two hostile classes in the same community. The coins now assume a pure Muslim type—some being struck at Deogir in Deccan. The architecture is of a Moorish type, unblended with Hindu designs or material; under this ruler, in fact begins the first decorated Pathán order, his beautiful gateway in the southern wall of the Kutab mosque has pointed arches of a horse-shoe character, and the cupola rests upon rich pendentives, all foreign to the ideas of the Hindu labourers, and beyond their mechanical skill.

Yet we hear of no relations between him and his non-Muslim subjects save what might be supposed to prevail between a huntsman and his hounds. Even when obedient the most they could expect was their food. The Sultan seldom consulted lawyers; but on one occasion he deigned to take an opinion as to the rights of a Muslim ruler over heathen subjects; and the answer was to this effect:—

By the strict theory, the people must either accept Islám or be killed: but the humanity of the school to which the learned man belonged had provided an alternative in the *Jazia* or capitation. When called on to pay this the Hindus should remember how highly they are favoured, and show becoming submissiveness. Should the collector be pleased to spit in their faces they are to receive it as an attention, and put no difficulties in his way by turning aside. Thus they are to stand; the object being to show their due obedience and to promote the glory of Islám. For what says Holy Scripture? "They must either accept Islám, or be killed, or become slaves." Only as followers of Abu Hanifa can we allow them the privilege of the capitation-tax. But the Sultan was far from agreeing in this humane view, or limiting the Hindu payments to a fixed poll-tax: and he issued ordinances by which —could they have been enforced—no Hindu would have had any property, only earning the flour and milk necessary to keep him alive and in working order.

Thus, amid much suffering, the Hindus under the Turkmán

and Pathán dynasties, followed their own laws and customs in the Punjab, in Hindustan, and in some of the outlying provinces. In the southern regions they were still less molested; in a great part of those countries they long maintained autonomous States; and, even in those provinces that were under Muslim Governments, Hindus rose to places of trust and power, and the two races were often on good terms. It must, however, be confessed that of these things we have little direct knowledge, unless as to those parts whose semi-legendary history has been collected by the patient if somewhat credulous enthusiasm of the British historian of Rajputána.* Elsewhere, we catch only passing glimpses of the indigenous races. It may be supposed that the bulk of the people lived a quiet, industrious, and frugal life, only interrupted, from time to time, by calls to arms from their native leaders, the "Rais and Ránas," who are sometimes mentioned as being chastised for rebellion. They would regard their foreign conquerers, generally, as a burden laid upon them by angry gods; and would pursue their avocations, agriculture and petty trade, under the necessity of living, which even Alá-uddin was fain to recognise. The origin of the *lingua franca*, mentioned in its proper place as dating from the latter part of this period, is an indication of intercourse between them and the Muslims; while the law-reform that occurred about the same time shows that they must have been left, as the people of Greece were under the Ottoman Empire, in the enjoyment of their own institutions.

We can form no exact estimate either of the numbers of the population, or the amount of the public revenue under the earlier Muslim Empire of Hindustan. We neither know the normal extent of its dominions, nor the actual purchasing power of its money. The integer of account was, usually, the *tanka*; a Turkish silver coin of that name still circulates in

---

* Lieutenant-Colonel J. Tod, "Annals and Antiquities of Rajasthan," two vols. second edition, Madras. 1873.

Central Asia, equivalent in value to four-tenths of a franc. The crazy Juna attempted to introduce a coinage of copper tokens, but he had to call them in after a short trial, and at a prodigious sacrifice. The same monarch also lost many of the outlying provinces. Under his successor, who was only partially successful in recovering those provinces, the annual revenue was sixty-five millions of tankas, but as these coins may have been of copper, of mixed metal, of silver, or even of gold, this statement gives no information. (At a somewhat later date the silver tanka was equivalent to the rupee). At the end of the period under notice the revenue of the Empire acquired by Bábar (1526) is estimated by Erskine as equivalent to £4,212,000 of modern sterling.

The sources of this revenue (under Juna's successor) were :— first, the *Khiráj*, a tithe on agriculture, payable by Muslims and non-Muslims alike ; second, the *Jazia*, a duplication of the above, payable by non-Muslims only; and third, a fifth of war-prize and of the yield of mines.

The population may have been somewhere about 5,000,000 of Muslims, and 25,000,000 of others ; or say 35,000,000 in all including aborigines.

SECTION 2.—With the conquest of Hindustan by Bábar, the foundation of a more civilised system was undoubtedly begun. It was not, indeed, due directly to any superior administrative ability of the Mughals, or Chaghtai Turks, of whose levity and indolence notice has been already taken ; and it is to a native Muslim usurper that the beginning of good government in Hindustan must be attributed. We have had occasion to show in CHAPTER V. how much that great man attempted in the way of uniting the various races of Hindustan under a sound and vigilant administration. After the Mughal restoration the seed that Sher Sháh had sown came up. Akbar, Mughal though he was, had been tutored in the school of adversity. Early in his reign he employed officials whom Sher Sháh had formed ;

and this advantage, joined to his own earnest and benevolent character, led to a general and most beneficial extension of Sher Sháh's system under Akbar. The year 1580 may be taken as the date from which the Empire began to exist in its consolidated form. The recalcitrant rulers of the remoter provinces north of the Narbada had been reduced to obedience, the supremacy of the sovereign had been acknowledged in a document which may be regarded to some degree at least, as "a written constitution." No conquests had as yet been attempted south of the Narbada of the twelve Provinces which made up the Empire of that date, we may borrow the account given by Abul Fazl, written some years later, premising that the rupee had now been made the monetary integer. It has not been thought necessary to complicate the matter by adding the figures from the detailed rent-rolls; apparently they were prepared at another time, yet they do not exceed the other estimates very seriously, and perhaps only so because they included omitted items of Customs.

Each Province was on the scale of an average European kingdom of those days. The EASTERN PROVINCE (or Provinces, for it might be so regarded) consisted of Bihár, Bengal, and Orissa, a tract of the size of France, and assessed—under Akbar—at about one kror and a half. It was chiefly in the plains of the Lower Ganges, with the Brahmaputra on the East and the Mahanadi on the west, with chains of considerable elevation to north and south, and provided everywhere with abundant streams of water. The chief towns were Patna, Lakhnauti (Gaur) and Sátgaon, afterwards Hugli.

Moving westward one came to ALLAHABAD and AUDH ("Oude"), often united under the same Viceroy, and each resembling Bihár in scenery, situation, and character: the total area of the two together being greater than that of Ireland. The aggregate land-revenue was about a *kror* and a third. The city of Allababad, called Prayág by the natives, was at the

1. Bengal.
2. Bahár.
3. Orissa.
4. Oudh.
5. Delhi.
6. Agra.
7. Allahábád.
8. Lahor.
9. Kábul.
10. Ajmir.
11. Multan.
12. Málwa.
13. Gujerát.
14. Khándes.
15. Berar.
16. Gondwana.
17. Aurangábad.
18. Bijapur.
19. Bidur.

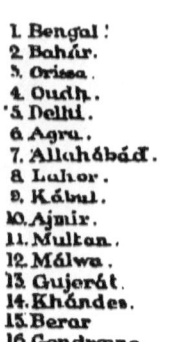

MAP of INDIA
(& the Deccan)
The Divisions of the Mughal Empire

junction of the Ganges and Jumna; and here Akbar built a great castle, still occupied by the British Government, and a place of strategic importance. Faizabad—near the ancient Hindu city of Ayodhya from which the Province took its name—was the capital of the Trans-Gangetic region.

AGRA—or Biána—was a compact division extending from Kálpi on the East to Riwári on the west—and from Aligarh, (Köel) to the southern limit of Narwar. The chief city—the Agar of the natives—was called Akbarábád, in honour of the Emperor. The fortress founded by him still subsists, and harboured the Christian residents and their followers during the troubles of 1857. The land-revenue from this large and fertile province was over two krors.

MALWA, a province formed out of a conquered kingdom, stretched from the borders of DEHLI and Gwalior (southern part of AGRA) to the GUJARAT frontier. The climate and fertility were famous: an ancient Hindi couplet avers that :—

"In Málwa land you are always fed,
One step water, next step bread."

MALWA was where Holkar now rules, and the chief towns in Akbar's time were Mandu and Ujain. The area was about equal to that of Audh (say, twenty-four thousand square miles), and the revenue about six hundred thousand rupees.

GUJARAT like MALWA, was an old Muslim kingdom annexed to the Empire in 1578. It was washed by the ocean, and contained the large peninsula of Kathiawár besides the province of Ahmadábad—on the mainland—in which the capital of the same name, was situated. The revenue exceeded a kror of rupees.

KHANDES, a small, but pleasant tract, lay between the Narbada and Tapti rivers : it was not wholly subjugated till 1601.

The so-called Subah of AJMERE was almost conterminous with the modern " Rájputána," and was held by various Hindu chiefs who may be regarded rather as allies than vassals. The country was hilly and unproductive; and the aggregate of the Rájas' tribute—estimated by Abul Fazl at five hundred and seventy-one thousand rupees—was only collected under compulsion. The Hindu chiefs were virtually independent, excepting that some of them were from time to time obliged to give their daughters in marriage to members of the Imperial house. They were there before the Mughals came, they are there after the Mughals have gone.

DEHLI was a province of average size, and the revenue from land was one and a half kror. The Khálsa, or demesne round the city, was valuable: in later reigns, indeed, it sometimes supplied almost all the needs of the Crown.

LAHORE was a province somewhat larger in extent, but yielding a nearly identical revenue: the capital—as in other cases—gave the province its name. It was a favourite residence with Akbar, and contained one of his fortified palaces.

MULTAN was a long strip of sandy country lying along the left bank of the Indus: the revenue was about four hundred thousand rupees. The capital—of the same name as the province—was a place of great strength, originally designed as a defence against invasion from the north-west.

THATTA gave the name to the valley of the Lower Indus which is now called Sindh. The revenue was not more than one hundred and sixty thousand rupees.

KASHMIR, with the adjoining hills of Swát, and Kábul, was the sub-alpine region of Asia's Italy: chiefly valued for climate and sport. The total revenue, in kind and specie, has been estimated at eight hundred thousand rupees. Balkh and Budakshán were outlying fragments inhabited by turbulent tribes, and of little account from the fiscal point of view.

Such was the Empire of Akbar, before he began to conquer in the Deccan: and the following further details may be noted as to the fiscal system.

A fixed standard of mensuration having been established, the soil was surveyed and classified, according as it might be waste, fallow, or under crop. The last of these classes formed the basis of assessment: that which produced cereals, vetches, or oil-seeds paying one-third of the estimated produce to the state, *in kind;* the rest was left the *Zamindár*—whom we may regard as a tenant-in-chief, or state-cultivator. But Akbar did all in his power to introduce cash payments into his service, and for this purpose—having little command of taxation proper or other revenue—he made a different sort of settlement on crops that were grown to be sold in the market; such as cotton and sugar. These paid *in specie*, at the same rate, only it was assessed on the estimated money value, instead of on the produce. This was a complete departure from the systems of his predecessors and later successors, who followed the law of Islám by virtue of which the non-Muslim subjects paid more than believers—about double it is thought.

Abul Fazl gives rates of pay, in cash, for all sorts of posts. Some of the high vassals, no doubt, were in possession of what may be called "fiefs," estates which they administered, and out of whose revenues they maintained the militia. It is related by Blochmann that when some of these nobles remonstrated with Akbar upon the great confidence that he reposed in Todar Mal, the Emperor good-humouredly replied by asking them, "who managed their estates?" and, on receiving the expected answer, said that he trusted that he also might have leave to confide the management of his estates to a Hindu.* In Akbar's reign, however, the chief military duties devolved on the regular army, who were paid in money, of which the purchasing power must be inferred from the recorded rates. The rupee was valued at forty *dáms*, and represented the value of three bushels of wheat, or half the price of an average sheep.† In the

---

* "Calcutta Review," vol. 52, p. 340.

† Akbar's rupee weighed 174·5 grains, and was nearly double the shilling of Elizabeth.

fortieth year of the reign (1596) the revenue "was fixed at the annual rental of 3,62,97,55,246 *dáms*, or Rs. 90,749,881. 2. 5." Adding up the detailed lists that followed we get a total of all but ten krors, and it seems that, excepting the miscellaneous items of customs which represent the difference between these two totals, the whole revenue was derived from land. A contemporary and fellow-official of Abul Fazl, by name Nizám-uddin Ahmad, says that it was "640 krors of *murádi tankas*," and as he must have meant much the same as his colleague, the integer he adopts may be taken as the indigenous copper *paisa* of the country, of which sixty-four went to the Rupee. Before the end of the reign, Khándes and Berar were annexed, yielding over two-and-a-half krors, and this explains the estimate of Coryat, in the following reign, that Jahángir succeeded, to a yearly revenue of "forty millions of crowns at six shillings each," say twelve krors of rupees.

Abul Fazl was a man of orderly mind, and his admiration for his hero is shown in minute detail of his public and private conduct, and otherwise than in the usual generalities of Oriental flattery. As a matter of course the information is not all of equal value. It is not important perhaps to know what was the price of ice, or how the household was supplied with drinking water; the general reader of three centuries later will hardly care whether the cheapest kind of velvet came from Gujarát, or from Europe. But we are more interested when we learn that the Emperor had an album containing portraits of all his chief officers, and that he openly expressed admiration for the art of portraiture, so generally discountenanced in Muslim countries. The manner in which his Majesty laid out his time, too, is fully stated, and bears the stamp of his character. He ate but once in the twenty-four hours, and sometimes abstained from flesh meat for months together. In the matter of sleep, Akbar was no less abstemious; sleeping a short time in the evening, and again before dawn, but passing the greater part of the night in debate or administrative business. In the last watch of the night there was a concert of music, after which the Emperor would rest till daybreak. He then rose and showed himself in a balcony, in front of which a crowd of people were collected; after that brief general audience, he would again retire. The forenoon was passed in the hall of state, where he received petitions, and dispensed justice. He had a sort of permanent Cabinet, many of his ministers being Hindus. The writer of another account confirms some of these statements. "Akbar," says the author of the *Dábistán*, "paid no regard to hereditary power or pedigree, but favoured those whom he found to excel in knowledge and in conduct." There was a peerage, a life peerage be it understood, of which the members were called *Mansabdárs*, classified according to the number of horsemen that they were supposed to lead; thus, princes of the blood were "leaders of five-thousand," and other degrees followed with lower numbers. The flower of the cavalry was a sort of bodyguard, consisting of gentlemen-cadets called "Ahdis," and corresponding to the "Exempts" of the old French monarchy; these were the sons or nominees of the peers, not entitled to succeed to hereditary dignity, yet having the advantage of beginning life in the Imperial household. Each of these young aspirants would be followed by one or more men-at-arms of inferior rank, they had the rank and pay of privates but were not liable to sentry or fatigue-duty. This is the corps of whose services we hear when the Emperor Jahángir was enlarged while Mahábat Khán was taking him to Kabul in 1625.

After describing the Empire as it was in the golden time of Akbar, Abul Fazl goes off into a description of other nations; and it is important to note that he particularly records a sympathetic account of the Hindus very different from the fastidious criticism of Babar, written about seventy years earlier. "The Hindus," says the friend and Minister of

Bábar's grandson, "are pious, affable, cheerful, given to study, lovers of justice, able in business, grateful, admirers of truth, and of an unbounded fidelity." He admits however, the grounds that had formerly existed for blaming their backwardness in material culture and comfort, and attributes a part of their advance to the care and wisdom of his master. Be this as it may, there is the indisputable fact that this foreign statesman evidently studied with kindly interest the tastes, thoughts, and habits of races hitherto treated with hatred and contempt. In doing so he obviously expected to please his Lord; and the appearance of the case goes some way to suggest that the manners of subject people are apt to be very much what their rulers make them.

It is for such reasons that the reign of Akbar, and the institutions that he founded or favoured, must be considered as typical. The reign of his son Jahángir was rather a period of negligence than of tyranny. He had his ideals, they stand on record in his own words, and they are not bad ones; though they have been severely criticised by Sir H. M. Elliot. He claims to have remitted transit-dues; but the evidence of European visitors of the period leads us to fear that this was rather of the nature of a "pious opinion" than of an actual measure of administration. The same doubt hangs over the assertion of measures for preventing highway robbery and the embezzlement of dead travellers' effects. The Emperor takes credit for promoting temperance among his subjects; unhappily he failed to practice that virtue in his own person. He says that he put down oppression; but Englishmen of Elizabethan times were not squeamish and some of them relate with loathing acts of oppression, done under the Emperor's orders, of which they were witnesses. Officials were forbidden to marry women in the districts under their authority without Government permission; a well-intentioned rule, though the Emperor broke it in his own case. His idea of public hospitals and dispensaries is to his credit: let us hope that it took effect. Of the remaining notions the like opinion holds good, they were useful if carried out, which we cannot be sure of; one of the most pleasing traits recorded of himself by Jahángir is the respect for his illustrious father's memory, of which he gave positive proof by a very fine mausoleum to be seen, near Agra, to the present day. Finch, an English traveller of that time says that the tomb was "much worshipped both by Moors and Gentiles, all holding Akbar for a great saint."*

Of the state of the country under Shahjahán something was said in our CHAPTER V., where it was shown that the Empire was in equipoise and that many favourable impressions were made upon Europeans competent to judge. The native historians are even more eulogistic; and, if we ought to judge a ruler by his own lights, their opinion is even more valuable, as showing the standard.

All that is vital and pregnant in the Muslim part of Indian history has now been reviewed: and the modern British administration has succeeded so far as it has taken hold of the ideas then introduced, in the three respects of revenue management, the employment of natives, and complete religious equality. We must now briefly notice the ill effects of a departure from sound views of these matters.

Shahjahán is said to have inherited a revenue of seventeen and a half krors; and the *Bádsháhnáma* gives that of twenty years later as twenty-two, adding the details for each Province.

By the middle of the reign of Álamgir all principles of moderation were flung to the winds: the Empire had reached its

* See article, by the late Prof. Blochmann, in "Calcutta Review" for 1869. He says "The memoirs of Jahángir do not contain one grand thought nor a trace that the author realised his exalted position": but that may be thought an overstatement.

extreme limits; but disaffection was rapidly loosening its cohesion. The map will show how great the nominal additions to the territory had been; for, excepting the extreme south of the Peninsula all India was under the nominal rule of the Mughal Empire: the Muslim kingdoms had been subverted, but their subversion had removed breakwaters against the rising tide of Mahratta ambition. North of the river Narbada a Hindu revival was being stimulated by persecution; the famous letter of Rána Ráj Singh, written about 1680, shows to what a pitch things were rising in the country of the chivalrous Rajputs, a people incapable of sympathising with the vulgar marauders of the Deccan, and by no means unwilling to be obedient subjects of the Emperors in whose veins ran so much of their blood. But the law of seven generations was at work, the impulse of the Mughals was exhausted. Their armies were cumbrous crowds of men-at-arms loosely disciplined and commanded by amateur officers. The Generals sate on elephants whose howdas were heavily plated with iron; whenever one of them was picked off by a hostile marksman his command dispersed; and if the chief leader fell the whole host fled and the fight was over. The artillery, except light culverins on camels, consisted of guns of position which were not moved without great delay and difficulty. The infantry consisted of archers, matchlockmen, and light companies armed with pikes. These hosts were constantly surrounded by the Mahratta horsemen, and could not move rapidly both by reason of their constitution and for want of supplies. When one or two chiefs had been disabled and the General-in-Chief was no longer visible in his howda, his men were wont to turn into a mob, only thinking of its own safety. "I am persuaded," said Bernier, at an early period of the reign, "that 25,000 veterans of Condé's army, led by a Turenne, would trample under foot all those armies." In point of fact, scarcely eighty years later, a force of 230 Frenchmen, with

REVIEW OF THE FOREGOING.   437

700 native infantry, but without either cavalry or guns, put to flight a Mughal army of 10,000 strong, horse, foot, and artillery, and took possession of their camp. This action took place near Madras in 1747, and was the foundation of all the later conquest of Europeans in India.

Álamgir's extended Empire makes a great show in the revenue estimates of the time. "Valuable MS. records" cited by E. Thomas, show the twenty-two krors of 1647 to have risen to twenty-four by 1655, and there are later estimates going as high as thirty-four krors. Manucci's detailed account may be compared with that given above for 1597. It will be observed that the assessments of Bengal and Gujarát had lately increased; and, as these were the provinces where the Portuguese and English had their treaty ports, the increase may be an indication of customs dues or other commercial profits. The total of the old Provinces answers fairly to the accounts given of Shahjahán's revenues. The annexations of Álamgir were recent when Manucci wrote, and are evidently not properly estimated.

Aurangabad, for example, which he calls Baglána, is shown by other writers to have ultimately borne a far higher assessment.

		Rs.
1.	BENGAL	4,00,90,000
2.	BIHAR	21,50,000
3.	ORISSA	57,07,500
4.	AUDH	1,00,50,000
5.	DELHI	1,25,50,000
6.	AGRA	2,22,03,550
7.	ALLAHABAD	77,38,000
8.	LAHORE	2,32,05,000
9.	KABUL	32,07,250
10.	AJMERE	19,00,000
11.	MULTAN	50,25,000

						Rs.
12.	MALWA	..	..	..	..	99,06,250
13.	GUJARAT	..	..	..	..	2,32,95,000
14.	KHANDES	..	..	..	..	1,11,05,000
15.	BERAR	..	..	..	..	1,58,07,500
16.	GONDWANA	..	..	..	..	Blank.
			TOTAL		..	21,67,10,550

Annexed by Alamgir.

17.	AURANGABAD	..	..	..	..	66,85,000
18.	BIJAPUR	..	..	..	..	5,00,00,000
19.	GOLKONDA	..	..	..	..	5,00,00,000
20.	BIDAR	..	..	..	..	72,00,000
			GRAND TOTAL		..	31,79,35,050

The last flicker of prosperity enjoyed by the House of Taimur was under the short reign of Aurangzeb's son. Then followed the bloodshed and confusion of the Sikh wars and the advance of the Mahrattas, the murder of one do-nothing sovereign after another, and the domineering of the king-making Sáyyads. A number of usurping provincials founded small states at the expense of the Empire, and when Nádir Sháh retired with the spoils of Delhi in 1738, the Empire was almost at its last gasp. Ten years later, when Muhamad Sháh died, a momentary flush arose from the success of his son over the invading Afgháns. But the country had almost ceased to be habitable by civilised men. A Persian traveller named Muhumad Házin had the fortune to go through the siege of Ispahán, and the Afghán conquest of his country, before taking refuge in India. He evidently thought his own country, under all its sufferings, preferable to Hindustan as a place of abode. "No man," he declared, "of his own choice will ever live in India; without compulsion he will never consent to a long residence there, . . unless he be one who unexpectedly arrives at wealth and distinction, and from lack of moral strength . . . becomes tranquil there, and habituates himself to the life."

SECTION 3.—Things, even then, were scarcely at their worst: the momentum of Government exhausted itself by slow degrees in Hindustan: in the Deccan its decay had taken place a little later, and the effects did not wear off so soon. Up to 1748, when the old Nizám died, the country about his capital of Haidarabad had been well ruled, so far as the constant greed and aggression of the Mahrattas would allow. But elsewhere the breakdown had already begun; and at the death of the Emperor Muhamad Sháh, in the same year, the whole of Hindustan was falling into anarchy. "After his demise," writes an able native historian, "everything went to wreck." Although the whole peninsula still owned the nominal sway of the Mughal Chancery of Delhi, no provinces remained in the actual possession of the Government officials, who only held a few districts on the left bank of the Sutlej, and a portion of the Upper Duáb. Gujarát was overrun by the Mahrattas; Málwa and Rajputána had ceased to pay tribute. The Játs were independent in the country between Agra and the Chambal River. About Gwalior and Ujain, Sindia was founding his power; the Bangash Patháns of Farrukhabad were in possession of the Central Duáb; Audh and Allahabad were ruled with quasi-royal state by Safdar Jang; the eastern provinces were subject to Ala Virdi and his line; the Mahrattas were supreme in the western Deccan; the rest of the South was under the rule or influence of the Nizám, save where the Hindu Rájas maintained a precarious autonomy.

But this revival of native local power was not the cause of much social welfare. With the example of the Nizám before mentioned the local dynasties did not concern themselves; and the country was in as wretched a condition as France after the Hundred Years' War. A native cited by Dow speaks of "every species of domestic confusion. Villainy," he adds, "was practised in all its forms; law and religion were trodden under foot, the bonds of private friendship and connection, as well as society and Government were broken, every individual, as if in a forest of wild beasts, could rely upon nothing but the strength of his own arm."

To a similar purpose is the testimony of another witness cited by Colonel Tod, the historian of Rajaputana:—

"The people of Hindustan at this period thought only of present safety and gratification. Misery was disregarded by those who escaped it, and man, centred only in himself, felt not for his kind. This selfishness, destructive of public and of private virtue, became universal after the invasion of Nadir Sháh."

The social degeneration went on almost to the end of the century. We are informed by Baillie Fraser on the authority of Colonel J. Skinner, C.B., who had trailed a pike in the service of Mahádaji Sindia from about 1790 to 1803, that Hindustan was actually becoming depopulated. "So reduced" he said, "was the actual number of human beings, and so utterly cowed their spirit, that the few villages that did continue to exist, at great intervals, had scarcely any communication with each other, and so great was the increase of beasts of prey that the little communication that remained was often cut off by a single tiger known to haunt the road."

Nor was the condition of Southern India much better. Of the moral character of the inhabitants of the Deccan we have the following opinion from a man of strong observation, but little given to strong language:—

"They are the most deceitful, mischievous race of people that I have ever seen or read of. I have not yet met with a Hindu who had one good quality; and honest Mussulmans do not exist." [Wellington's "Supplementary Despatches," 1797, etc.]

When we look at the India of to-day, North and South

REVIEW OF THE FOREGOING.

alike, we find a difficulty in believing that it is peopled by the near descendants of the beings thus described. The population is dense, almost too much so, but it is free from crime and orderly to an unusual degree. Roads, canals, railways, and busy manufacturing and commercial communities are everywhere to be seen. Five universities and nearly one hundred thousand public schools provide all grades of instruction; a large revenue is raised with a very low rate of incidence. The country has passed, in a few generations, from anarchy to the reign of law.

How great the work has been must be learned from the next volume. Our present task has been to show how great the need was, and in what difficult conditions it was begun. The first impression on anarchy in Hindustán, was made before Lake's conquest, by officers acting under Mahádaji Sindia.*

After the blinding of Sháh Álam by Ghulam Kadir, and when the new-model army had been thoroughly organised, General de Boigne held land at Aligarh; the pay of the officers and men being a first charge upon the rents: and this estate was gradually increased until it became a quasi-principality.

The time of the conquest Perron held as follows:—

		RUPEES.
Resumed Jagirs, 7; with yearly income		375,248
Talukas in Duáb, 4; ,, ,,		84,047
Districts W. of Jumna, 3; ,, ,,		65,000
In Saháranpore, 18; ,, ,,		478,089
In Duáb (original); ,, ,,		2,083,287
N. of Jumna (original) ,, ,,		1,031,852
	Total, say,	4,112,523

---

* v. "Madhava Ráo, Sindhia," Rulers of India series; Oxford, 1892. The spelling of the name in the text is taken from an authentic seal in possession of Mr. L. Bowring, C.S.I.

The original holding was of the value of some twenty lakhs (say two millions sterling) per annum; gradually increased to more than double of that income; and with that security for their pay and confidence in the honour and promises of their Savoyard chief, the troops became patterns of good conduct. In an English newspaper of the time we are told that the men submitted to General de Boigne's " discipline and civilisation, and . . . the rapacious licence which had formerly been common . . . came at last to be looked upon as infamous even by the meanest soldier " (" Bengal Journal," 1790.) The "civilisation" introduced among the troops would form a type for the surrounding population; naturally mild and orderly, and finding themselves no longer robbed or oppressed by their professed guardians, they would turn to their squalid homes and long-neglected fallows with some hope of finding a profit in honest industry. Like the great Pathán ruler, Sher Sháh, the General knew that the proper price of a high position is strenuous and increasing labour. He rose at dawn and continued at work nearly all day; surveying stores and factories, inspecting troops, hearing reports from civil officials and passing orders thereon, receiving visitors, carrying on diplomatic business, and attending to his own private concerns. Yet we have undoubted evidence that all this industry was unavailing to the production of any great change in the immediate present of the people. The attention of the foreign administrator—in the direction of civil work—must have been much absorbed by the collection of the revenue; for that was the keystone of every duty and interest committed to his charge. Crime might elude punishment, decree-holders might have to wait for the execution of their decrees; but a village in arrear could not be allowed to set an example the following whereof might mean bankruptcy, mutiny, and total failure. The usual method employed was farming to the highest bidder, who naturally rack-rented the cultivators; and the same plan must have affected the lands held in recompense of feudal service—though these latter were in the immediate neighbourhood of Aligarh, they perhaps benefited from their nearness to headquarters. But a brigade was always quartered at Sikandrábad, a few miles south of Delhi, for the express purpose of aiding in the collection of revenue; and if any farmer who was in balance refused to pay up he brought on his village the penalty of plunder and destruction; life being often sacrificed in these violent fiscal measures. The arrangements for judicial work were of the crudest; there was a native official whose duty it was to collect the reports of the local revenue-officers, and, so far as these might contain penal matters, submit them for the General's final decision : no formal confronting of accused and witnesses being attempted, before he passed his sentence. [The Governor of a British Presidency had at one time a similar jurisdiction: sentences of death and of acquittal being confirmed in Council, after deliberation, with closed doors, down to 1793.] Nor did anyone venture on a show of wealth or display of personal comfort: such a possession as a masonry-built house, even in Aligarh itself, being regarded as an index to taxation. Even in De Boigne's time "people lived in a low state, both as regards food and clothes; their marriages were not costly, and none of their females dared wear jewels. The well-to-do accumulated money and could not enjoy it: they buried it under ground; and often died without letting their family know the place of its concealment . . . The bazaar street of the city was very narrow in Perron's time: neither he nor De Boigne ever paid any attention to the improvement of the people." ("History of Aligarh, by an old resident." *)

The "old resident" was writing from tradition, and, perhaps, did scant justice to De Boigne, whose turn was for benevolent ædileship, as he sufficiently showed at Chambéri after his return to his native country.† But the general impression remains,

---

* "Delhi Gazette," 5th June, 1874.

† v. "Mémoire," etc., by his son, Count C. de Boigne, Chambéri, 1829; also Tod's "Rajasthan," vol. 1, p. 765.

with the feeling that, if well-intentioned European officers could do no more for the people, the country must have fared still worse under the Muslim and Hindu chiefs of that bad time. The Talukdárs of Hindustan, as a matter of fact, were a set of robber-barons, who levied contributions right and left, so that it was hardly worth while either to raise or to distribute produce. So late as the second quarter of the nineteenth century the "Meerut Universal Magazine" stated that in Begam Samru's principality of Sardhana armed soldiers had to patrol the fields to enforce cultivation; and it is on record that she levied transit dues on every kind of goods entering or leaving her territory down to her death in 1836. .

From State-papers written so near the close of the anarchic period as 1808 we obtain confirmation of the above-recorded descriptions. A Board having been formed to construct a system of administration for the "ceded and conquered Provinces," reports were called for from local officials which show the miserable condition into which the land had fallen. The Collector of Aligarh recommended cautious measures in regard to the appraisement of assets for the purpose of fixing the State's demand; stating that the land, owing to long misrule, famine, and war, had lapsed into a quasi-wild condition. He anticipated an increase of cultivation and of revenue—should six years of peace follow—which he reckoned at 32 per cent. In Etáwa, lower down the Duáb, matters were no better. "Foreign invasion," wrote the District-officer, "and intestine tumult, had materially checked population, whilst the poverty of the country and the capacity of its governors had almost annihilated commerce. Elsewhere it was noted that "the form of Government which had existed had not operated to relieve the necessities of the subject or to improve the resources of the Empire by the encouragement of husbandry and commerce. The exertions of the yeomanry have been discouraged and means of cultivation denied them. Agriculture, as a consequence, has languished and declined." Every Talukdár had his "customs-platform," where goods in transit were systematically stopped and taken toll of. "It is a matter of fact," says a good authority, "that in those days the highways were unoccupied, and the travellers walked through bye-ways." Skinner and Gardner, two good officers from the Mahratta service, patrolled the roads with parties of horse; but the gangs broke out as soon as their backs were turned under the Ját and Bargoojuar chieftains.

In the southern part of India matters were, if possible, worse. Writing of the period between 1763 and 1783, the able author of Forbes's "Oriental Memoirs" says that the Mahratta Governor of Poona was inattentive to the misery of the people, whom "his deputy oppressed in a cruel manner. Venality and corruption guide the helm of State and pervade all departments. From the chieftains and nobles to the humblest peasant in a village, neither the property nor the life of a subject can be called his own." He confirms the resident of remote Aligarh as to the fear of show; the man who has saved a little hoard "makes no improvement, lives no better than before, and buries it in the earth without informing his children of the concealment."* On the other side of the country Mountstuart Elphinstone records a curious conversation with a begging friar near the temple of Jagannath so late as 1801. "He spoke to us without any respect . . . called us to him, but would not let us pass his boundary. When we were near he said ' Listen ! When will you take this country ? This country wants you. The Hindus are villains. When will you take the country?' We answered ' Never !' He said ' Yes, you will certainly take it.'"

* "Oriental Memoirs," 2 vols. London, 1813. Further information as to the condition of various parts of Hindustan are to be found in "Aleegurh Statistics," by Hutchinson and Sherer; Roorkee, 1856, and "Selections from Revenue Records," Allahabad, 1873.

"The country wants you," that was the true saying of an unaccredited but competent representative. It would be unbecoming for British writers to lay stress on the fact. And it must be confessed that the assumption of power in India by Clive and Wellesley was not usually an unbiassed answer to the appeal of the suffering masses. Nevertheless it was a good deed, and bore the promise of salvation to the people of India.

The glimpses that our narrative has afforded of the condition of the natives in the past have shown us a people afflicted with chronic warfare and misrule. In spite of the experts, we cannot exactly compare the taxation of by-gone times with more recent demands.* But we know that Akbar took off fifty-eight minor items, and cut down the land-revenue—his chief remaining resource—to a demand of one-third of the gross produce. Yet the result was an annual income of one hundred millions of rupees, each rupee being equivalent to over a hundred-weight of corn, or the food of a man for three months. The addition of four more Provinces and the imposition of the Hindu poll-tax brought up the revenue in 1697 to nearly fourfold that amount; so that without customs, opium, stamps, and other modern resources, and with money worth three times its present local value, the Mughals raised, from the comparatively small population subject to them, considerably more, in actual amount, than the British Government derives from the same source.†

But instead of drawing comparisons with the administra-

---

* v. conflicting statements in "Imperial Gazetteer," vol. VI., 2nd edit., 299-300. See also revised statements and notice by Mr. Stanley Lane Poole in "Indian Empire," by Sir W. Hunter; 3rd edit., 1893.

† The land revenue of British India has been nearly stationary for some years, at about two hundred and thirty millions of rupees per annum. The wage of unskilled labour and the pay of a soldier have trebled since. 1590, as has also the price of food.

tion of the Mughals, which had ceased before British rule began, let us confine our attention to the conditions of the last century. We may then feel less unwilling to accept the complimentary sentiments expressed by a distinguished Russian publicist now, unhappily, departed.*

"In reality," wrote the late Michael Katkoff—in spite of his being the accredited champion of the narrower Muscovite patriotism—"the English have been the saviours of India. During whole centuries the history of India presents one continued spectacle of murder and devastation. The bloody era terminates with the conquest of India by the English, whose rule has been incomparably more mild, human, and just, than all the Governments under which the Hindus have ever lived."

What the Russian publicist rightly considers the beginning of the new era in India was entered upon when Lord Mornington destroyed French influence, beat down Tipu, and made all Native States accept the arbitration and political control of his Government. This is distinguishable, no doubt, from a "conquest of India," which has never been either possible or desired. But the foundations were laid for a social and political fabric in which the various populations of the vast peninsula should hereafter meet in unity and order; and the work was not the less certain because it was in a future, however remote; nor the less grand and imposing because it was done in the name of a commercial syndicate.

Nor had these unprecedented results been due solely, or even chiefly, to the vain resistance of the people. The native armies, indeed, had been frequently conquered; but we have seen what those armies were, tumultuous disorganised throngs of mercenaries, without patriotism, cohesion, or good general-

---

* M. Katkoff died 1st August, 1887, having made his paper, "The Moscow Gazette," the most influential journal in Russia. It is from this journal that the above sentences are quoted.

ship. Two thousand years had passed since Hippocrates pointed out the secret of such successes as those of Themistocles: "Oriental armies," he said, "fought only for their master, whereas Europeans fought for themselves." And so it was still; and it may be fairly doubted whether the bulk of Tipu's forces felt a stronger interest in the prosperity of the "God-sent State" than did the French adventurers who drilled the infantry of that—or any other—Indian power.

Neither had there been—at least, up to the time of Lord Mornington—any deliberate design of becoming paramount on the part of the rulers of England. Clive had restored the territories of the Audh Nawáb when he had beaten him at Baksár; and he laid down the rule that British authority in Bengal ought never to pass the Karamnása; a little stream bounding the old Province of Bihar on the north-west. Warren Hastings made over the district of Guntoor to the Nizám's brother, and was ready to surrender the Northern Sirkars. Cornwallis proposed to make Bombay a treaty-port; and in 1782, the Home-Government was prepared to abandon Fort St. George and the Carnatic to the Nawáb. And yet the god Terminus continued to advance; here, provoked by jealousy of France, there pushed on by the need of resistance to other powers; until, at length, the chief of the Calcutta counting-house had become the arbiter among a crowd of princes, and and supreme disposer of the fortunes of many millions of humble human beings.

Yet, for all that had been done, there was still no national unity; India, like medieval Italy, was but "a geographical expression." To give some notion of the multiplicity of divisions existing when Mornington assumed the government, a list is appended, taken from the work published at the time by the Surveyor-General.*

---

* Rennell's "Map of India," (v. inf.)

REVIEW OF THE FOREGOING. 449

BRITISH POSSESSIONS.—Bengal, Bihar, and Benares; northern Sirkars and Guntoor, Báramahal and Dindigal, Jágir of Madras, Calicut and Palikat.

BRITISH ALLIES.—Audh, Carnatic, Travancore, Tanjore.

MAHRATTA STATES. — Poona Mahrattas, Khandés, Gujarát, Bijápur, Duáb of the Krishna and Tunga-Bhudra rivers.

ALLIES AND FEUDATORIES.—Sindia's dominions and the Delhi territories, Rajputána, Bundelkhand, Bhopál, Minor States.

BERAR STATES.—(Nagpur, Orissa, etc.)

THE NIZAM.—The Deccan, with Cadapa, Gooti, and other districts taken from Tipu.

TIPU.—Mysore and parts of Malabar.

[Besides the Sikh and Rohilla states in the north and northwest, and the country round Bhurtpore held by the Játs.]

From which it appears that, in addition to scattered possessions of their own (inhabited by races whose speech was not intelligible to each other) the British held two Muslim and two Hindu principalities in subsidiary alliance; i.e., virtual dependence. There were, under Mahratta rule no less than eleven vast and various countries; while two powerful and well-armed Muhamadan princes ruled the remainder of the southern region.

If, therefore, up to the point at present reached, there has been but little information as to the social state and progress of the people, and our narrative has seemed to dwell almost exclusively on the wars and intrigues of selfish or contentious public men, let it be considered that we have been necessarily confined to such matters by the very nature of the case. In the next portion of our study—though we shall not be entirely free from such subjects—we shall have the satisfaction of observing the unmistakable advance of the Indian races to a united nationality and a common civilisation.

G G

[Some curious, and often wonderfully correct, information as to the pre-British condition of the peninsula will be found in "Memoir of a Map of Hindustan," &c., by James Rennell, F.R.S., late Major of Engineers, and Surveyor-General of Bengal, 4to, London, 1793. See also Tieffenthaler; "Description de l'Inde," 3 v., 4to, Berlin, 1788.]

END OF VOL. I.

INDEX TO VOL. I.

Abdáli; or Ahmad Sháh, Dauráni, invades Hindustan, 184; returns (1757), 200; again enters India, 208.

Abul Fazl; introduced at Court, 130-2; sent to Deccan, where he conquers Ahmadnagar, and is murdered on his way back, 141; account of Hindus by, 142.

Adham Khán; half-brother of Akbar, his crimes and punishment, 128-9.

Ahalia Bai; good and popular Lady of Indore, 224; decline of her faculties and consequent increase of Tukáji's power, 300.

Aibak; v. Kutb-ud-din.

Ain Akbari; Institutes of Akbar, 141-3; (v. Abul Fazl.)

Akbar; accession, 127; adopts system of Sher Sháh, 131; religious liberalism, 131-3; reasons of failure, 134-5; employment of Hindu generals, 137; decline and death of, 141-2; principal events of Akbar's reign (1556-1605), 127-42.

Akbar Mirza; son of Aurangzeb, 169-70, 172.

Akbar Sháh; succeeds Sháh Álam (1806), as King of Delhi and titular Emperor, 386; his futile attempts to get increased allowances, 398.

Álamgir; title of Aurangzeb, 157; revenue at accession (1659), 158; character of early administration, 159-60; absence of facts regarding, 161; trouble with Hindus, 163, 167; date of bad fortune, 165; persecutes, 167-9; troublous close of reign, 170-3; state of India under, 173-5.

Alá-ud-dín, Khilji; murders his uncle and becomes Sultan at Delhi (1296), 75; his mad pride, 76; success in military business, 77; death (1315), 78.

Alexander; invasion of India, 30.

Aligarh; stormed by General Lake, 361.

Ali Gauhar; Mirza, v. Sháh Álam II., 208.

Ambér; v. Jaipore.

Amir Khán; chased by Lake, 375; associated with Jaswant Ráo, Holkar, in plundering Rájput States, 387; warned off from Nágpore by Minto, 397.

Aryans; their migrations, 22-23.

Asaf-ud-daula; Nawáb of Audh, succeeds Shujá (1775), 233; his weakness, 238, 299; death (1797), 311.

Asai; v. General A. Wellesley.

Asoka; his reign and edicts, 34-36.

Audh; principality founded (c. 1731), 181, under Barlow, 387, 406 (v. Shore).

Aurangzeb; son of Sháh Jahán, his rebellion, 157; v. Álamgir.

Bábar; Záhir-ud-din, 96; invades Punjab (1524), 97; encounters army of Hindustan at Pánipat (1526), 98; victorious, 100; his memoirs, *id.*; war with Sanga Ráno, 101-3; takes Chandairi,

104; founds Empire, 105; death and burial, 106.
Bahádur Sháh; conquers his brother near Agra (1707) and assumes Empire, 176.
Bahlol Lodí; his reign (1451-88), 94.
Báhmaní; Muslim Kingdom, breaks up (1527), 114.
Baillie; defeat of, at Pollilore (1780), 260-1.
Bájí Ráo; becomes Peshwa (1796), 310.
Baksár; battle of, and consequent treaty, 220.
Balban; rise, 66-7; ministry, 68; becomes Sultan, 69; reign and conquests, 70-71; death, 72.
Barlow, Sir George; his accession and character, 383; opposed by Lake, 384; Minto's views of him, 389; Governor of Madras, *id.*
Begam Samru, or **Sombre**; succeeds to Samru's jágir, 239; harsh, but efficient administration, 359, 444.
Benares; policy of W. Hastings towards Rája of, 240-1; successful opposition to police-rate (1812), 407.
Bengal; (v. Bihár), annexed to Delhi (1324), becomes independent (1351), 89-113; v. table at 116; foundation of dynasty at Murshidabad, 181; invasion by Mahrattas (1742), 183; how ruled from Clive to Warren Hastings, 222; severe famine (1770), 223; v. Permanent settlement.
Bhagwán Dás, Bihári Mál, Mán Sinh, three Rájput chiefs patronised by Akbar, 129-30.
Bihár and **Bengal**; early dynasties, 49.
Bijainagar; v. Vijainagar.
Black Hole; v. Siráj-ud-daula.
Boigne, Benoit de, Savoyard general in service of Sindia,
269-275; remodels the army (1789), 294-5; conquers Mughal-Mahratta confederacy at Pátan and Merta, 295-8; beats Holkar's army at Lakhairi, 301; retires, succeeded by Perron, 314.
Brahmans; their origin, 20-22.
Buddhism: its origin, 27-29.
Bundelkhand; pacification of, under Minto, 390, *f.f.*
Bussy, M. de; tranquilising influence in Deccan, 192; illtreated by Nizám Ali, 195; recovers power, 196; leaves Deccan, 205; returns to India (1783), 265; death of, *id.*
Buxar; v. Baksár.

Calcutta; early history, 192-3; could not be a treaty port, 193; conferred by Imperial patent (1717), 194; attacked by Nawáb (June, 1756), 194-5.
Camac, Col.; commands against Sindia (1781), 237.
Canals; Hindustan, 6.
Carnac; British commander; relations with Mir Kásim and Sháh Alam, 214-5; commands after Baksár, 220; failure at Wadgáon (1779), 235.
Carnatic; disputed succession, 190; English recover influence (1752-4), 191; Nawáb mediatised (1801), 333; v. Haidar, Madras, Nizám, Tipu.
Chandernagore; captured by Clive (Feb. 1757), 198.
Chinese Pilgrims; 41-43.
Clive; his first appearance as a soldier, 190; fights French (1751-2), 191; sent to relieve Bengal, 196; advances on Plassy, 202; assumes government, 204; settles Bengal (1765), 220; retires (1767), 221.
Company, E.I.; 150, change in its policy (1773), 266; Charter (1793), 290.

INDEX. 453

Coote, Sir Eyre; beats Lally at Wandewash, 207; irritates Mir Kásim (1761), 215; acts against Haidar in Carnatic, 262, *f.*

Cornwallis; comes to Calcutta as Governor (1786), 268; support of British Ministry, 272; seeks friendship of Poona, 279; moves in strength upon Mysore (1792), 281; revenue reforms, 283, *f.f.*; other reforms, 290; retirement, 291; second administration, 377-83.

Dára; Sultan, son of Sháh Jahán, assumes regency (1657), 156; defeated at Samoghar, 157; decapitated, 158.

Dáyabhága; Hindu code of Bengal, 107.

Deccan; 8, 11, 40; state in Middle Ages, 72–4; divisions and dynasties in Middle Ages, 73-4, 85, 108, and 110; v. also Note at p. 111, and table 116, *f.f.*; Muslims of; mediæval wars and revolutions, 108-111; disputed succession to Nizám, 189.

Deogiri; in Deccan, become tributary to Delhi (1309), 77; becomes seat of a Muslim government (1312), 78.

Diwáni; grant of; v. Baksar.

Dupleix; Governor of French India, 189-191.

Dutch; rise and fall of power in India, 150.

Dynasties, of India before Mughal Empire, 116, *ff.*

Dynasty or Constitution; its average duration, 420.

East India Company; rise, 150-1; changes in position, 232, 266, 410.

Elphinstone, Mountstuart; sent as Envoy to Sháh Shujá, 396.

English; v. East India Company, 150.

Erskine; indirect apology for administration of W. Hastings, 267.

Fa Hian; v. Chinese pilgrims.

Fatehpur-Sikri; palace of Akbar, 131, 132.

Firoz Tughlak; accession (1351) 87; founds city of Firozábád near Delhi, 88; limits of his Empire, *id.*; love of public works and beneficent reign, 89; abdicates (1388) 90.

Forde, Col.; conquers Northern Sirkars, 205-6.

French; in India, 152; v. Carnatic, Dupleix, Lally, Madras, Pondicherry.

Ghází-ud-din, the younger; in power at Delhi (1753) 200; murders Emperor Alamgir II. and flies (1759) 208.

Goa; described, 149.

Goddard; British Commander, his march and victories, 235.

Gujarát; Muslim State (founded 1376), 114; (1531), 120; settled by Lord Cornwallis, 299; conquered for Akbar (1561), 128.

Gupta dynasty, 39.

Gwalior; campaign of 1780-1, 236-7.

Haidar "Naik"; or Hyder Áli, born (1722), 186; origin and rise, 248-9; beats Madras army, 251-2-3; Treaty of 1769, 253; conquers Coorg, 254; submits to Raguba, 255; threatens the Company, 256; insults Madras envoy (Gray), 257; invades the Carnatic, 258; defeats Col. Baillie, 261; devastates country, 262; defeated by Coote, 263; dies, 264.

Hampi; (Bijainagar or Vijainagar), in Middle Ages, 107.

INDEX.

Hariána; under Thomas, 326; settled by Minto, 392.

Harris, Gen.; Mil. Sec. to Gen. Medows (1762), 280; his loyal efforts to prepare for war against Tipu, 317; neglected by Governor-General, 321.

Hassan Gangu; founds dynasty in Deccan (1347), 86; death of (1358), 108.

Hastings, Warren; Governor of Bengal (1772), 231; Governor-General under Regulating Act, 232; aids Nawáb against Rohillas, 232-3; disputes with Francis, 234; duel with ditto, 242; character of his administration, 242-3-6; succeeded by Macpherson, 268.

Hému; a Hindu chandler, commands army of Patháns, 126; defeat and death of, 127.

Hindu drama; picture of manners, 42-50.

Hinduism; rise and character, 46-48; its abuses and need of reform, 108.

Hindus; their chiefs recognised by Delhi Sultans, 81.

Hindustan; condition in 1761-4, 218-9.

Hindustáni; language, its origin, 82.

Hippocrates; view of difference of Oriental and Western armies, 448.

Hiwen Tsiang; v. Chinese pilgrims.

Holkar (Tukáji); his rise, 226-300; war with Sindia, 301; death, 315.

Jaswant Ráo; his rise, 315-335; victory over Sindia's army at Poona, 340; provokes war (1804), 375; makes treaty with Lake, 385; plunders Rájputs, 387-8; his drunken habits, 388; death, 401.

Hoysala Ballálas; obscured by Muslim conquest in Deccan (1347), 113.

Humaiun, Emperor; wars, exile, and restoration, 120-6.

India; described generally, 1, *f.f.*; northern region, 5-7; southern region, v. Deccan; ethnology, 12-16.

Intervention, and non-intervention, 387-8, 390.

Ibrahim Lodi; his reign, 95, 100.

Iltimsh; Sultan at Delhi, 61-64.

Jáfir Ali; v. Mir Jáfir.

Jáfir Khán, viceroy of Daulatábád, v. Hassan Gangu.

Jahándár Sháh; Emperor (May, 1711), short reign, 178.

Jahángir (Mirza Salim); succeeds Akbar, by title of, 143; his futile reign, 143-4; dies in camp, 145.

Jaipore, or Jaipur, Rájput State, formerly called Ambér, 129: capital removed by Jai Sinh II., 181.

Jai Sinh I.; ruler of Ambér, or Dhundar, commands army for Dára, 157; dies, 165.

Jai Sinh, II.; founds Jaipore, 177: death (1743), 184.

Jalal-ud-din (v. Khiljis), murdered (1290-6), 74,5.

Jaswant Ráo, v. Holkar.

Jaswant Sinh; Rája of Márwar or Jodhpore, shares command of army (1664-5), 165, dies at Kábul (1678), 167.

Játs; first efforts of, near Agra, 171; join Hindu confederation (1759), 209; subdued by Mirza Najaf, 233.

Jaunpore; Muslim power at (1393-1478), 114.

Juna, or Muhamad Tughlak; succeeds his father, 84; founds Daulatábád (1328), 85; crazy administration, *id.*; death and burial, 86.

INDEX. 455

Kafur; General under Alá-ud-din, his rise, 77 ; and fall (1312), 78.
Kai Kobád; Sultan (1287-90), 72.
Kámbaksh; younger son of Alamgir, defeated and killed, 176.
Kanishka; great Buddhist council under, 37.
Kardla; defeat of Nizám Ali at, (1795), 309.
Kásim Ali Khán; Nawáb of Bengal, v. Mir Kásim.
Katkoff, M.; Russian journalist, on British India, 447.
Khafi Khán; nature of his narrative, 161-2.
Khiljis; rise of dynasty, 72 ; their system, 81.
Khizr Khán; founds Sayyid dynasty, 93; succeeded by Mubárak, *id.*
Khurram; Sultan, v. Sháh Jahán, 144.
Khusru, Malik; assumes power at Delhi (1321), 79 ; overthrown and killed (August, 1321), 81.
Kutb-ud-din Aibak. 59, 61.

Lake; his great campaign (1803-4), 361, *f.f.*; fails at Bhurtpore, 377 ; crippled by Barlow, 384-6.
Lally, Count ; his character and relations with the civilians of Pondicherry, 205 ; besieges Madras (1758-9), 206; retreats to Wandewash, and is there defeated by Coote, 207.
Lodi; dynasty at Delhi, founded by Sultan Bahlol, 93-4 ; appreciation of specie under, 95 ; overthrown by Bábar (1526), 98-100.

Macpherson, Sir J.; succeeds Hastings in India, 268.
Madhu Ráo Naráyan; infant Peshwa, scandal as to his paternity, 293 : visited by Sindia, 300-302 ; death, 310.
Madras; (Fort St. George), foundation of factory and fort (1639), 151 ; taken by La Bourdonnais (1746), 188 ; restored under treaty of Aix-la-Chapelle, *id.*; besieged by Lally, 206 ; general incapacity and misconduct at (from 1766 to 1789), 250, 262, 265, 279, etc. ; relations with the Carnatic, 249, 255 ; mutiny of officers (1809), 398, *f.f.*
Mahábat Khán, or Zamánat Beg ; a General under Jahángir, captures Emperor and Empress, and on their freeing themselves flies to the Deccan, 145.
Mahmud of Ghazni; the iconoclast, 54.
Mahrattas; rise (1636), 163 ; affairs at Alamgir's death, 176 ; constitution during eighteenth century, A.D., 183 ; invade Bengal, 183; threaten Hindustan and Punjab, 201. Confederacy, how constituted, 293 ; virtually dissolved, 343.
Malcolm, John; employed in disbanding French force at Haiderabad, 315 ; Envoy to Persia (1800), 333 ; a second mission (1807), 397.
Málwa; united to Mamelukes (or Slave-dynasty), subverted, 72 ; given to Hindu Viceroy afterwards reduced by Mahrattas (1732), 181 ; Hasám-ud-din founds Mándu, 115 ; conquered by Rána of Chittore, 115.
Megasthenes; resides at Palibothra, 31 ; his account of India. 32-34.
Metcalfe, Charles; Envoy to Ranjit Sinh (1808), 393 ; his great success, 395 ; Resident at Court of Delhi, 397.
Minto, Earl of; takes charge of Government (1807), 389 ; his views, and difficulties, 390-3 ; takes Mauritius, 402 ; and Java, 403, *f.f.*; troubles with missionaries, 408, *f.f.*; superseded,

410; ill-success in finance and revenue, 411, *f.f.*
Mir Jáfir; betrays his master (1758), 202; made Nawáb of Bengal by Clive, 204; deposed by Calcutta Council, 211.
Mir Kásim; made Nawáb by Calcutta Council, 211; murders Ellis and defies British, 217; flies to Audh, *id.*; death (1777), 233.
Mitákshara; digest of Hindu law so-called, 111.
Moira, Earl of; useful to Prince-Regent, 405, 410; takes charge from Minto (1813), 419.
Monson, Colonel the Hon. W.; his disaster in Rajputan, 376.
Mornington, Earl of; arrives to take charge of Government of India (May, 1798), 313; made a Marquess for conquest of Tipu Sultan, 321; tenders resignation (1802), 334.
Mountstuart Elphinstone; *v.* Elphinstone.
Mughals; their original character, 91; the new Mughals, 96; characteristics of new, 120; defeated by Patháns under Sher Sháh (1540), 122, *f.f.*; restoration (1555), 126; Empire, establishment and equilibrium (1556-60), 127-60; decline, 160, *f.f.*; provinces and revenues, under Akbar, 428; under Álamgír I. (Aurangzeb), 437; breaking-up, 439; note on revenues under Akbar, Jahángír, and Sháh Jahán, 147; relations with Europeans, 155.
Muhamad-bin-Sám; conquers Punjab, 57; murdered by Ghakkárs, 59.
Muhamad Sháh; Emperor (1719-48), 179-81.
Munro, Hector; British Commander, *v.* Baksár, *v.* Baillie.
Munro, Thomas; his views on land-revenue favoured by Lord W. Bentinck when Governor of Madras, 416; adopted in great part of the territory, 417.
Muslims; early movements, 51; invasions of Upper India, 52-57.
Mysore; Hindu State in South India, 185-6; *v.* Haidar and Tipu.

Nádir Sháh; invades Hindustan (1738), plunder of Delhi and consequences, 182.
Najaf Khán; Mirza, advises Emperor on recommendation of Clive (1760), 223; Governor of Kora (1766), 224; quarrels with the Mahrattas (1773), 227; administration, 229, 239.
Najíb Khán (afterwards Najíb-ud-daùla); Minister at Delhi, 210; dies (October, 1770), 225.
Nána Farnavís; Mahratta statesman, 237, 293; tenders resignation (1793), 302; hostility to Sindia, 303; decline of influence, 310, 323.
Nand Kumar; first appearance (1757), 198; patronised by Mir Kásim, 221; his intrigues and death, 234.
Násir-ud-dín; his reign, 65-9
Nizám; Chin Killich Khán, Asaf Jáh, founds State, under the title at Haidarábád, Deccan, 179; departs from Court at Delhi, 180; good government, 180-4; dies (1748), 185.
Nizám Áli; son of Asaf Jáh, succeeds, and attempts to assert authority in Carnatic, 249; *v.* Kardla, also Raymond.
North-West Provinces; beginnings of settlement, 415, 417-18.
Nur Jahán; wife of Emperor Jahangir, 144.

Orangal; capital of Hindu king-

INDEX. 457

dom of Telingána, 73-4; taken by Sultan Alá-ud-din (1309), 77; taken again (1323), 83; recovered by Hindus, 85, 93; destroyed by Muhamad Báhmani (1422), 113.
Orissa; famine of, 1770, 222.

Pánipat; great fight between Muslims and Mahrattas (ends January 13, 1761), 213-14.
Pathán Kings of Delhi; who so called, 80.
Permanent Settlement; revenue policy of Cornwallis in Bengal, 284, *f.f.*
Perron; French officer in Sindia's service, succeeds De Boigne, 314; his great apparent position, faults, and weakness, 323; troubled by insubordination of officers, 324-5; ambitious projects, 327; imprudent conduct. 330; plan of campaign against British, 349; surrenders, and leaves Hindustan, 357; his landed estates, 441.
Pigot, Lord; Governor of Madras, his troubles and death, 255.
Pindáris; harboured in Nimár, make incursions into the Company's territory (1812), 406.
Pitt; his India Bill passes (1784), 243-4.
Plassy; v. Siráj-ud-daula.
Police Rates; difficulties attending (1812-13), 407.
Pondicherry; station of French East India Company (1719-44), 187; paramount under Dupleix, 190; taken by Coote (Jan. 15, 1761), 214.
Popham; takes Gwalior (1780), 236; rescues Hastings, 241.
Portuguese; dealings with Zamorin of Calicut, and founding of Goa, 148; foundation and loss of Hugli, 149-53.
Puránas; date and contents, 45.

Ragoba; v. Rugnáth Rao.
Rájput States; abandoned by Barlow, 384; exposed to plunder, 385-7.
Ranjit Sinh; first mention, 306; obtains Lahore from Afgháns (1798), 314; supports Lake with regard to Jaswant Holkar, 385; Minto negotiates with, 393; Metcalfe obtains treaty from, 395.
Raymond, Michel; French officer in service of Nizám, 308-9; dies, (March, 1798), 313.
Raziya; Sultana at Delhi, 64-5.
Rohillas; make treaty with Nawáb of Audh (1772), 228; glance at their case, 230; refuse to pay stipulated money, 230; defeated at Katra (April, 1774), 233.
Rughnáth Ráo; uncle of Peshwa, becomes Regent at Poona, 224; aided by British from Bombay. 229; arrangement set aside by Calcutta Council, 234.

Saádat Khán; head of Irán party. sent to Audh, defeats the Mahrattas (1732), 181.
Salbai; treaty (1781), 267.
Salim Sháh; son of Sher Sháh. 125.
Samru; Walter Reinhardt, military adventurer. 216; his death and successor (1778), 239; v. Begam Samru.
Satnámi; movement of Hindu sect (c. 1680), 166.
Sayids; Ministers and Kingmakers (1716-19), 179.
Seringapatam; taken (1799), 319-21.
Shaháb-un-din, or Gházi-ud-din II.; Minister at Delhi, 200; murders Emperor Alamgir II. (1759).
Sháh Álam; attacks Bengal (1760), 210; settles at Allahabad, 223; restoration, 227; goes towards

Ajmir, 276; blinded by Ghulám Kádir, 277; dies, 386.
Sháh Jahán; rise of, 144; reign, 145; deposition, 147, 157.
Sheodasheo Ráo, Bháo; cousin of Peshwa, commands expedition in Deccan (1759), 208; takes Delhi (1759), 212; fights the Muslim league (1760), 212-13; disappears at Pánipat, 214.
Sher Sháh; rise, progress, and rule, 121-125.
Shore, Sir John; Governor-General, 308-9; vigorous conduct in regard to Audh succession, 311; returns to Europe (1798), 313.
Shujá-ud-daula; Nawáb of Audh (1754), 208; assists Sháh Álam, 210; joins the Muslim combination (1759), 212; harbours Mir Kásim, and wars with East India Company, 219-20; treaty with Clive, 220; death (Jan., 1775), 233; v. Rohillas, and Hastings, Warren.
Sikandar Lodi; Sultan (d. 1510), 94-5.
Sikhs; their rise and character of their religion, 177; beaten by Munáim Khán (1710), 177; outbreak of (1716), 178; interfere in Delhi affairs, 233; rebel (1778), 238; defeated and expelled (1779), 239; relations with Abdáli's son and with George Thomas, 304-5.
Sindia, Mahádaji; consenting party to Sháh Álam's restoration, 226; receives Carnac's surrender at Wadgáon, 235; attacked by W. Hastings (1780), 237; makes peace, 237; supreme at Delhi, 245; rebuked for demanding Bengal tribute, 269, 301; dies, 303.
Sindia, Daulat Ráo; succeeds to the power of his great-uncle (1794), 304; his misconduct, 316; complains of treaty of Basain, 343; joins Berár, 346, 350; power broken by Wellesley, 352, *f.f.*; makes peace at Anjangáon, 370; supplemental treaty (1806), 385.
Siraj - ud - daula; succeeds Alá Wirdi as Nawáb of Bengal (1756), 194; takes Calcutta (Black-Hole), 194-5; beaten at Plassy, 203; killed, 204.
Siváji; rise and early progress, 164, *f.f.*; death, 169.
Subsidiary system; favoured by Wellesley, its errors shown by Munro, 380; extended inconsistently by Barlow, 388.
Summary, or Review of first part, 420, *f.f.*

Taimur (Amir); his origin, 91; invades India (1398), 92; Daulat Khán Lodi professes to rule as his vassal, 93.
Táj; mausoleum of Empress, at Agra, designed by G. Verroneo, 153.
Tamerlane; v. Taimur.
Tanjore; coerced by Nawáb of Carnatic, 249; plundered twice (1773), 255; becomes a British dependency, 307.
Thomas, George; an Irish sailor, makes war and governs on his own account in Hindustan, 305, 323; opposes Perron, and offers service to Wellesley, 326-7; overthrown by Perron, 328-9.
Tipu; succeeds Haidar as Sultan of Mysore, 264; excluded from list of British allies by Cornwallis, 269; makes war against General Medows (1790), and repulses Cornwallis (1791), 279-81; is reduced to submission and surrenders territory (1792), 282; his temper, 291; sends to France and Afghanistán for help against British, 298; character. 307;

struggling (1797), 312; sends for help to Mauritius and France, 313; considered dangerous by Mornington, 316; Harris sent against him, 318; killed in storm of Seringapatam, 320; importance of conquest, 321.

Todar Mal; Akbar's Hindu Minister, 129-35; his military service, 137; refuses title, 138; Revenue-administration, 139.

Travancore; British alliance with, and Tipu's threatened attack, 279; valiant defence (1789), 280; troubles in Minto's time, 398.

Tughlak; rise of dynasty, 81; first Sultan of line, 82; murdered by his son Juna (1323), 84.

Tughlak dynasty; decline of, 90; extinguished, 92.

Udaipore, or Méwar; a Gahlot-Rájput State, 115; religious persecution by Alamgir, 169; plundered by Amir Khán, 387.

Ulagh Beg; v. Balban.

Ulagh Khán; original name of Sultan Juna, or Muhamad Tughak, 83.

Vallabhi dynasty, 39.

Vansittart; successor to Clive in Bengal, 215; negotiates with Mir Kásim, 216.

Vedic Aryans; laws and language, 16-18, 26; religion, 19-21.

Vellore; mutiny at (1806), 389.

Vijainagar; Narsingh, State of, founded (1350), 90; wars of (1365—1527), 113; fall, 129. (v. Hampi.)

Vikram Adítya; his era, 37-39.

Visáji; Mahratta Quarter-master-general; invades Hindustan, 224.

Wadgáon; convention of; v. Carnac: Sindia.

Wellesley, Marquess of; v. Mornington; defects of his character, 322; policy towards the Peshwa, 336; prepares for war with Sindia, 337; concludes treaty with Basain, 341, f.f.; ultimatum to Sindia and Berár, 347; recalled, and relieved by Cornwallis, 377; review of his administration, 378, 381.

Wellesley, General A.; campaign in Deccan, 363-8; his Minute on policy of 1803, 343-378.

Zamindárs; their *status* misunderstood, 285, 414-5; v. Permanent Settlement.

Zulfikár; general under Álamgir, opposes Bahádur Sháh, defeated, pardoned, and employed, 176; killed, 178.

FINIS.

WORKS BY
Mr. H. G. KEENE, C.I.E., B.C.S., &c.

The Fall of the Moghul Empire. From the Death of Aurungzeb to the overthrow of the Mahratta Power. A New Edition, with Corrections and Additions. With Map. Crown 8vo. 7s. 6d.

> This work fills up a blank between the ending of Elphinstone's and the commencement of Thornton's Histories.

Administration in India. Post 8vo. 5s.

Peepul Leaves. Poems written in India. Post 8vo. 5s.

Fifty-Seven. Some Account of the Administration of Indian Districts during the Revolt of the Bengal Army. Demy 8vo. 6s.

The Turks in India. Historical Chapters on the Administration of Hindostan by the Chugtai Tartar, Babar and his Descendants. Demy 8vo. 12s. 6d.

Verses. Translated and Original. Fcap 8vo. 3s. 6d.

LONDON:
W. H. ALLEN & CO., LIMITED, 13, WATERLOO PLACE.

www.ingramcontent.com/pod-product-compliance
Lightning Source LLC
Chambersburg PA
CBHW021425300426
44114CB00010B/646